LOVE MANGA?
LET US KNOW WHAT YOU THINK!

OUR MANGA SURVEY IS NOW
AVAILABLE ONLINE. PLEASE VISIT:
VIZ.COM/MANGASURVEY

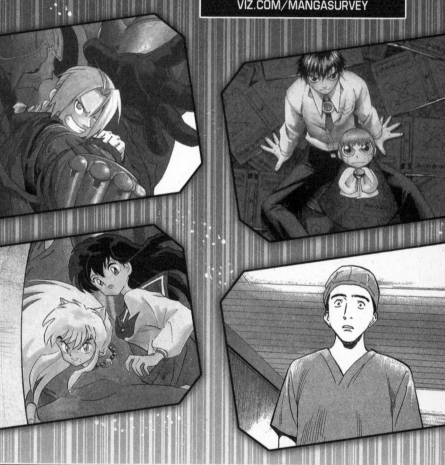

HELP US MAKE THE MANGA
YOU LOVE BETTER!

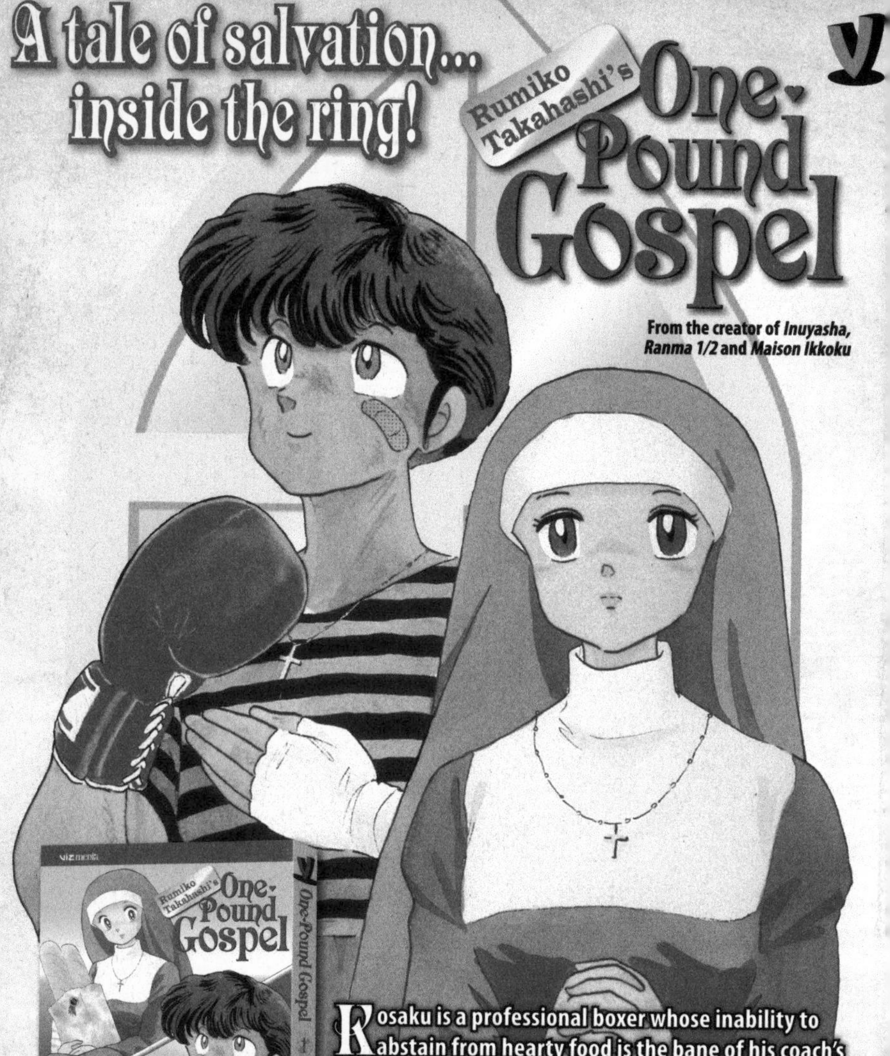
A tale of salvation... inside the ring!
Rumiko Takahashi's One-Pound Gospel
From the creator of *Inuyasha*, *Ranma 1/2* and *Maison Ikkoku*
Rumiko Takahashi's One-Pound Gospel
One-Pound Gospel
Rumiko Takahashi
Kosaku is a professional boxer whose inability to abstain from hearty food is the bane of his coach's existence. Sister Angela is a young, dedicated and fairly naive nun who catches Kosaku's eye. Can her faith redeem his gluttony?
Find out in the *One Pound Gospel* manga series—buy yours today!

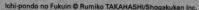

INUYASHA

VOL. 40

Shonen Sunday Edi

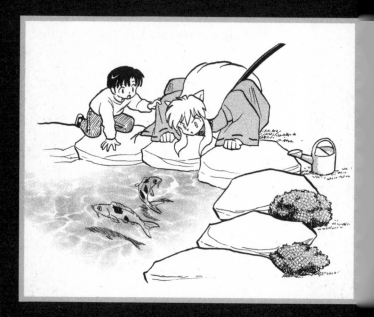

STORY AND ART BY
RUMIKO TAKAHASHI

CONTENTS

Long ago, in the "Warring States" era of Japan's Muromachi period (*Sengoku-jidai*, approximately 1467-1568 CE), a legendary dog-like half-demon called "Inuyasha" attempted to steal the Shikon Jewel—or "Jewel of Four Souls"—from a village, but was stopped by the enchanted arrow of the village priestess, Kikyo. Inuyasha fell into a deep sleep, pinned to a tree by Kikyo's arrow, while the mortally wounded Kikyo took the Shikon Jewel with her into the fires of her funeral pyre. Years passed.

Fast-forward to the present day. Kagome, a Japanese high school girl, is pulled into a well one day by a mysterious centipede monster and finds herself transported into the past—only to come face to face with the trapped Inuyasha. She frees him, and Inuyasha easily defeats the centipede monster.

The residents of the village, now 50 years older, readily accept Kagome as the reincarnation of their deceased priestess Kikyo, a claim supported by the fact that the Shikon Jewel emerges from a cut on Kagome's body. Unfortunately, the jewel's rediscovery means that the village is soon under attack by a variety of demons in search of this treasure. Then, the jewel is accidentally shattered into many shards, each of which may have the fearsome power of the entire jewel.

Although Inuyasha says he hates Kagome because of her resemblance to Kikyo, the woman who "killed" him, he is forced to team up with her when Kaede, the village leader, binds him to Kagome with a powerful spell. Now the two grudging companions must fight to reclaim and reassemble the shattered shards of the Shikon Jewel before they fall into the wrong hands...

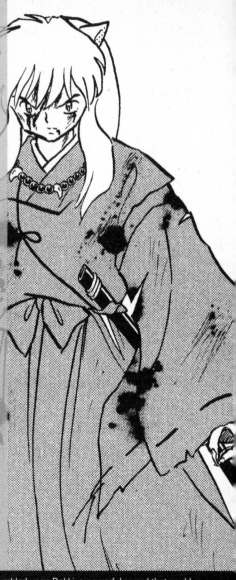

THIS VOLUME Inuyasha and the gang have stumbled upon Dakki, a powerful sword that could help them defeat the evil Midoriko and Naraku. But first they must face the sword's creator, Toshu, a human infected with demonic power. Dakki possesses a unique ability that could spell defeat for Inuyasha and his sword Tetsusaiga...

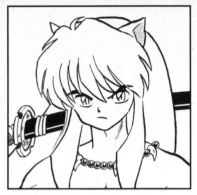

INUYASHA
Half-demon hybrid, son of a human mother and demon father. His necklace is enchanted, allowing Kagome to control him with a word.

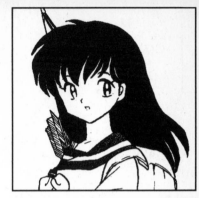

KAGOME
Modern-day Japanese schoolgirl who can travel back and forth between the past and present through an enchanted well.

NARAKU
Enigmatic demon-mastermind behind the miseries of nearly everyone in the story.

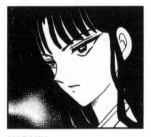

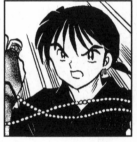

MIROKU
Lecherous Buddhist priest cursed with a mystical "hellhole" in his hand that's slowly killing him.

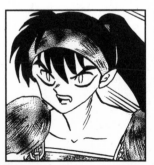

KOGA
Leader of the Wolf Clan, Koga is himself a Wolf Demon and, because of several Shikon shards in his legs, possesses super speed. Enamored of Kagome, he quarrels with Inuyasha frequently.

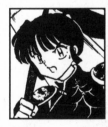

SANGO
"Demon Exterminator" or slayer from the village where the Shikon Jewel was first born.

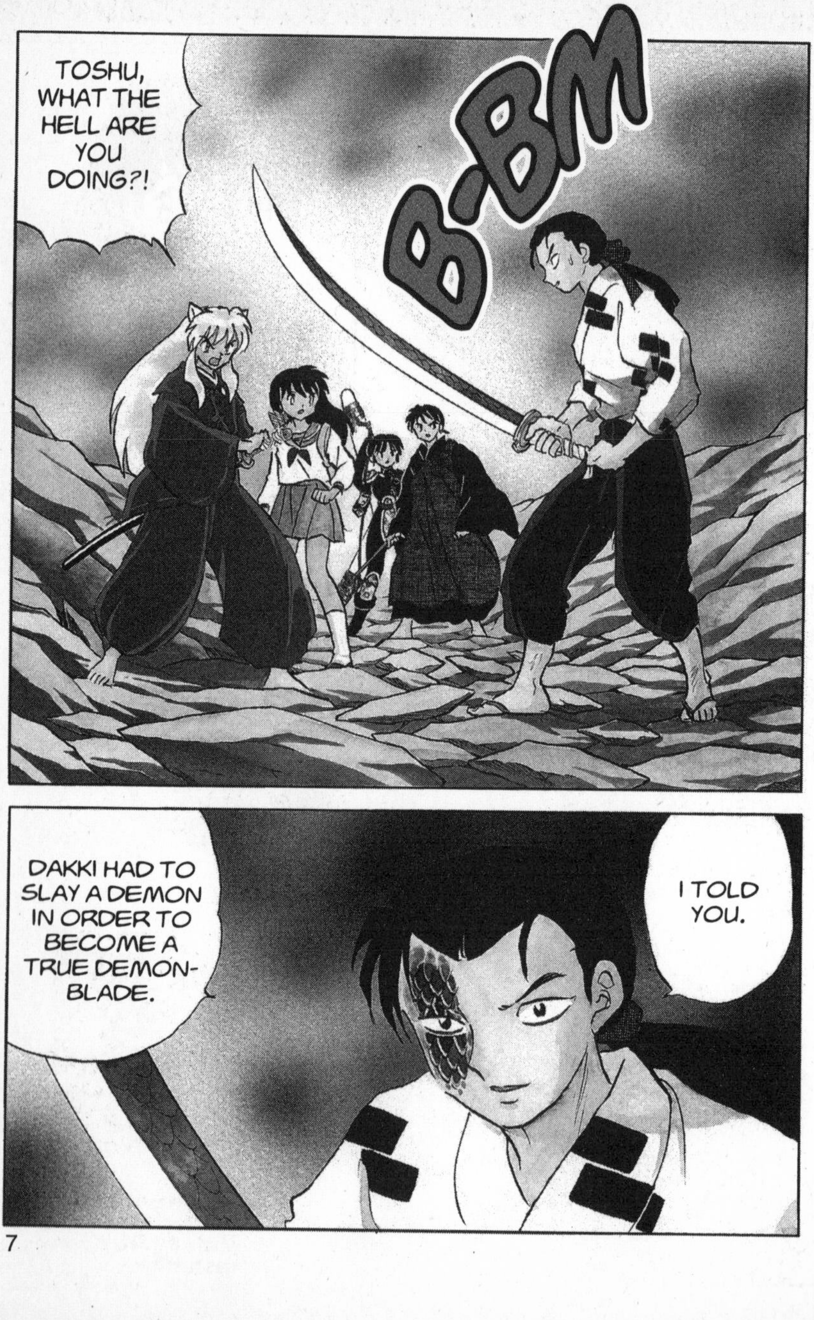
B-BM
TOSHU, WHAT THE HELL ARE YOU DOING?!
I TOLD YOU.
DAKKI HAD TO SLAY A DEMON IN ORDER TO BECOME A TRUE DEMON-BLADE.

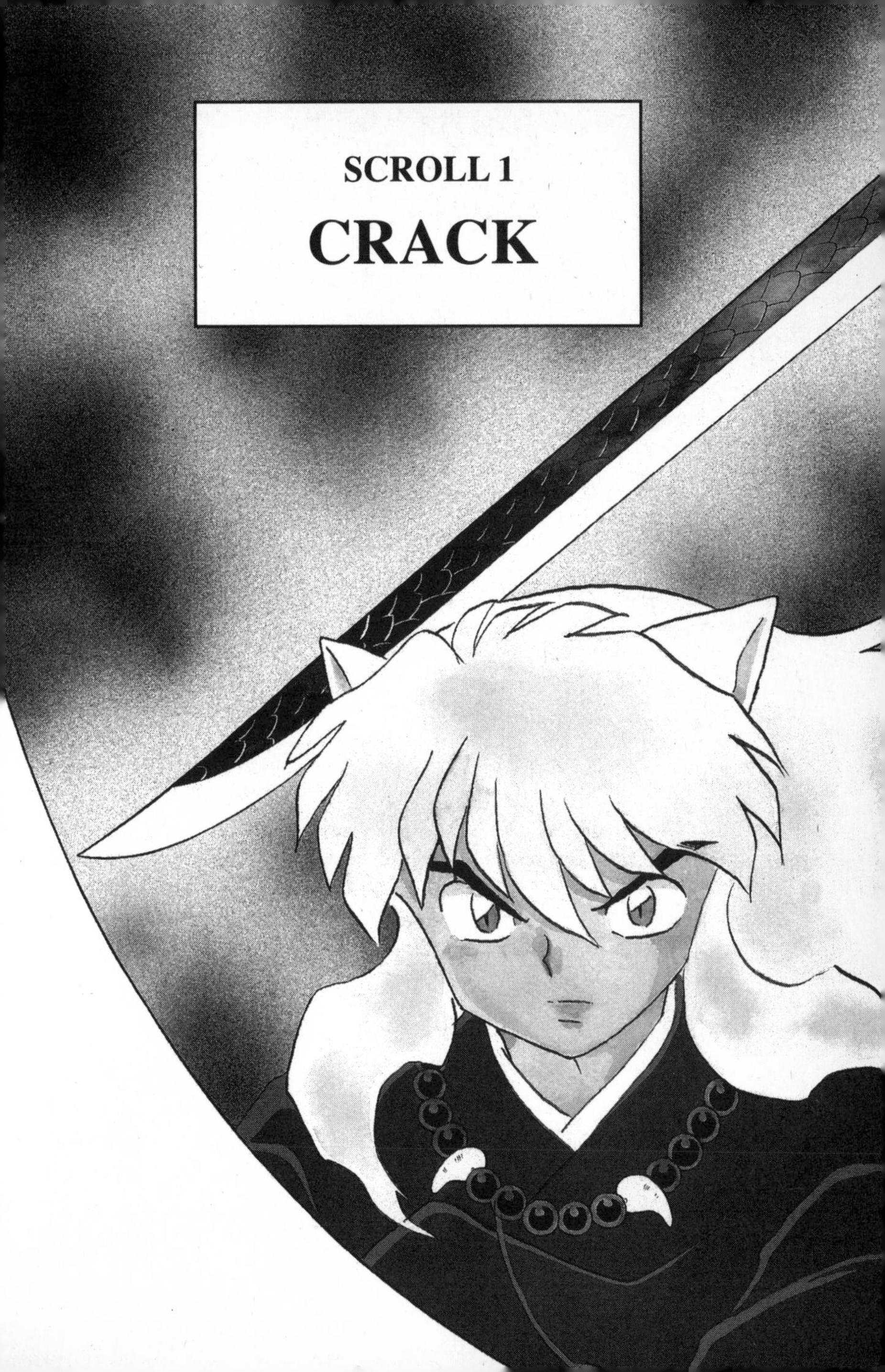
SCROLL 1
CRACK

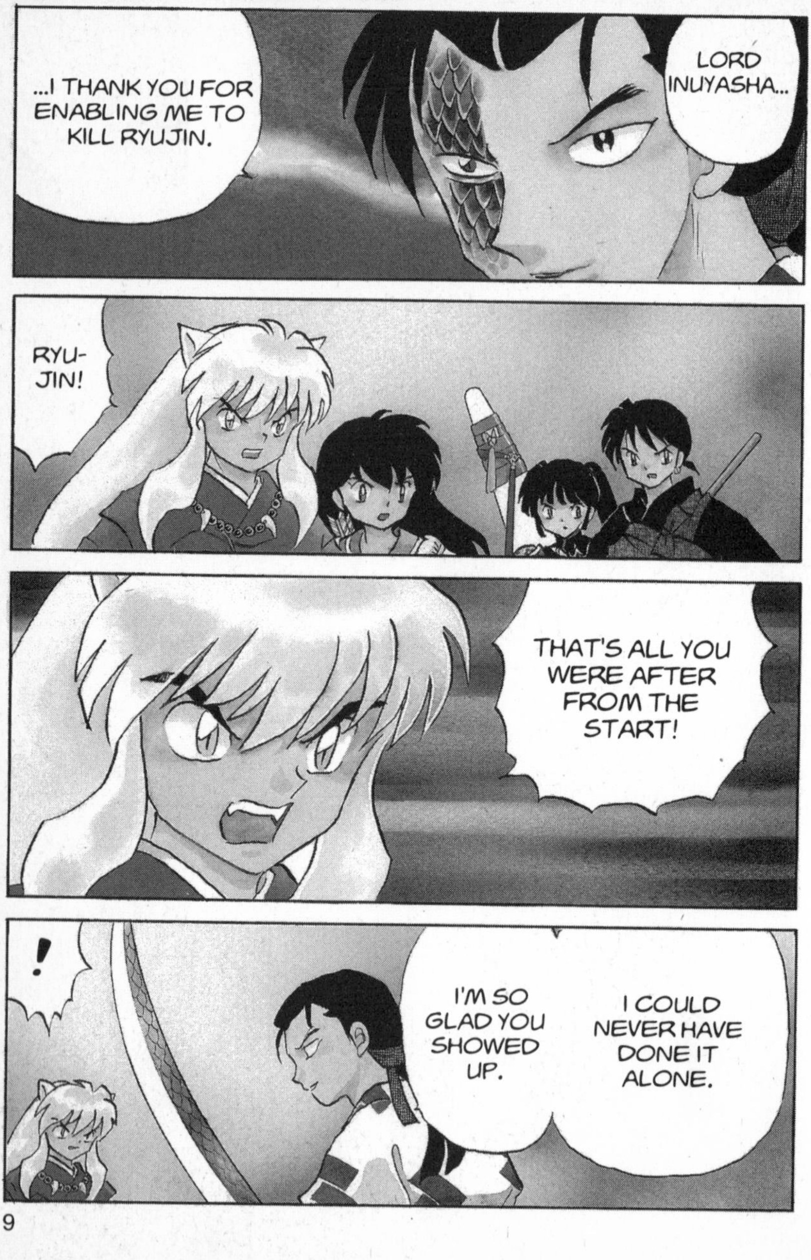
LORD INUYASHA...
...I THANK YOU FOR ENABLING ME TO KILL RYUJIN.
RYU-JIN!
THAT'S ALL YOU WERE AFTER FROM THE START!
I COULD NEVER HAVE DONE IT ALONE.
I'M SO GLAD YOU SHOWED UP.
!

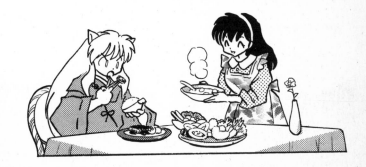

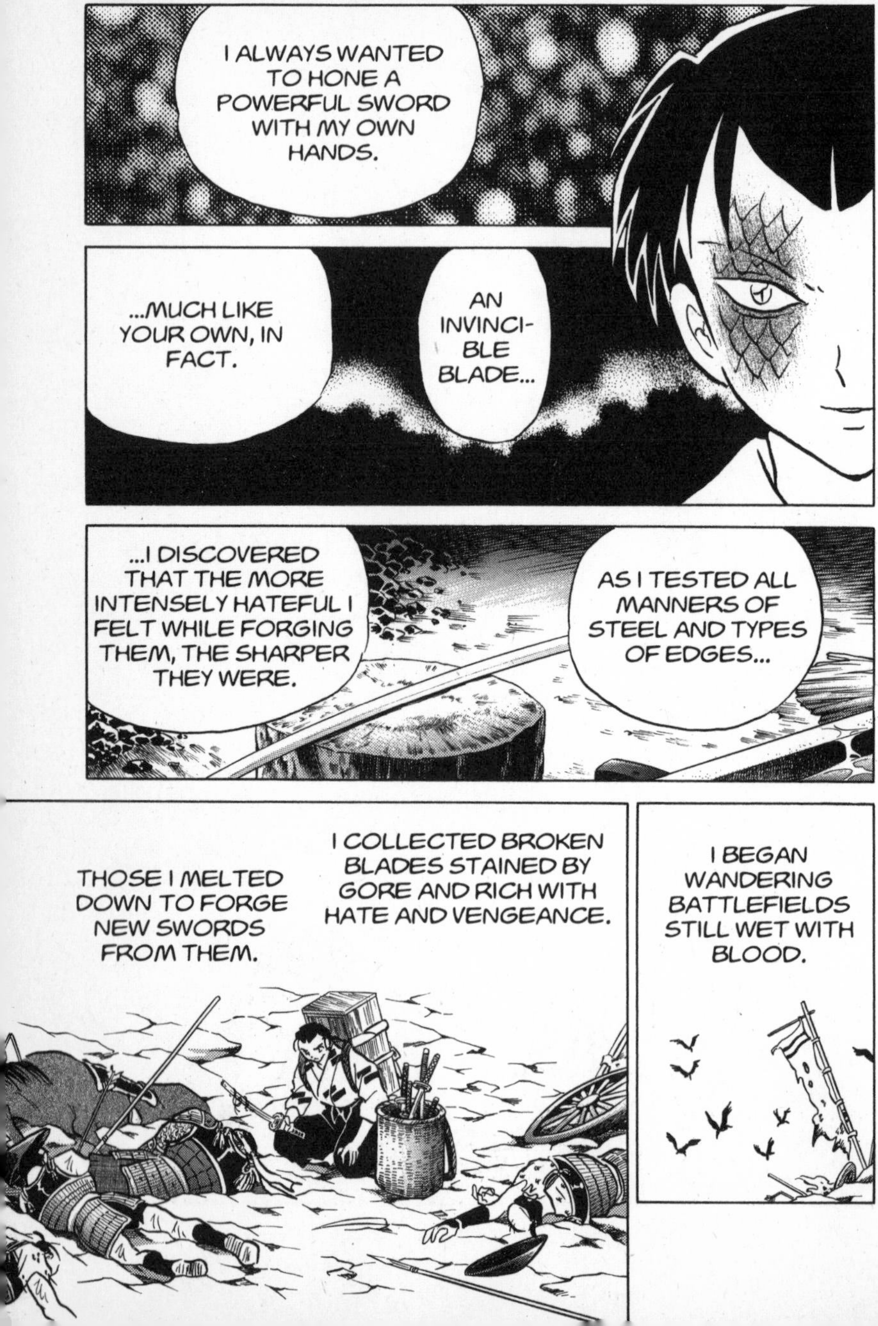
I ALWAYS WANTED TO HONE A POWERFUL SWORD WITH MY OWN HANDS.
AN INVINCI-BLE BLADE...
...MUCH LIKE YOUR OWN, IN FACT.
AS I TESTED ALL MANNERS OF STEEL AND TYPES OF EDGES...
...I DISCOVERED THAT THE MORE INTENSELY HATEFUL I FELT WHILE FORGING THEM, THE SHARPER THEY WERE.
I BEGAN WANDERING BATTLEFIELDS STILL WET WITH BLOOD.
I COLLECTED BROKEN BLADES STAINED BY GORE AND RICH WITH HATE AND VENGEANCE.
THOSE I MELTED DOWN TO FORGE NEW SWORDS FROM THEM.

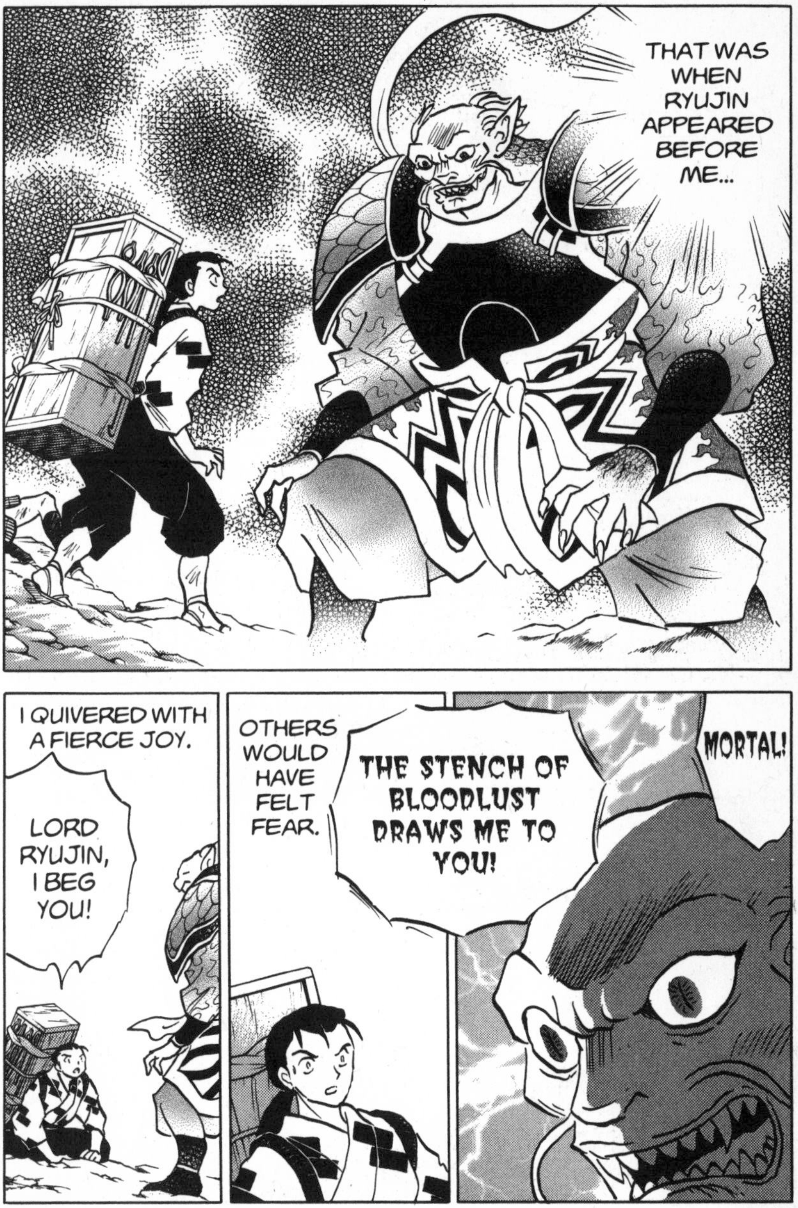
THAT WAS WHEN RYUJIN APPEARED BEFORE ME...
MORTAL!
THE STENCH OF BLOODLUST DRAWS ME TO YOU!
OTHERS WOULD HAVE FELT FEAR.
I QUIVERED WITH A FIERCE JOY.
LORD RYUJIN, I BEG YOU!

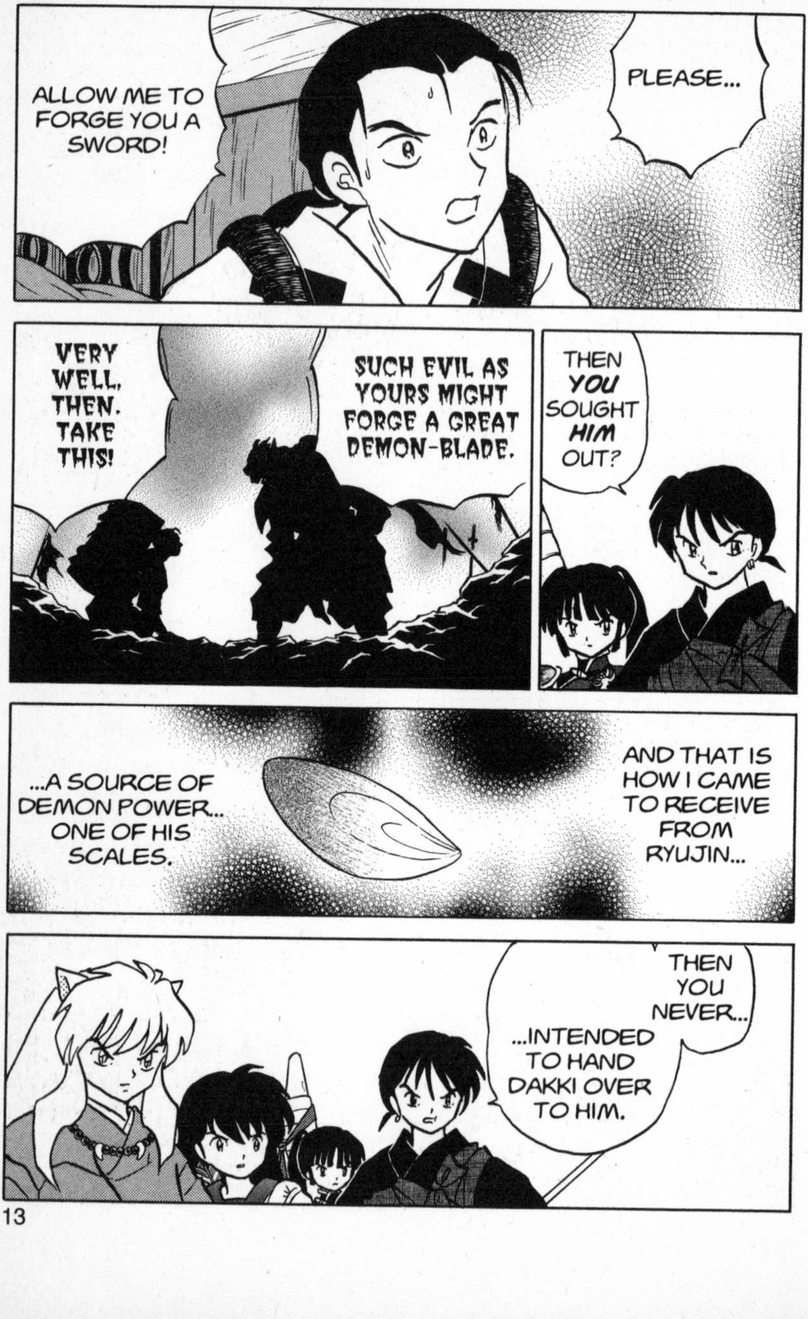
PLEASE...
ALLOW ME TO FORGE YOU A SWORD!
THEN YOU SOUGHT HIM OUT?
SUCH EVIL AS YOURS MIGHT FORGE A GREAT DEMON-BLADE.
VERY WELL, THEN. TAKE THIS!
AND THAT IS HOW I CAME TO RECEIVE FROM RYUJIN...
...A SOURCE OF DEMON POWER... ONE OF HIS SCALES.
THEN YOU NEVER...
...INTENDED TO HAND DAKKI OVER TO HIM.

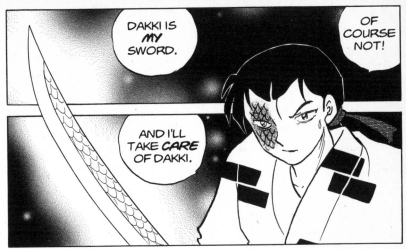

OF COURSE NOT!
DAKKI IS MY SWORD.
AND I'LL TAKE CARE OF DAKKI.
LORD INUYASHA... THAT BLADE OF YOURS...
!
...I CAN FEEL THE DEMON-POWER.
DAKKI WANTS TO DRINK YOUR SWORD'S POWER.
SORRY.

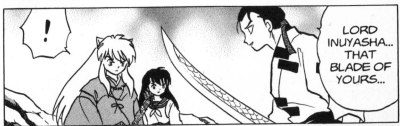

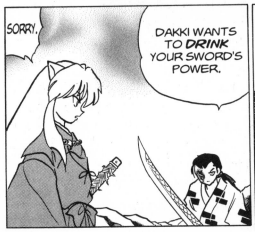

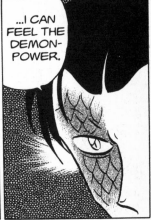

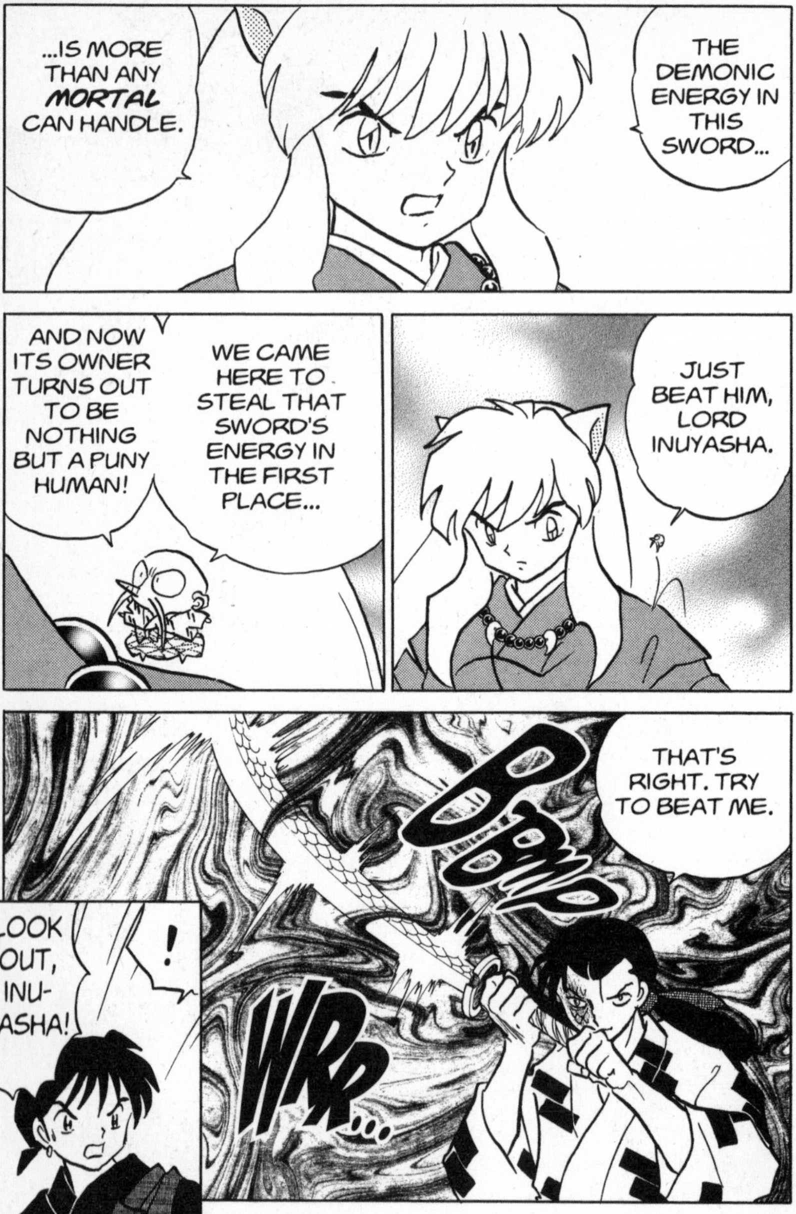
THE DEMONIC ENERGY IN THIS SWORD...
...IS MORE THAN ANY MORTAL CAN HANDLE.
JUST BEAT HIM, LORD INUYASHA.
WE CAME HERE TO STEAL THAT SWORD'S ENERGY IN THE FIRST PLACE...
AND NOW ITS OWNER TURNS OUT TO BE NOTHING BUT A PUNY HUMAN!
THAT'S RIGHT. TRY TO BEAT ME.
BDOMP
WRR...
!
LOOK OUT, INU-YASHA!

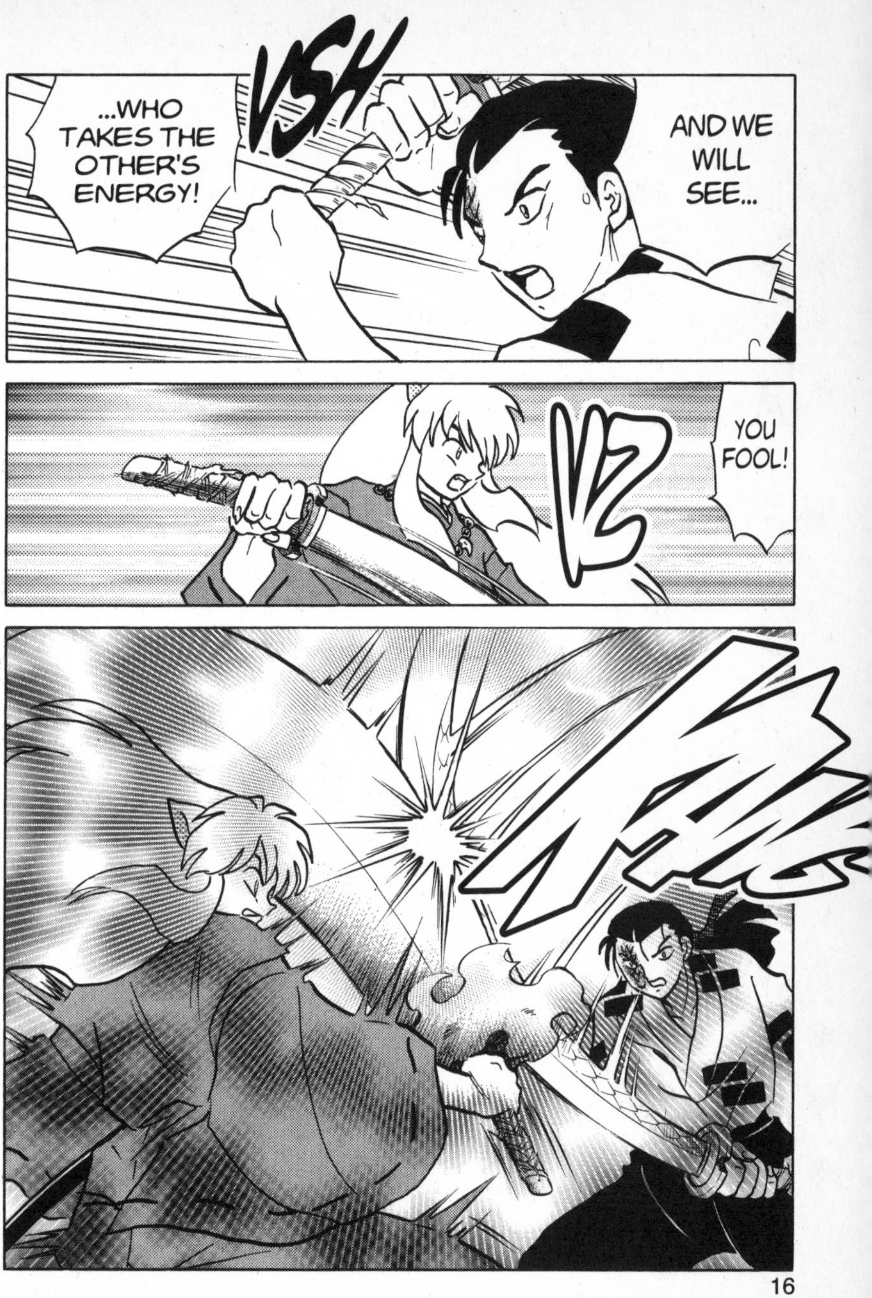
AND WE WILL SEE...
VSH
...WHO TAKES THE OTHER'S ENERGY!
YOU FOOL!

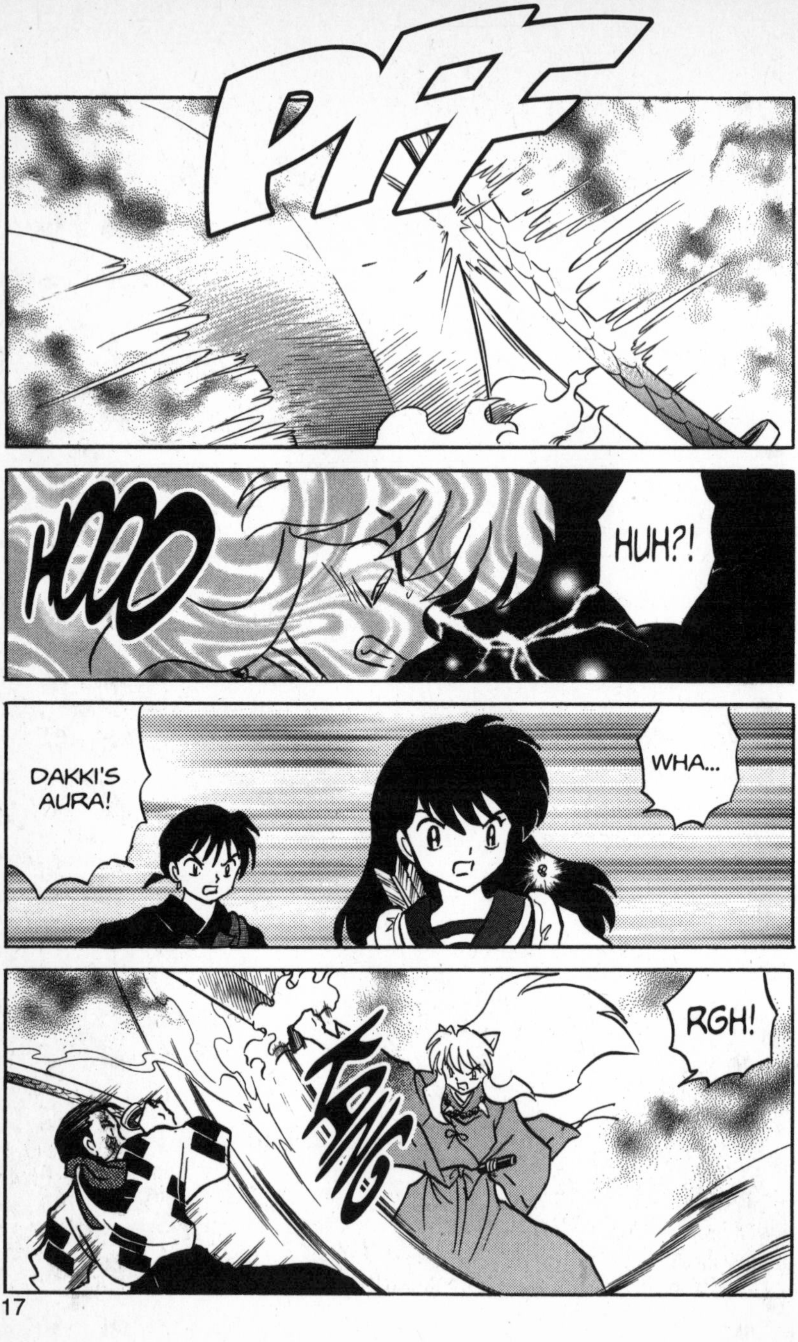
PFF
HUH?!
HOOO
WHA...
DAKKI'S AURA!
RGH!
KANG

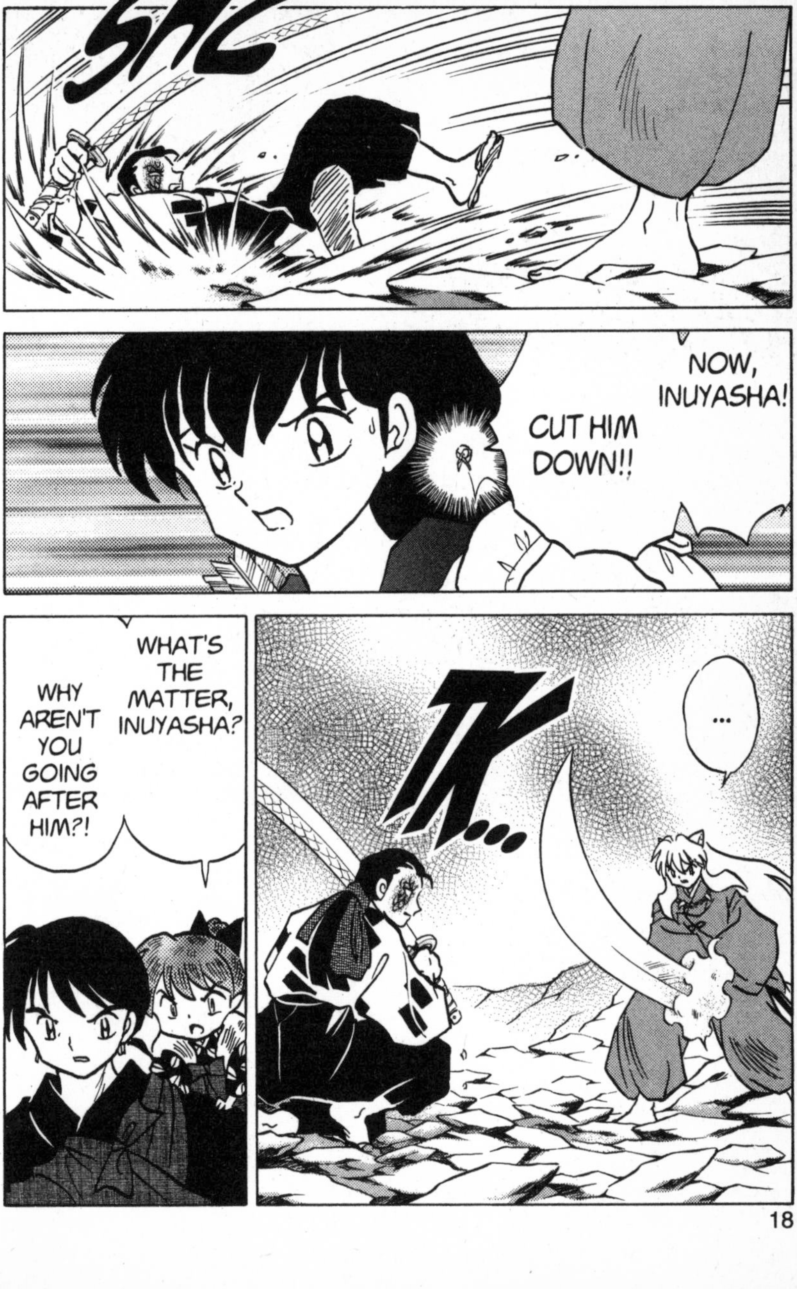
SHZ
NOW, INUYASHA!
CUT HIM DOWN!!
TK...
...
WHAT'S THE MATTER, INUYASHA?
WHY AREN'T YOU GOING AFTER HIM?!

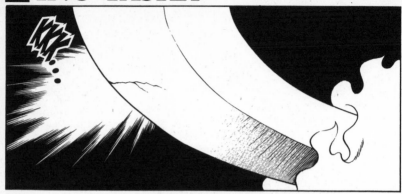

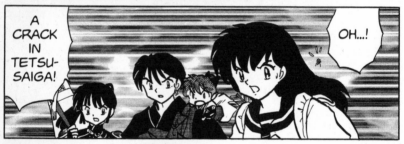

A CRACK IN TETSU- SAIGA!

OH...!

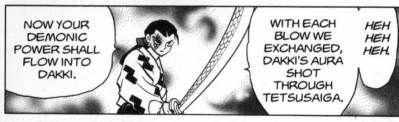

NOW YOUR DEMONIC POWER SHALL FLOW INTO DAKKI.

WITH EACH BLOW WE EXCHANGED, DAKKI'S AURA SHOT THROUGH TETSUSAIGA.

HEH HEH HEH.

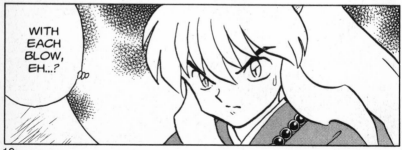

WITH EACH BLOW, EH...?

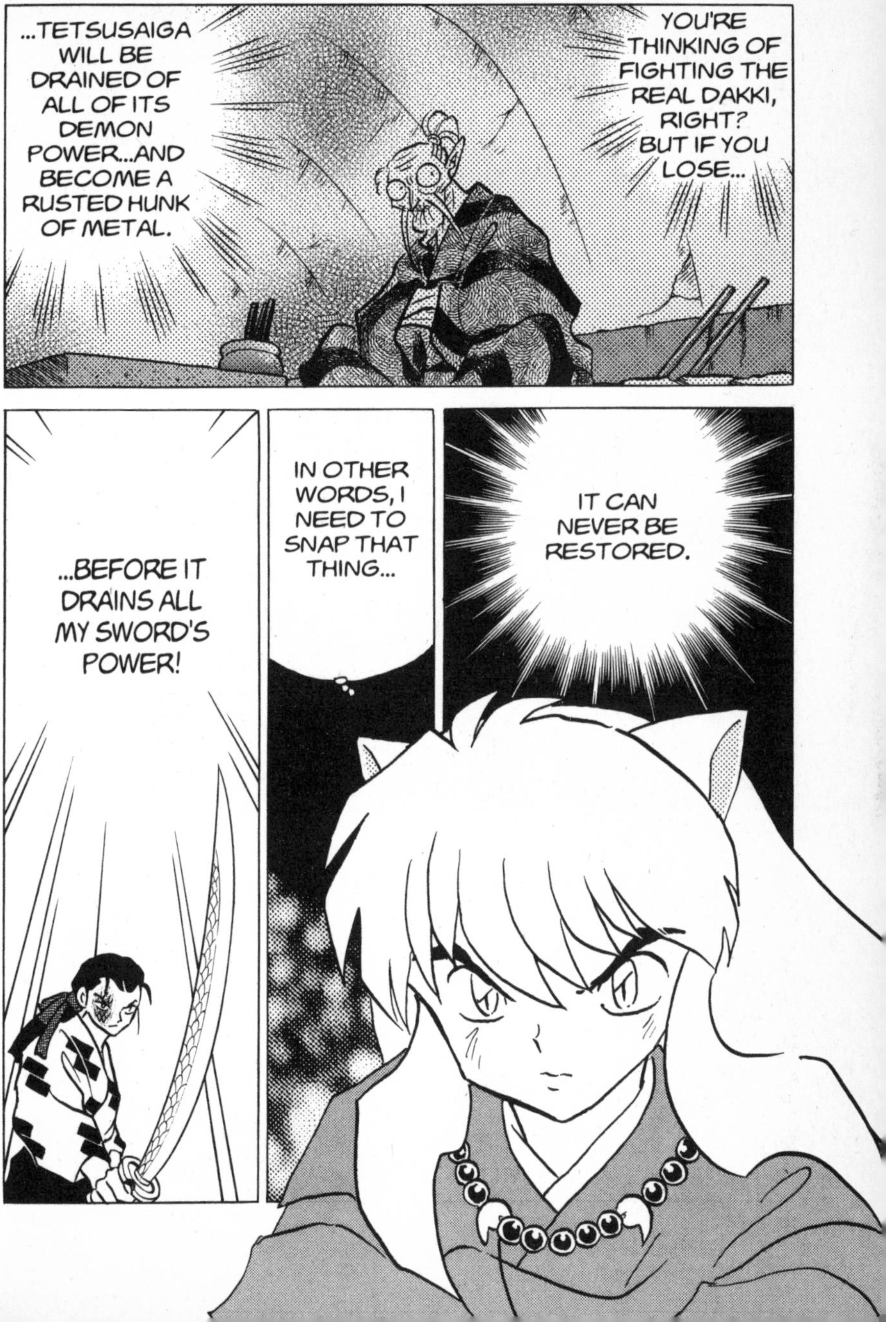
YOU'RE THINKING OF FIGHTING THE REAL DAKKI, RIGHT? BUT IF YOU LOSE...
...TETSUSAIGA WILL BE DRAINED OF ALL OF ITS DEMON POWER...AND BECOME A RUSTED HUNK OF METAL.
IT CAN NEVER BE RESTORED.
IN OTHER WORDS, I NEED TO SNAP THAT THING...
...BEFORE IT DRAINS ALL MY SWORD'S POWER!

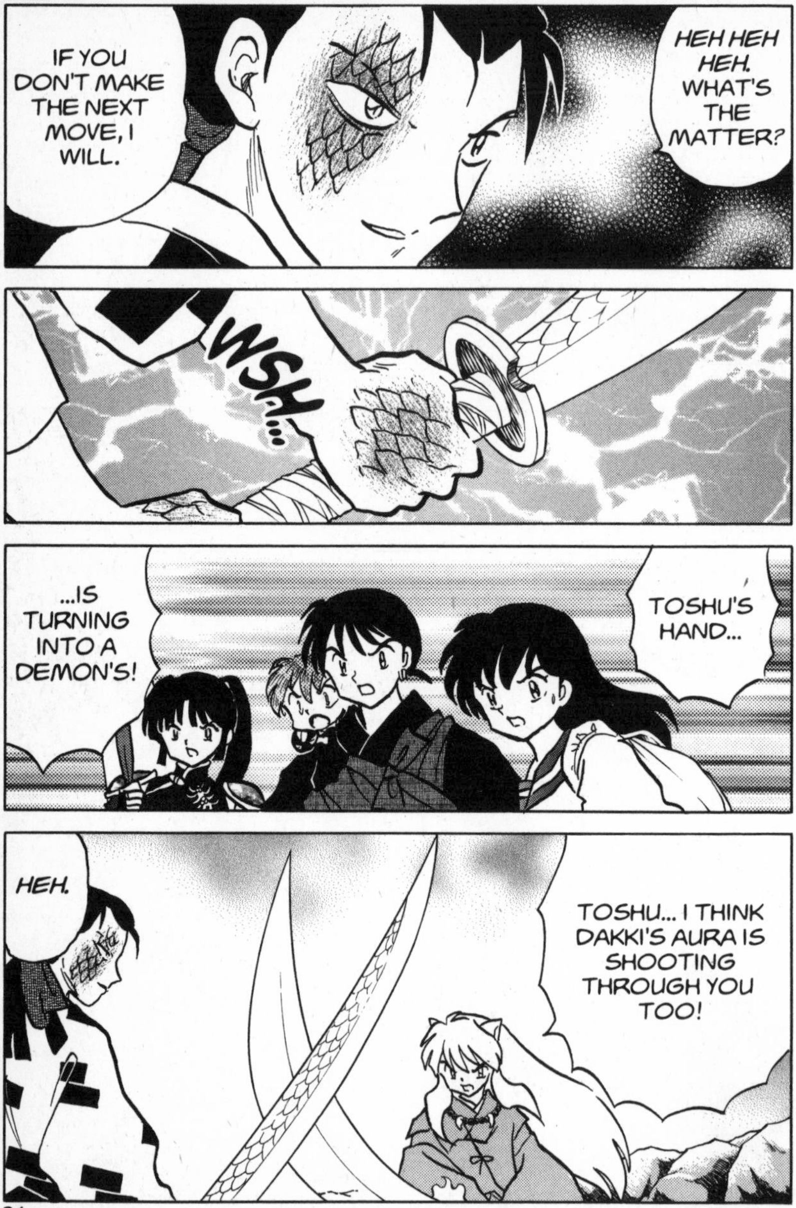
HEH HEH HEH. WHAT'S THE MATTER?
IF YOU DON'T MAKE THE NEXT MOVE, I WILL.
WSH...
TOSHU'S HAND...
...IS TURNING INTO A DEMON'S!
TOSHU... I THINK DAKKI'S AURA IS SHOOTING THROUGH YOU TOO!
HEH.

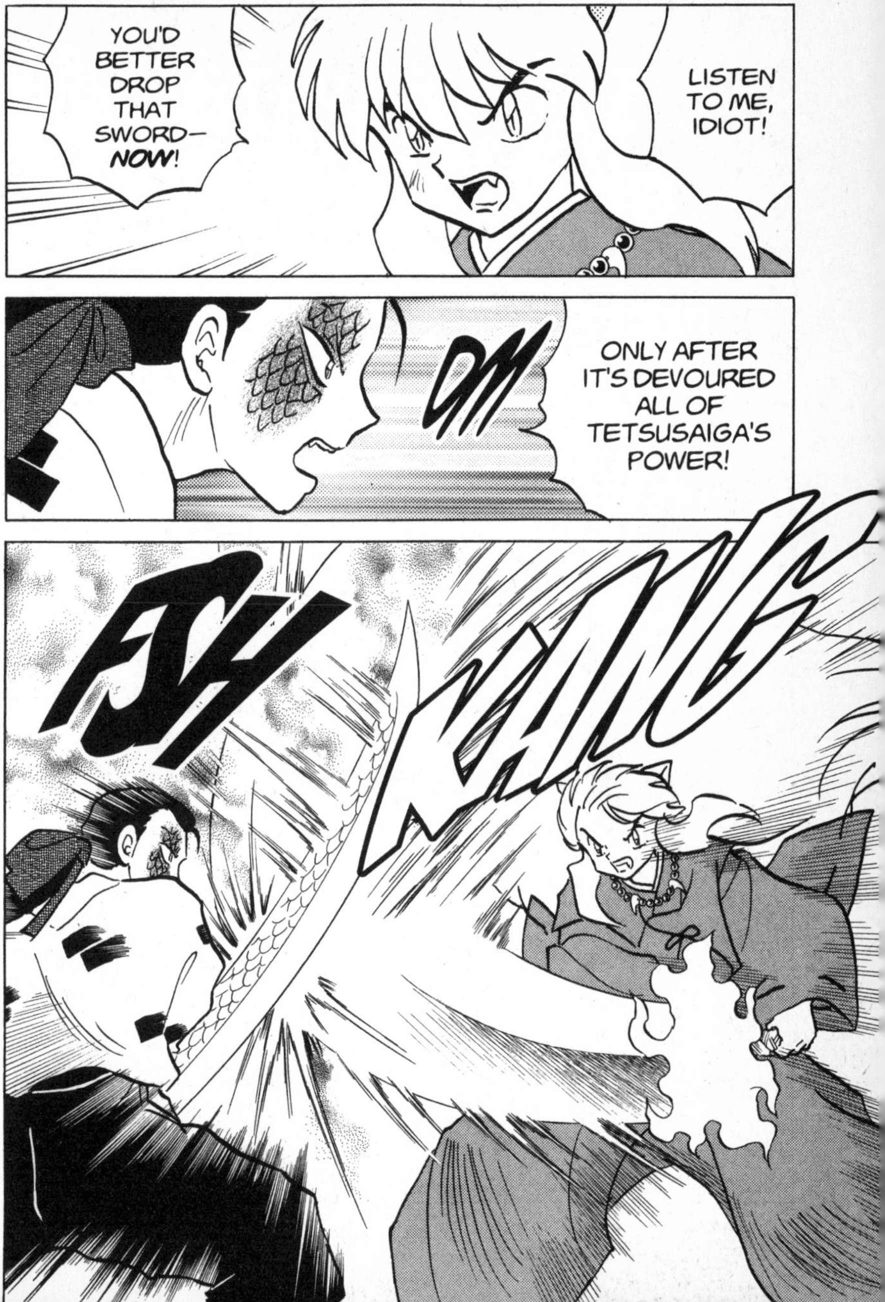
LISTEN TO ME, IDIOT!
YOU'D BETTER DROP THAT SWORD—*NOW*!
ONLY AFTER IT'S DEVOURED ALL OF TETSUSAIGA'S POWER!

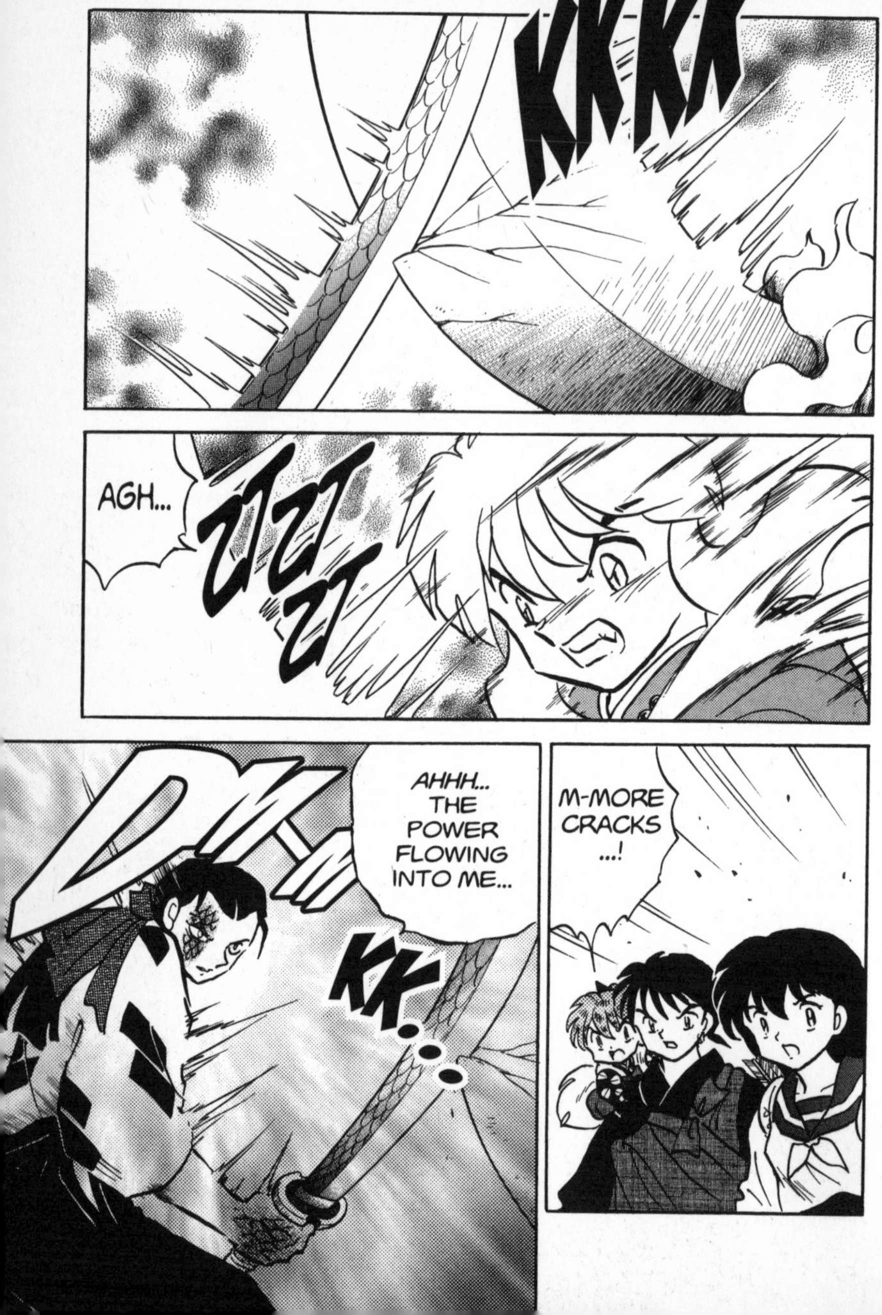
KKKX
AGH...
M-MORE CRACKS ...!
AHHH... THE POWER FLOWING INTO ME...
KK...

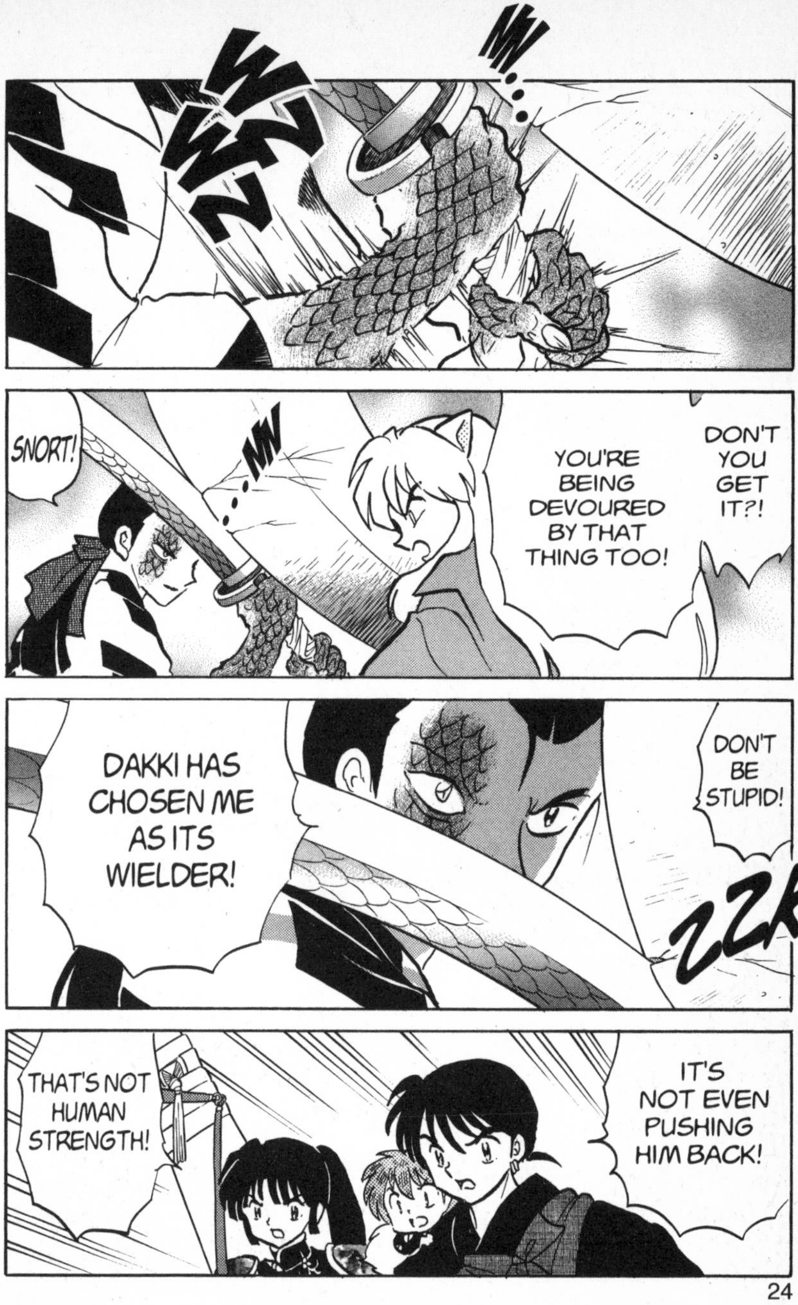
DON'T YOU GET IT?!
YOU'RE BEING DEVOURED BY THAT THING TOO!
SNORT!
DON'T BE STUPID!
ZZK
DAKKI HAS CHOSEN ME AS ITS WIELDER!
IT'S NOT EVEN PUSHING HIM BACK!
THAT'S NOT HUMAN STRENGTH!

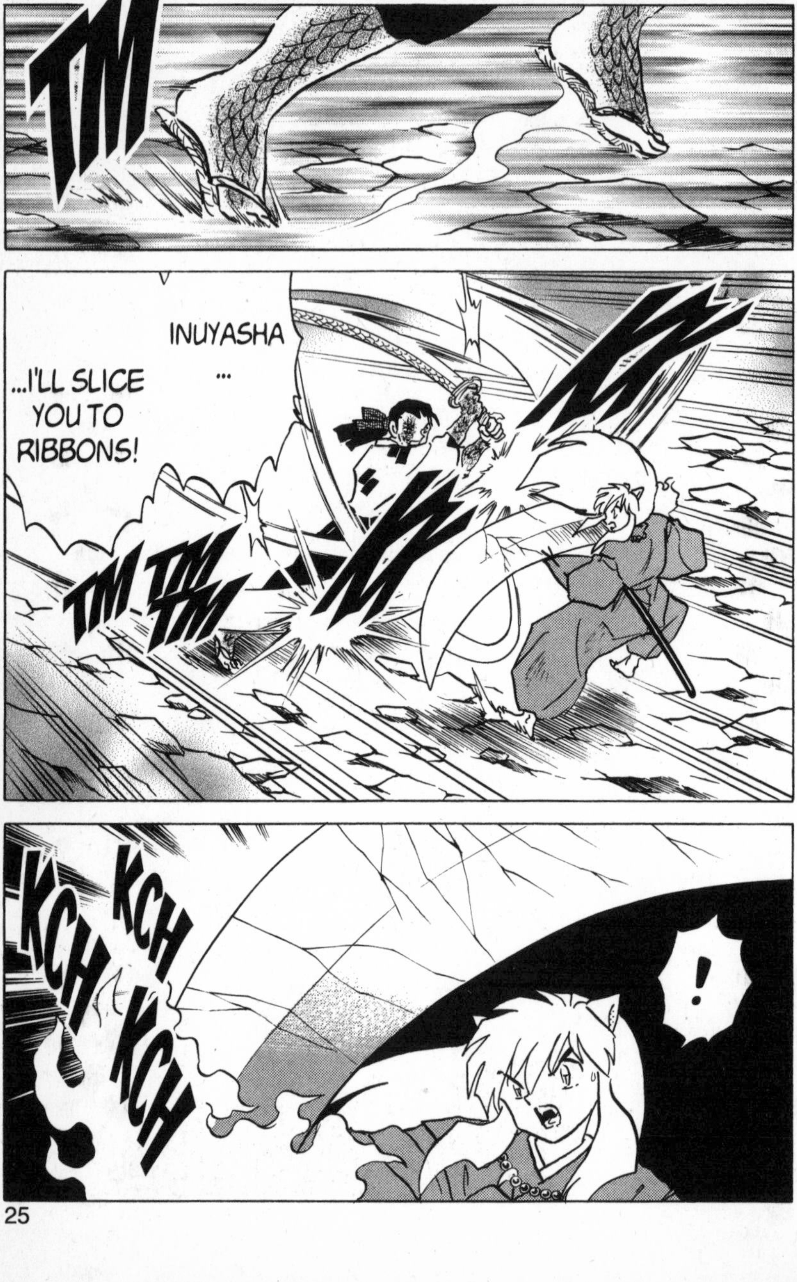
TM
INUYASHA ...
...I'LL SLICE YOU TO RIBBONS!
TM TM TM
!
KCH KCH
KCH KCH

IT'S GOING TO BREAK!
NNH!
IF YOU LOSE, TETSUSAIGA WILL BECOME A RUSTED HUNK OF METAL...
IT CAN NEVER BE RESTORED.
!
B-BM
TETSU-SAIGA ...?!
WRRR

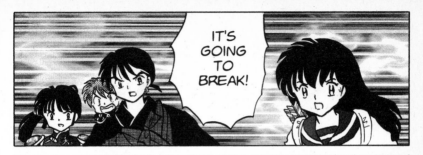

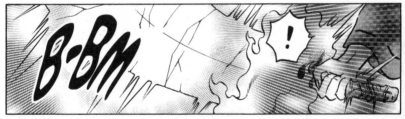

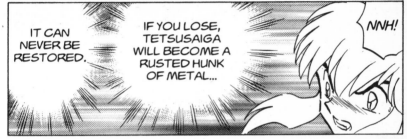

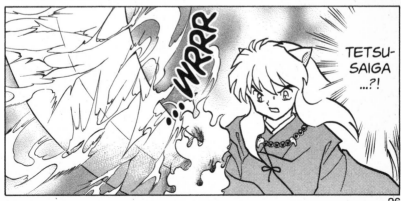

SCROLL 2
RESIGNATION

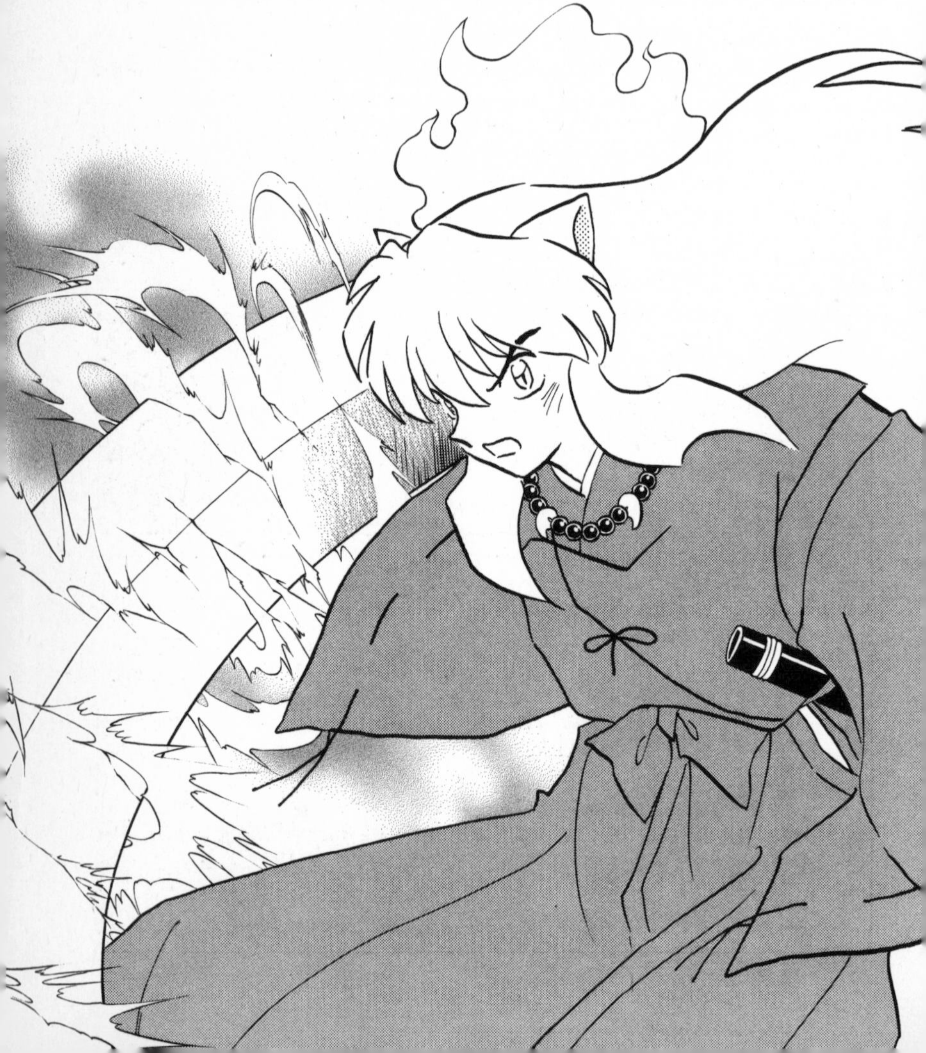

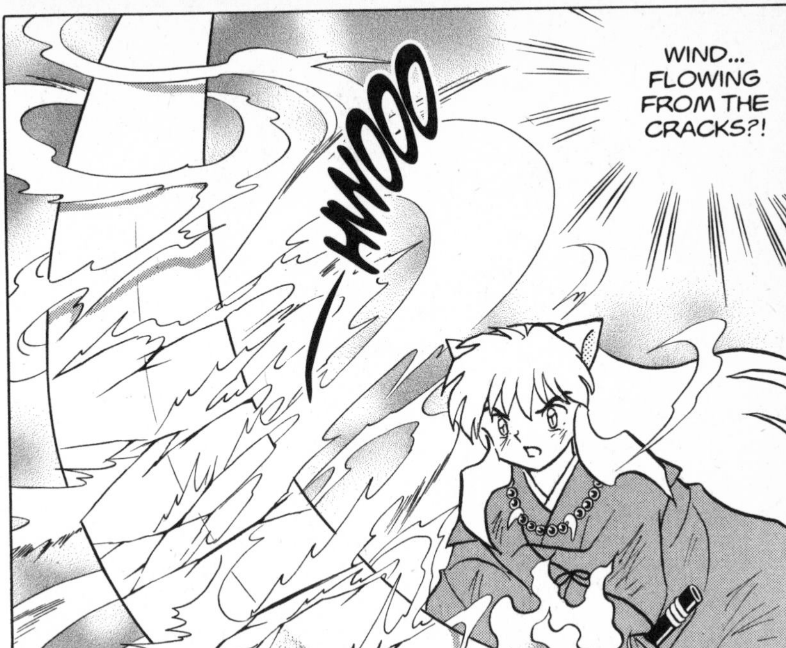
WIND... FLOWING FROM THE CRACKS?!
HWOOO

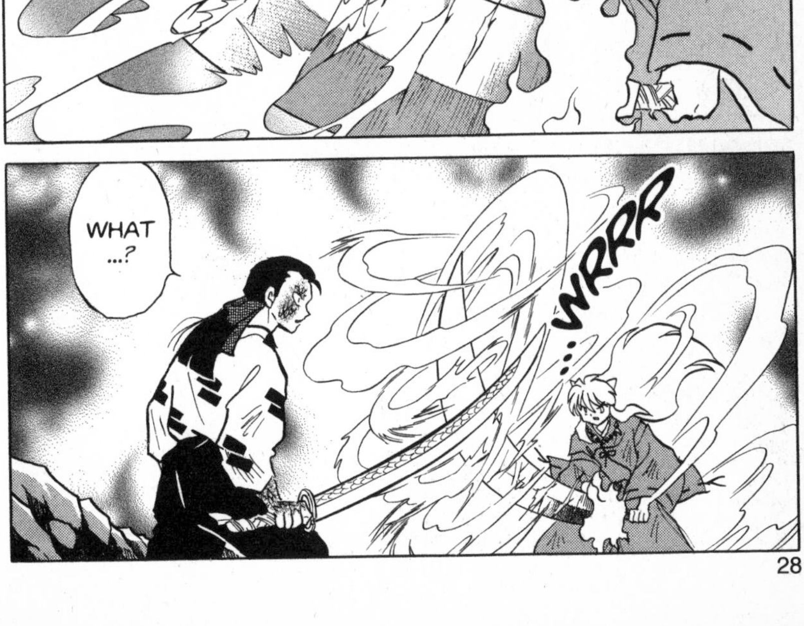
WRRR
WHAT ...?

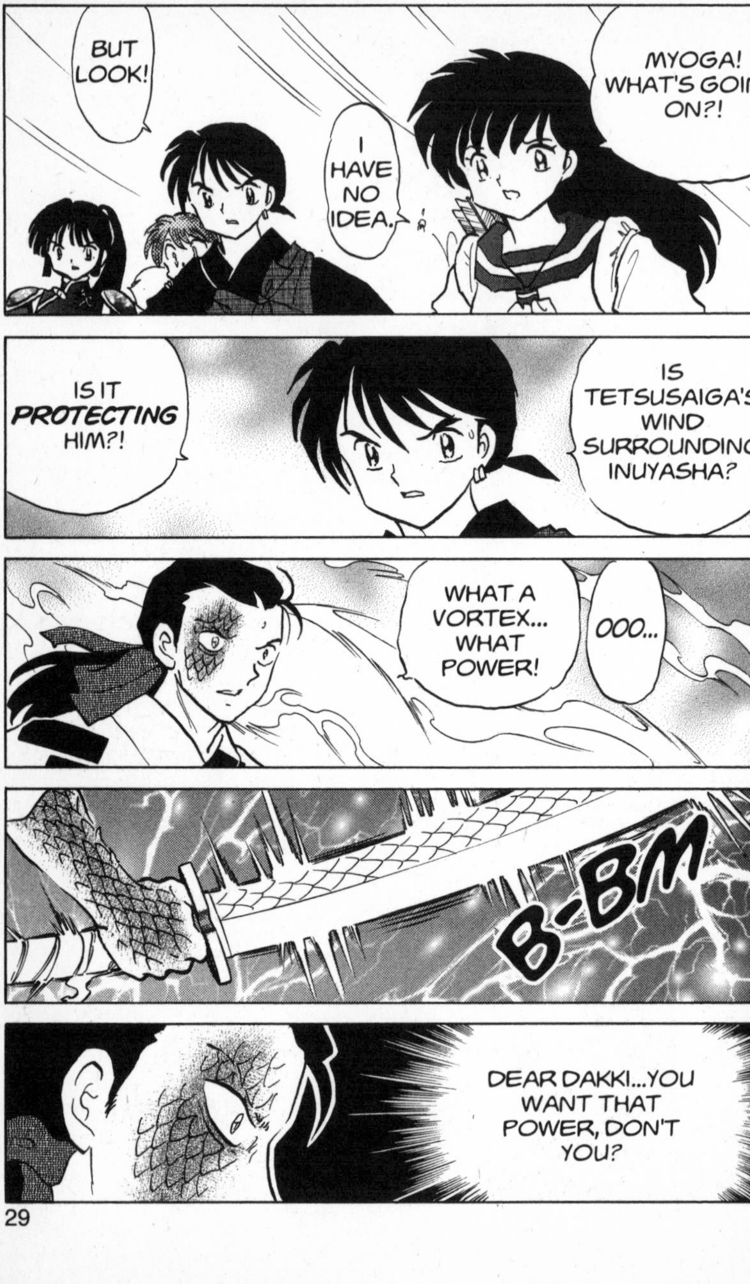
MYOGA! WHAT'S GOING ON?!
I HAVE NO IDEA.
BUT LOOK!
IS TETSUSAIGA'S WIND SURROUNDING INUYASHA?
IS IT *PROTECTING* HIM?!
OOO...
WHAT A VORTEX... WHAT POWER!
B-BM
DEAR DAKKI...YOU WANT THAT POWER, DON'T YOU?

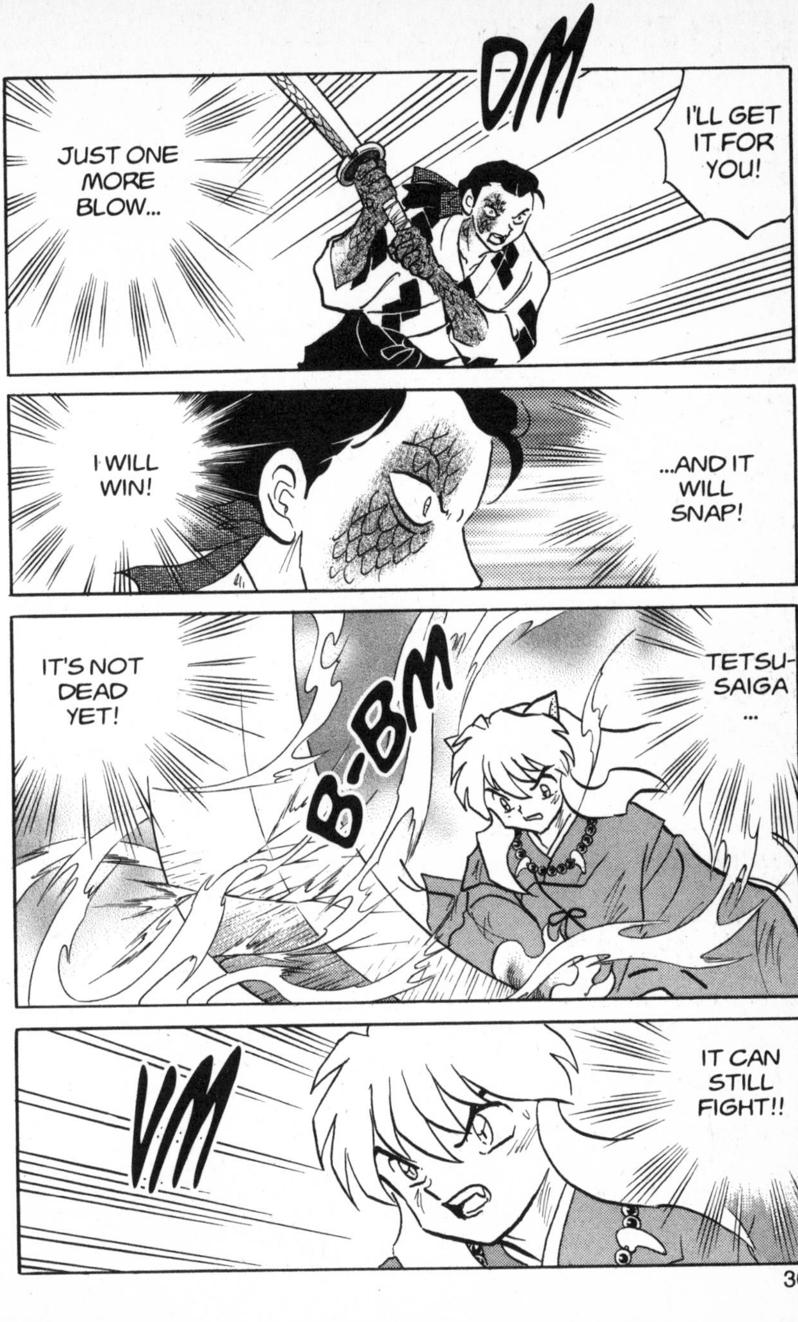
DM
I'LL GET IT FOR YOU!
JUST ONE MORE BLOW...
...AND IT WILL SNAP!
I WILL WIN!
TETSU-SAIGA...
B-BM
IT'S NOT DEAD YET!
IT CAN STILL FIGHT!!
VM

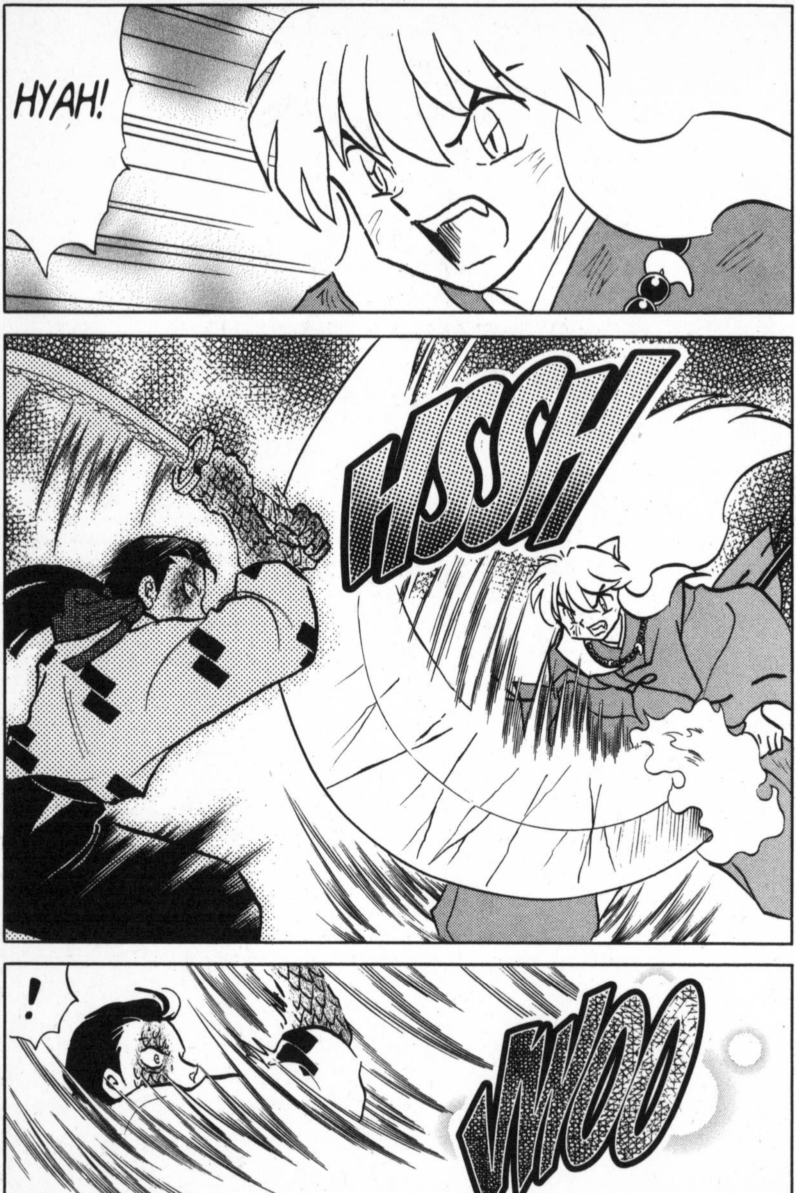
HYAH!
HSSH
!
WHOO

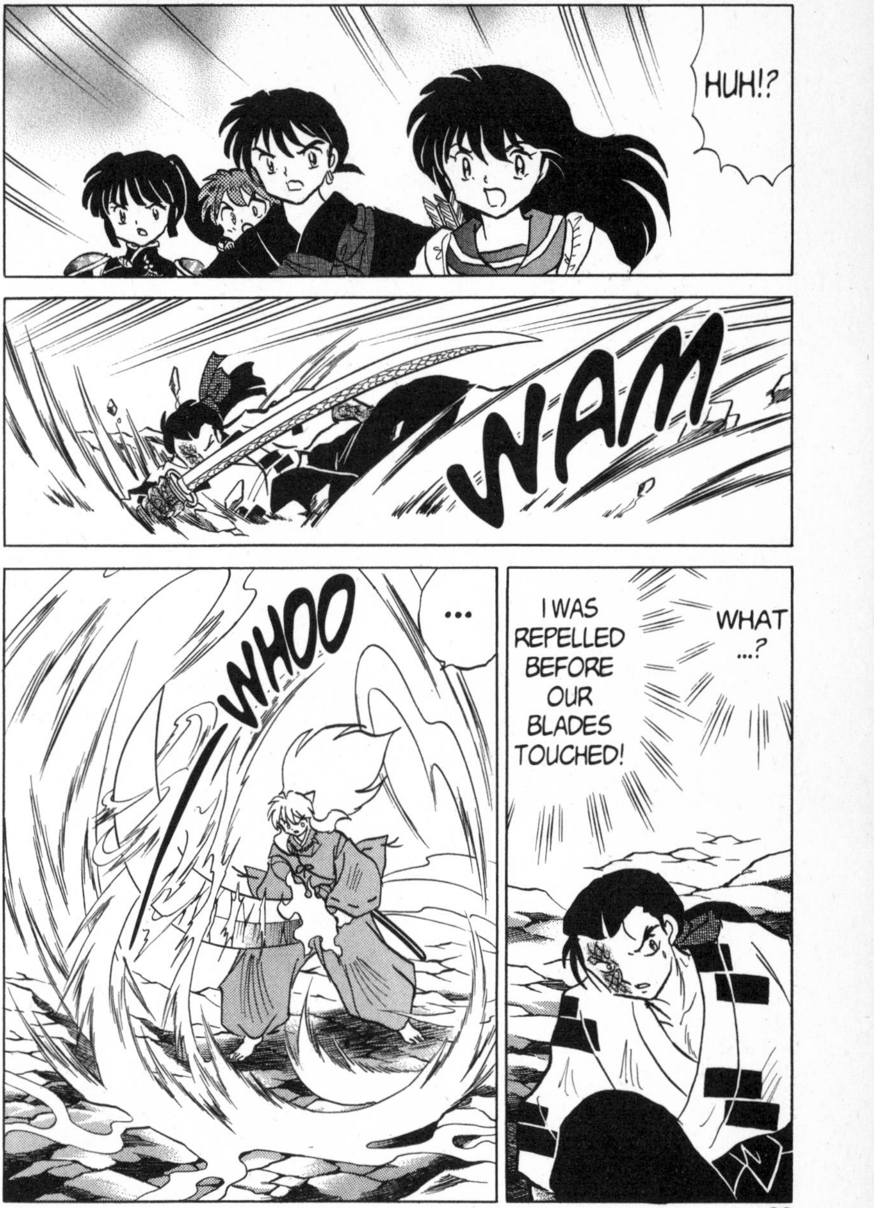
HUH!?
WAM
WHAT ...?
I WAS REPELLED BEFORE OUR BLADES TOUCHED!
...
WHOO

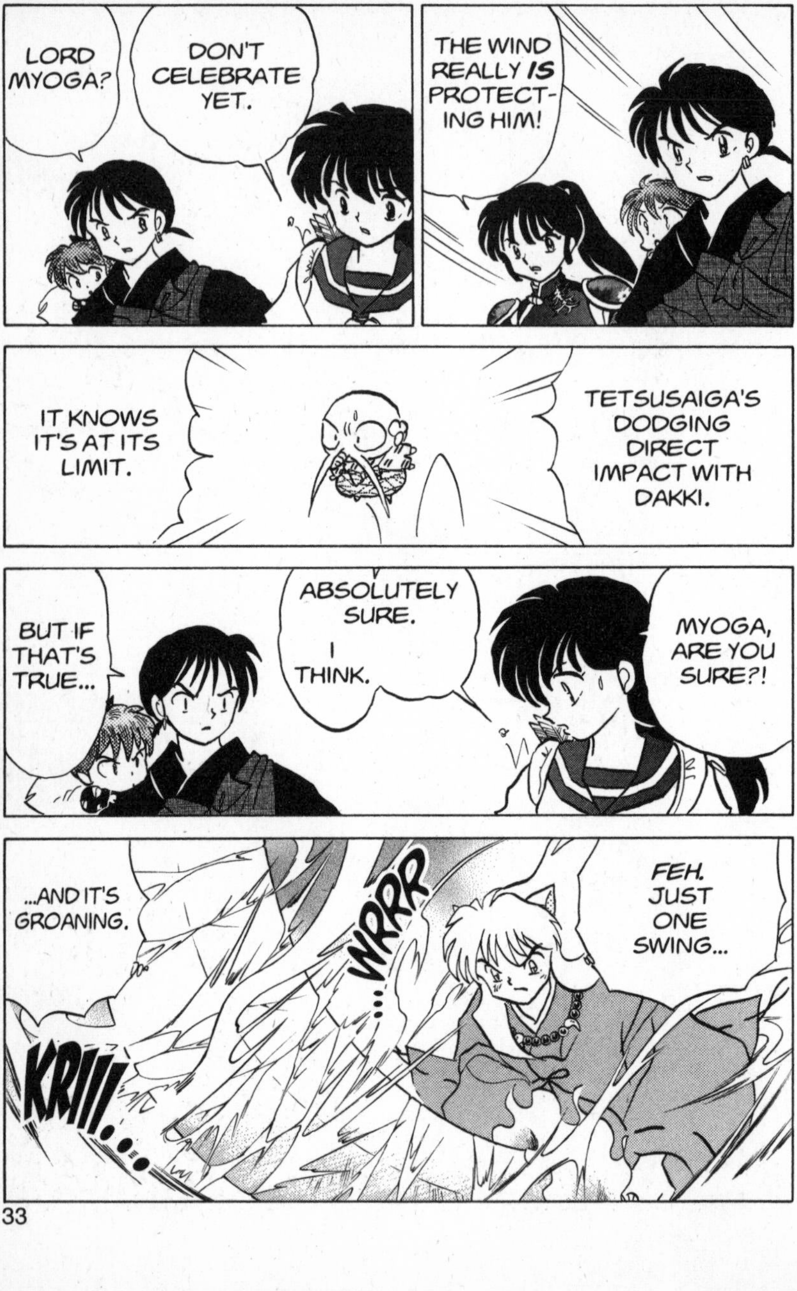
THE WIND REALLY **IS** PROTECTING HIM!
DON'T CELEBRATE YET.
LORD MYOGA?
TETSUSAIGA'S DODGING DIRECT IMPACT WITH DAKKI.
IT KNOWS IT'S AT ITS LIMIT.
MYOGA, ARE YOU SURE?!
ABSOLUTELY SURE.
I THINK.
BUT IF THAT'S TRUE...
FEH. JUST ONE SWING...
...WRRR
...AND IT'S GROANING.
KRIII...

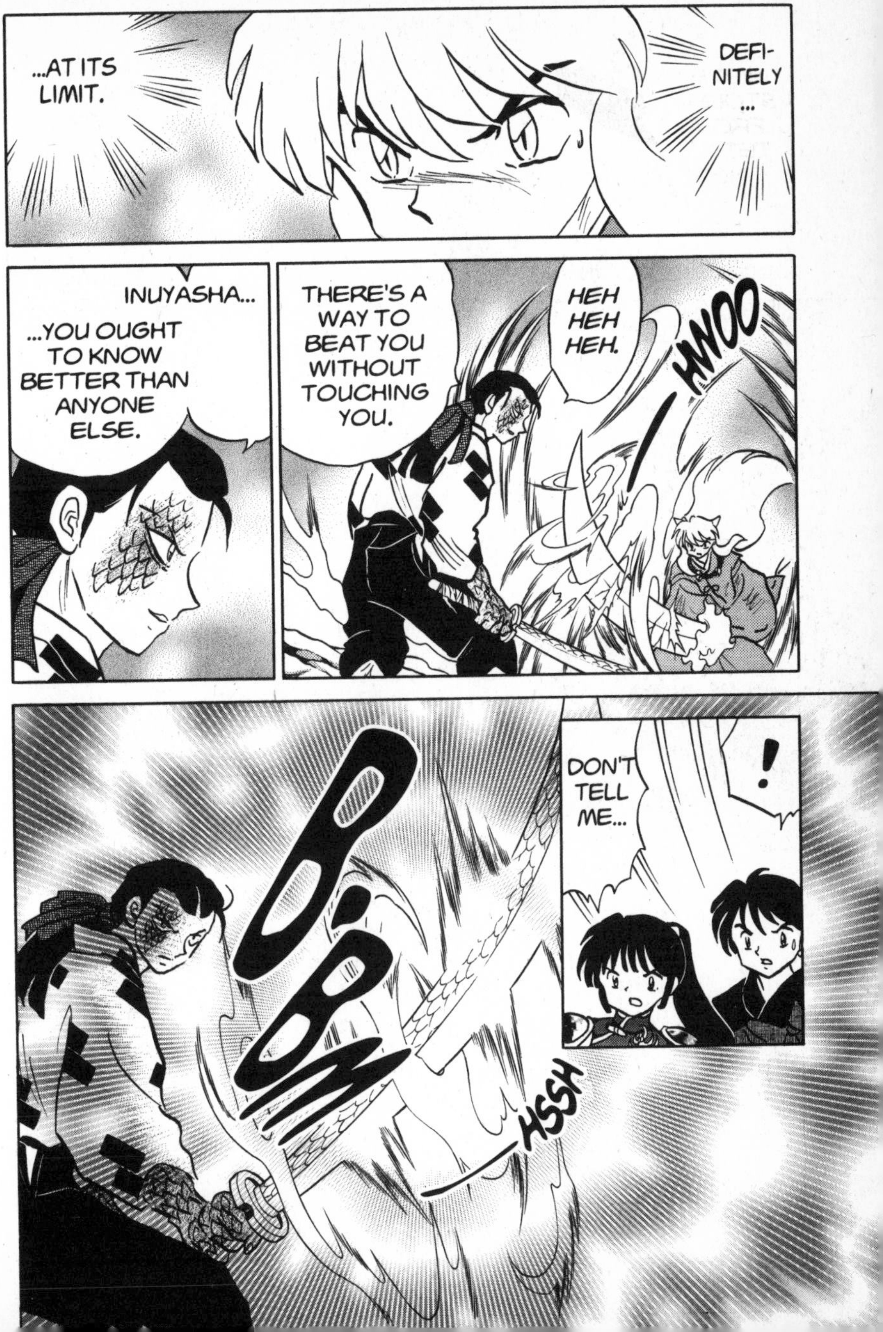
DEFINITELY...
...AT ITS LIMIT.
HWOO
HEH HEH HEH.
THERE'S A WAY TO BEAT YOU WITHOUT TOUCHING YOU.
INUYASHA...
...YOU OUGHT TO KNOW BETTER THAN ANYONE ELSE.
!
DON'T TELL ME...
BOOM
HSSH

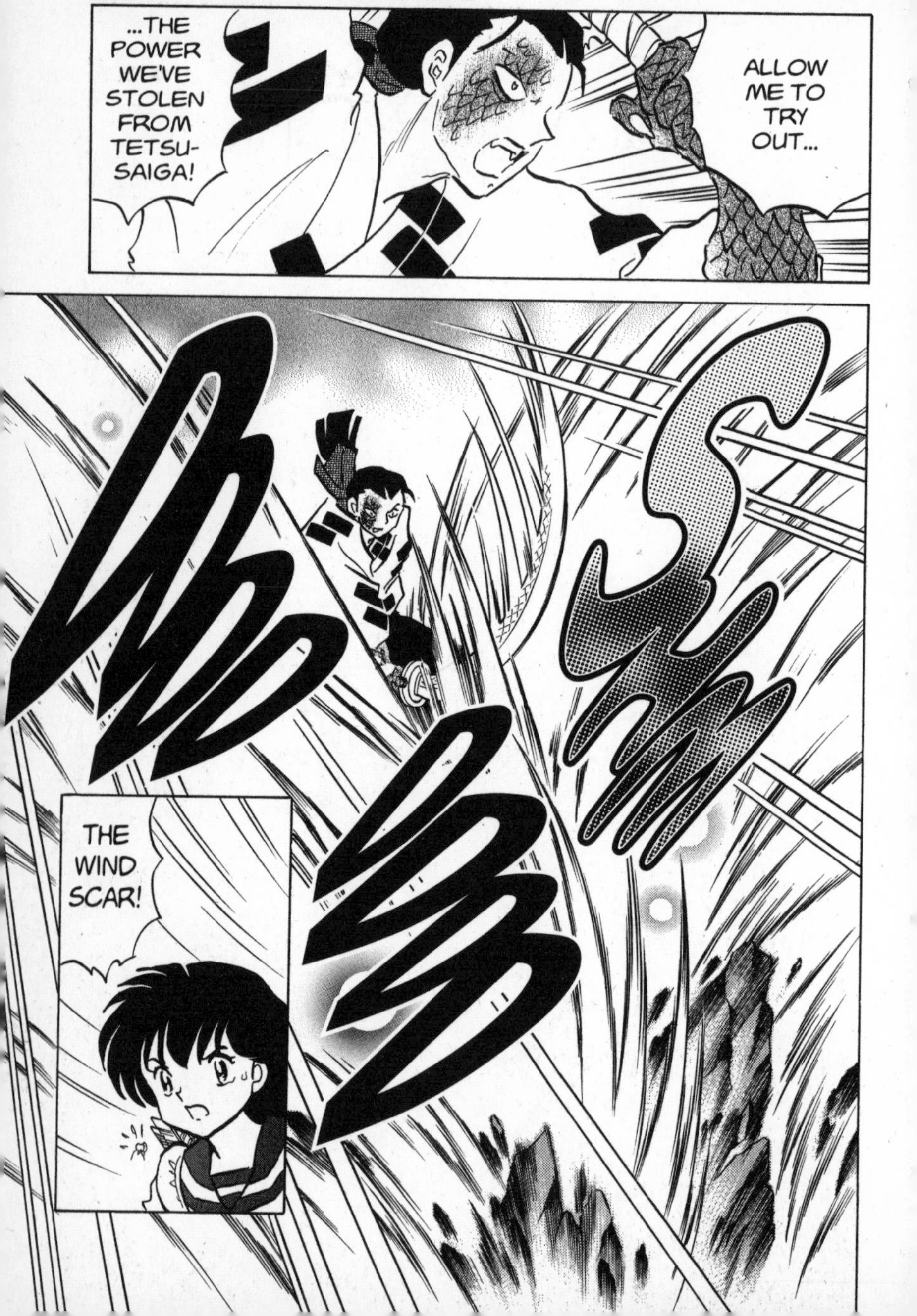
ALLOW ME TO TRY OUT...
...THE POWER WE'VE STOLEN FROM TETSU-SAIGA!
THE WIND SCAR!

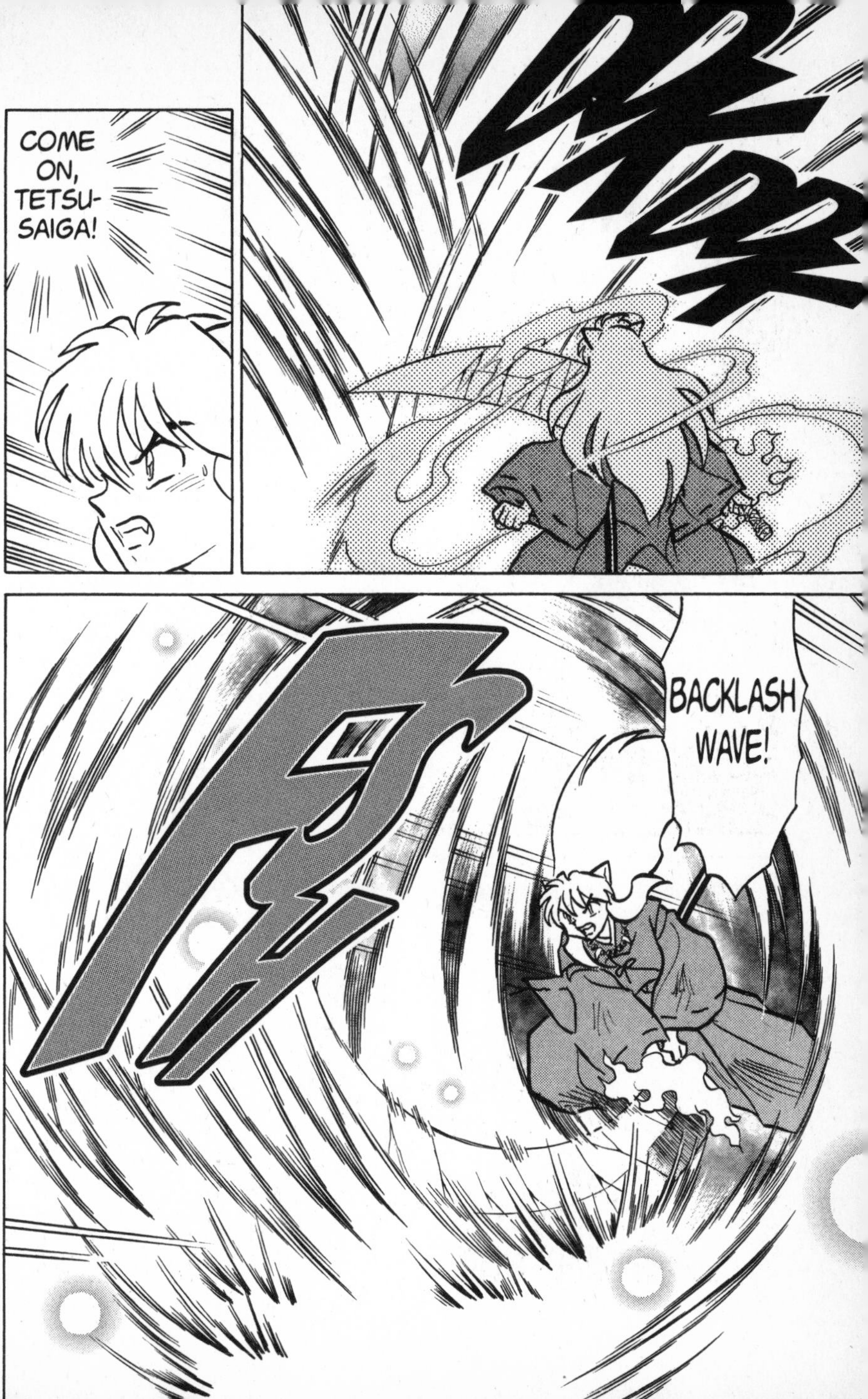
COME ON, TETSU-SAIGA!
BACKLASH WAVE!

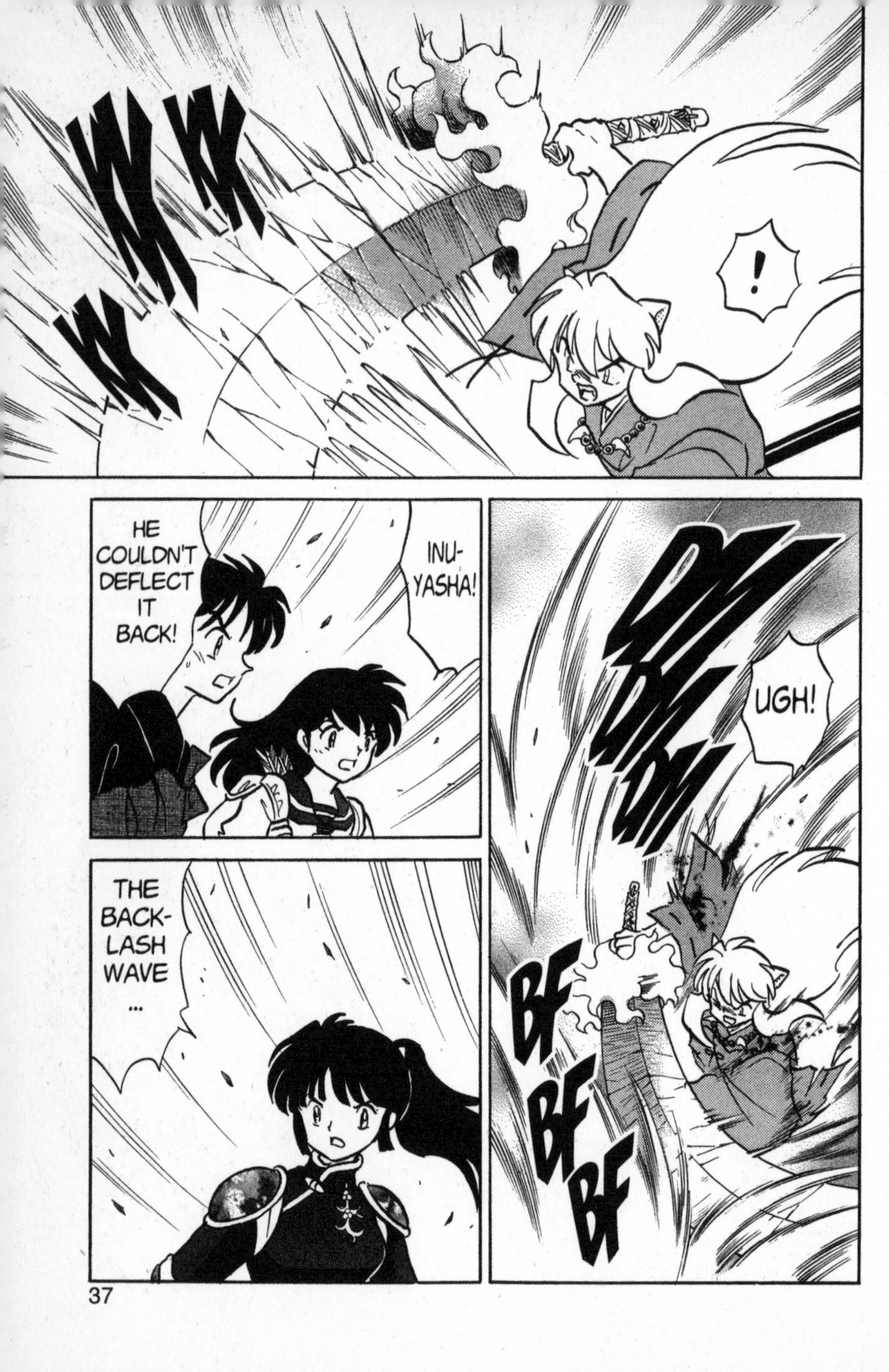
!
UGH!
BF BF BF BF
INU-YASHA!
HE COULDN'T DEFLECT IT BACK!
THE BACK-LASH WAVE ...

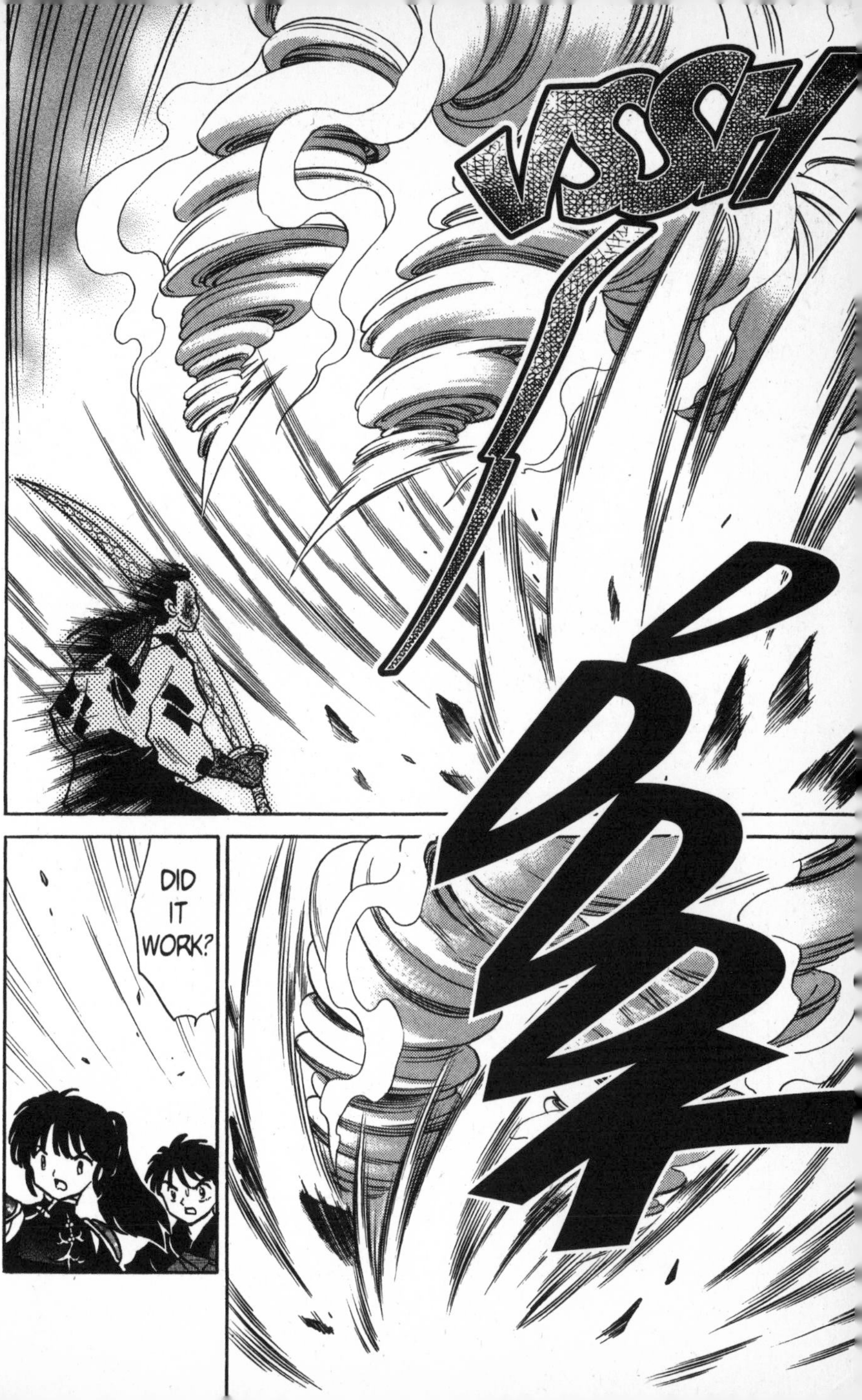
VSSCH
DID IT WORK?

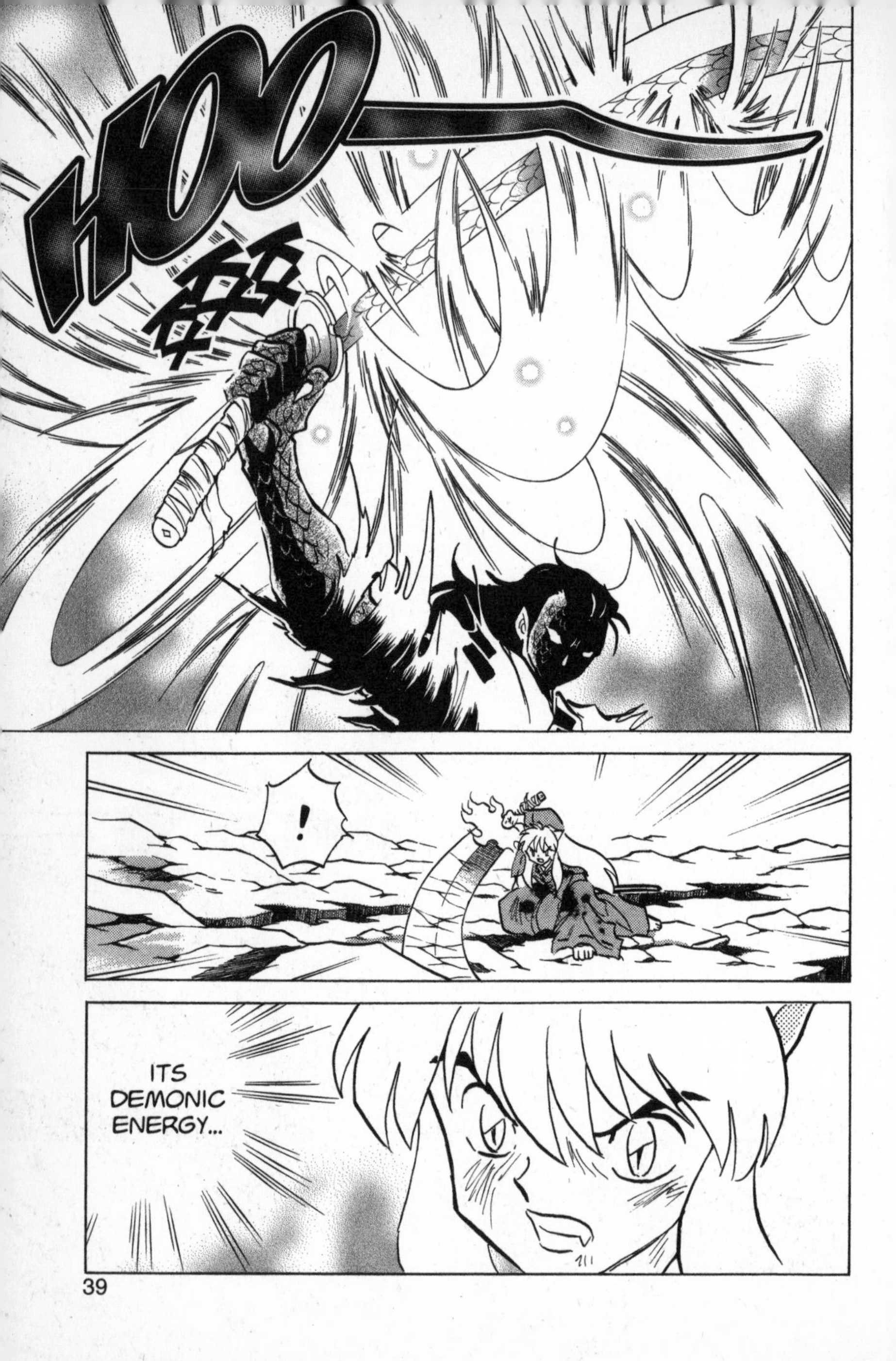
HOO—
!
ITS DEMONIC ENERGY...

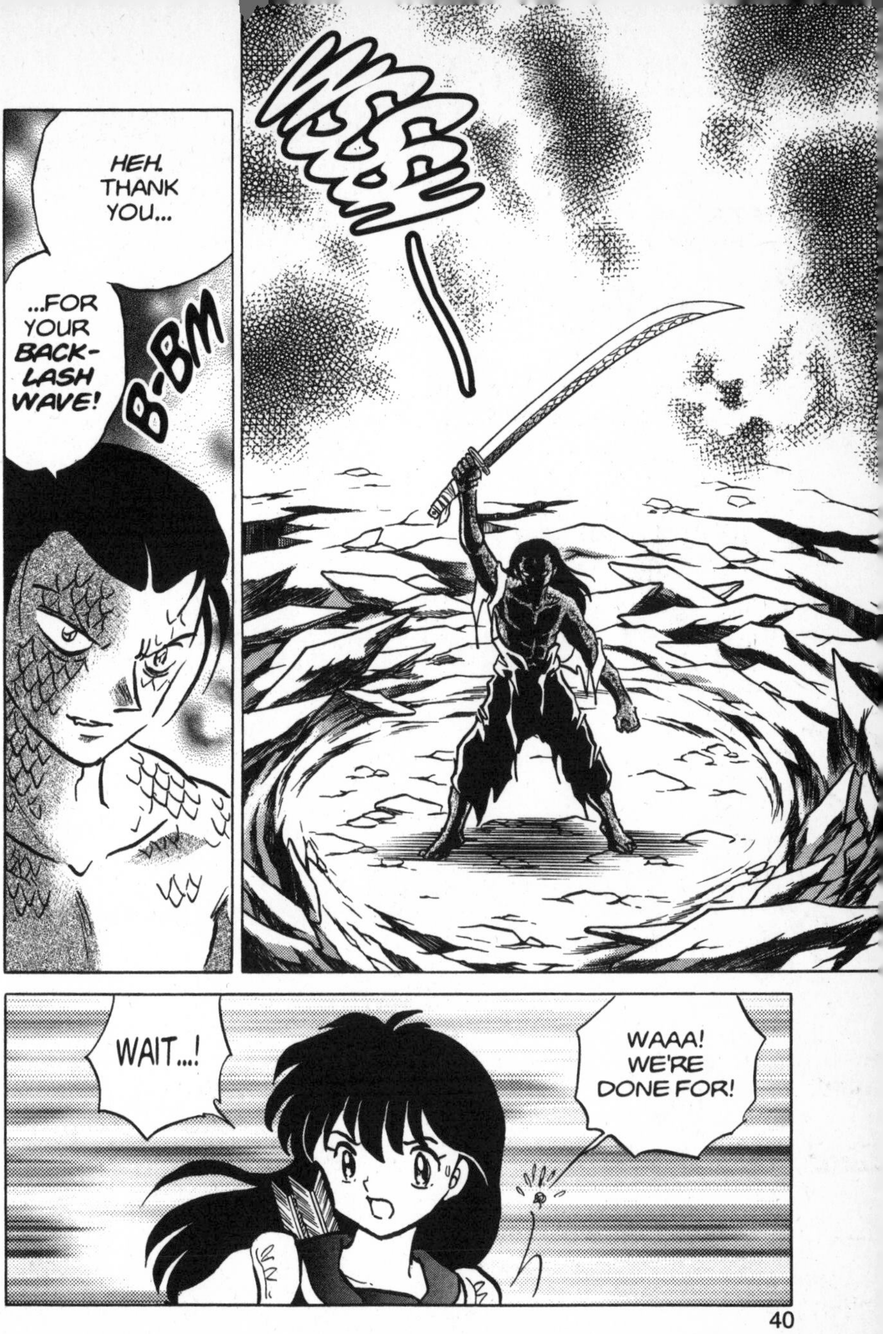
HEH. THANK YOU...
...FOR YOUR BACK-LASH WAVE!
B-BM
WAAA! WE'RE DONE FOR!
WAIT...!

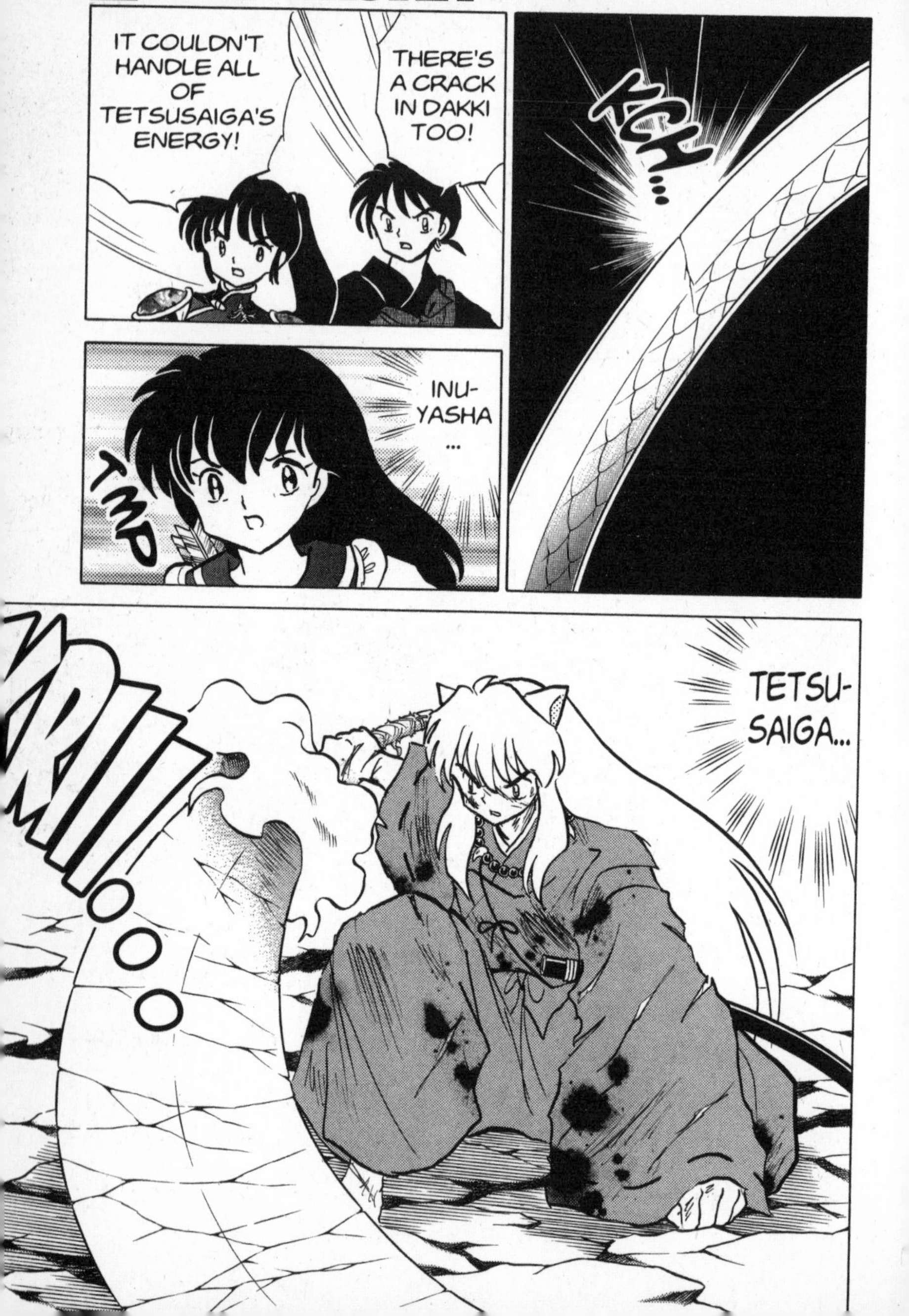
KCH...
THERE'S A CRACK IN DAKKI TOO!
IT COULDN'T HANDLE ALL OF TETSUSAIGA'S ENERGY!
INU-YASHA ...
TMP
TETSU-SAIGA...

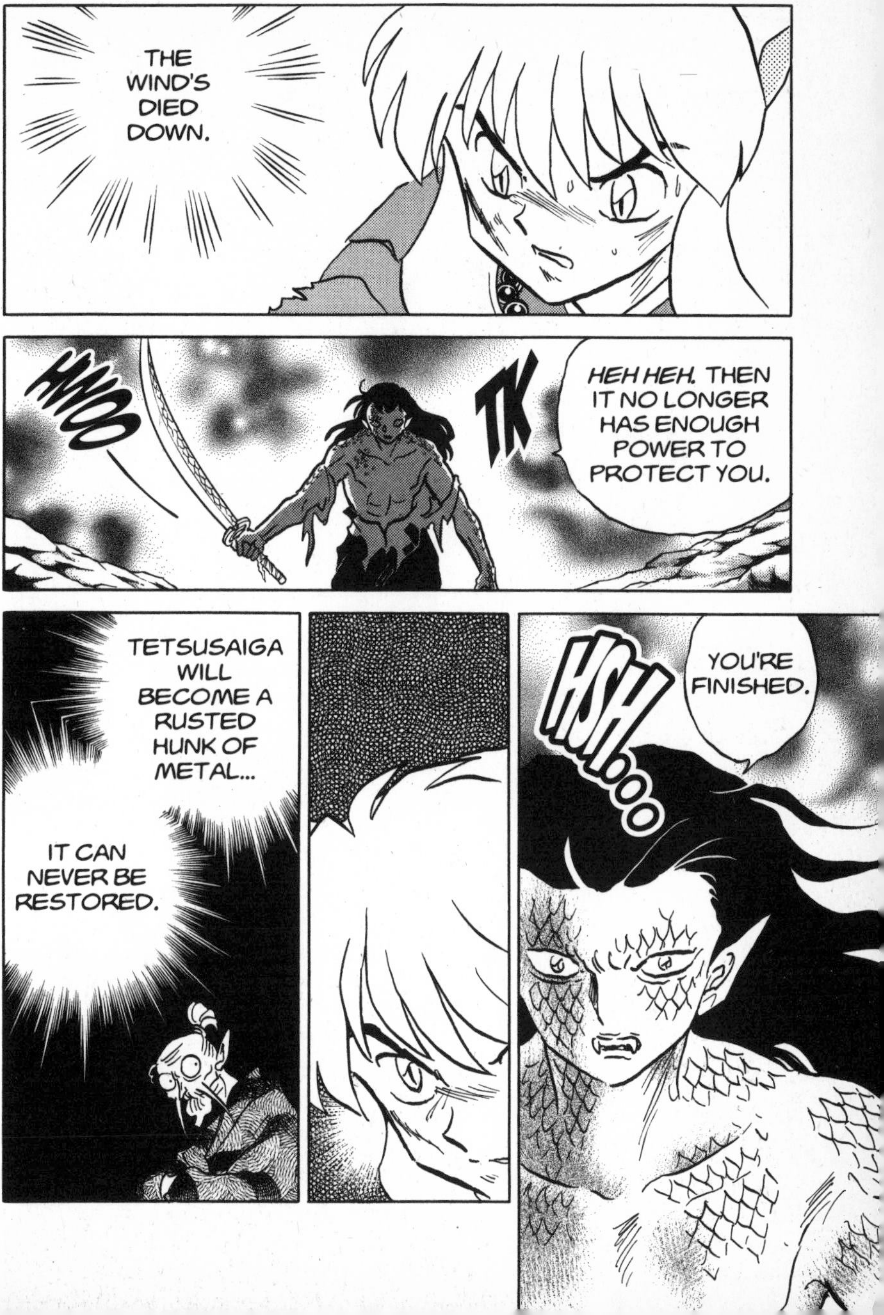
THE WIND'S DIED DOWN.
HEH HEH. THEN IT NO LONGER HAS ENOUGH POWER TO PROTECT YOU.
TK
HWOO
YOU'RE FINISHED.
HSH...OOO
TETSUSAIGA WILL BECOME A RUSTED HUNK OF METAL...
IT CAN NEVER BE RESTORED.

ARE YOU WILLING TO TAKE THAT RISK, INUYASHA?

IT'S NOT OVER YET.

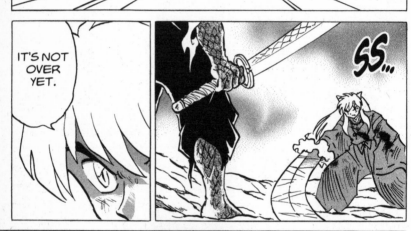

SS...

SO LONG AS I LIVE... *TETSUSAIGA LIVES!*

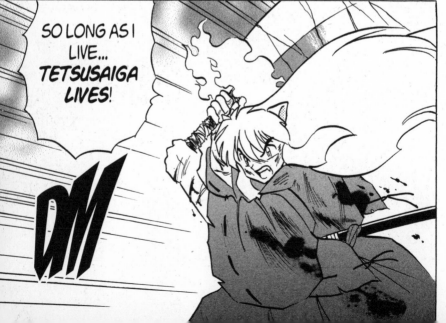

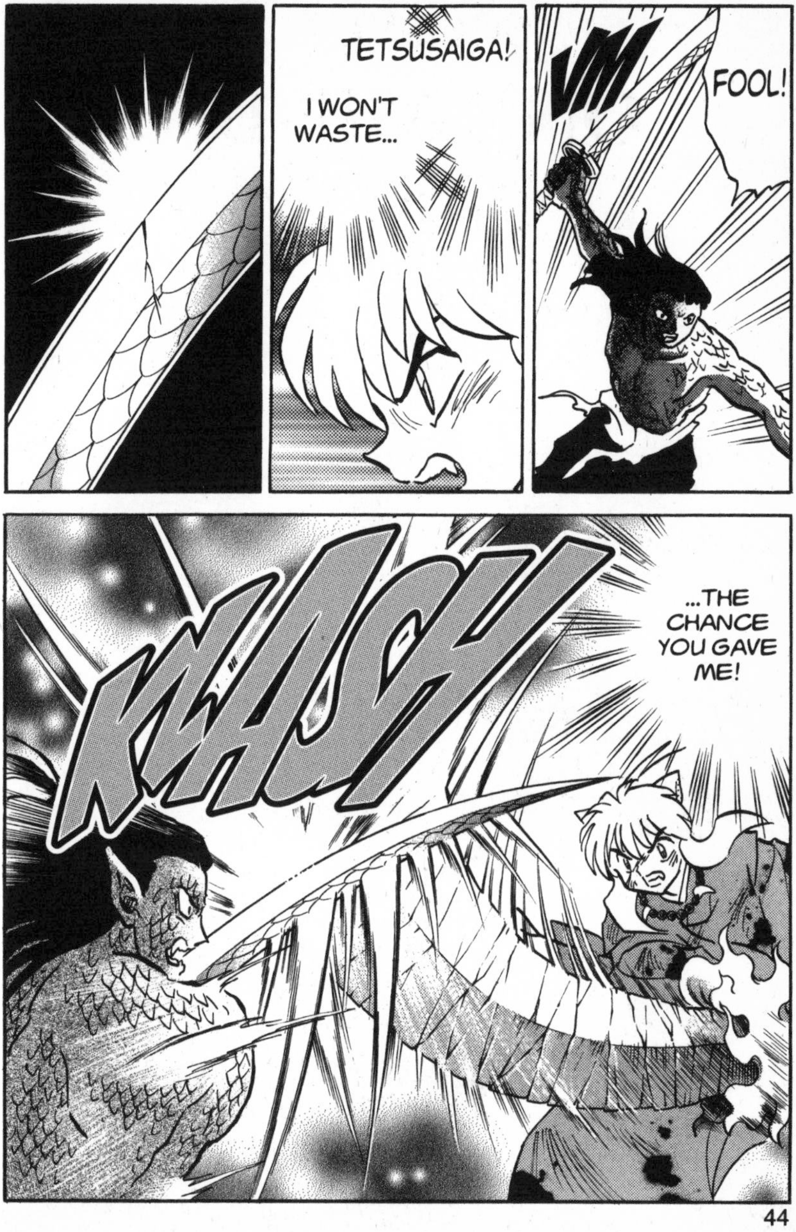
VM
FOOL!
TETSUSAIGA!
I WON'T WASTE...
...THE CHANCE YOU GAVE ME!

SCROLL 3

ONE MIND, ONE BODY

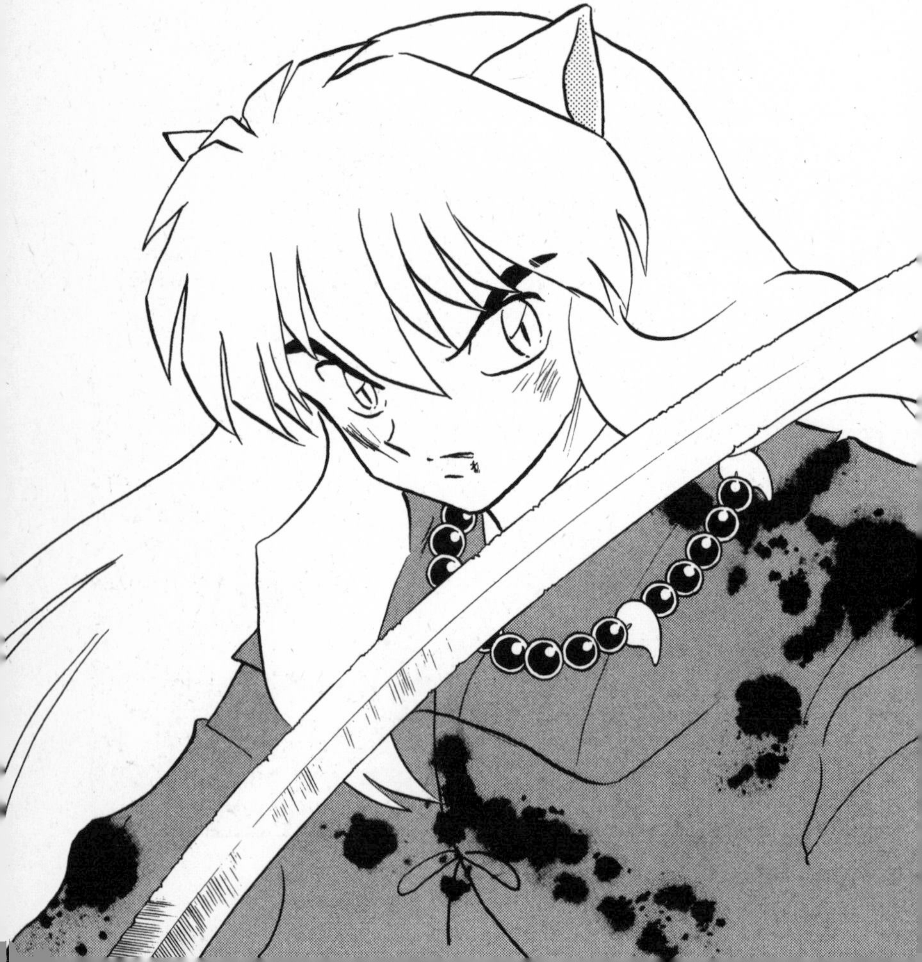

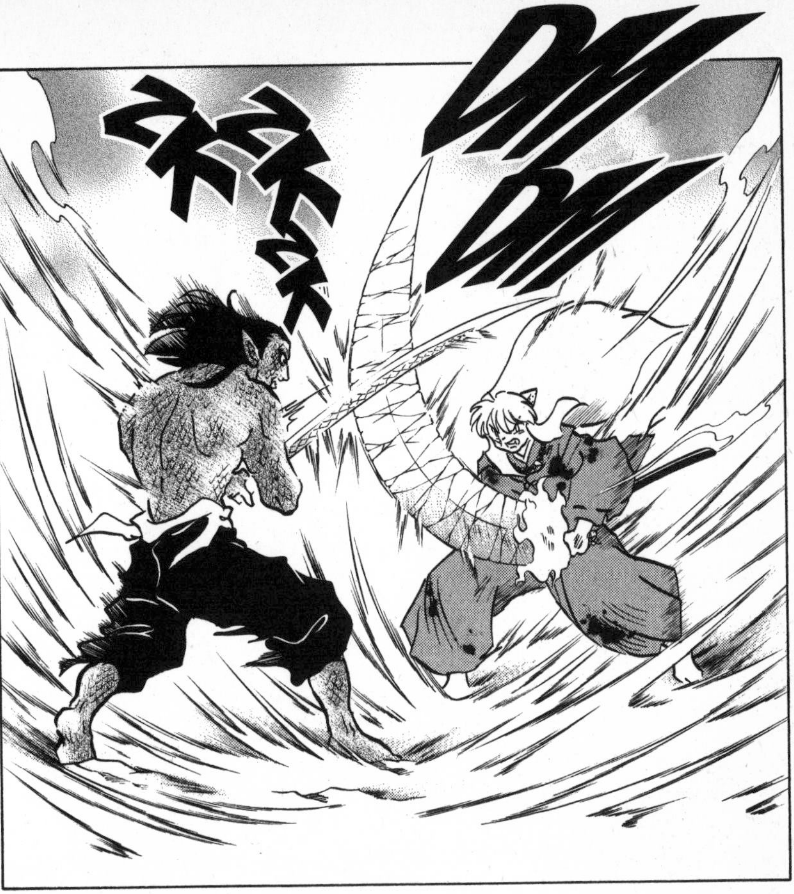
DM
DM

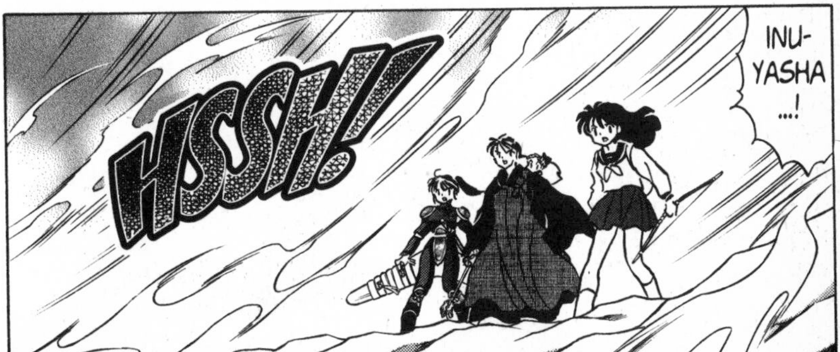
INU-YASHA ...!
HSSH!

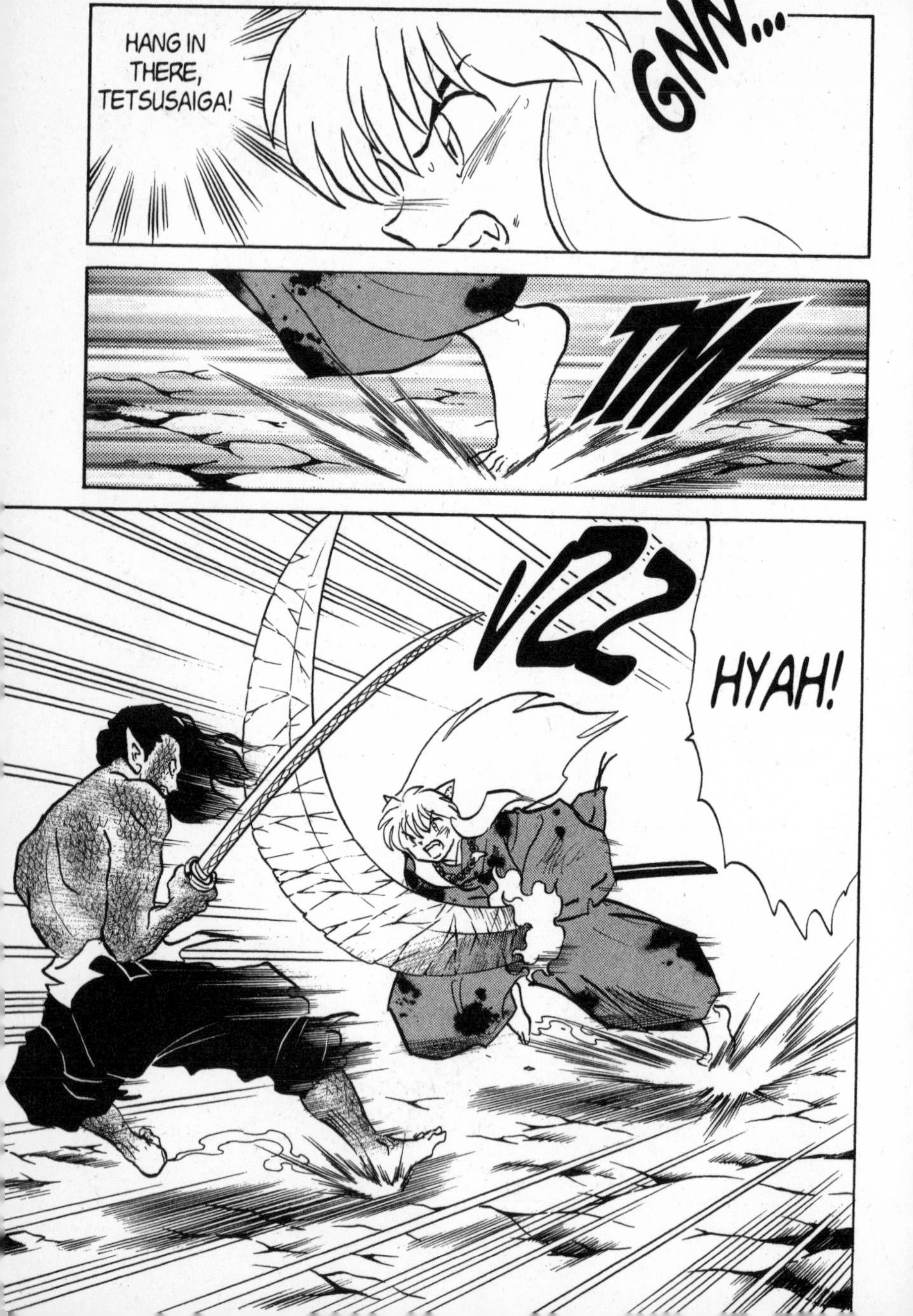
GNN...
HANG IN THERE, TETSUSAIGA!
TM
VZZ
HYAH!

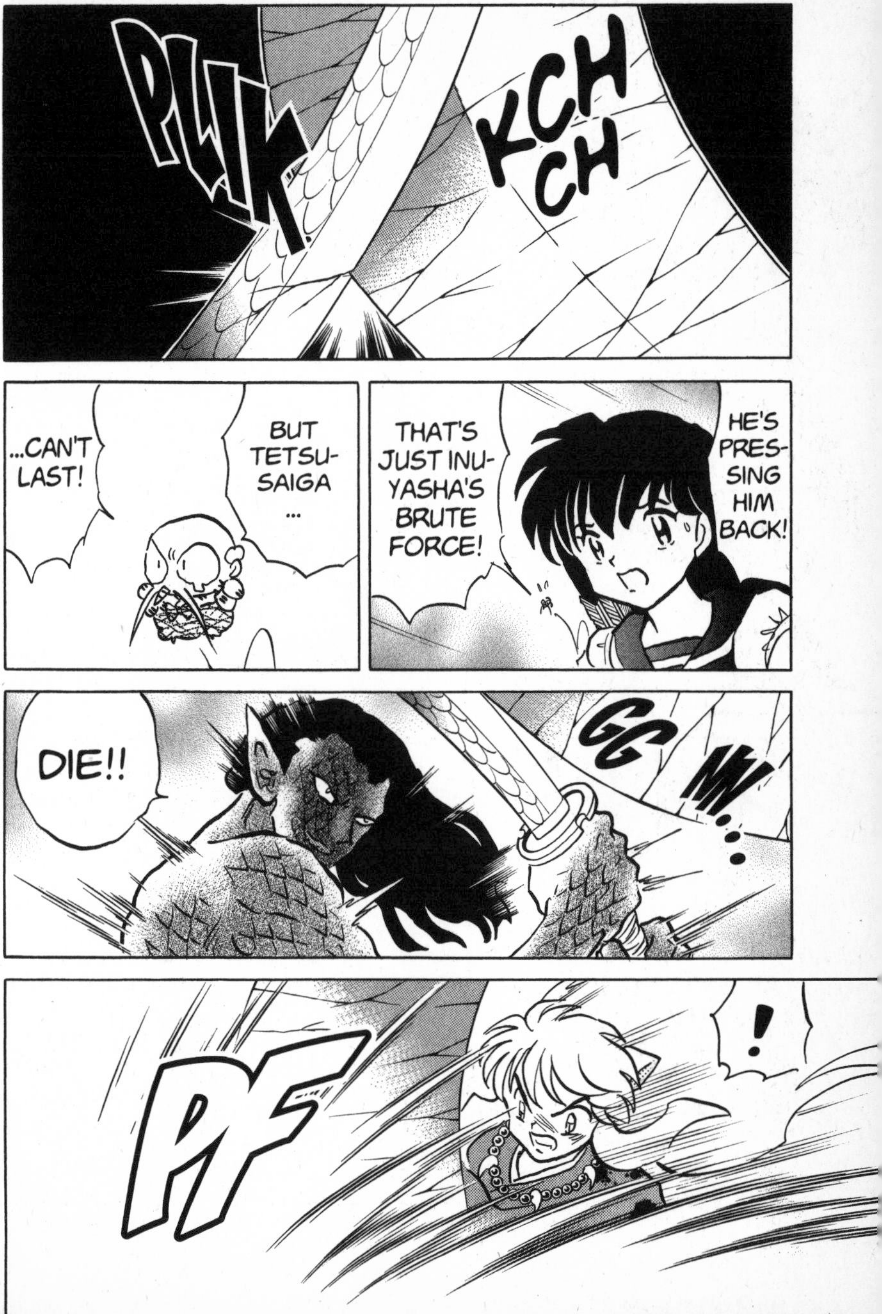
KCH CH
PLIK
HE'S PRES-SING HIM BACK!
THAT'S JUST INU-YASHA'S BRUTE FORCE!
BUT TETSU-SAIGA ...
...CAN'T LAST!
GG MN...
DIE!!
!
PF

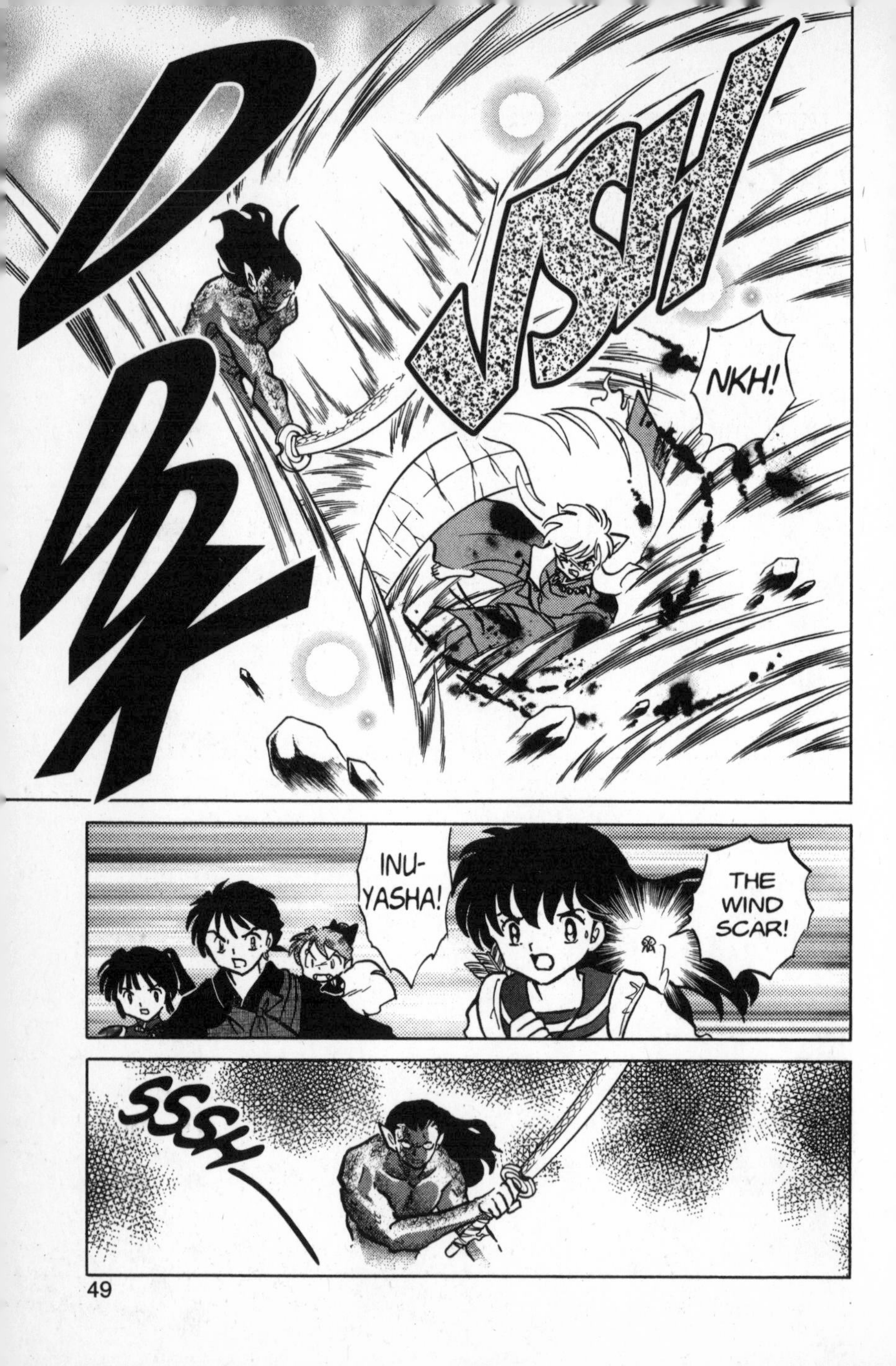
VSH
NKH!
THE WIND SCAR!
INU-YASHA!
SSSH—

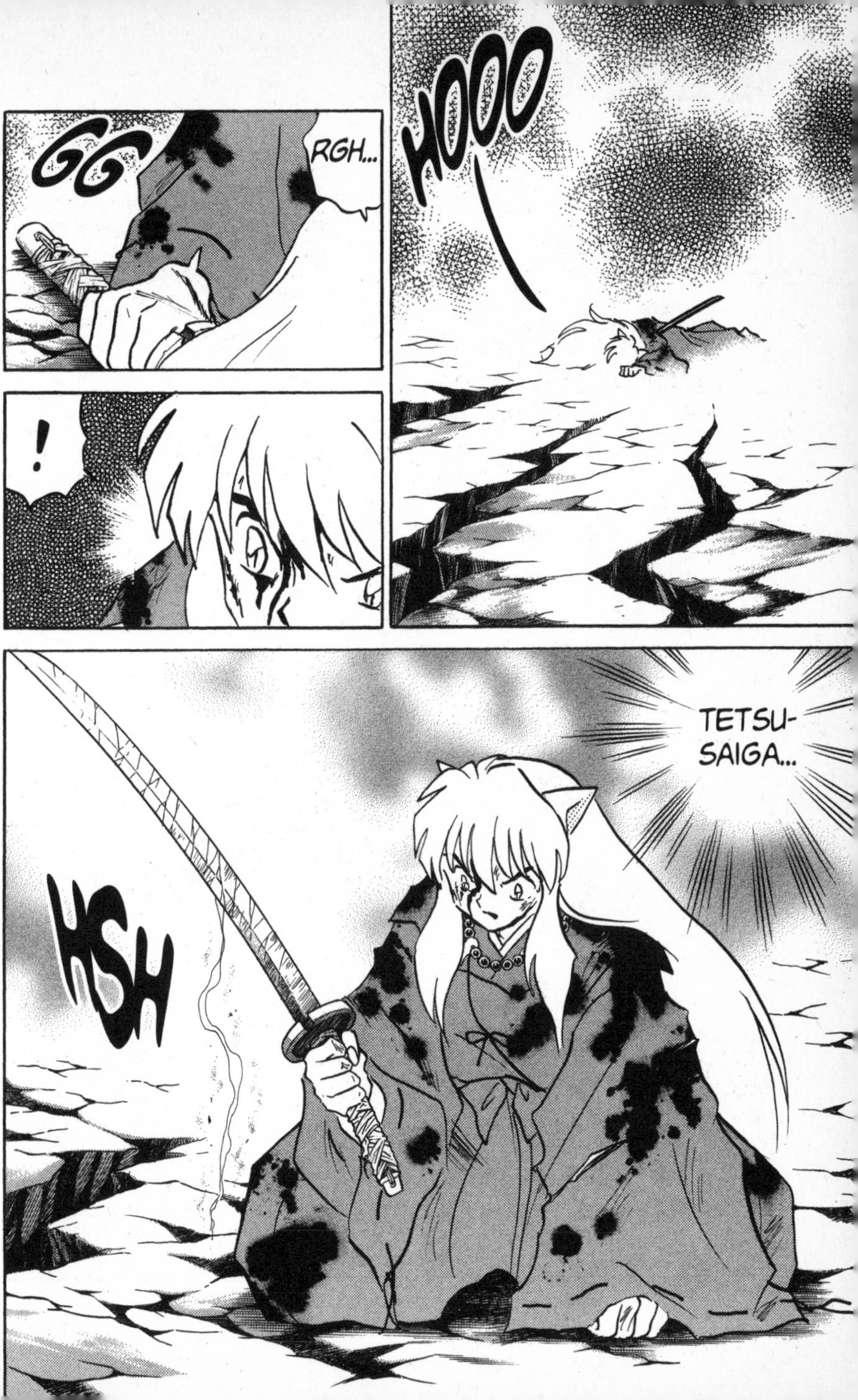
HOOO
GG
RGH...
!
TETSU-
SAIGA...
HSH

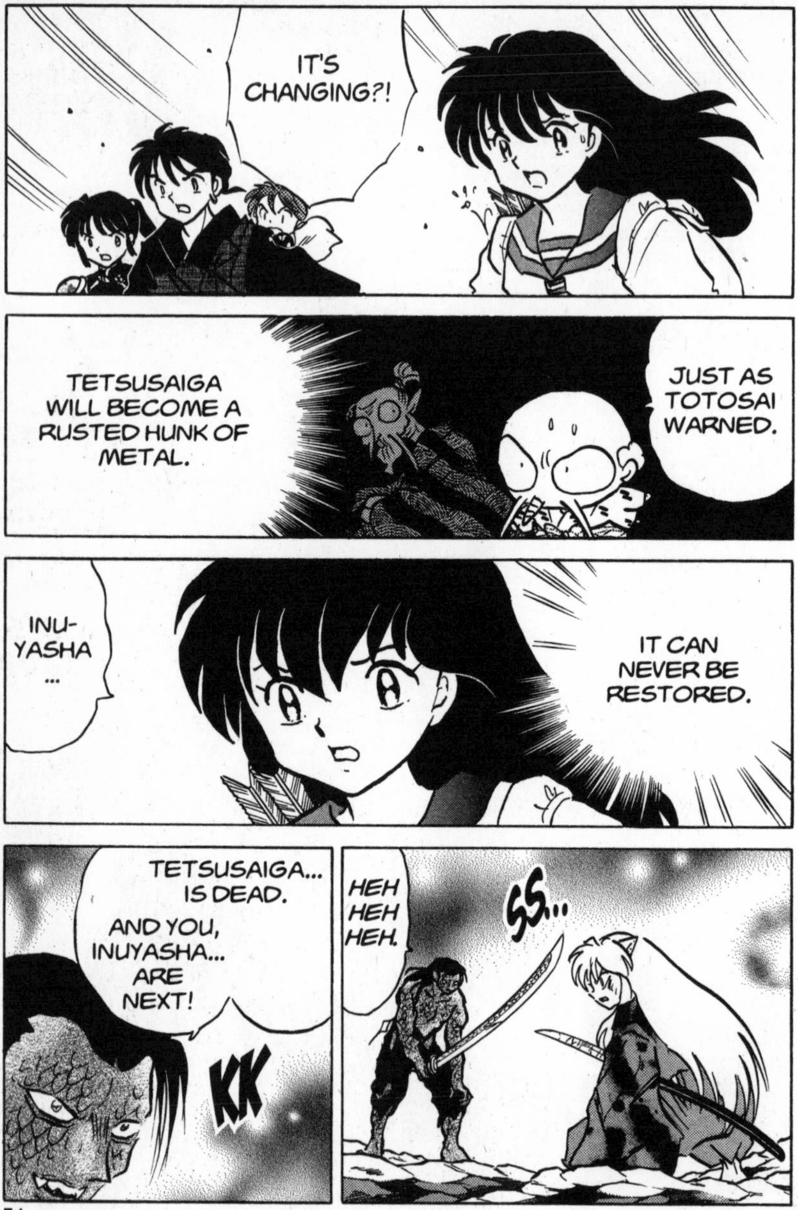
IT'S CHANGING?!
JUST AS TOTOSAI WARNED.
TETSUSAIGA WILL BECOME A RUSTED HUNK OF METAL.
IT CAN NEVER BE RESTORED.
INU-YASHA ...
HEH HEH HEH.
SS...
TETSUSAIGA... IS DEAD. AND YOU, INUYASHA... ARE NEXT!
KK

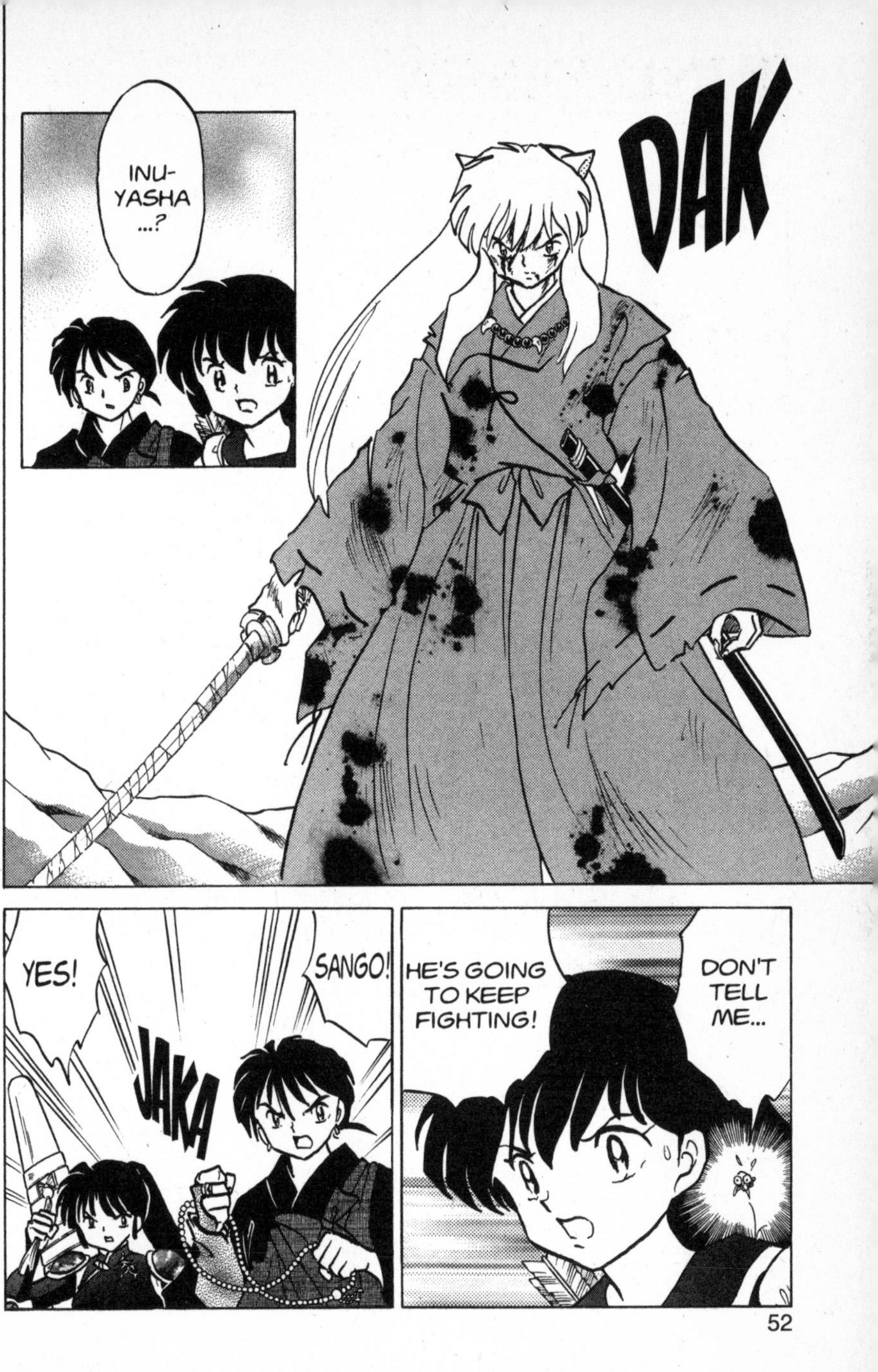
DAK
INU-YASHA ...?
DON'T TELL ME...
HE'S GOING TO KEEP FIGHTING!
SANGO!
JAKA
YES!

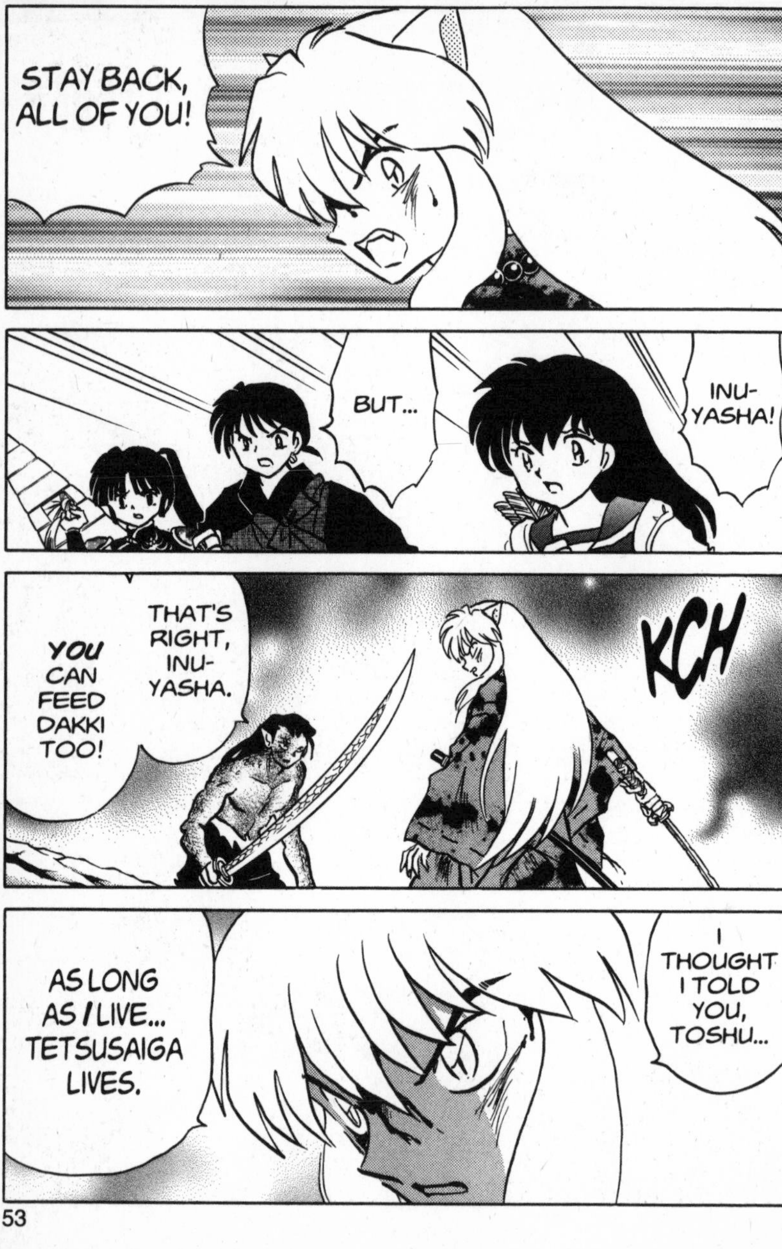
STAY BACK, ALL OF YOU!
INU-YASHA!
BUT...
KCH
THAT'S RIGHT, INU-YASHA.
YOU CAN FEED DAKKI TOO!
I THOUGHT I TOLD YOU, TOSHU...
AS LONG AS I LIVE... TETSUSAIGA LIVES.

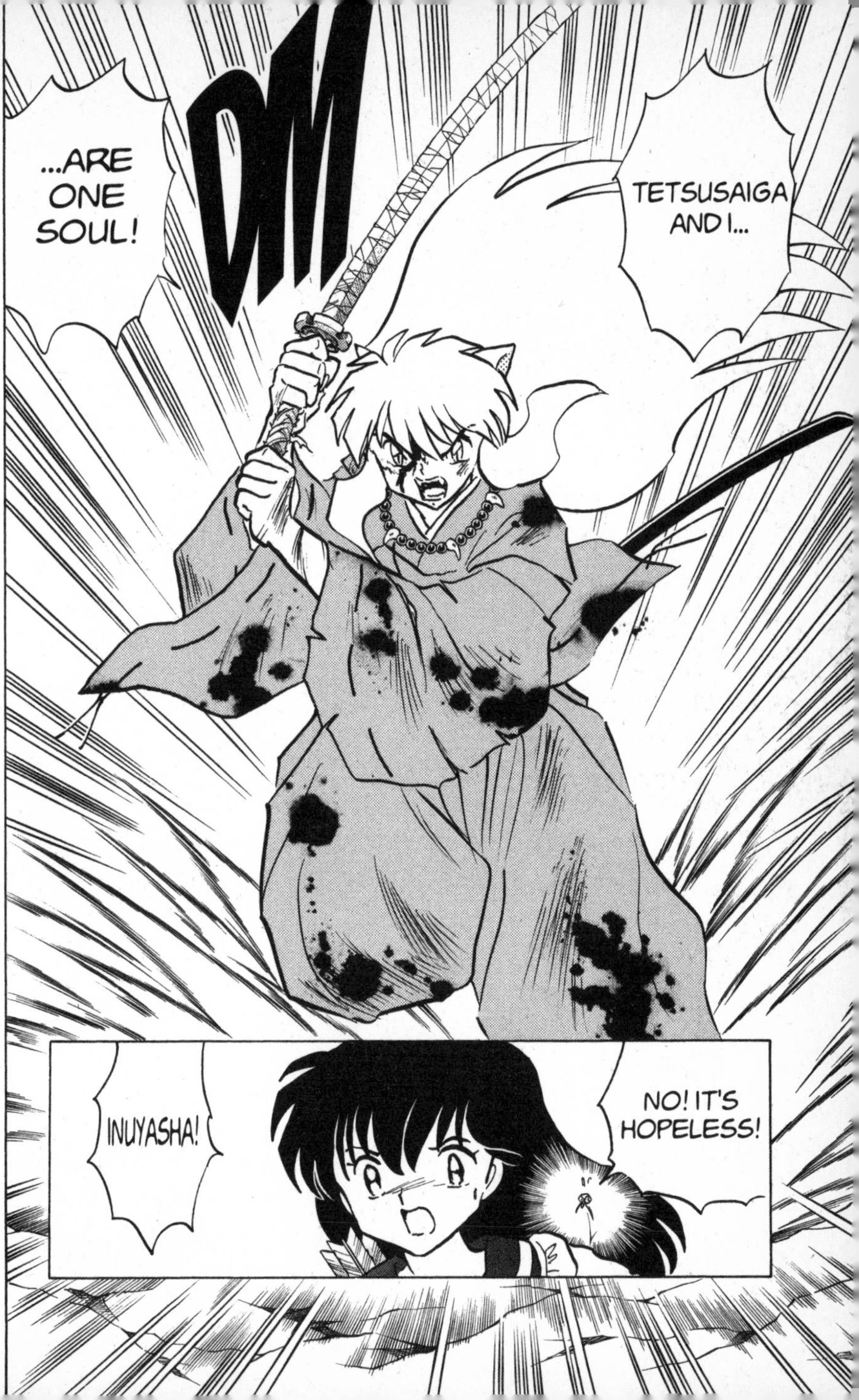
TETSUSAIGA AND I...
DM
...ARE ONE SOUL!
NO! IT'S HOPELESS!
INUYASHA!

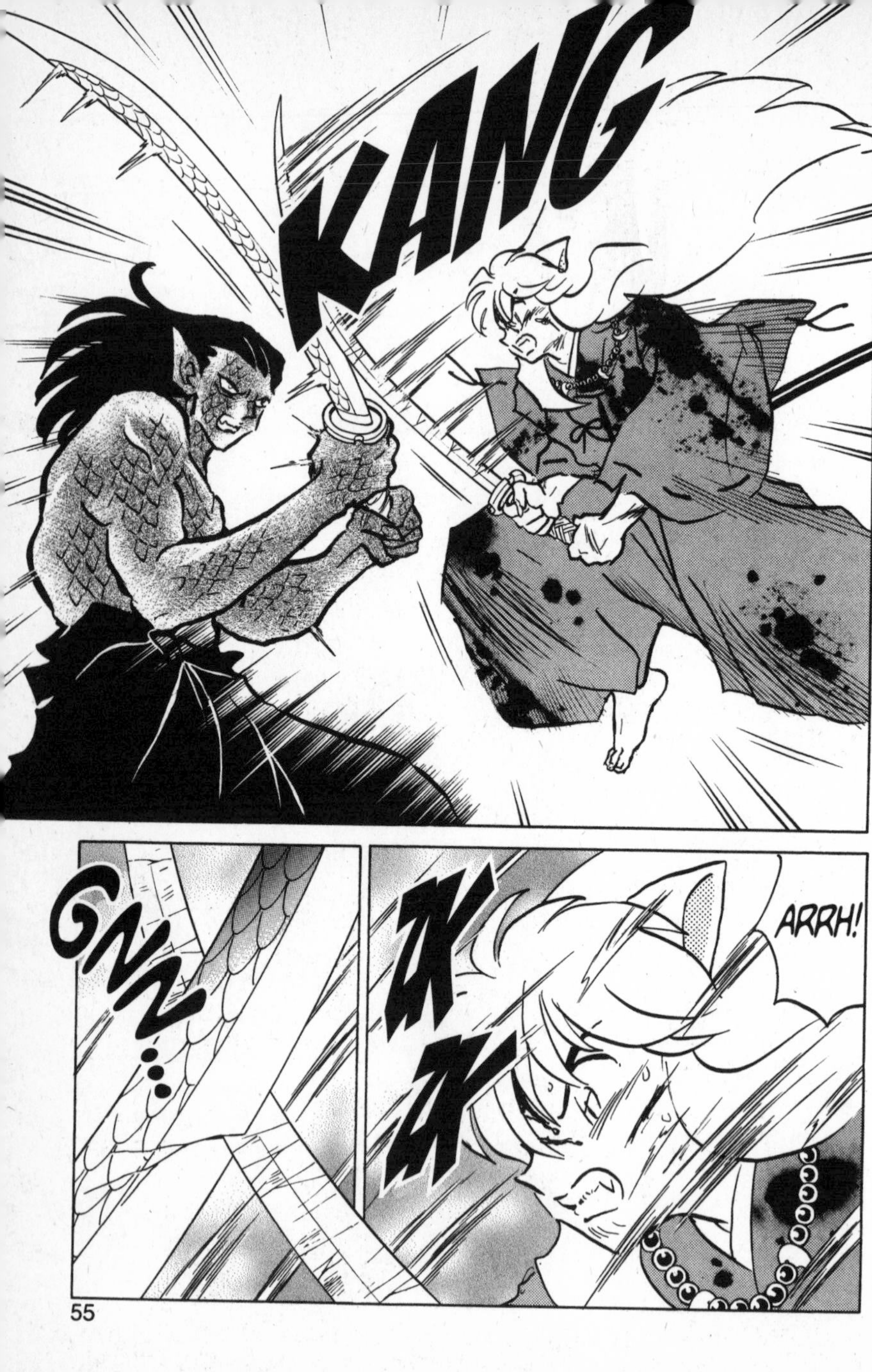
KANG
ARRH!
GNN...

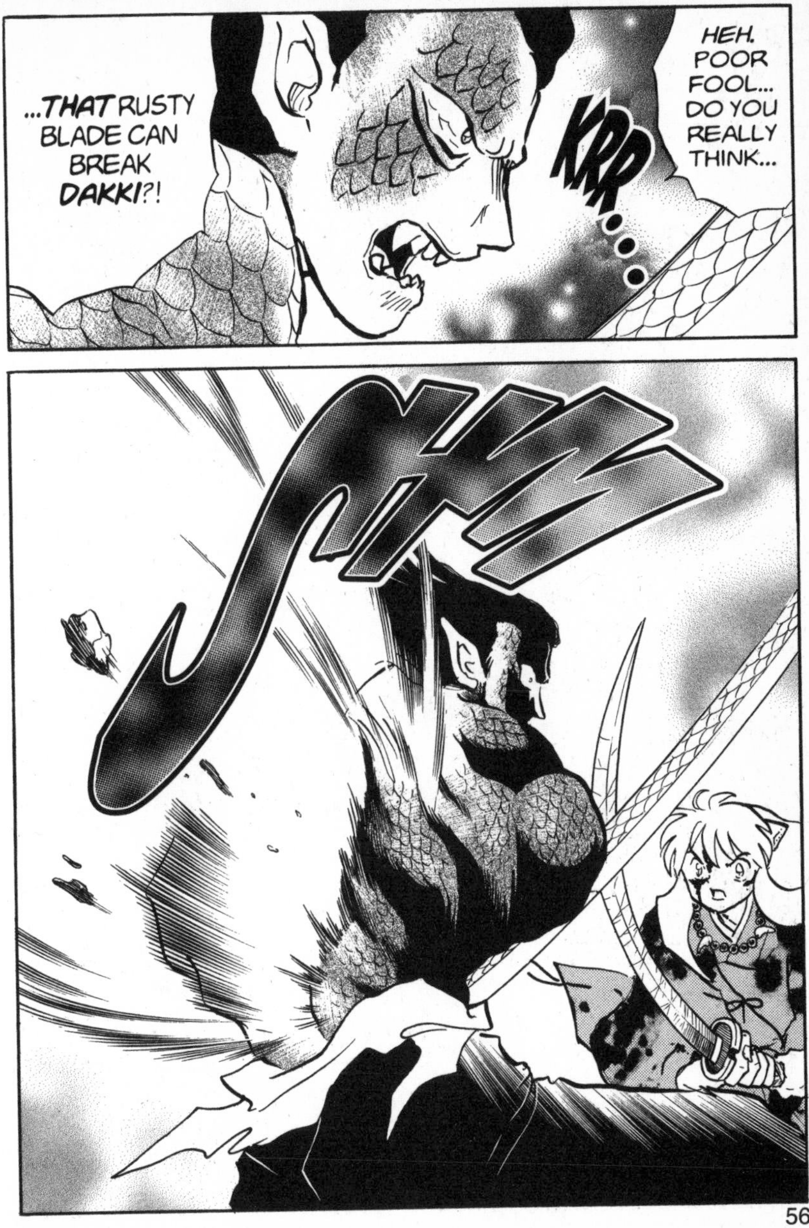
HEH. POOR FOOL... DO YOU REALLY THINK...
KRR...
...THAT RUSTY BLADE CAN BREAK DAKKI?!

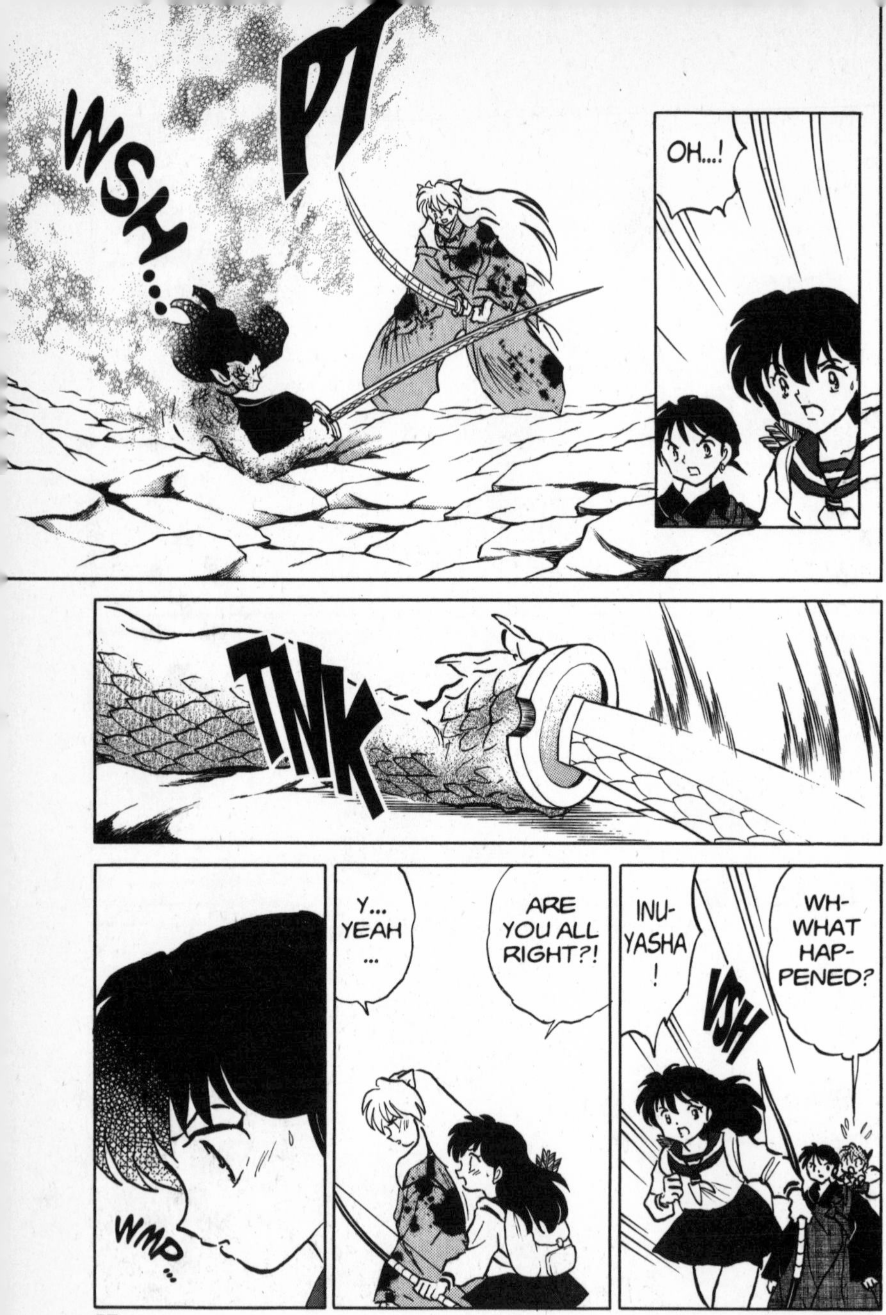

OH...!
WSH...
PT
TINK
WH- WHAT HAP- PENED?
VSH
INU- YASHA !
ARE YOU ALL RIGHT?!
Y... YEAH ...
WMP...

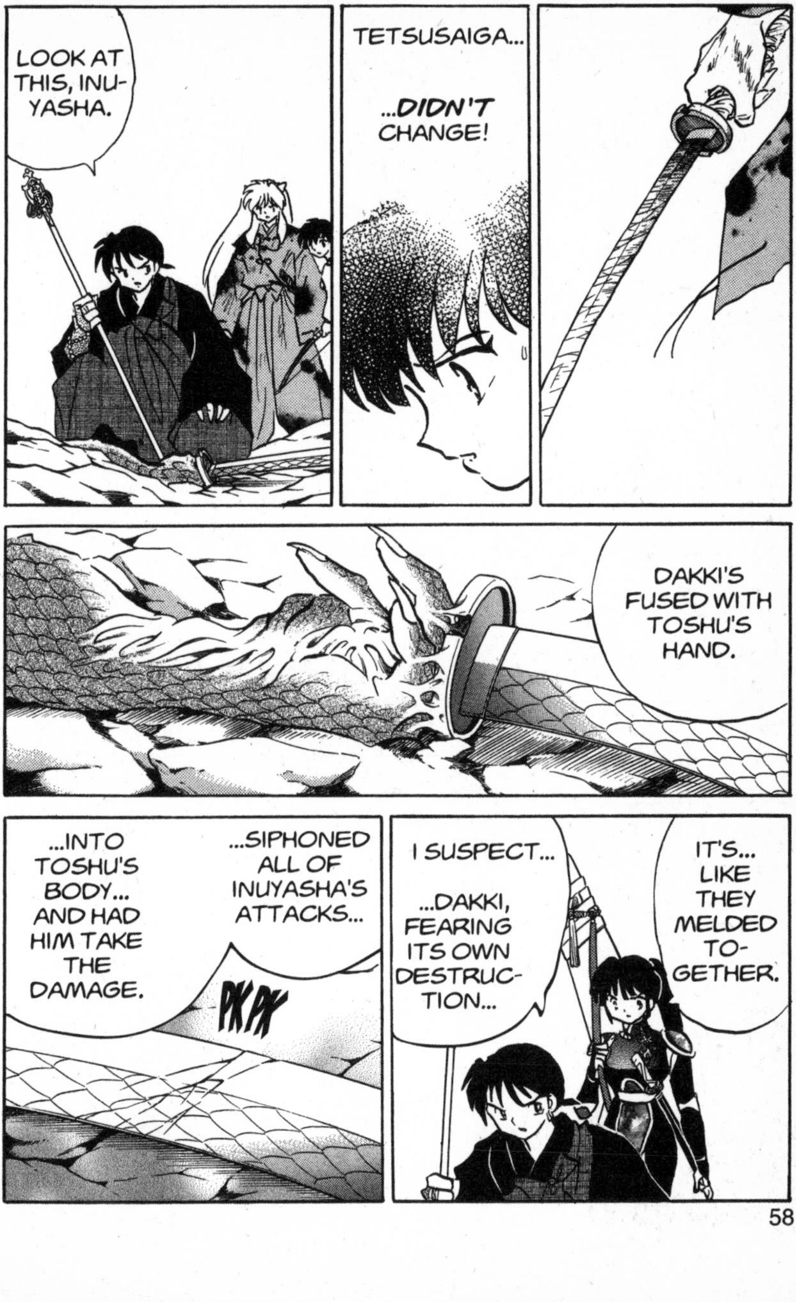
TETSUSAIGA...
...DIDN'T CHANGE!
LOOK AT THIS, INU-YASHA.
DAKKI'S FUSED WITH TOSHU'S HAND.
IT'S... LIKE THEY MELDED TO-GETHER.
I SUSPECT...
...DAKKI, FEARING ITS OWN DESTRUC-TION...
...SIPHONED ALL OF INUYASHA'S ATTACKS...
...INTO TOSHU'S BODY... AND HAD HIM TAKE THE DAMAGE.
PK PK

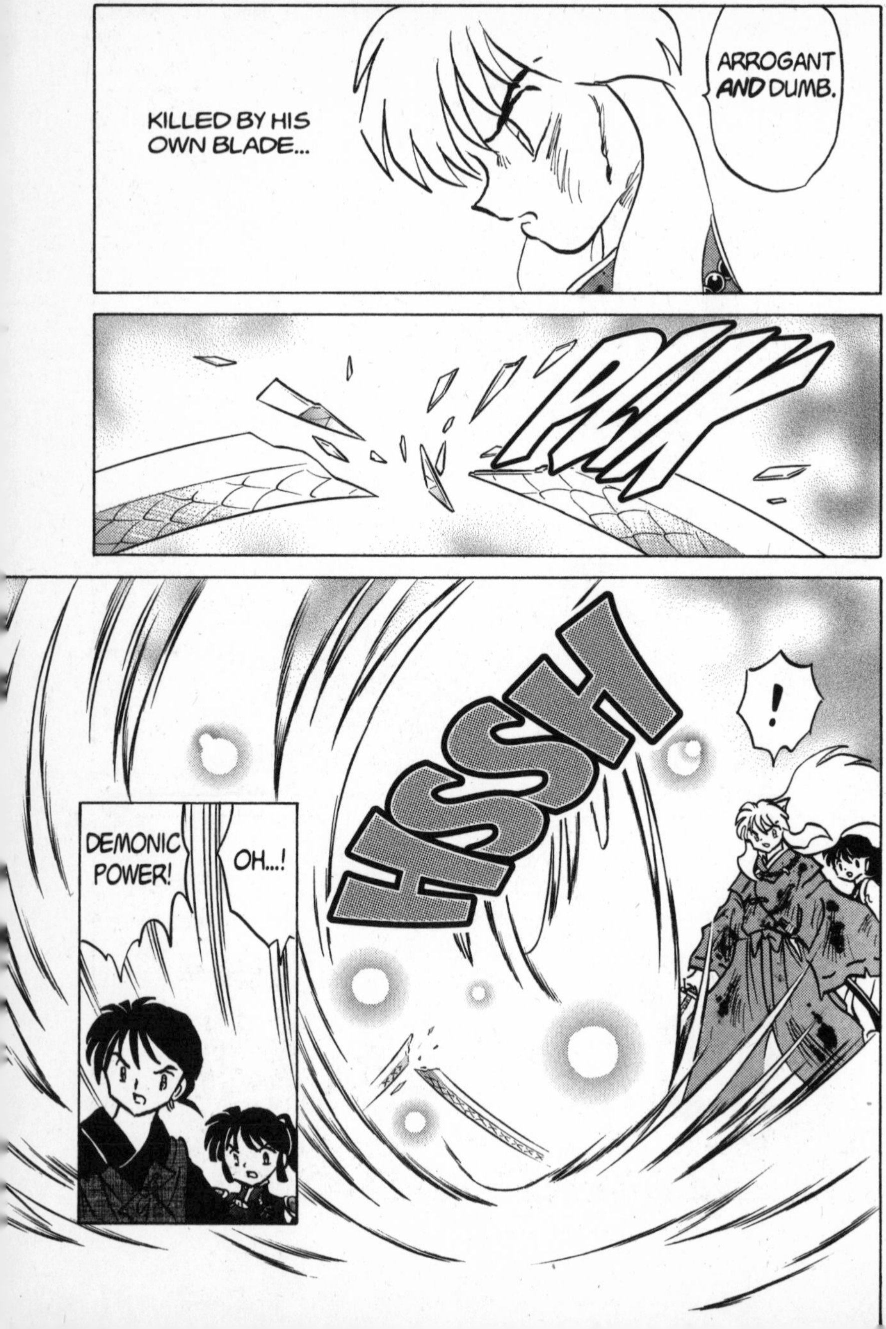
ARROGANT AND DUMB.
KILLED BY HIS OWN BLADE...
PAK
!
HISSH
OH...!
DEMONIC POWER!

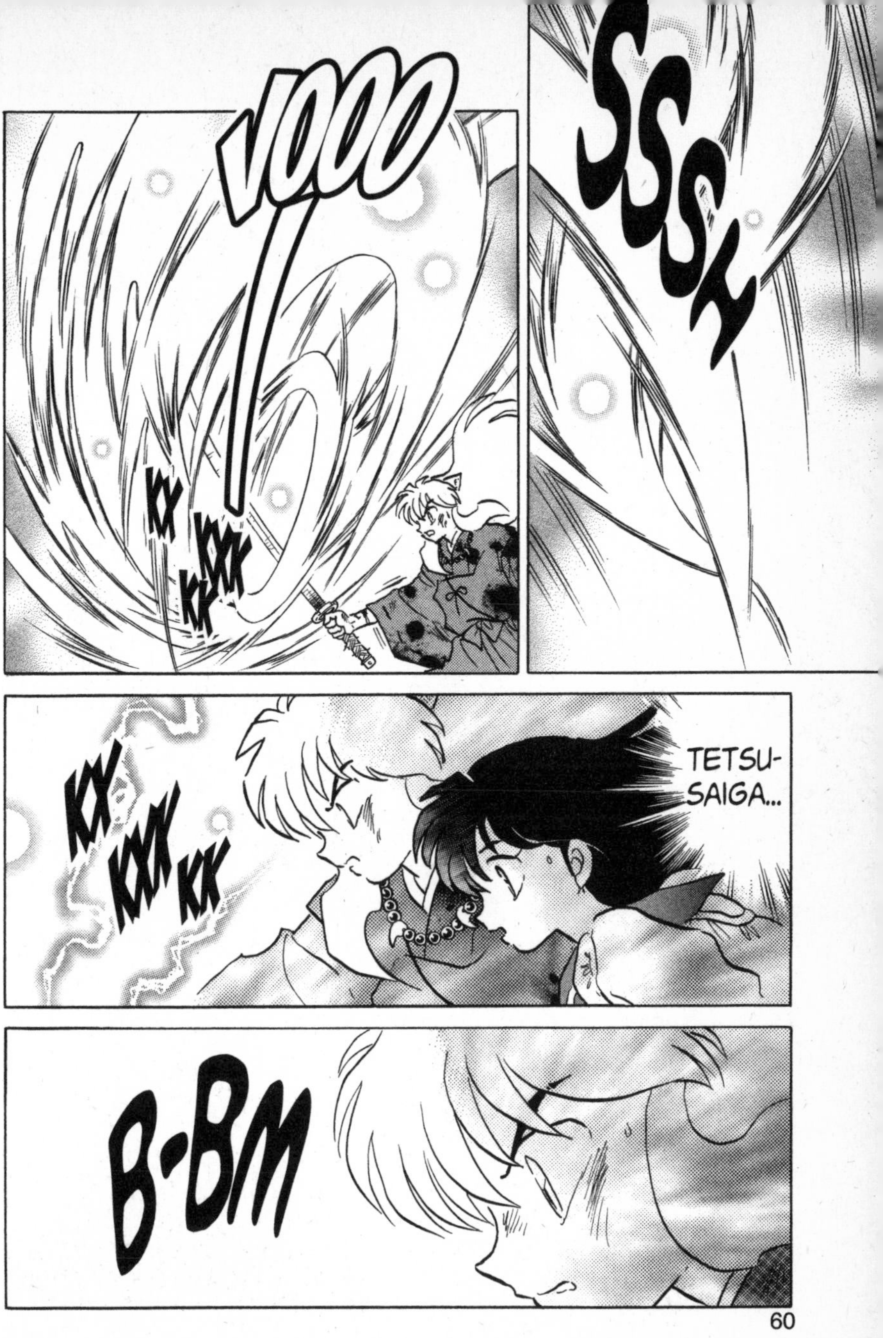
SSSH
VOOO
KY
KKKK
KK
TETSU-SAIGA...
B-BM

SCROLL 4
A PEACEFUL MEAL

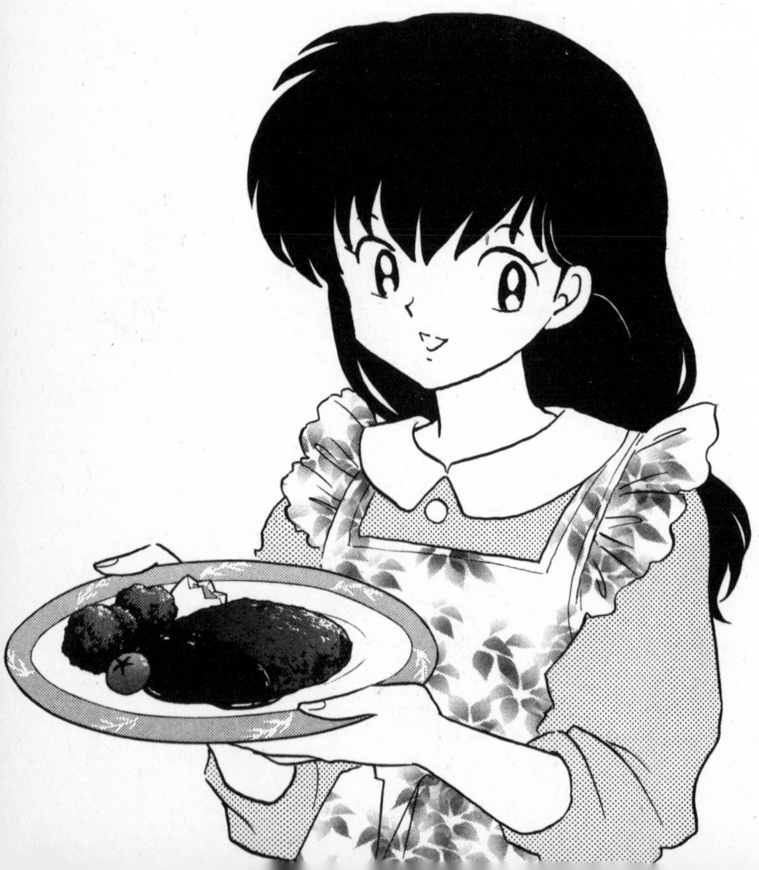

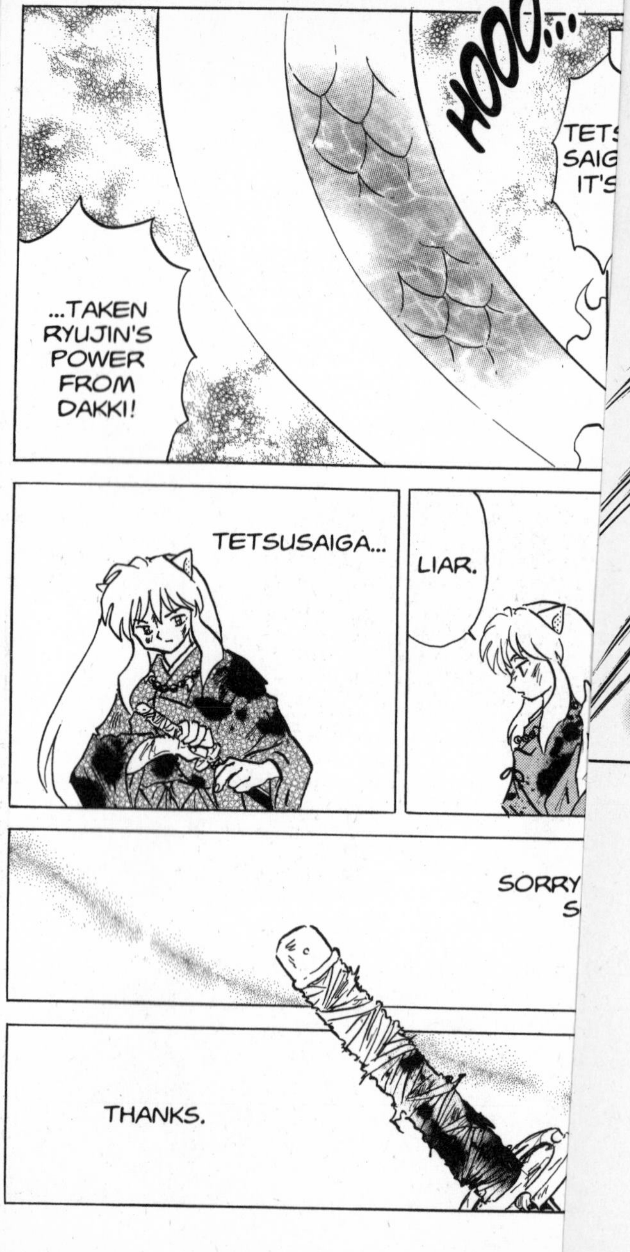
HOOO...
TETS
SAIG
IT'S
...TAKEN RYUJIN'S POWER FROM DAKKI!
LIAR.
TETSUSAIGA...
SORRY
THANKS.

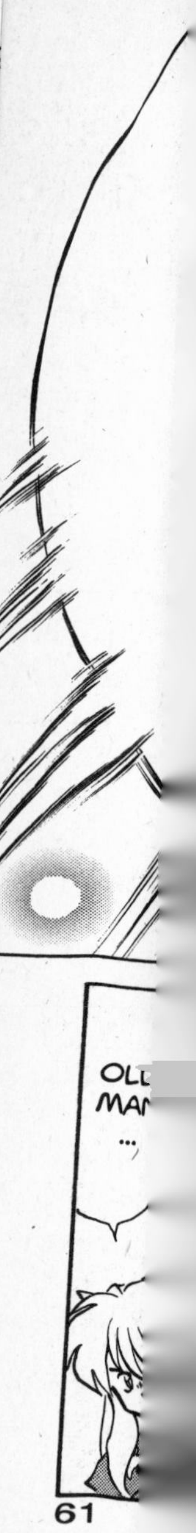

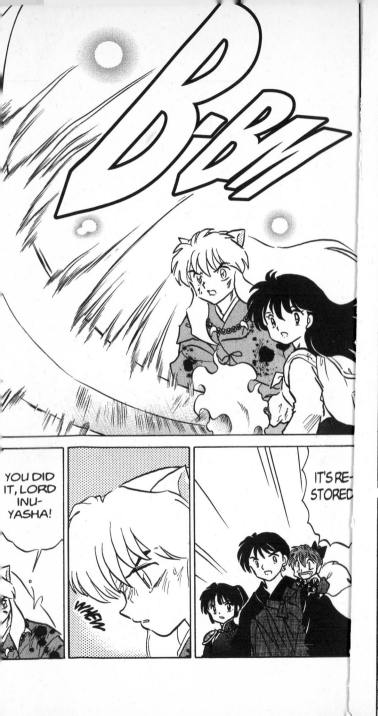

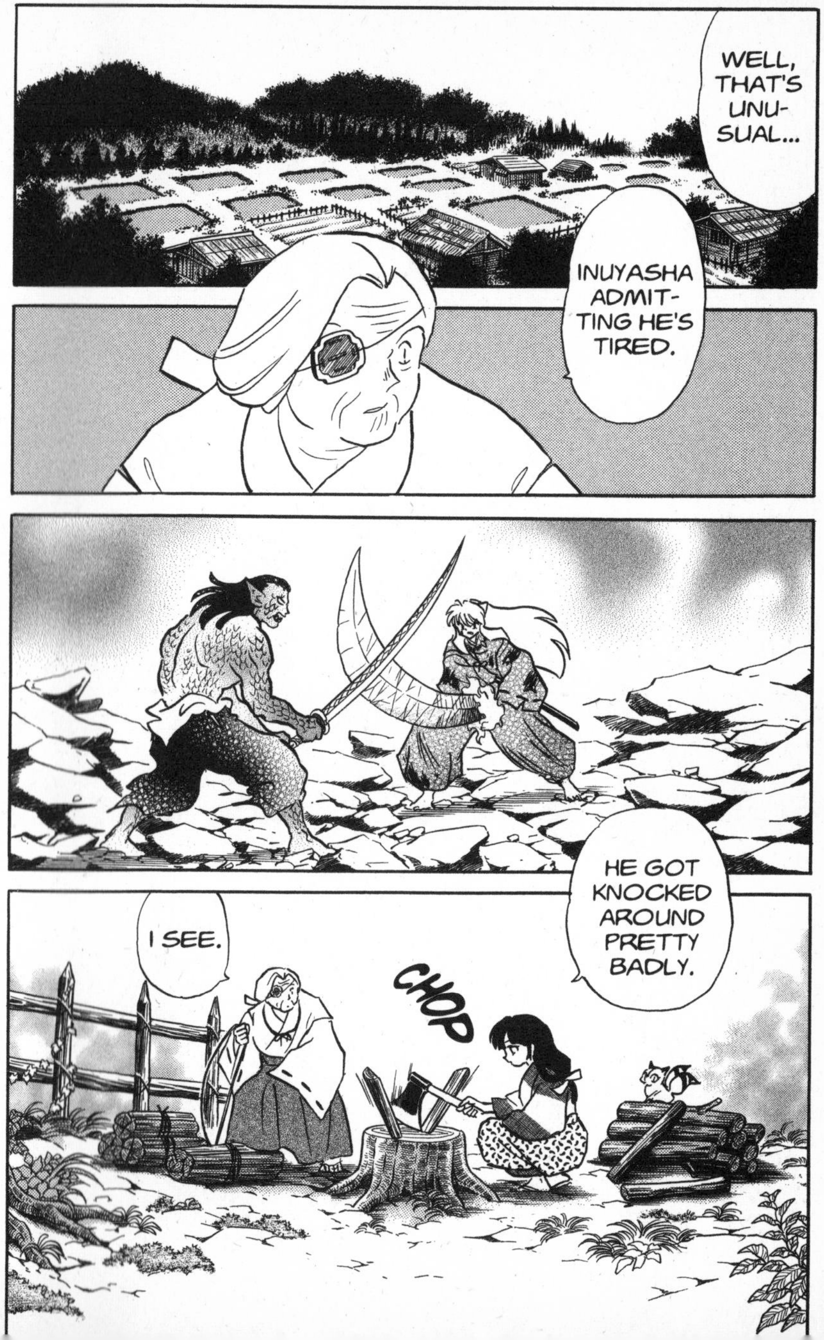
WELL, THAT'S UNU-SUAL...
INUYASHA ADMIT-TING HE'S TIRED.
HE GOT KNOCKED AROUND PRETTY BADLY.
I SEE.
CHOP

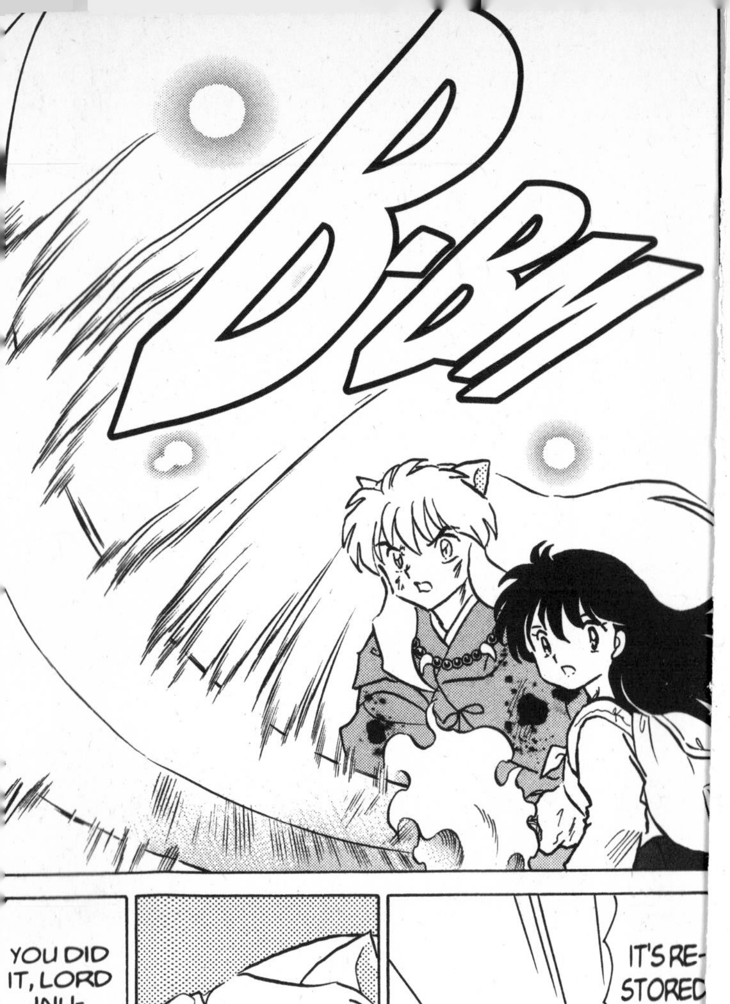
BEM
IT'S RE-STORED
WHEW
YOU DID IT, LORD INU-YASHA!

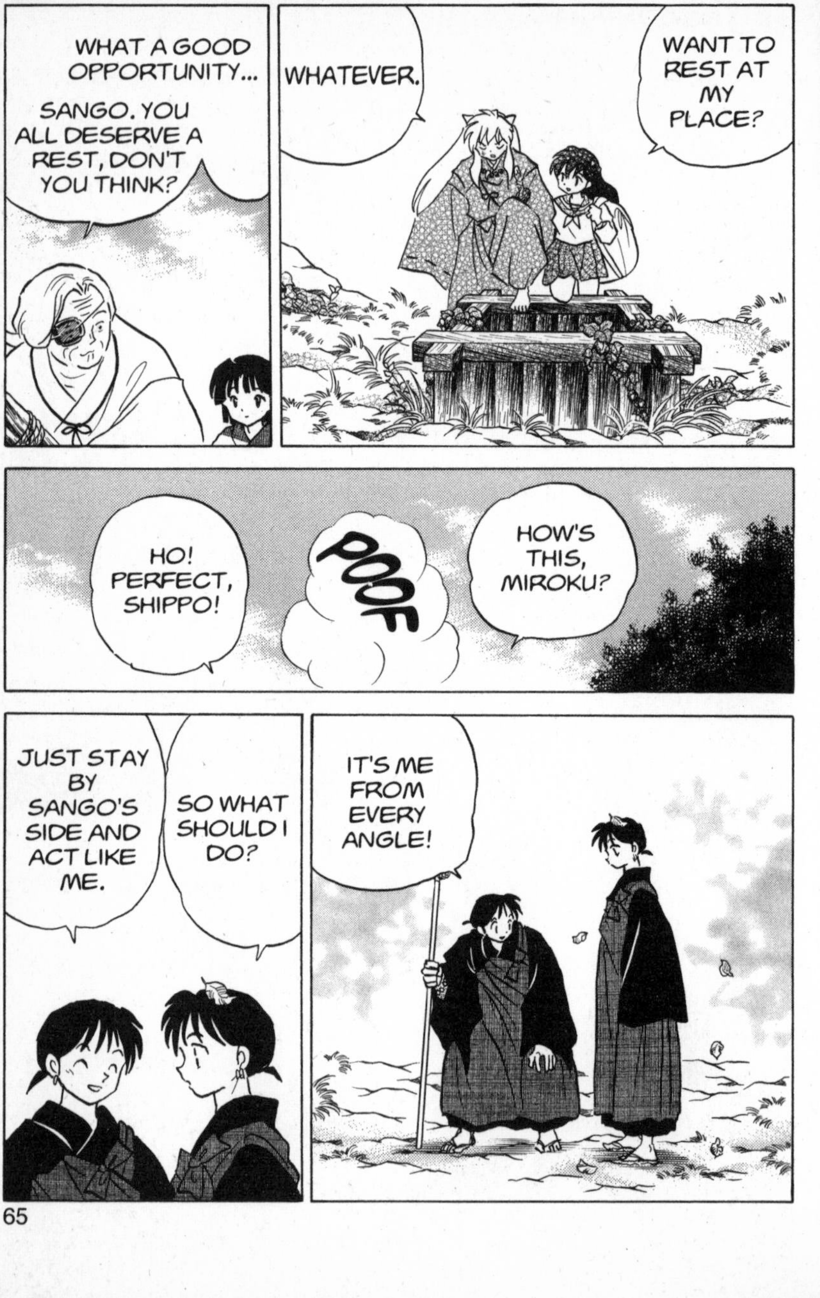
WANT TO REST AT MY PLACE?
WHATEVER.
WHAT A GOOD OPPORTUNITY...
SANGO. YOU ALL DESERVE A REST, DON'T YOU THINK?
HOW'S THIS, MIROKU?
POOF
HO! PERFECT, SHIPPO!
IT'S ME FROM EVERY ANGLE!
SO WHAT SHOULD I DO?
JUST STAY BY SANGO'S SIDE AND ACT LIKE ME.

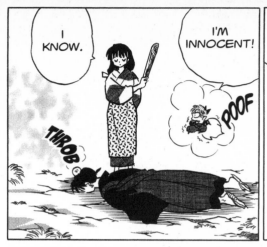

I KNOW.

I'M INNOCENT!

THROB

POOF

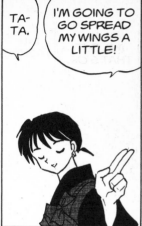

TA-TA.

I'M GOING TO GO SPREAD MY WINGS A LITTLE!

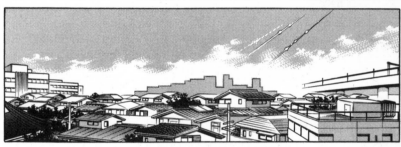

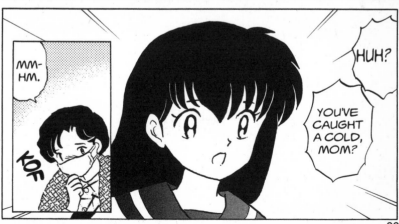

MM-HM.

KOF

HUH?

YOU'VE CAUGHT A COLD, MOM?

66

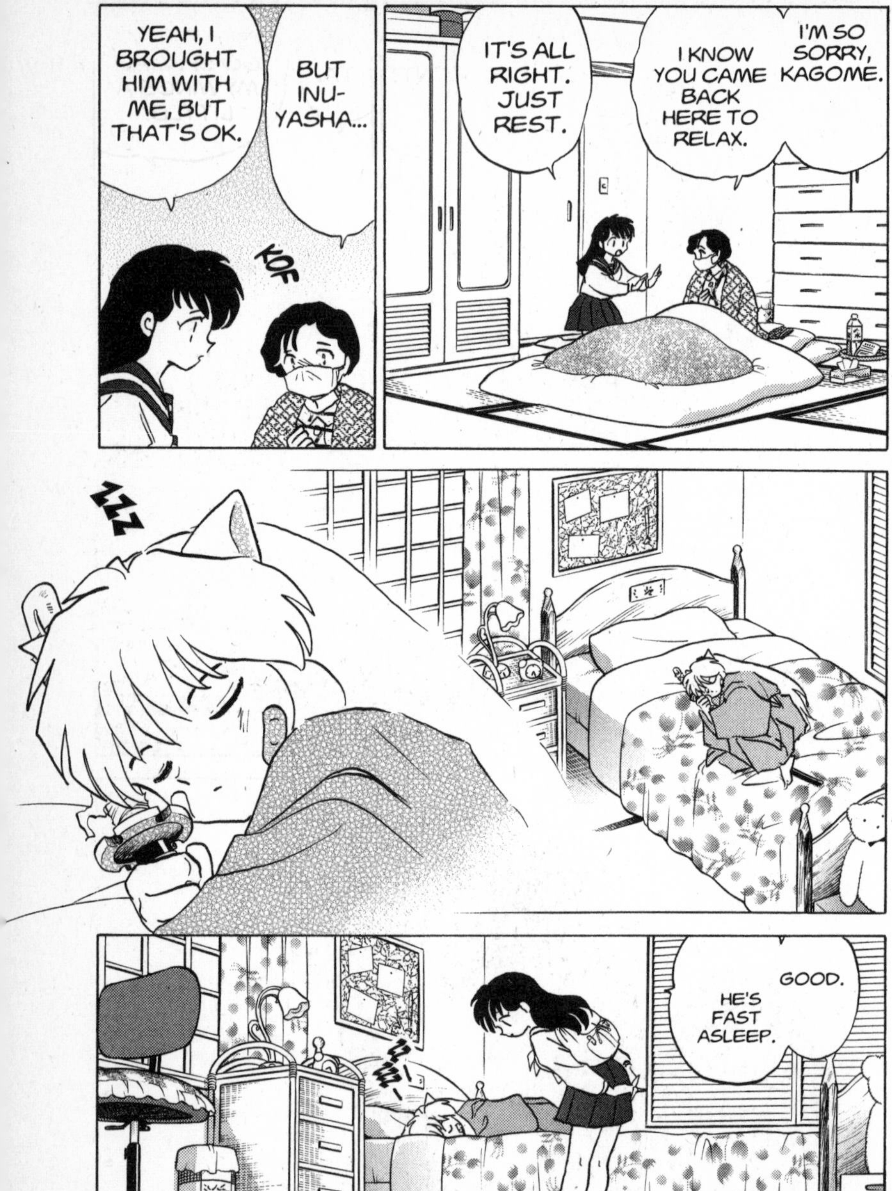
I'M SO SORRY, KAGOME.
I KNOW YOU CAME BACK HERE TO RELAX.
IT'S ALL RIGHT. JUST REST.
BUT INU-YASHA...
YEAH, I BROUGHT HIM WITH ME, BUT THAT'S OK.
KOF
ZZZ
GOOD.
HE'S FAST ASLEEP.

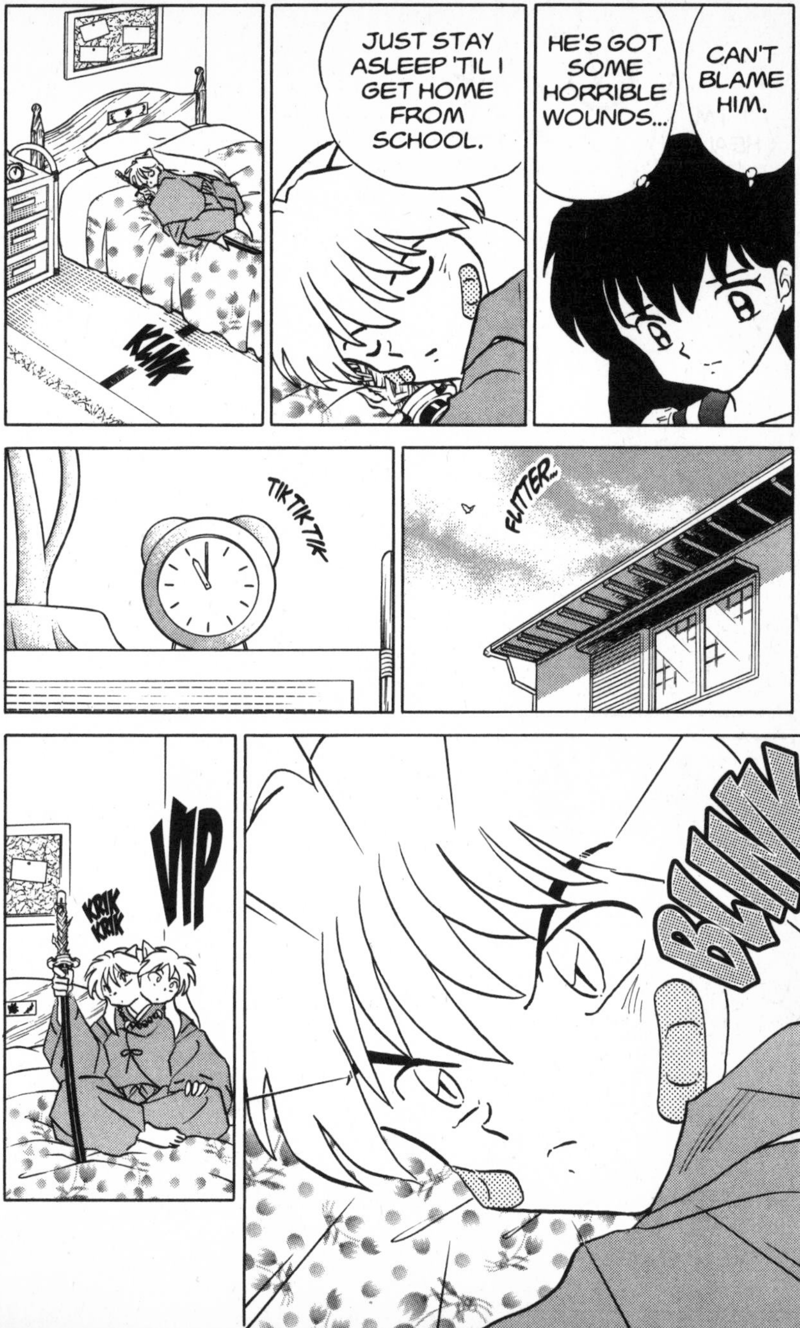

CAN'T BLAME HIM.
HE'S GOT SOME HORRIBLE WOUNDS...
JUST STAY ASLEEP 'TIL I GET HOME FROM SCHOOL.
KLINK
FLUTTER...
TIKTIKTIK
BLINK
VIP
KRIK KRIK

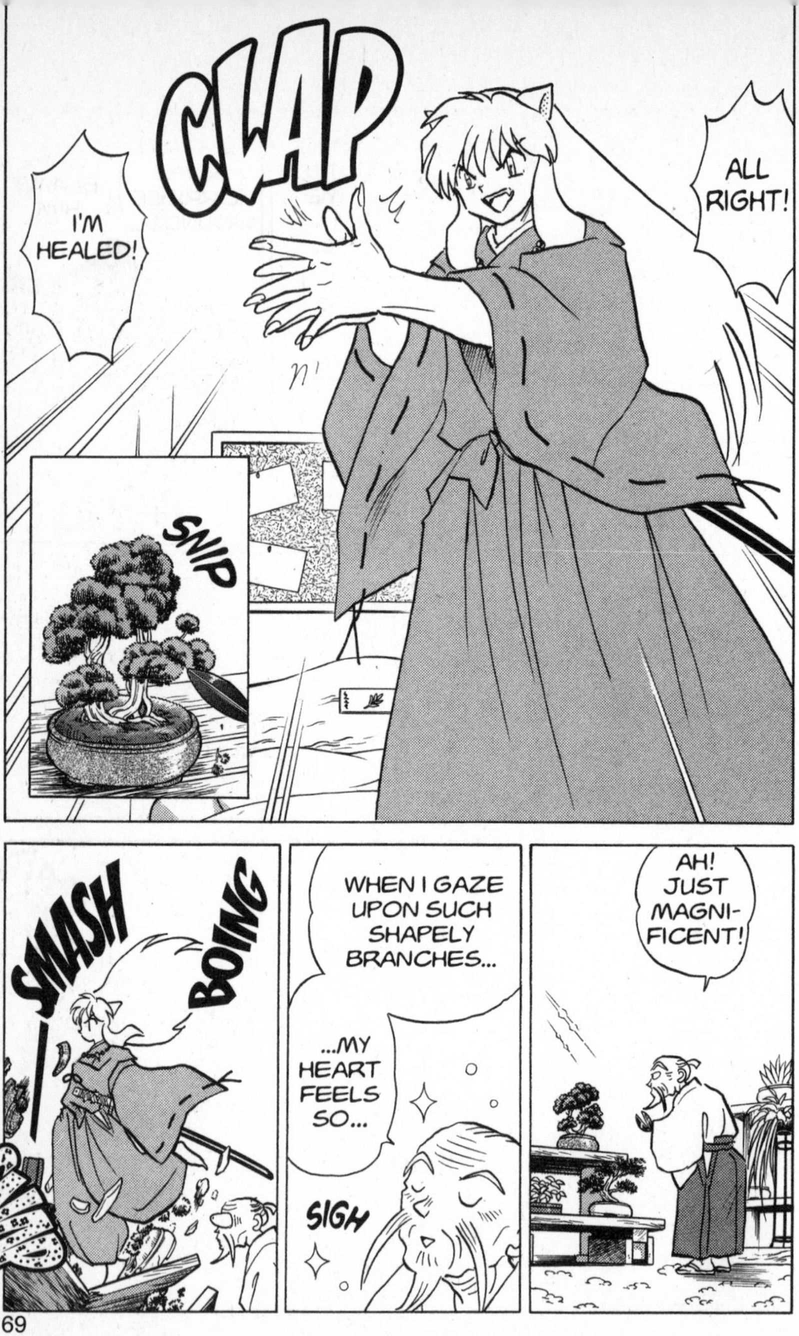
ALL RIGHT!
CLAP
I'M HEALED!
SNIP
AH! JUST MAGNI- FICENT!
WHEN I GAZE UPON SUCH SHAPELY BRANCHES...
...MY HEART FEELS SO...
SIGH
BOING
SMASH

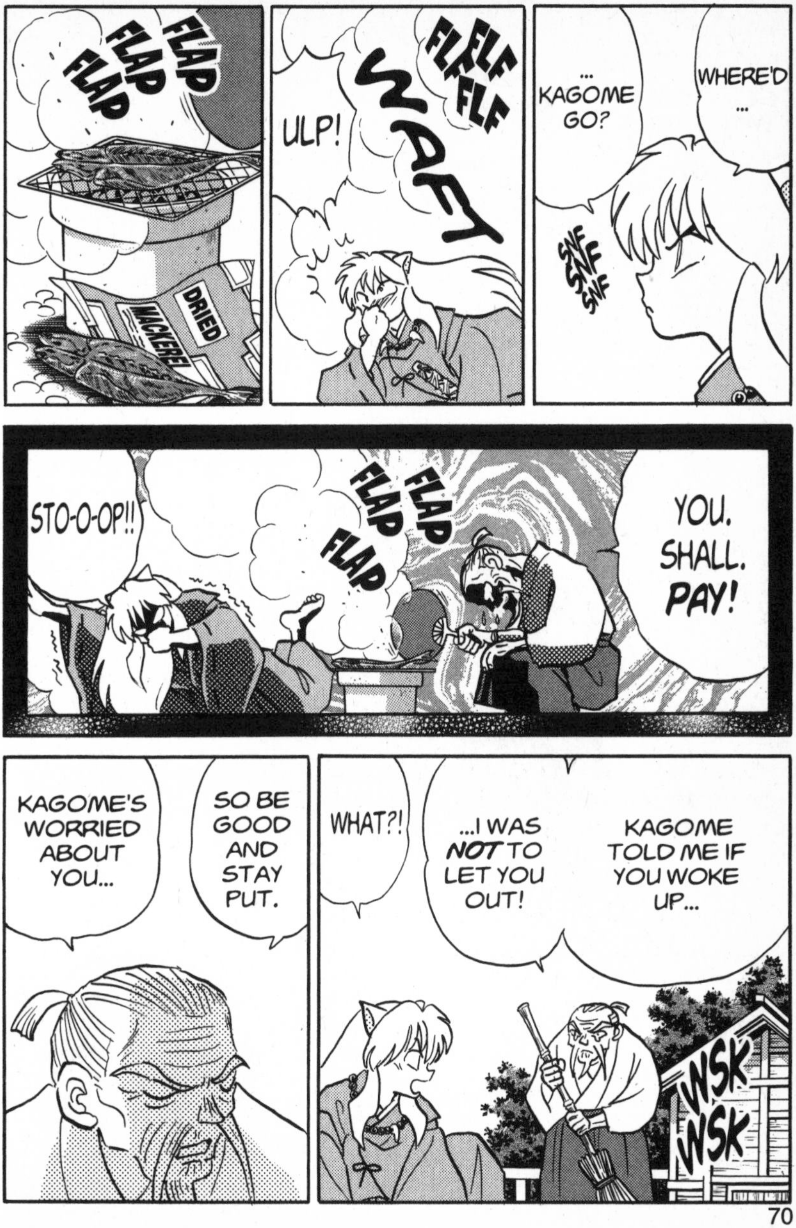
WHERE'D ...
... KAGOME GO?
SNF SNF SNF
FLF FLF FLF
WAFT
ULP!
FLAP FLAP FLAP
DRIED MACKEREL
YOU. SHALL. PAY!
FLAP FLAP FLAP
STO-O-OP!!
KAGOME TOLD ME IF YOU WOKE UP...
...I WAS NOT TO LET YOU OUT!
WHAT?!
WSK WSK
SO BE GOOD AND STAY PUT.
KAGOME'S WORRIED ABOUT YOU...

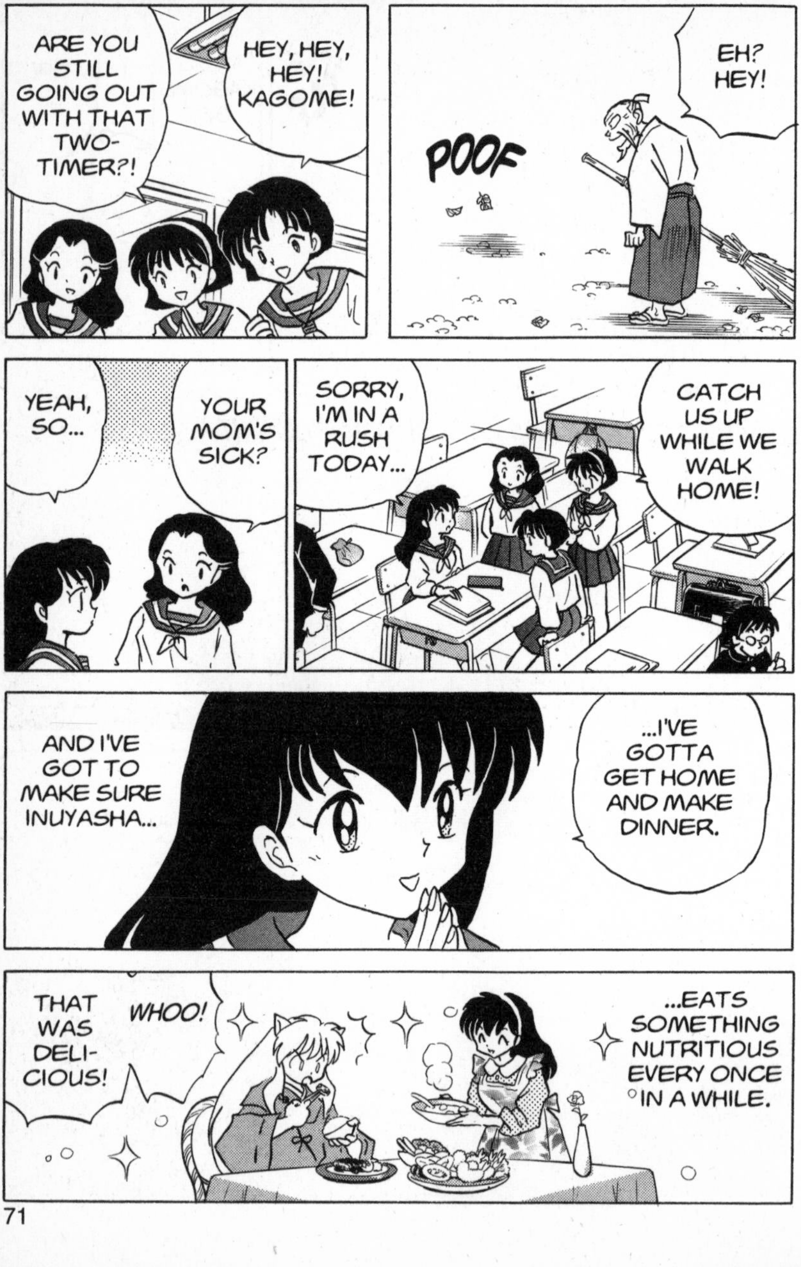
EH? HEY!
POOF
HEY, HEY, HEY! KAGOME!
ARE YOU STILL GOING OUT WITH THAT TWO-TIMER?!
CATCH US UP WHILE WE WALK HOME!
SORRY, I'M IN A RUSH TODAY...
YOUR MOM'S SICK?
YEAH, SO...
...I'VE GOTTA GET HOME AND MAKE DINNER.
AND I'VE GOT TO MAKE SURE INUYASHA...
...EATS SOMETHING NUTRITIOUS EVERY ONCE IN A WHILE.
WHOO!
THAT WAS DELI-CIOUS!

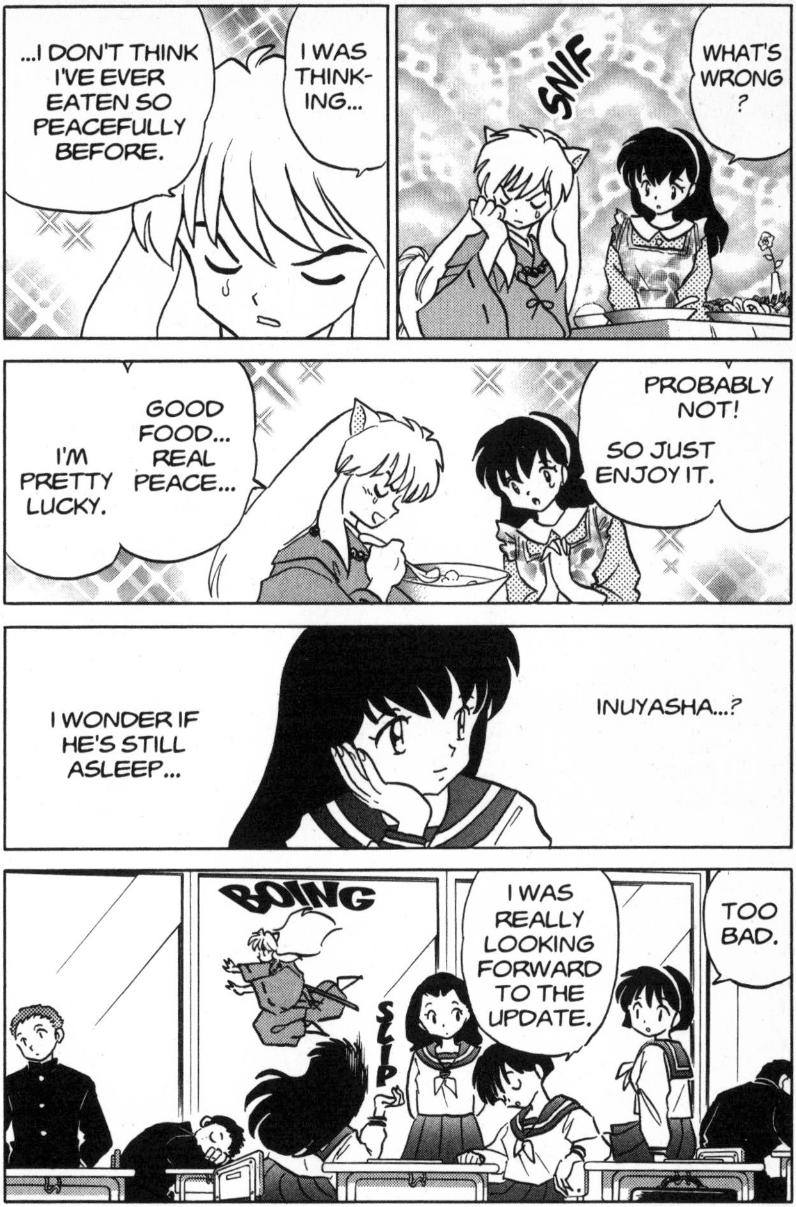
WHAT'S WRONG ?
SNIF
I WAS THINKING...
...I DON'T THINK I'VE EVER EATEN SO PEACEFULLY BEFORE.
PROBABLY NOT!
SO JUST ENJOY IT.
GOOD FOOD... REAL PEACE...
I'M PRETTY LUCKY.
INUYASHA...?
I WONDER IF HE'S STILL ASLEEP...
TOO BAD.
I WAS REALLY LOOKING FORWARD TO THE UPDATE.
BOING
SLIP

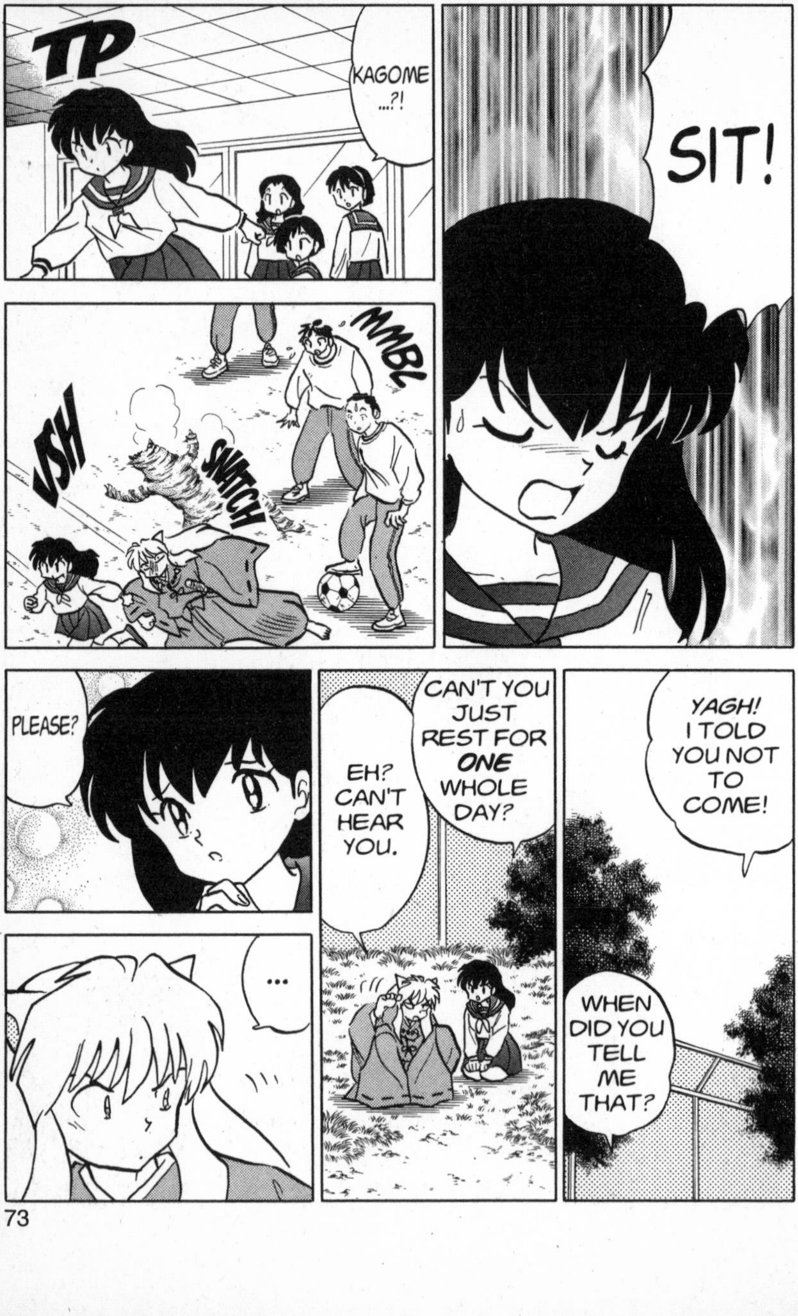
SIT!
KAGOME ...?!
TP
MMBL
SNATCH
VSH
YAGH! I TOLD YOU NOT TO COME!
WHEN DID YOU TELL ME THAT?
CAN'T YOU JUST REST FOR ONE WHOLE DAY?
EH? CAN'T HEAR YOU.
PLEASE?
...

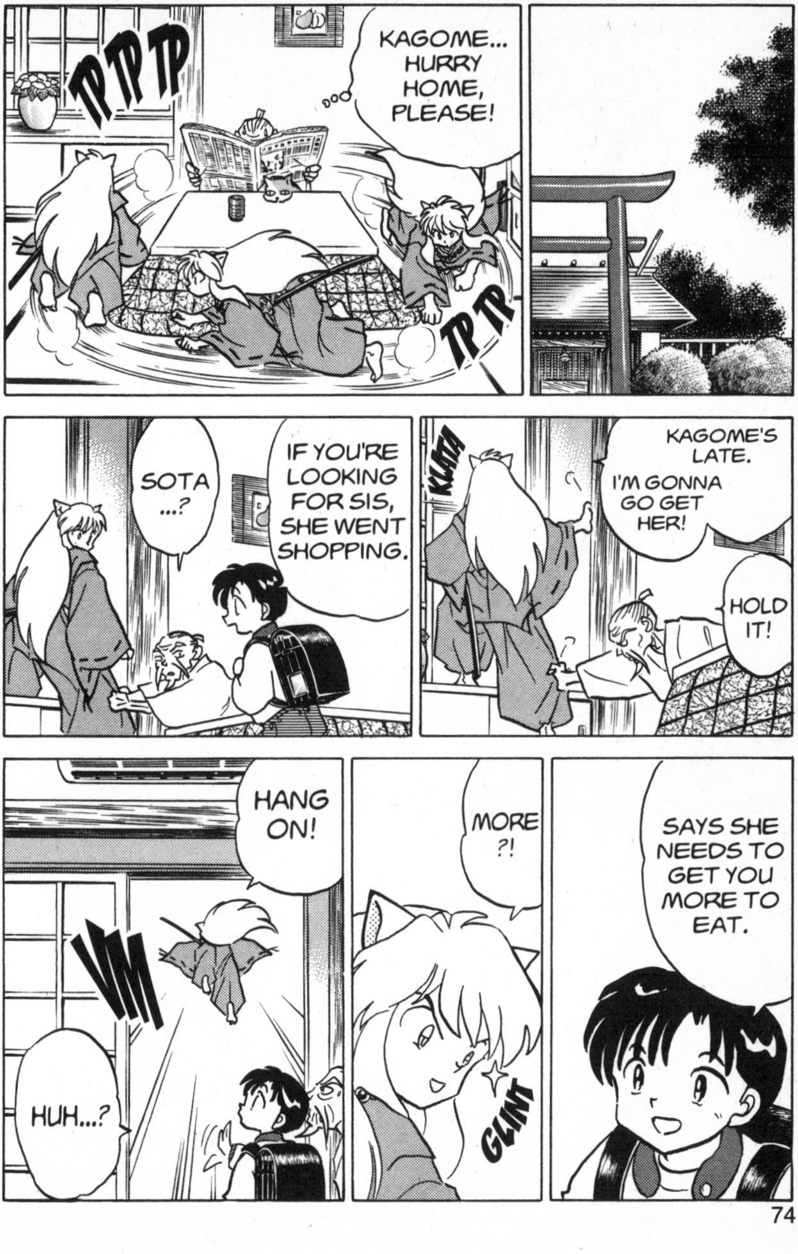
KAGOME... HURRY HOME, PLEASE!
TP TP TP
TP TP
KAGOME'S LATE.
I'M GONNA GO GET HER!
KLATA
HOLD IT!
IF YOU'RE LOOKING FOR SIS, SHE WENT SHOPPING.
SOTA ...?
SAYS SHE NEEDS TO GET YOU MORE TO EAT.
MORE ?!
GLINT
HANG ON!
VM
HUH...?

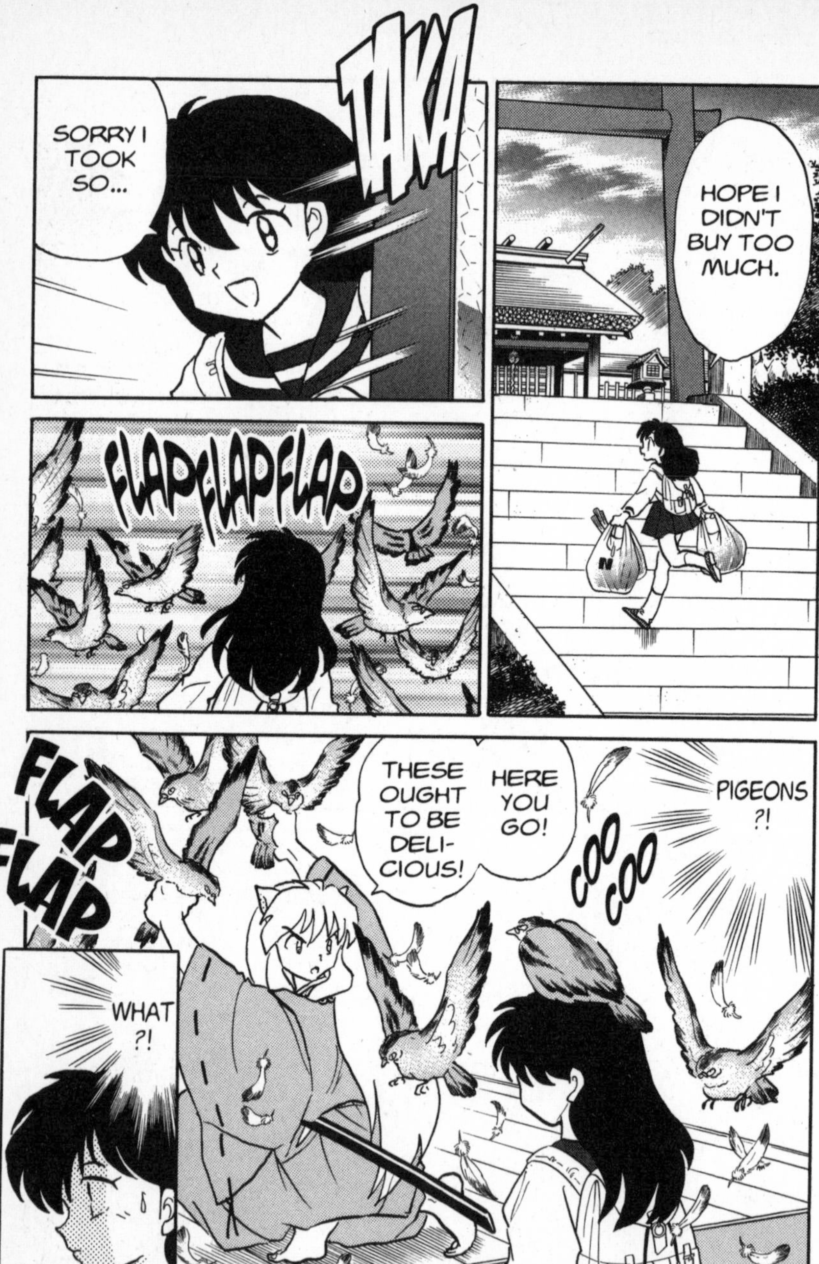
HOPE I DIDN'T BUY TOO MUCH.
TAKA
SORRY I TOOK SO...
FLAPFLAPFLAP
PIGEONS ?!
COO COO
HERE YOU GO!
THESE OUGHT TO BE DELICIOUS!
FLAP FLAP
WHAT ?!

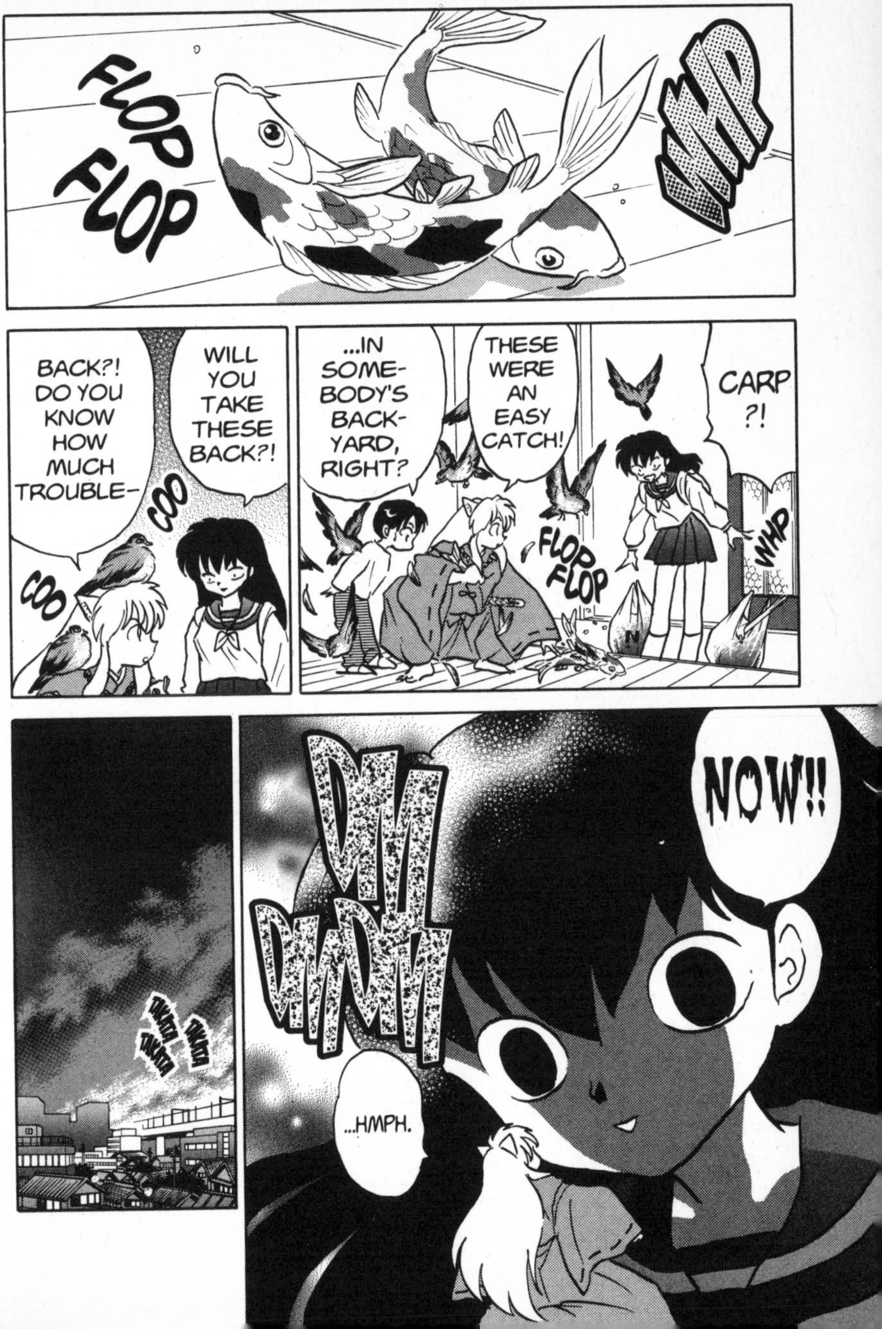
WHP
FLOP FLOP
CARP?!
THESE WERE AN EASY CATCH!
...IN SOMEBODY'S BACKYARD, RIGHT?
WHP
FLOP FLOP
WILL YOU TAKE THESE BACK?!
BACK?! DO YOU KNOW HOW MUCH TROUBLE-
COO
COO
NOW!!
DMM DMMDMM
...HMPH.

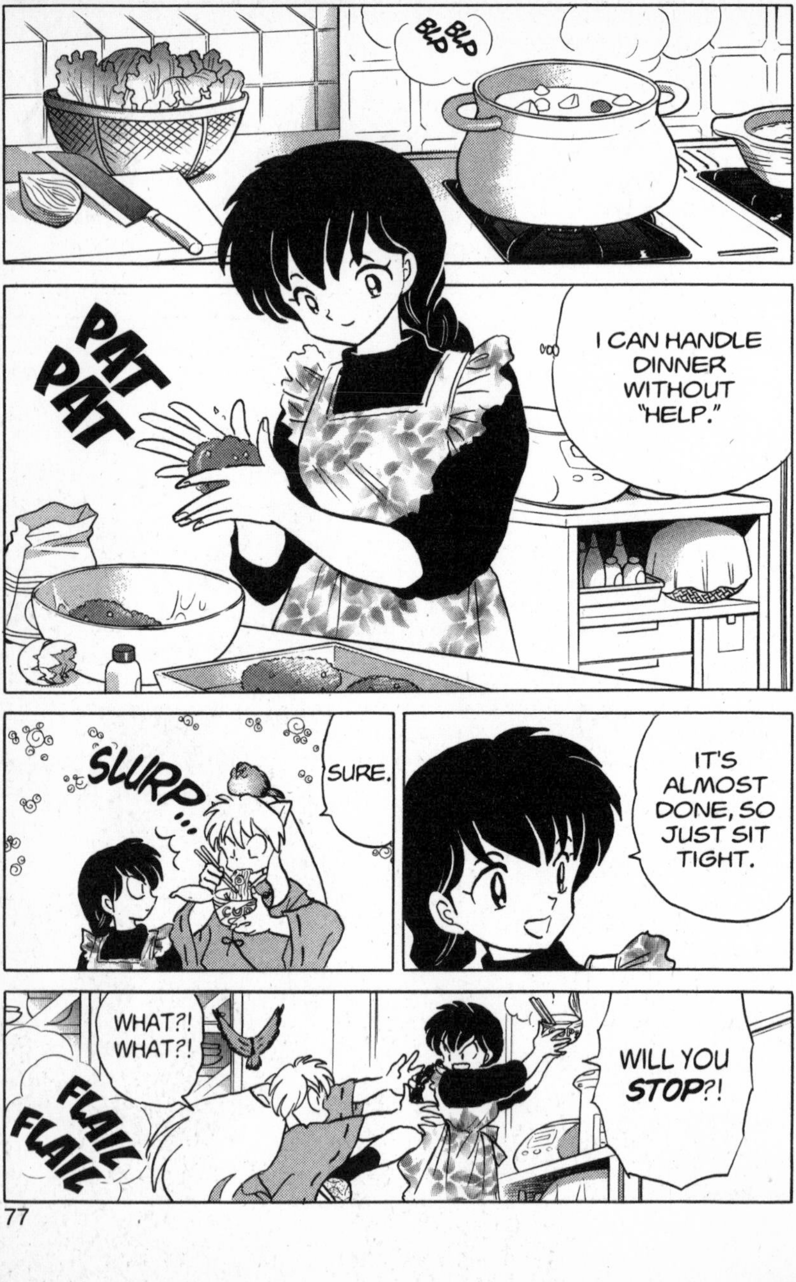
BLP BLP BLP
I CAN HANDLE DINNER WITHOUT "HELP."
PAT PAT
IT'S ALMOST DONE, SO JUST SIT TIGHT.
SURE.
SLURP...
CUP
WILL YOU STOP?!
WHAT?! WHAT?!
FLAIL FLAIL

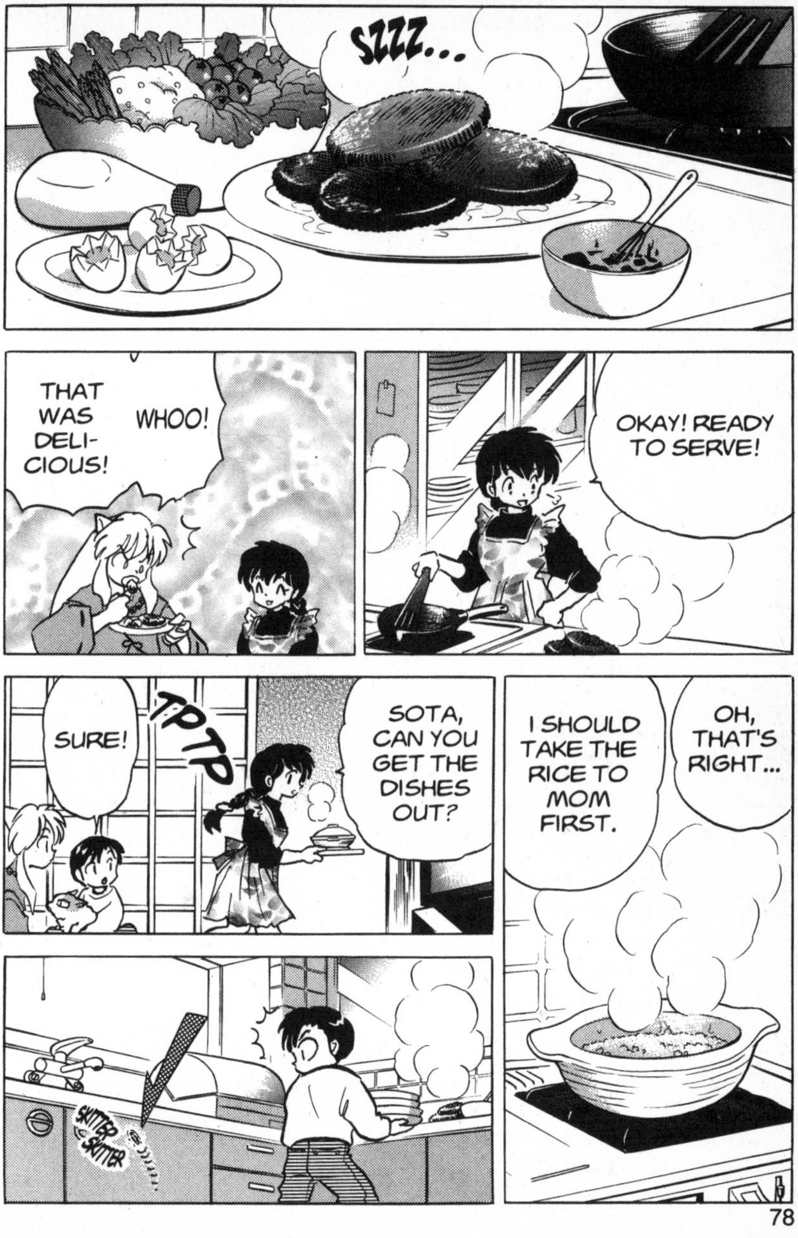
SZZZ...
OKAY! READY TO SERVE!
WHOO!
THAT WAS DELICIOUS!
OH, THAT'S RIGHT...
I SHOULD TAKE THE RICE TO MOM FIRST.
SOTA, CAN YOU GET THE DISHES OUT?
TP TP
SURE!
SKITTER SKITTER

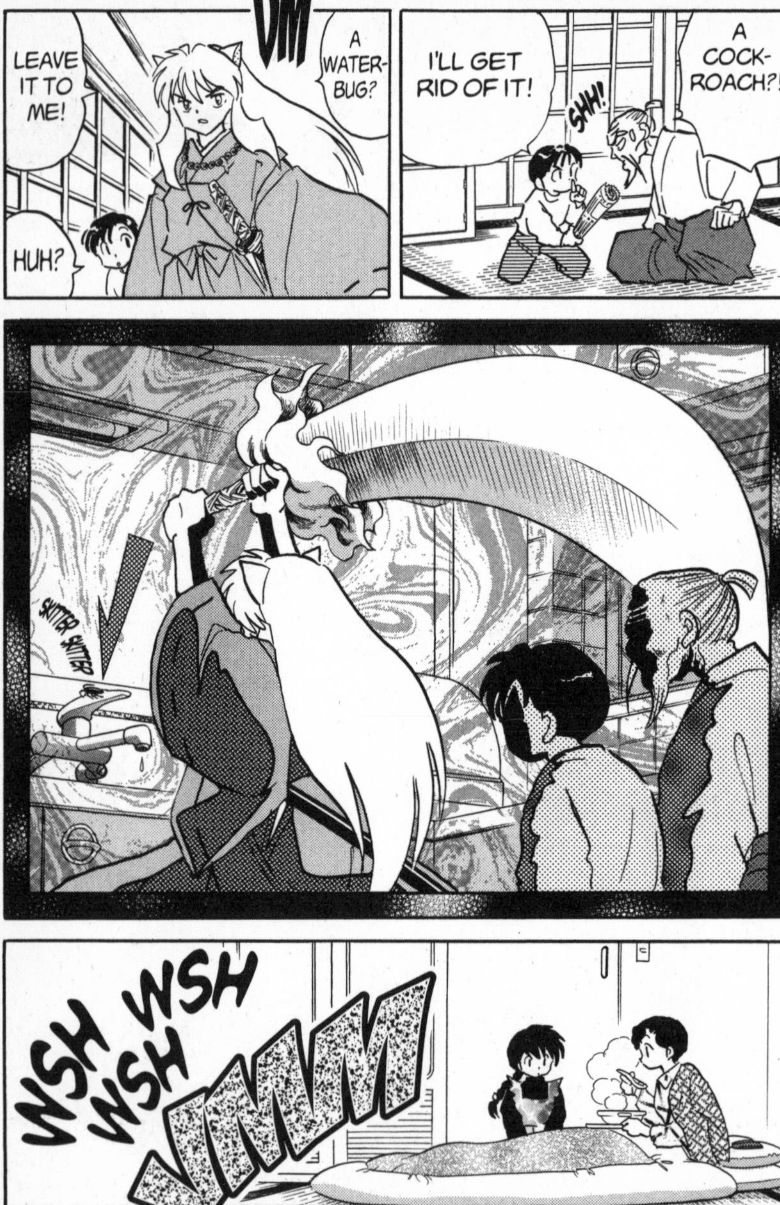
A COCK-ROACH?!
SHH!
I'LL GET RID OF IT!
A WATER-BUG?
DM
LEAVE IT TO ME!
HUH?
SKITTER SKITTER
WSH WSH WSH
VMMM

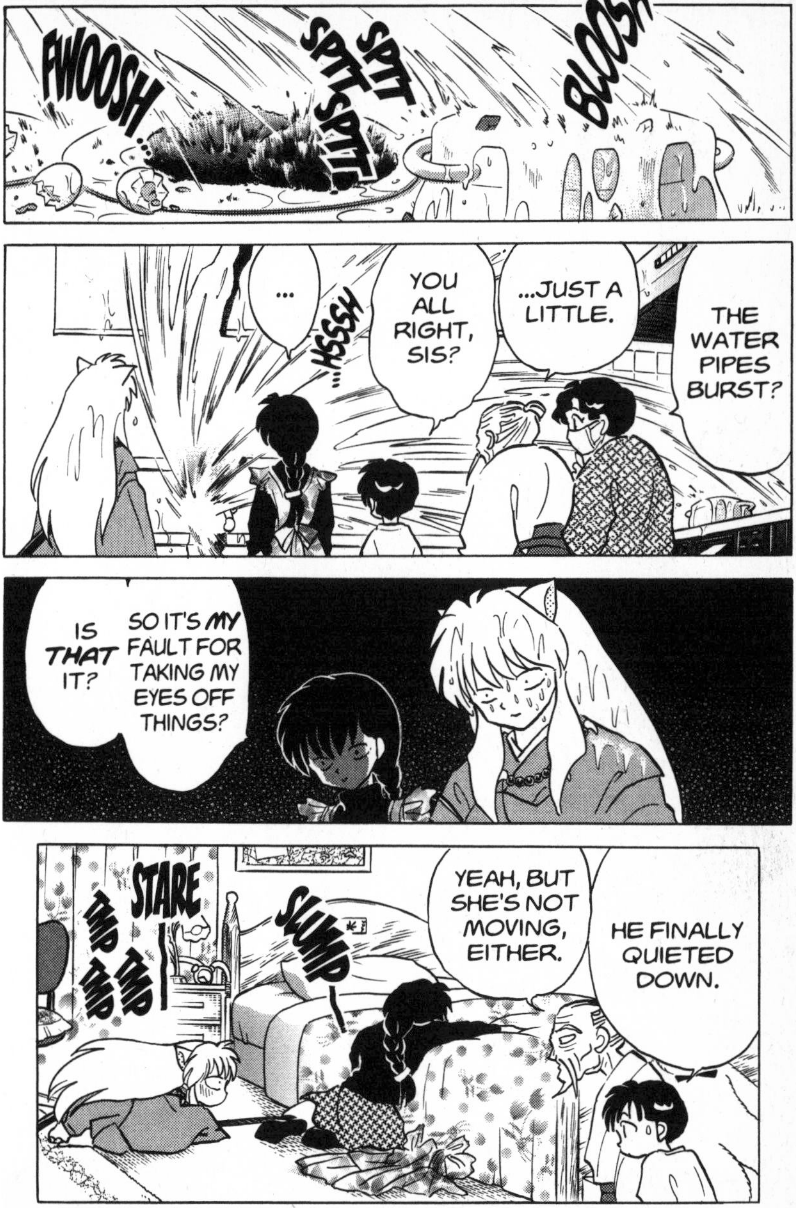
BLOOSH
SPTT SPTT SPTT
FWOOSH...
THE WATER PIPES BURST?
...JUST A LITTLE.
YOU ALL RIGHT, SIS?
HSSSH...
...
SO IT'S *MY* FAULT FOR TAKING MY EYES OFF THINGS?
IS *THAT* IT?
HE FINALLY QUIETED DOWN.
YEAH, BUT SHE'S NOT MOVING, EITHER.
SLUMP—
STARE—
TMP TMP TMP

SCROLL 5

THE NUNNERY

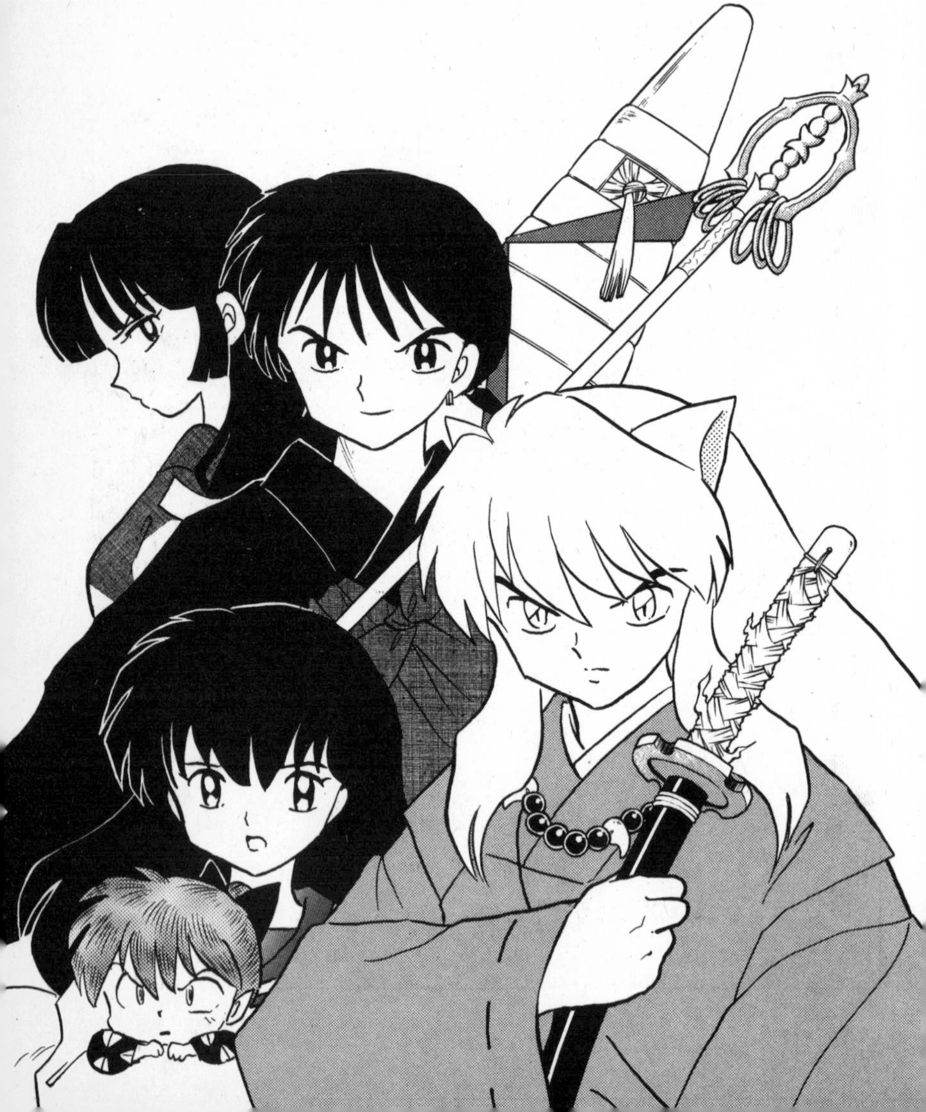

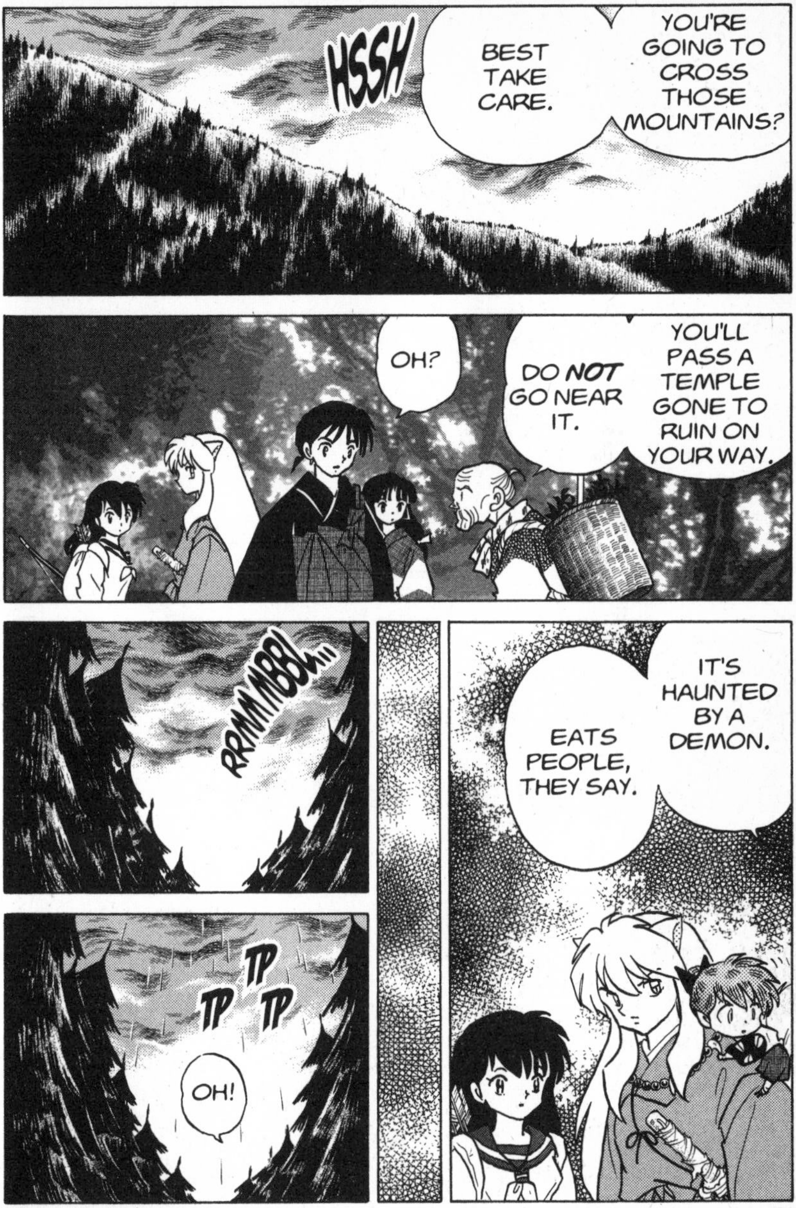
YOU'RE GOING TO CROSS THOSE MOUNTAINS?
BEST TAKE CARE.
HSSH
YOU'LL PASS A TEMPLE GONE TO RUIN ON YOUR WAY.
DO **NOT** GO NEAR IT.
OH?
IT'S HAUNTED BY A DEMON.
EATS PEOPLE, THEY SAY.
RRMMMBBL...
TP TP TP
OH!

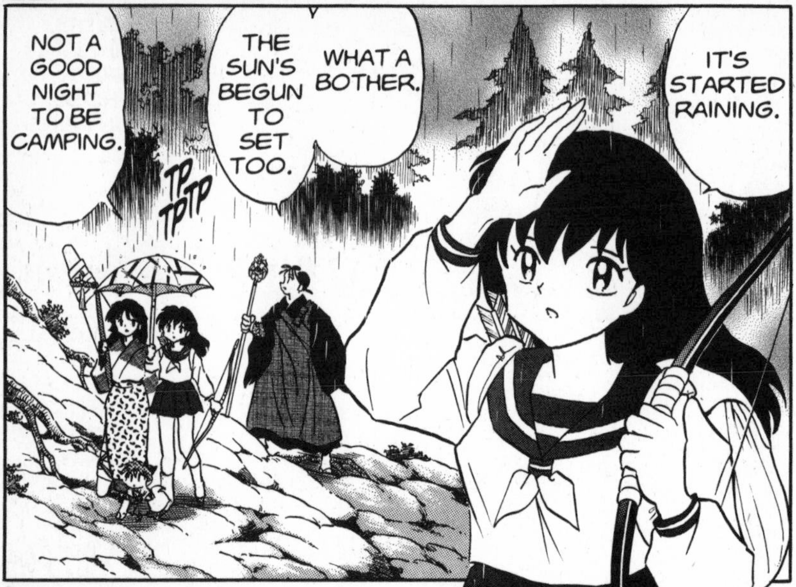
IT'S STARTED RAINING.
WHAT A BOTHER.
THE SUN'S BEGUN TO SET TOO.
NOT A GOOD NIGHT TO BE CAMPING.
TP TPTP

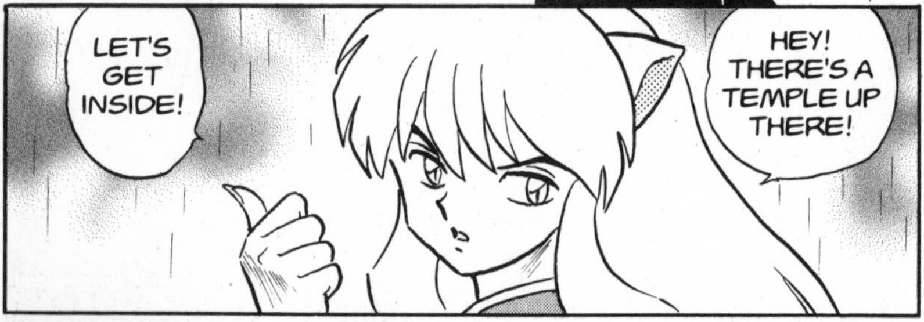
HEY! THERE'S A TEMPLE UP THERE!
LET'S GET INSIDE!

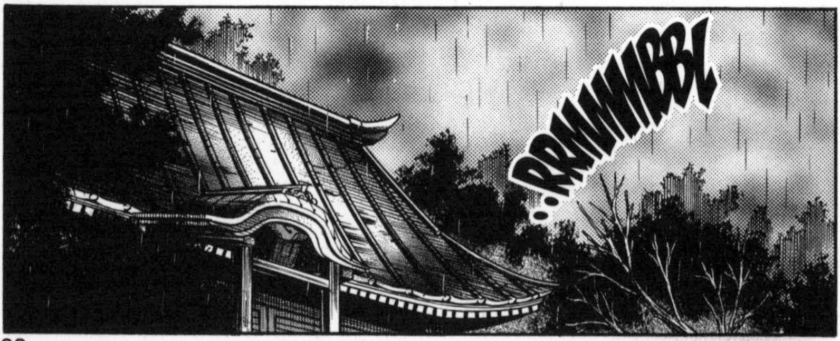
..RRMMMBBL

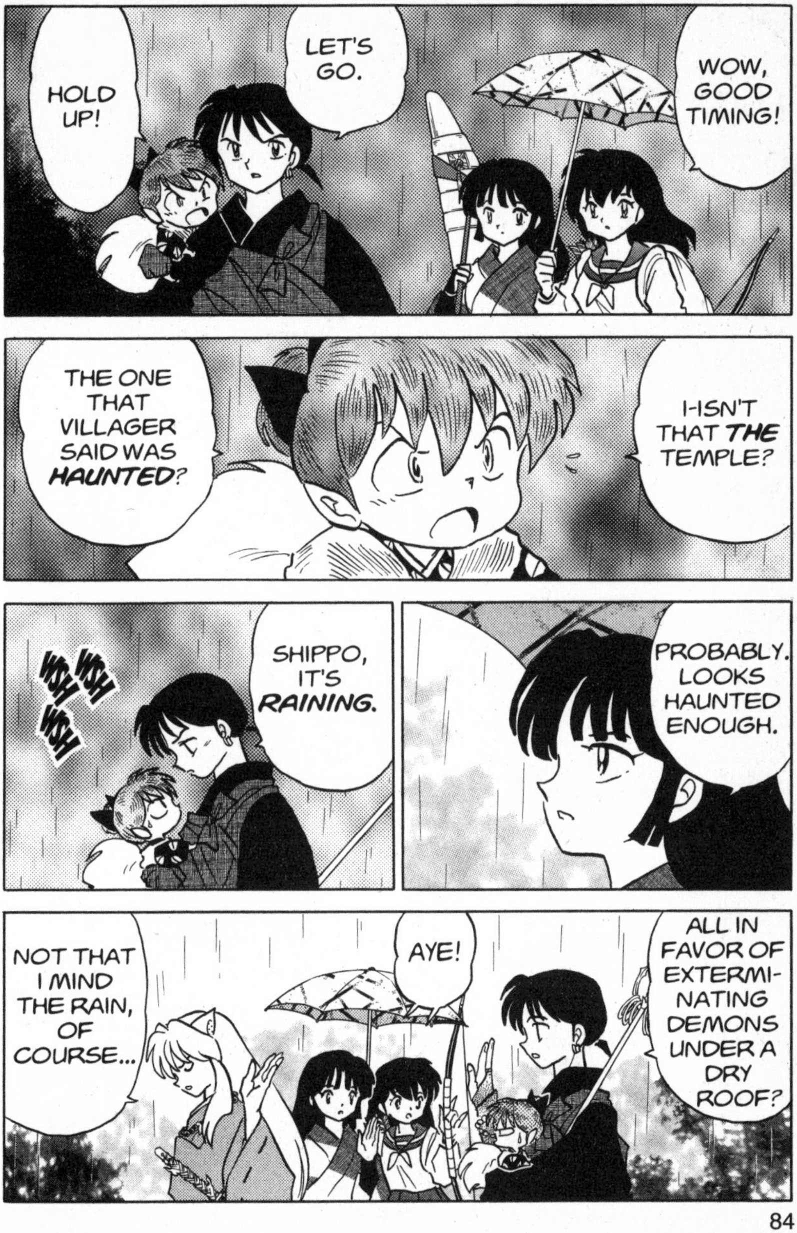
WOW, GOOD TIMING!
LET'S GO.
HOLD UP!
I-ISN'T THAT *THE* TEMPLE?
THE ONE THAT VILLAGER SAID WAS *HAUNTED*?
PROBABLY. LOOKS HAUNTED ENOUGH.
SHIPPO, IT'S *RAINING*.
WSH WSH WSH
ALL IN FAVOR OF EXTERMI-NATING DEMONS UNDER A DRY ROOF?
AYE!
NOT THAT I MIND THE RAIN, OF COURSE...

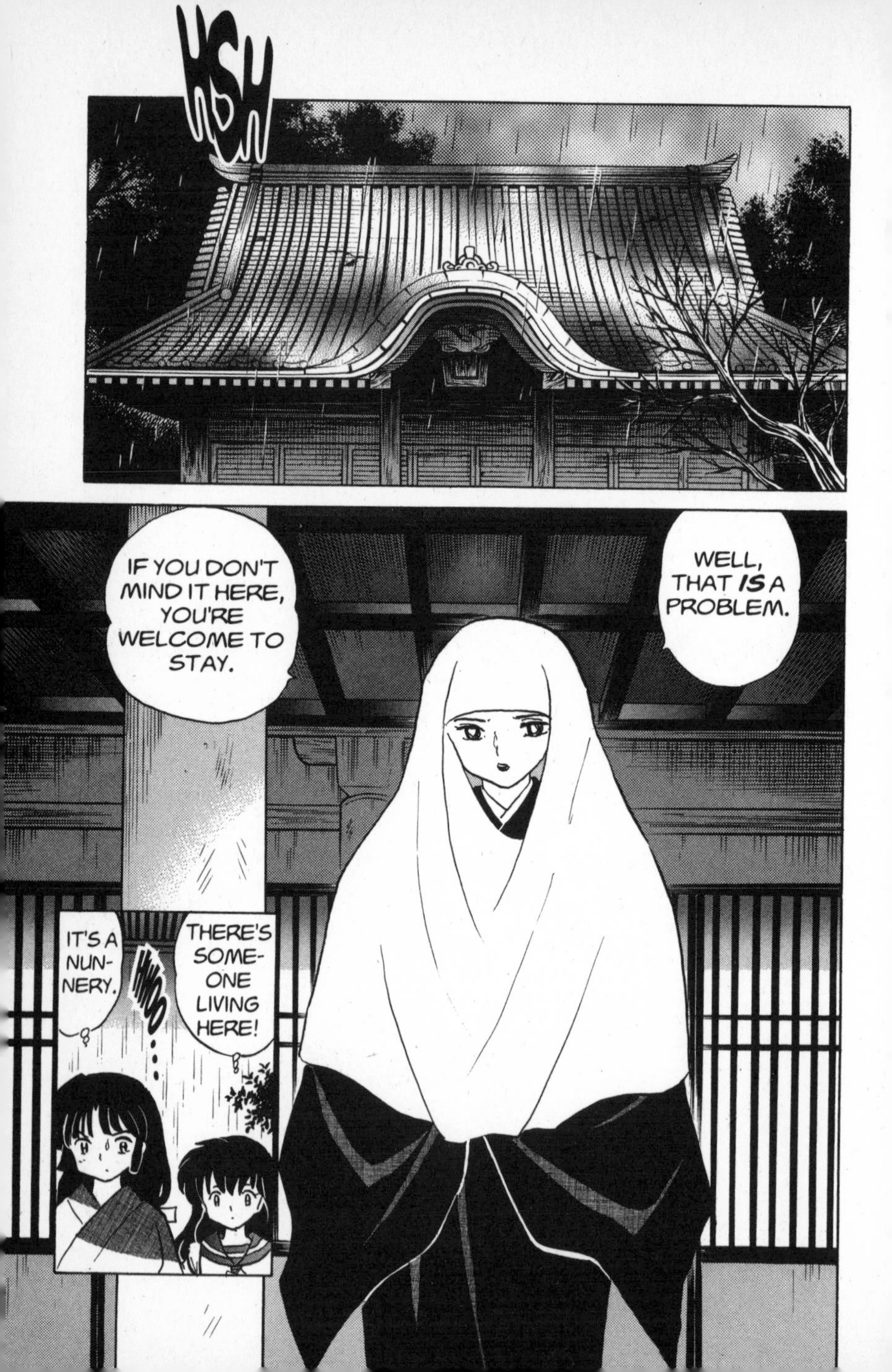
HSH
WELL, THAT *IS* A PROBLEM.
IF YOU DON'T MIND IT HERE, YOU'RE WELCOME TO STAY.
THERE'S SOME-ONE LIVING HERE!
HWOO...
IT'S A NUN-NERY.

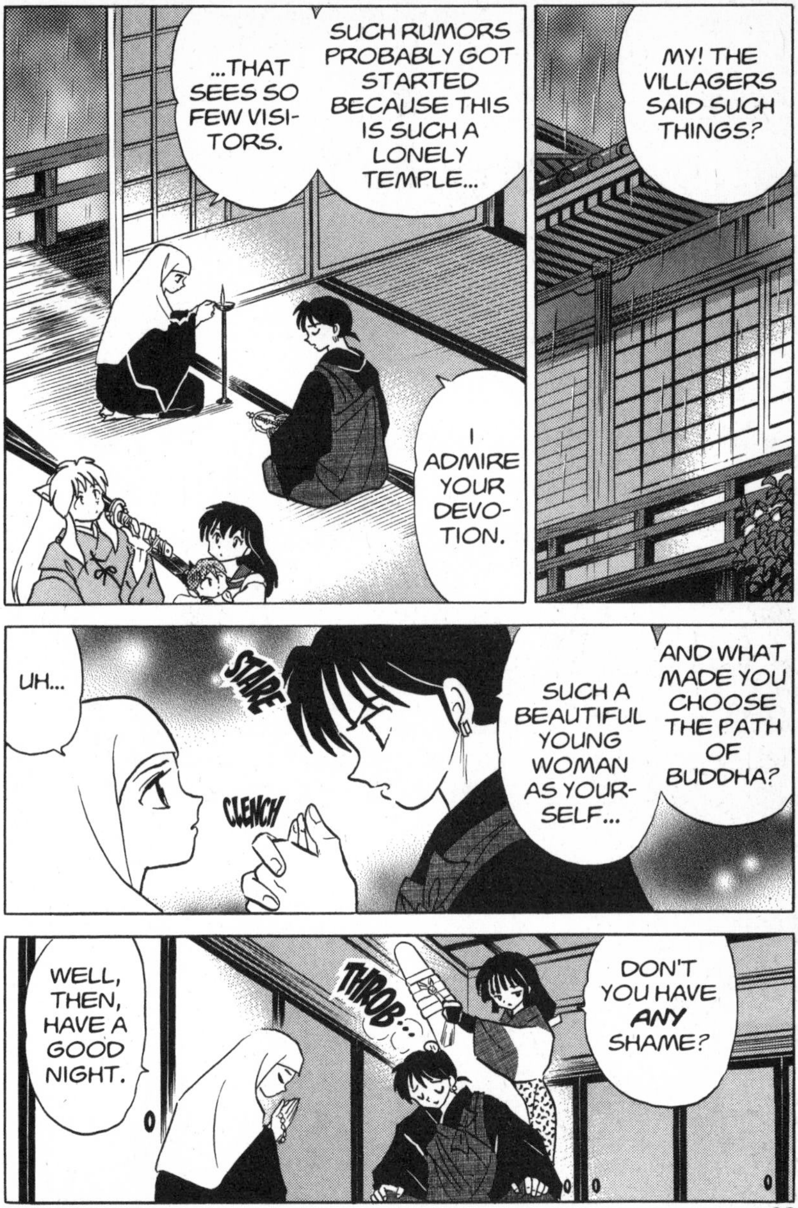
MY! THE VILLAGERS SAID SUCH THINGS?
SUCH RUMORS PROBABLY GOT STARTED BECAUSE THIS IS SUCH A LONELY TEMPLE...
...THAT SEES SO FEW VISI-TORS.
I ADMIRE YOUR DEVO-TION.
AND WHAT MADE YOU CHOOSE THE PATH OF BUDDHA?
SUCH A BEAUTIFUL YOUNG WOMAN AS YOUR-SELF...
STARE
CLENCH
UH...
DON'T YOU HAVE ANY SHAME?
THROB...
WELL, THEN, HAVE A GOOD NIGHT.

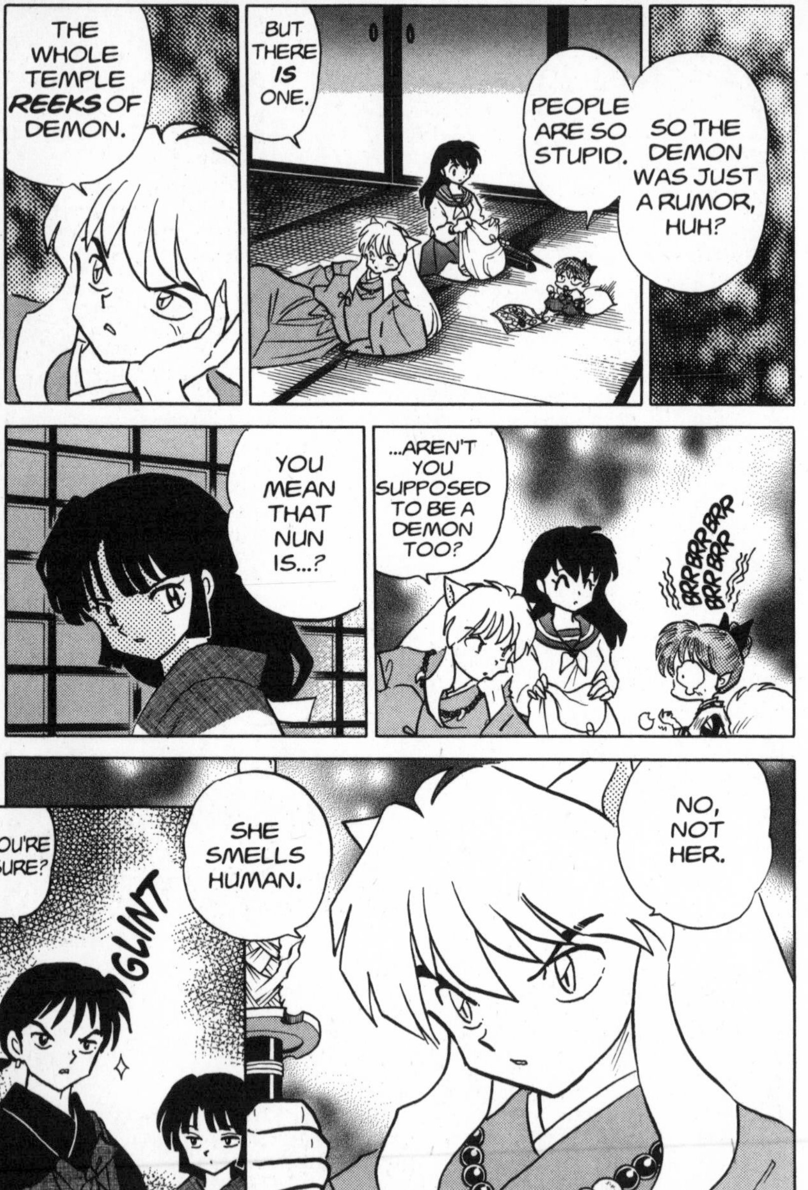
SO THE DEMON WAS JUST A RUMOR, HUH?
PEOPLE ARE SO STUPID.
BUT THERE IS ONE.
THE WHOLE TEMPLE REEKS OF DEMON.
...AREN'T YOU SUPPOSED TO BE A DEMON TOO?
BRRBRRBRR BRRBRR
YOU MEAN THAT NUN IS...?
NO, NOT HER.
SHE SMELLS HUMAN.
GLINT
YOU'RE SURE?

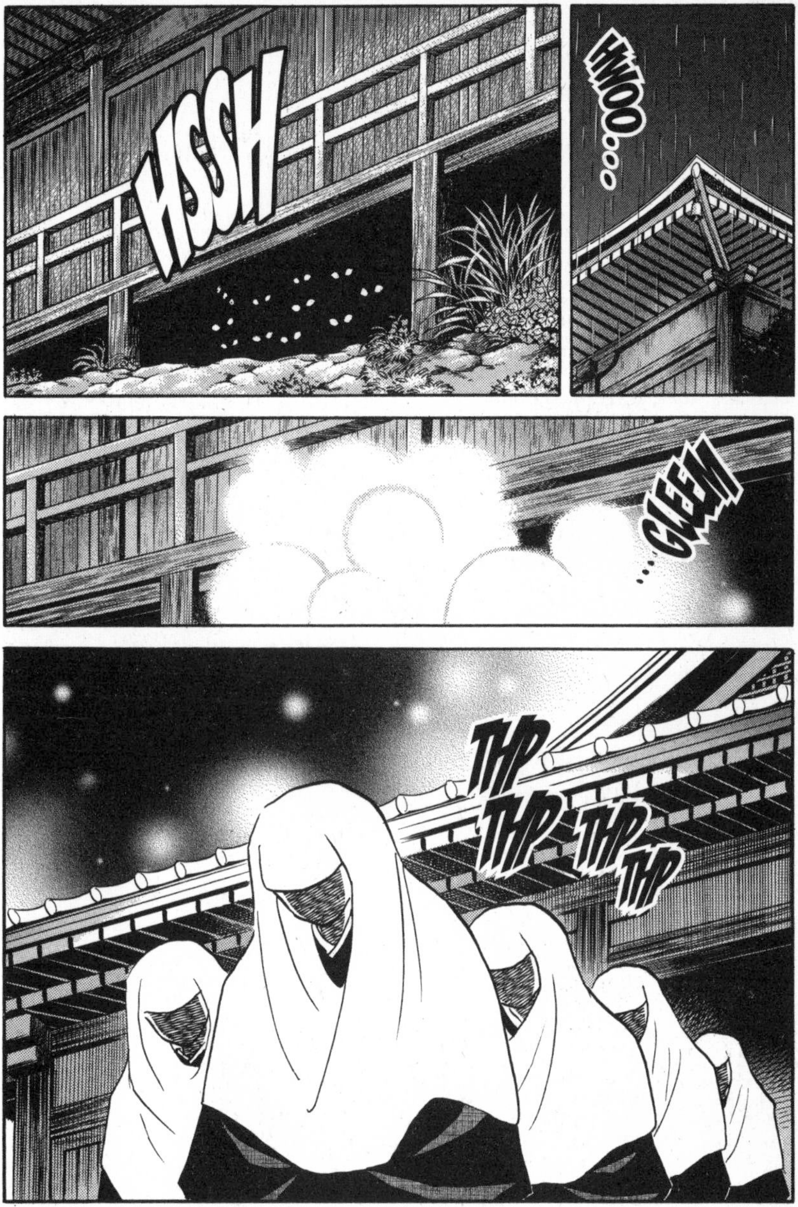
HWOOO...
HSSH
...GLEEM
THP THP THP THP

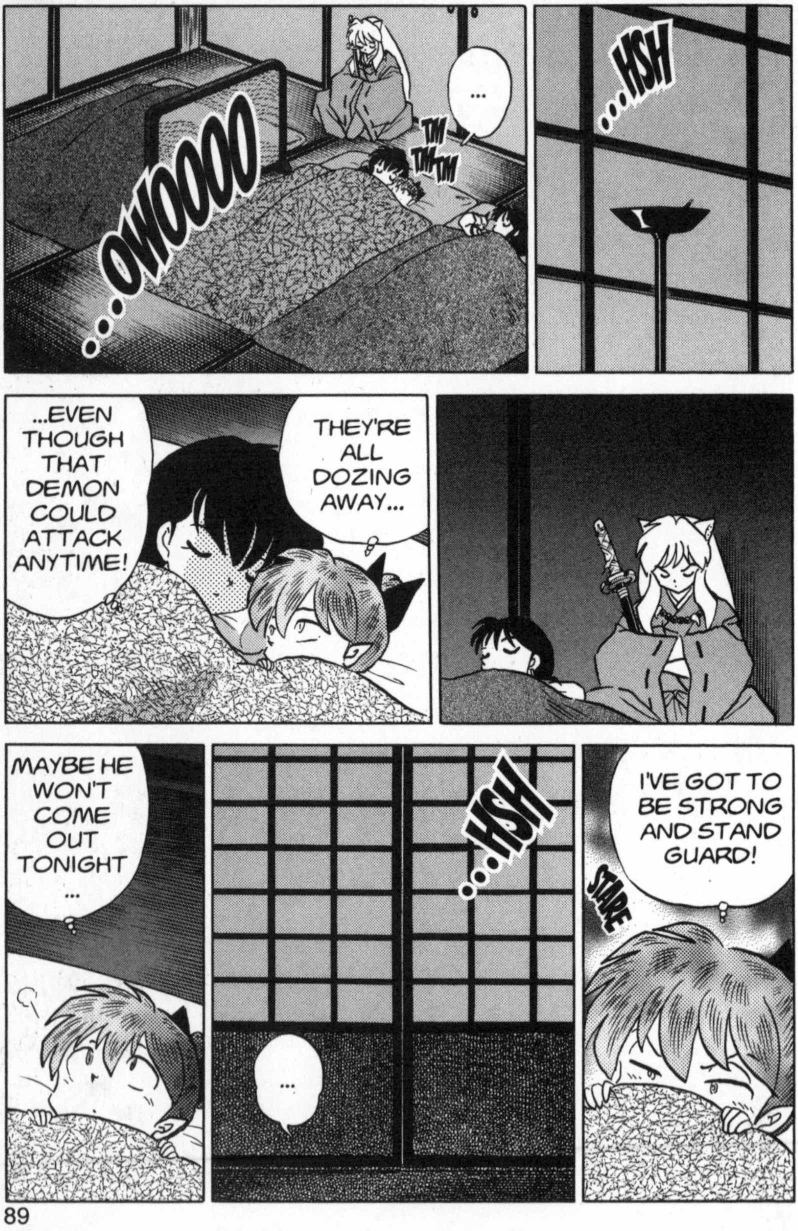
...HSH
...
TM TM TM TM
...OWOOOO
THEY'RE ALL DOZING AWAY...
...EVEN THOUGH THAT DEMON COULD ATTACK ANYTIME!
I'VE GOT TO BE STRONG AND STAND GUARD!
STARE
...HSH
...
MAYBE HE WON'T COME OUT TONIGHT ...

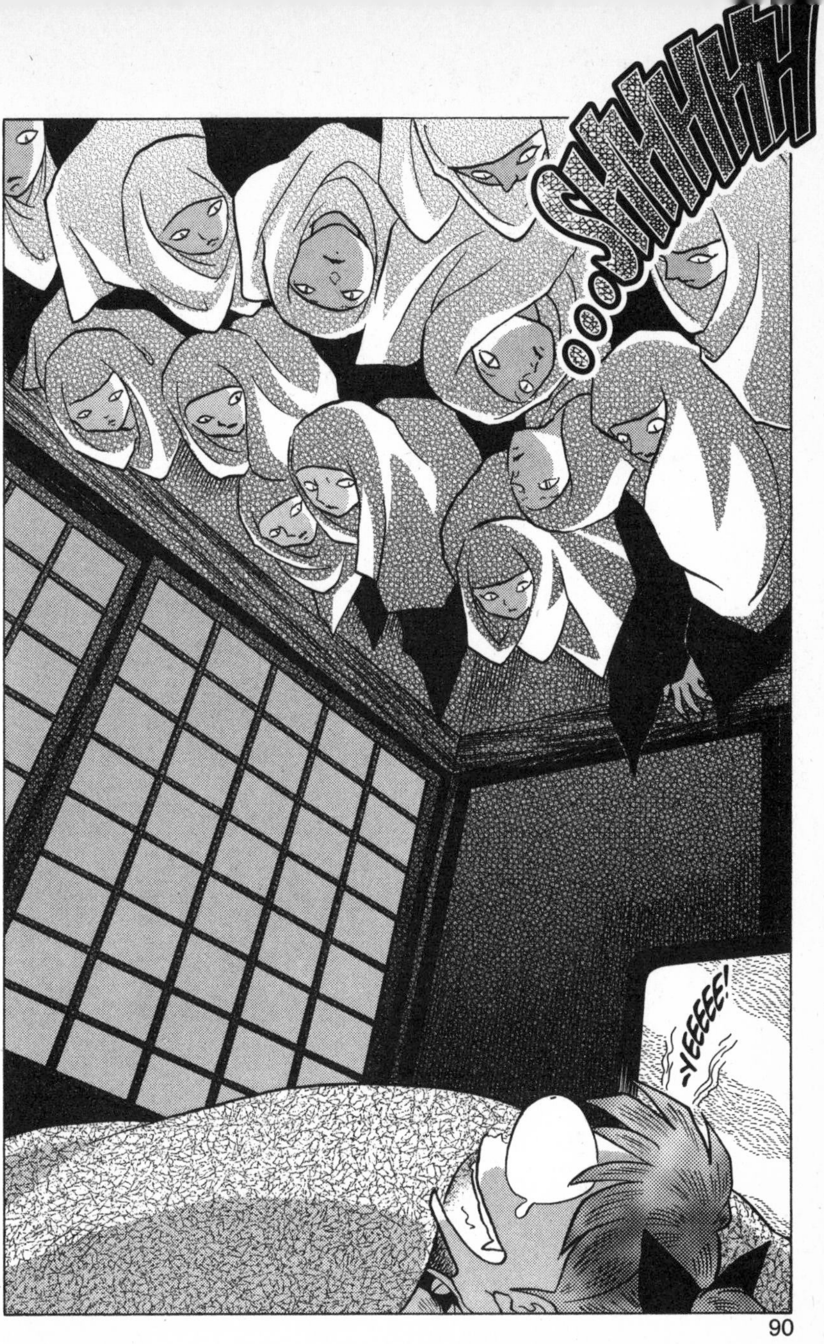
...SHHHHH
-YEEEEE!

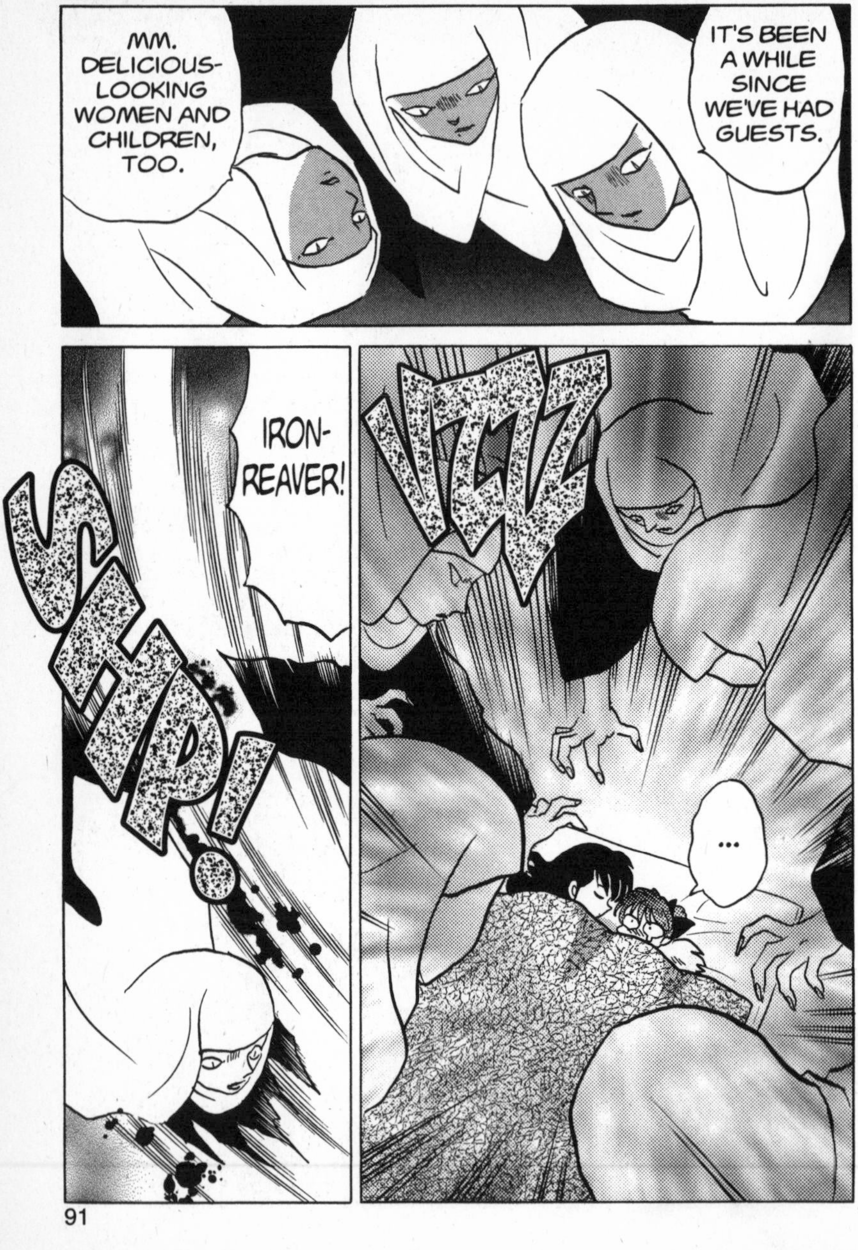
IT'S BEEN A WHILE SINCE WE'VE HAD GUESTS.
MM. DELICIOUS-LOOKING WOMEN AND CHILDREN, TOO.
VZZZ
...
IRON-REAVER!
SHHP!

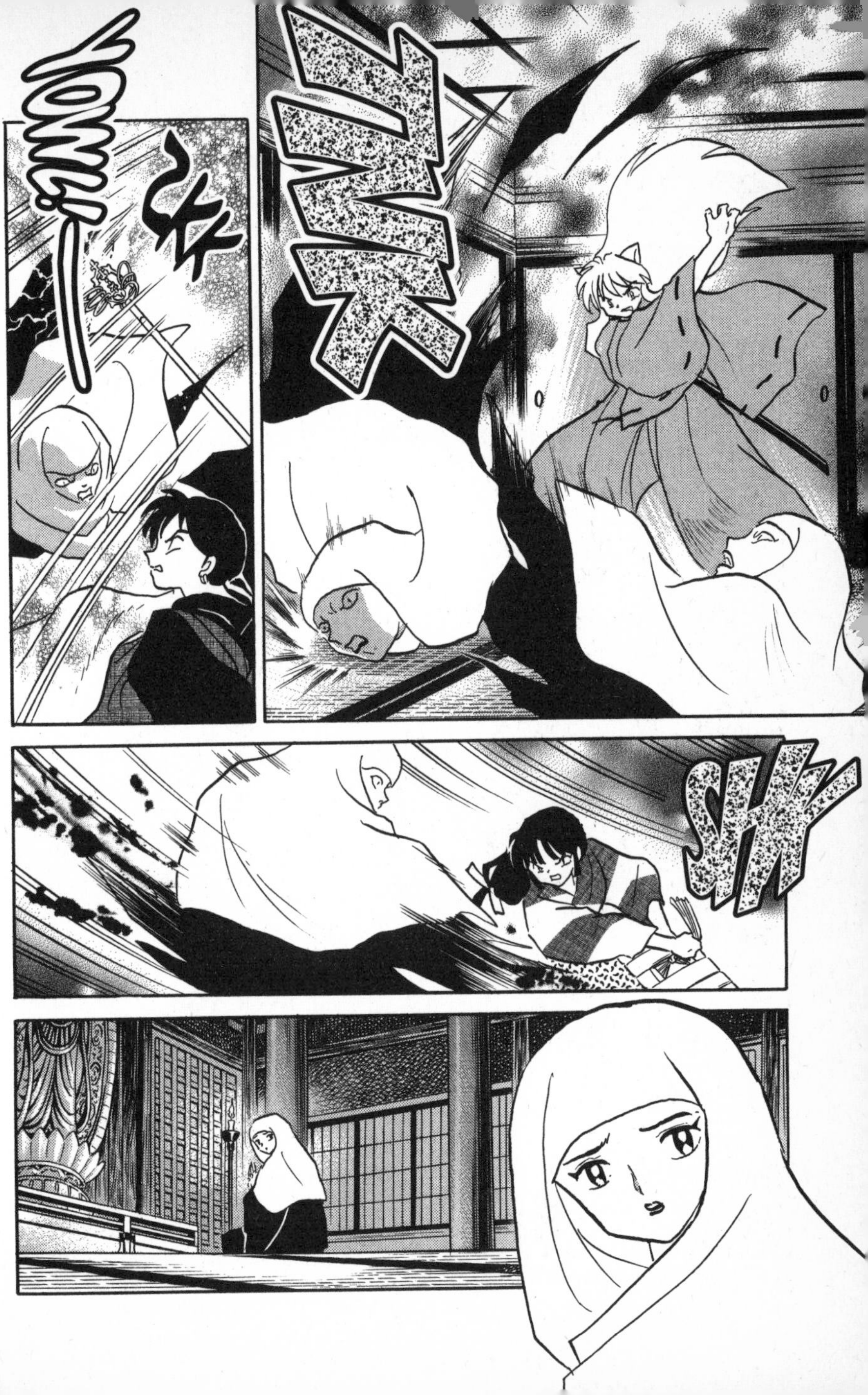
ZNK
ZKK
YOWL!!—
SHK

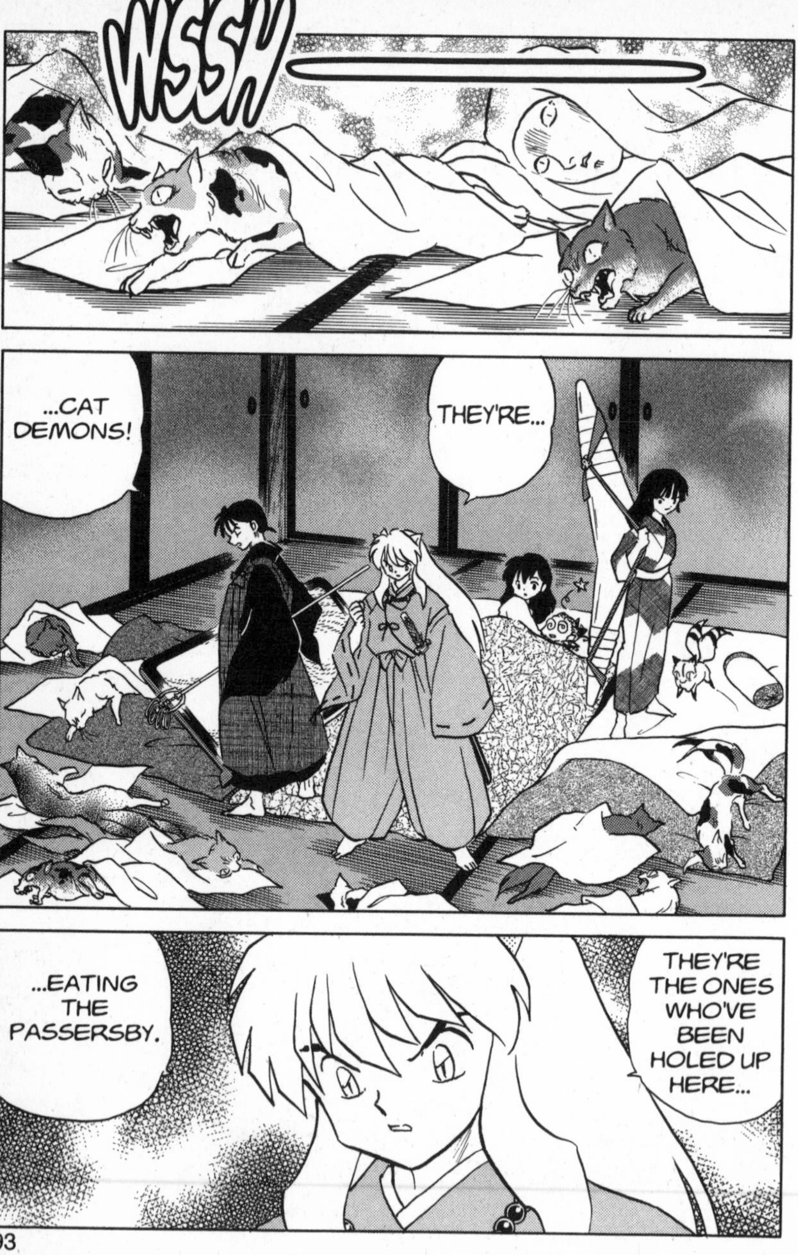
WSSH
THEY'RE...
...CAT DEMONS!
THEY'RE THE ONES WHO'VE BEEN HOLED UP HERE...
...EATING THE PASSERSBY.

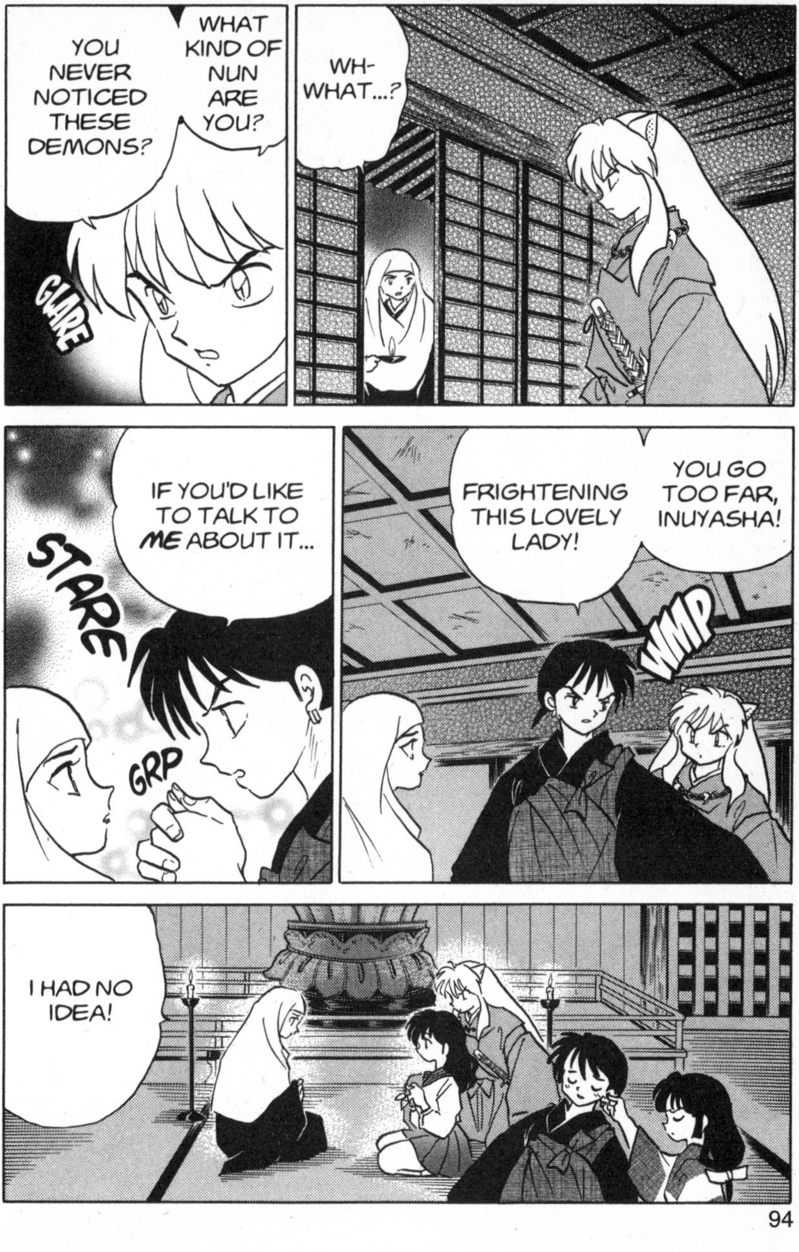
WH-WHAT...?
WHAT KIND OF NUN ARE YOU?
YOU NEVER NOTICED THESE DEMONS?
GLARE
YOU GO TOO FAR, INUYASHA!
FRIGHTENING THIS LOVELY LADY!
WMP
IF YOU'D LIKE TO TALK TO ME ABOUT IT...
STARE
GRP
I HAD NO IDEA!

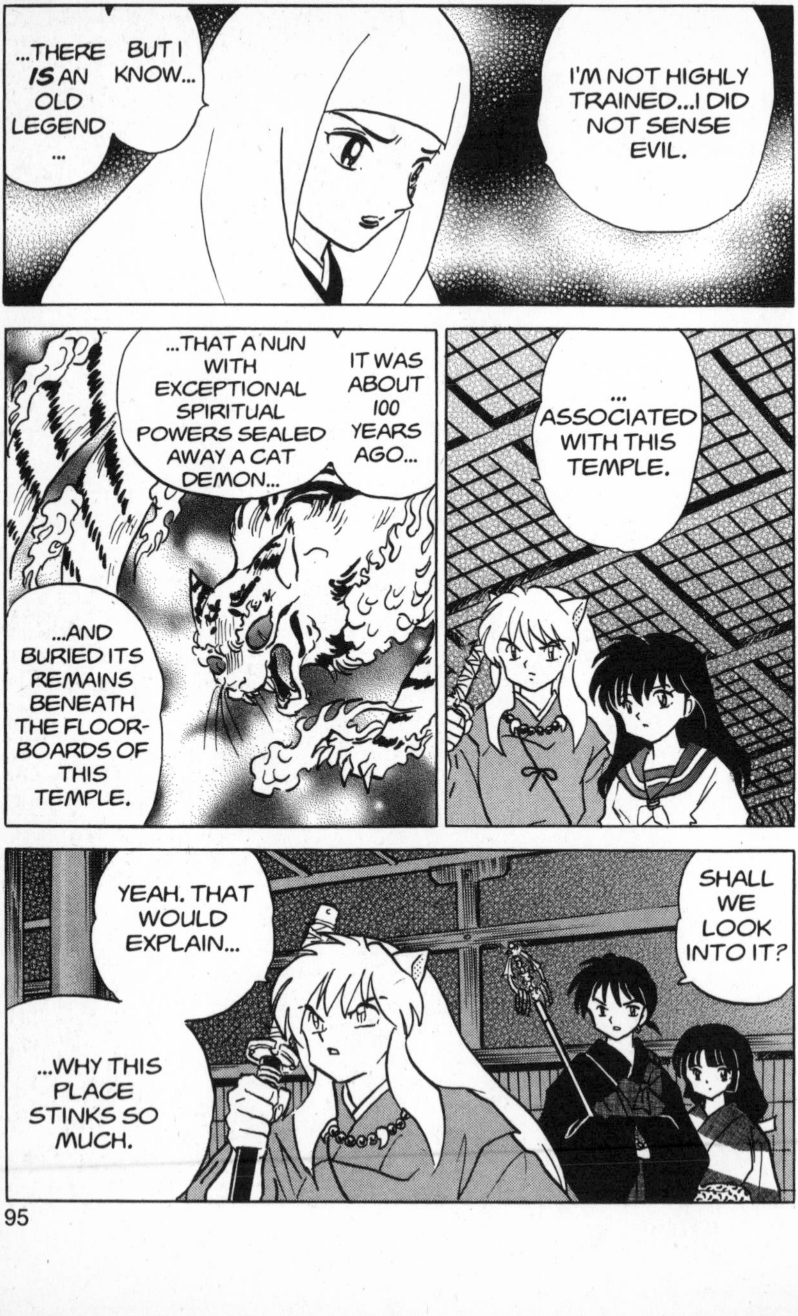
I'M NOT HIGHLY TRAINED...I DID NOT SENSE EVIL.
BUT I KNOW...
...THERE *IS* AN OLD LEGEND ...
... ASSOCIATED WITH THIS TEMPLE.
IT WAS ABOUT 100 YEARS AGO...
...THAT A NUN WITH EXCEPTIONAL SPIRITUAL POWERS SEALED AWAY A CAT DEMON...
...AND BURIED ITS REMAINS BENEATH THE FLOOR-BOARDS OF THIS TEMPLE.
SHALL WE LOOK INTO IT?
YEAH. THAT WOULD EXPLAIN...
...WHY THIS PLACE STINKS SO MUCH.

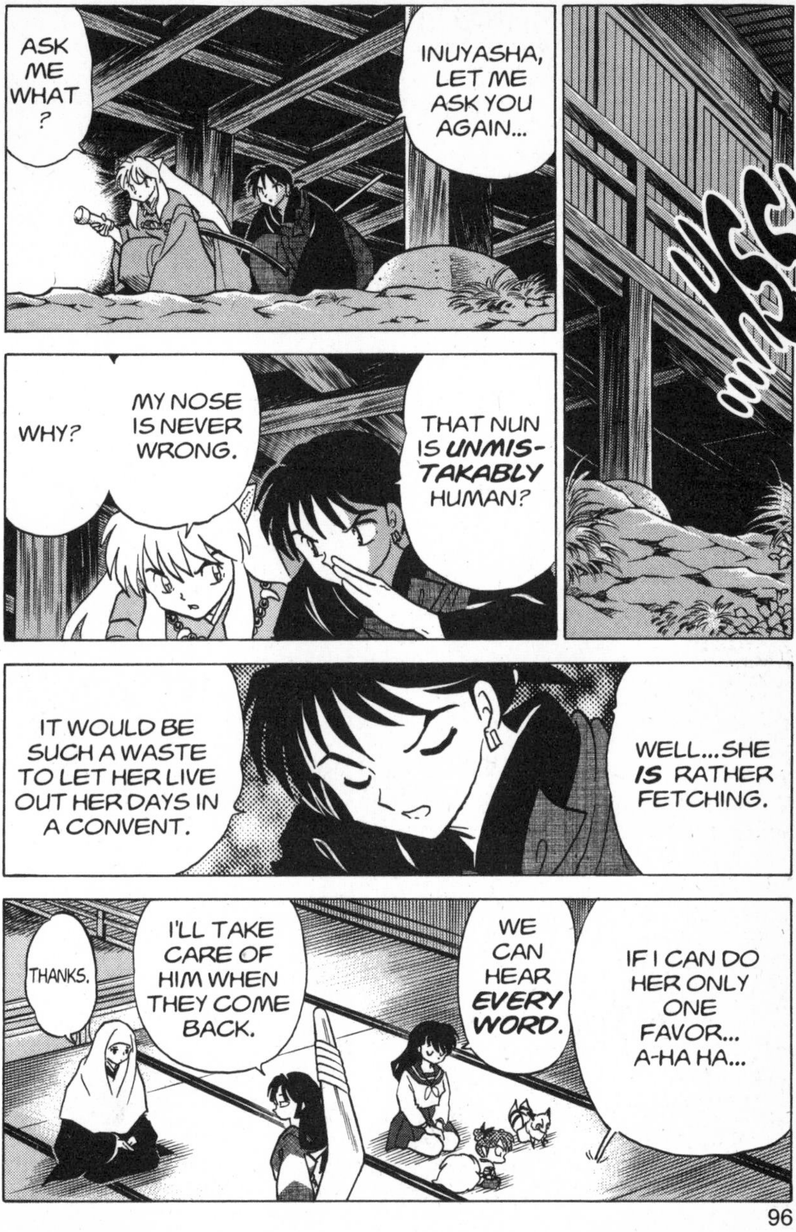
INUYASHA, LET ME ASK YOU AGAIN...
ASK ME WHAT?
THAT NUN IS *UNMIS-TAKABLY* HUMAN?
MY NOSE IS NEVER WRONG.
WHY?
WELL...SHE *IS* RATHER FETCHING.
IT WOULD BE SUCH A WASTE TO LET HER LIVE OUT HER DAYS IN A CONVENT.
IF I CAN DO HER ONLY ONE FAVOR... A-HA HA...
WE CAN HEAR *EVERY WORD*.
I'LL TAKE CARE OF HIM WHEN THEY COME BACK.
THANKS.

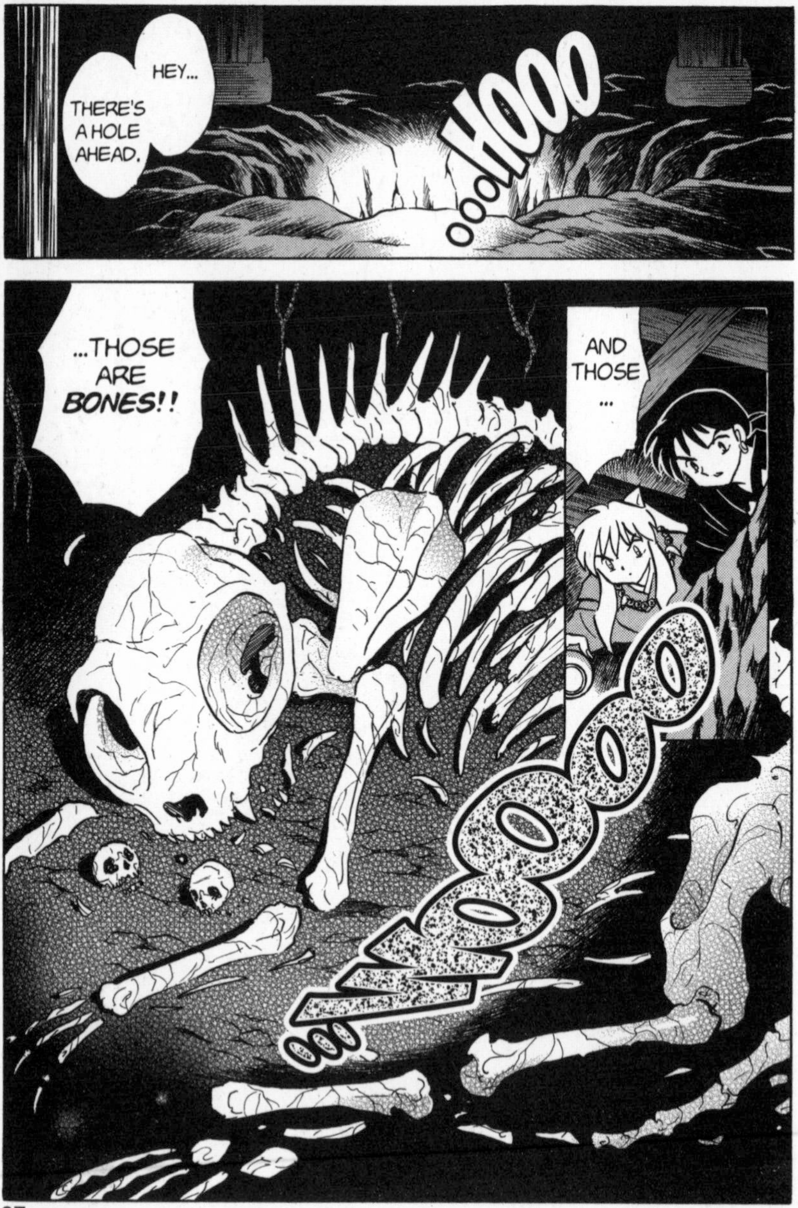
HEY...
THERE'S A HOLE AHEAD.
OOOHOOO
AND THOSE ...
...THOSE ARE BONES!!
...WOOOOOOO

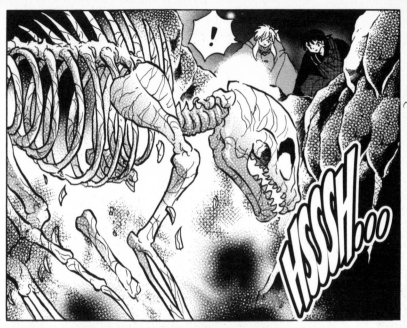

INUYASHA AND MIROKU SURE ARE TAKING THEIR TIME...

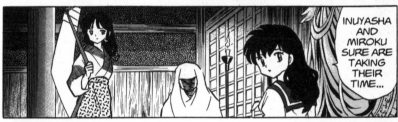

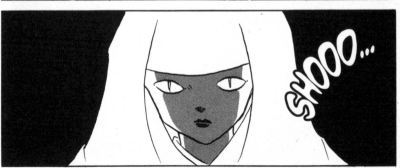

98

SCROLL 6

CAT DEMON

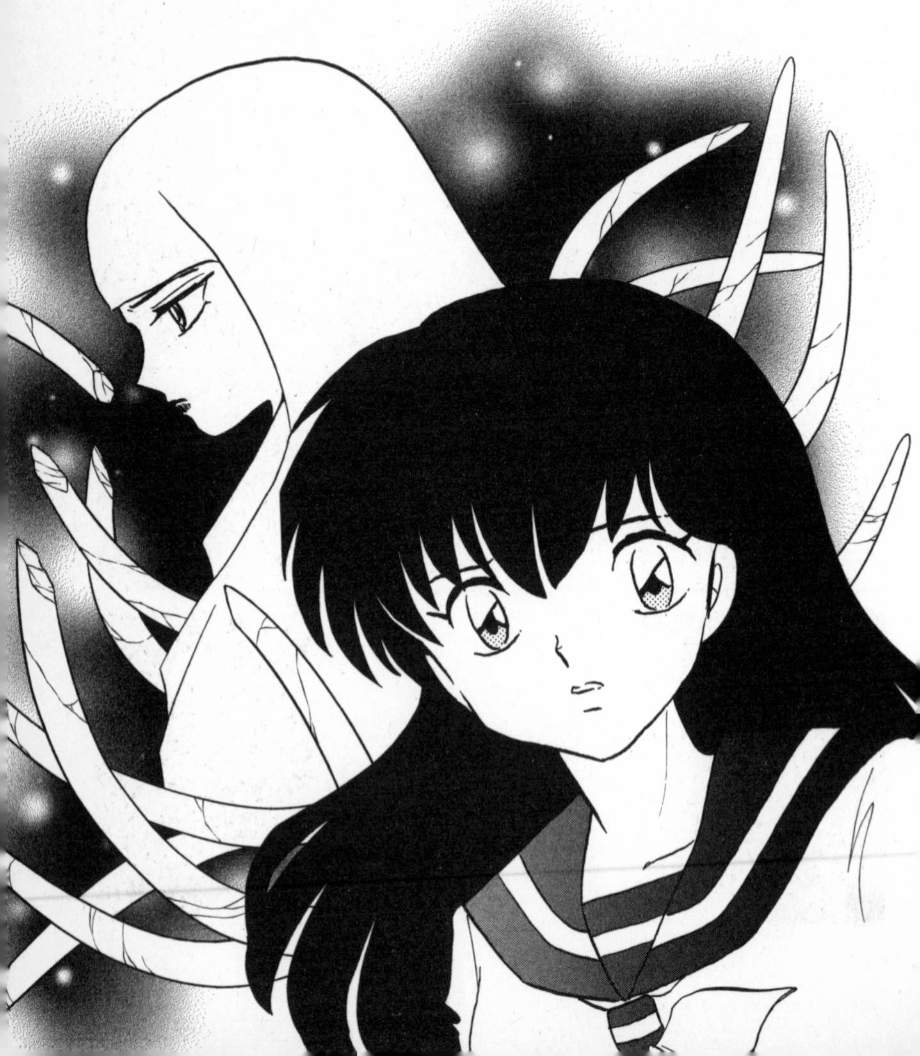

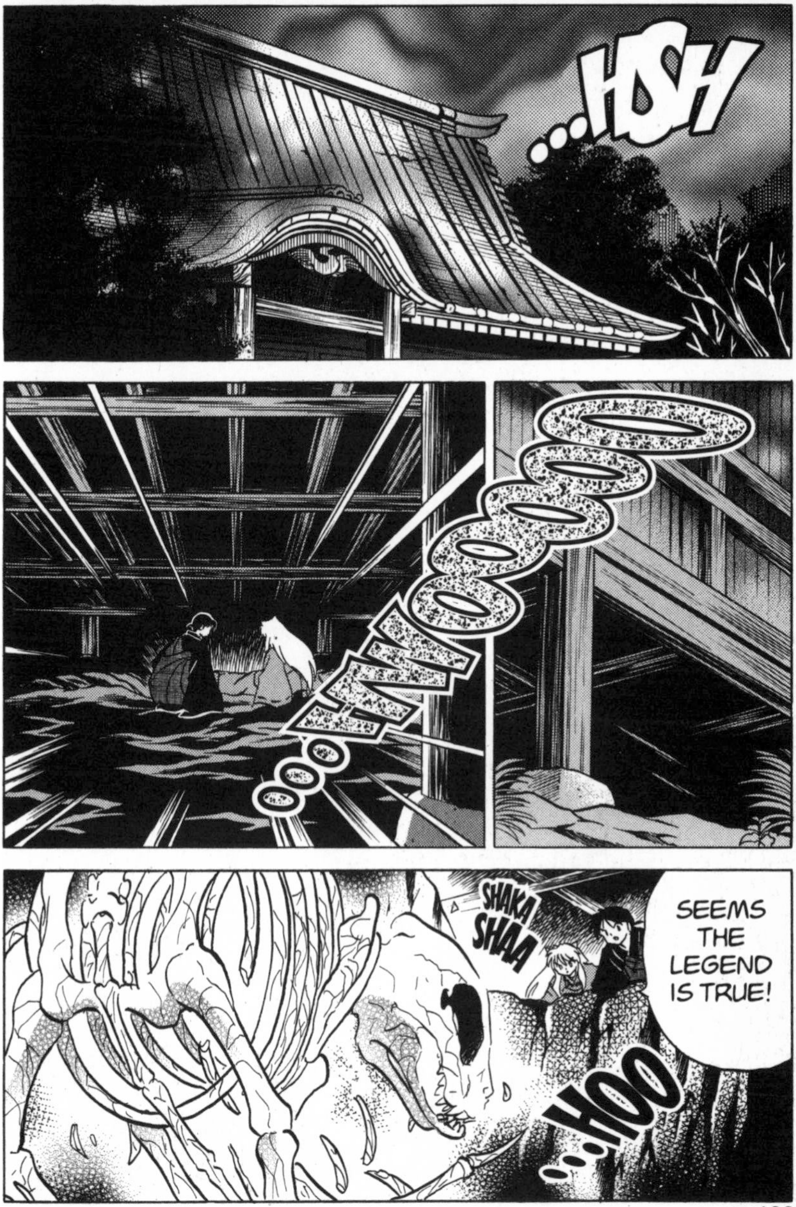
...HSH
...HWOOOOO
SEEMS THE LEGEND IS TRUE!
SHAKA SHAA
...HOO

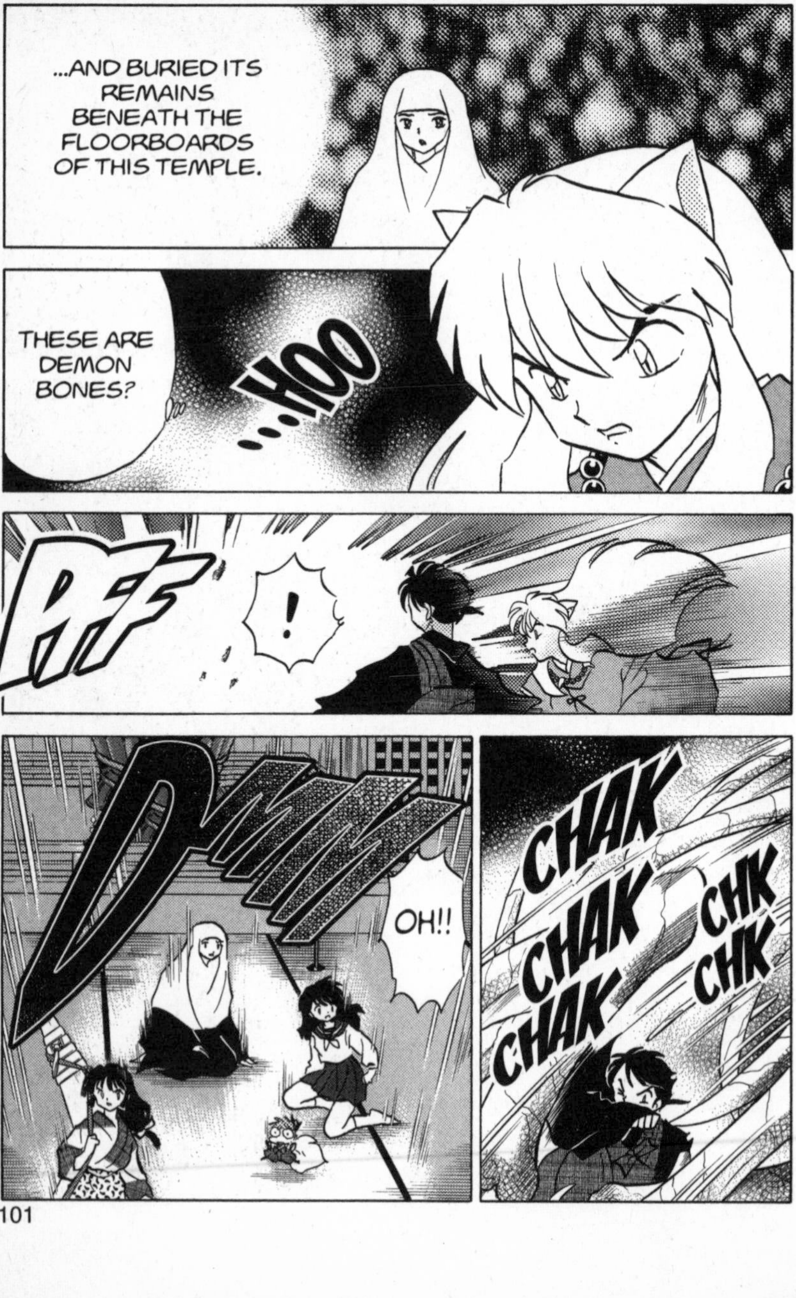
...AND BURIED ITS REMAINS BENEATH THE FLOORBOARDS OF THIS TEMPLE.
HOO...
THESE ARE DEMON BONES?
!
PFF
CHK
CHK
CHAK
CHAK
CHAK
DMMM
OH!!

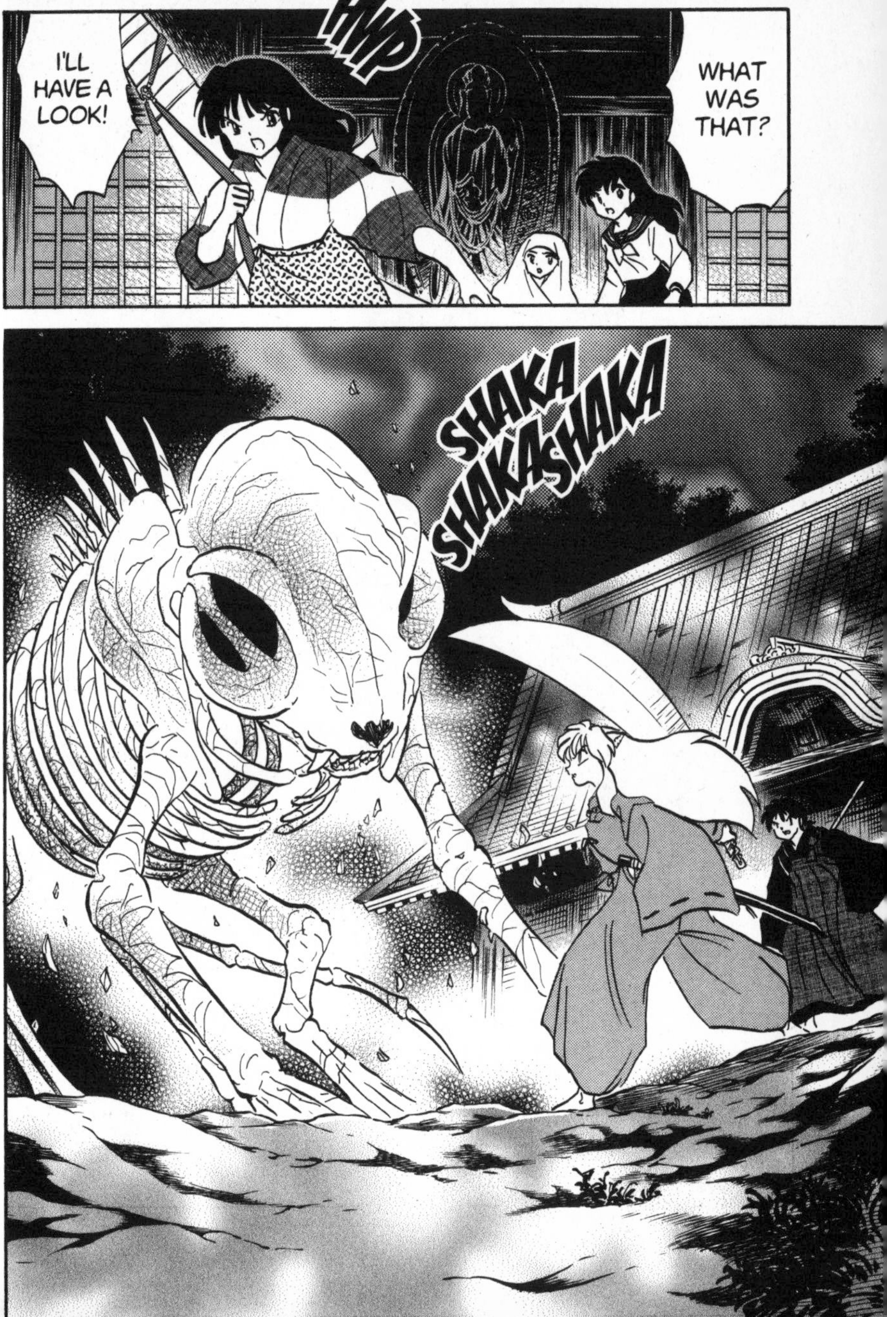
WHAT WAS THAT?
HMP
I'LL HAVE A LOOK!
SHAKA SHAKASHAKA

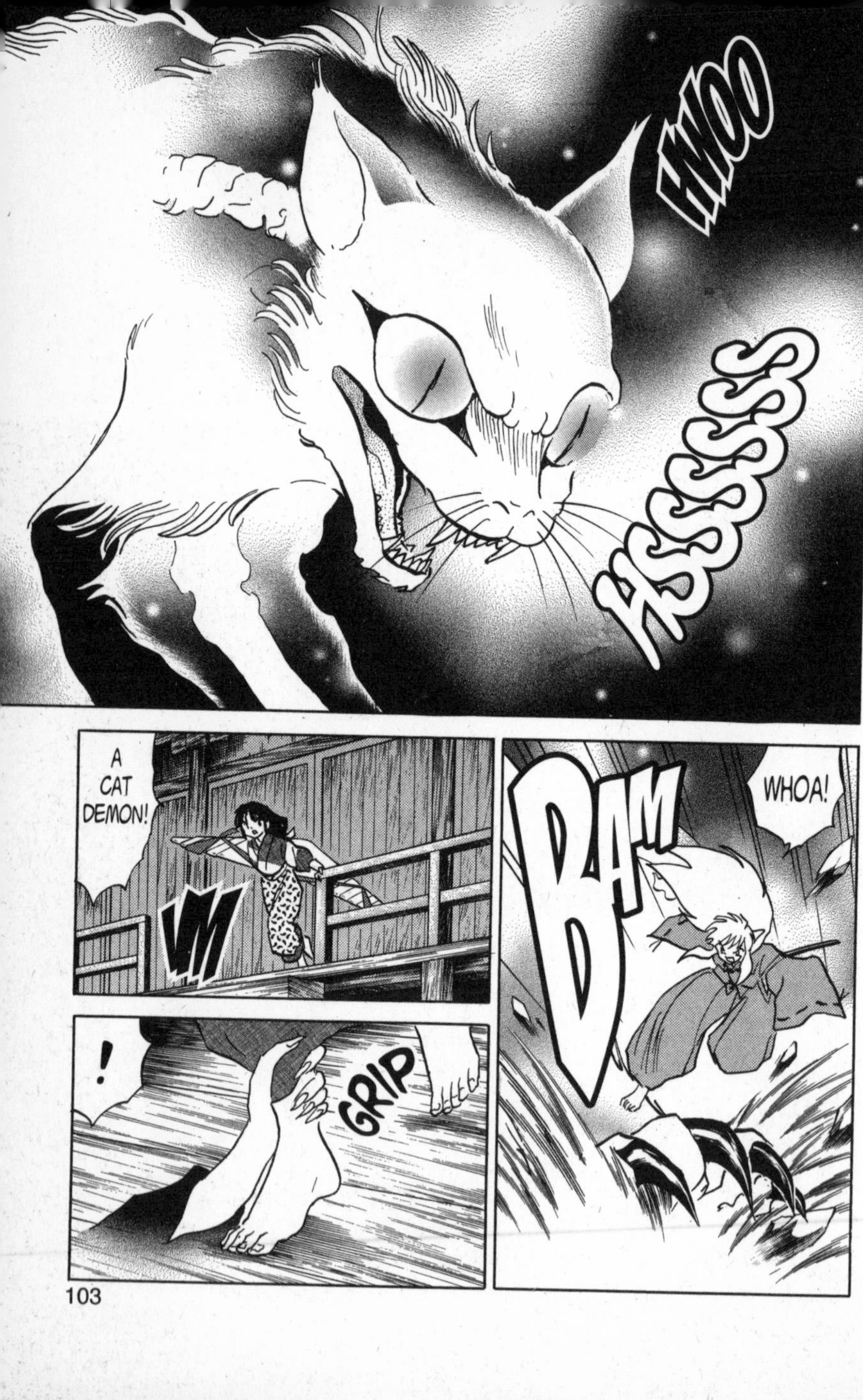

HWOO
HSSSSSS
BAM
WHOA!
A CAT DEMON!
VM
!
GRIP

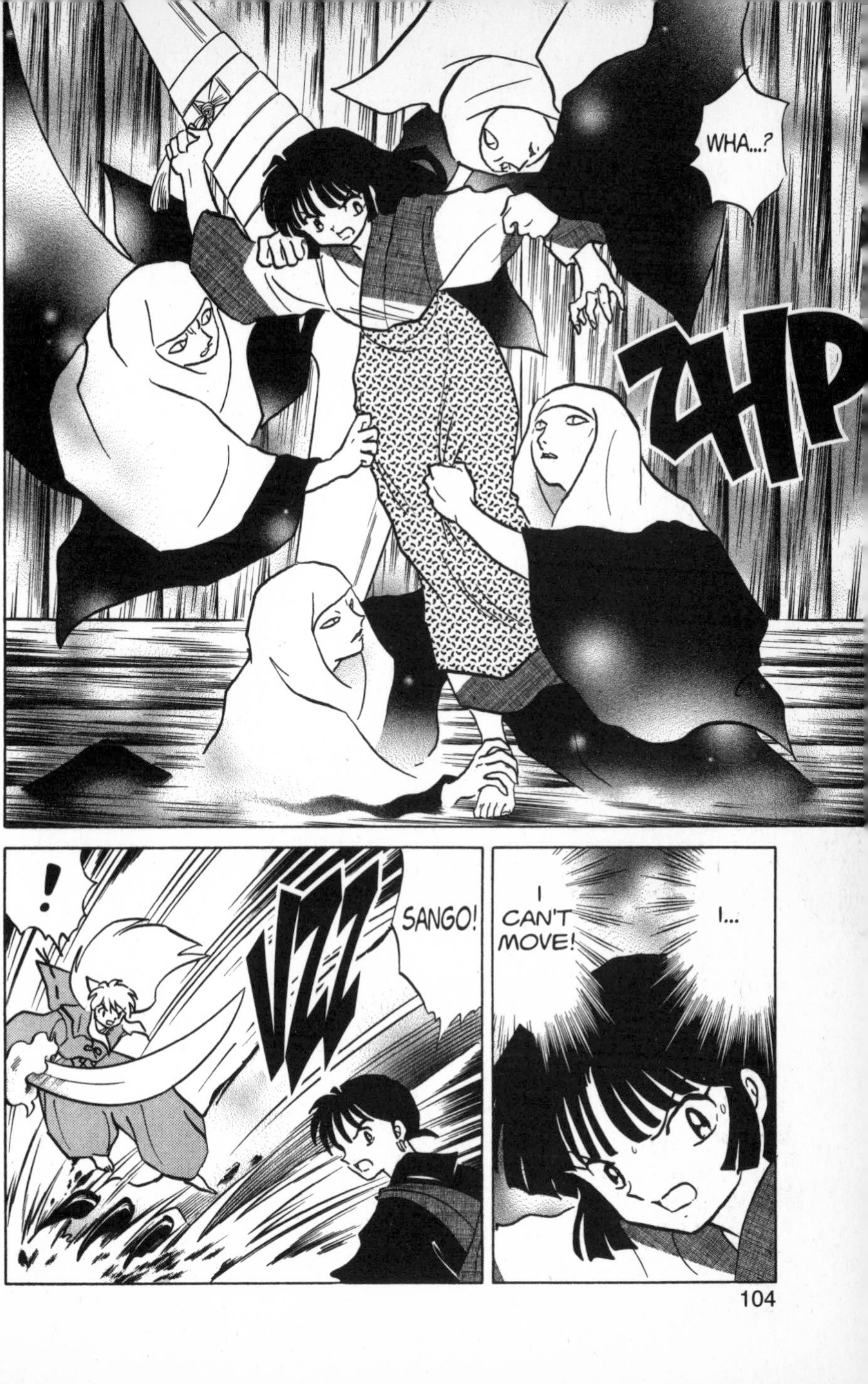
WHA...?
ZHP
I...
I CAN'T MOVE!
SANGO!
VZZ
!

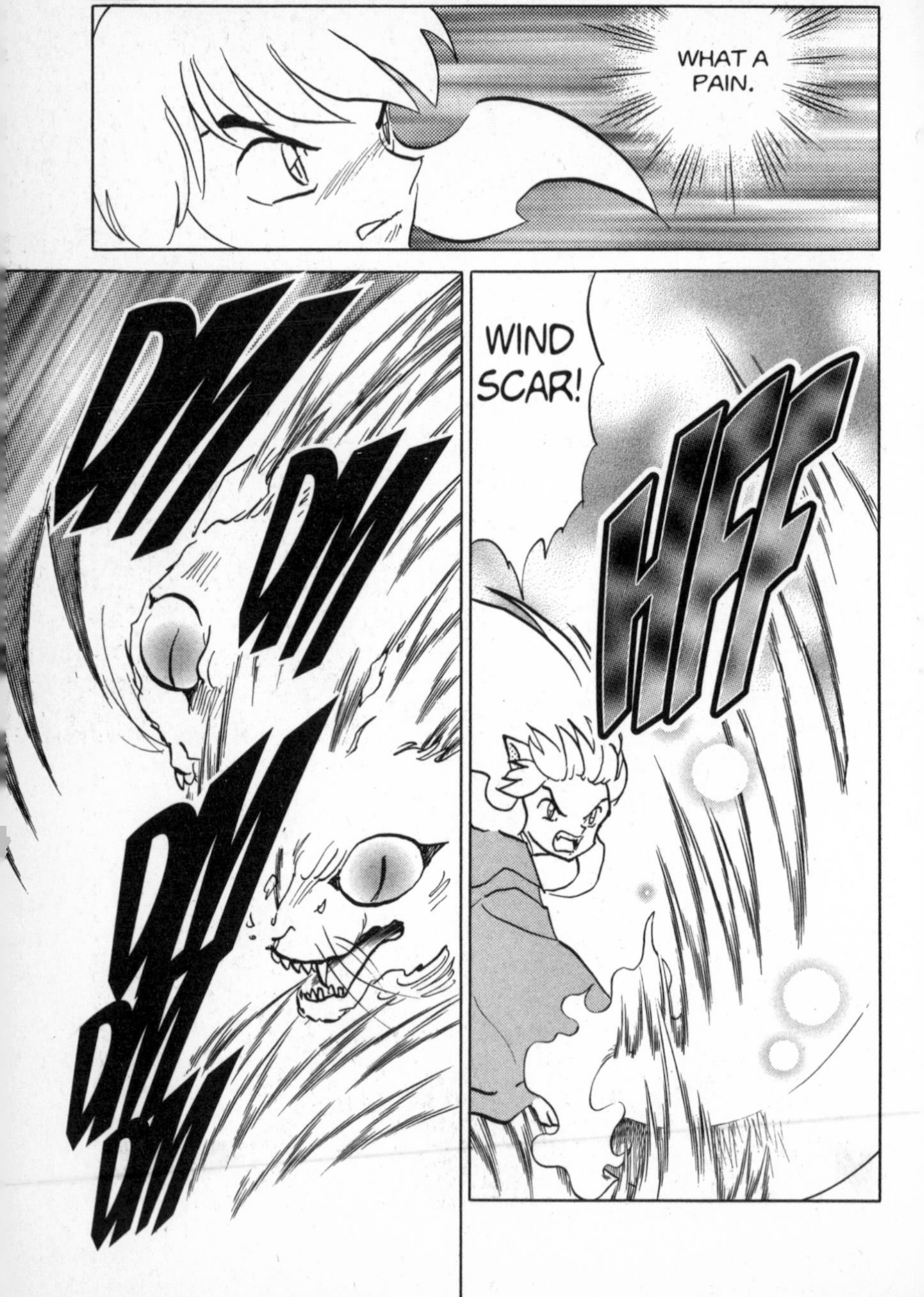
WHAT A PAIN.
WIND SCAR!
HIFF
DN DN
DN DN DN

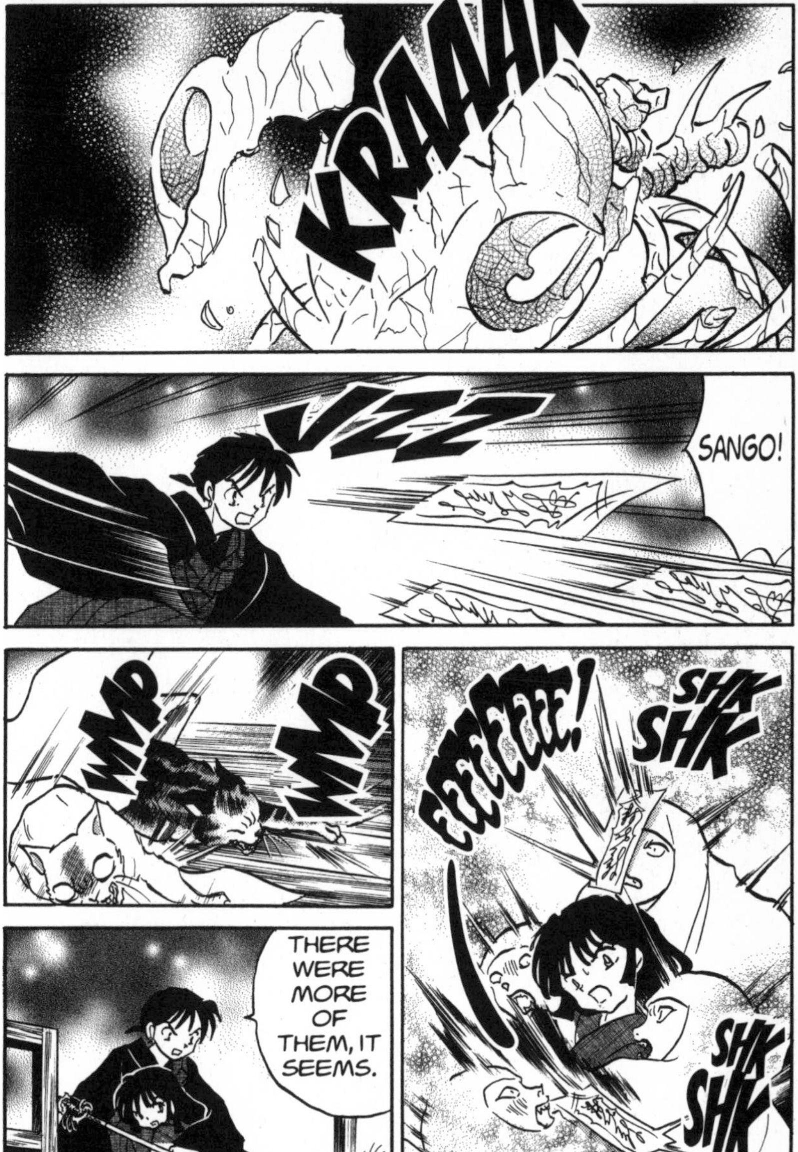
KRAAAK
SANGO!
VZZZ
EEEEEEEE!
SHK SHK
SHK SHK
WMP
WMP
THERE WERE MORE OF THEM, IT SEEMS.

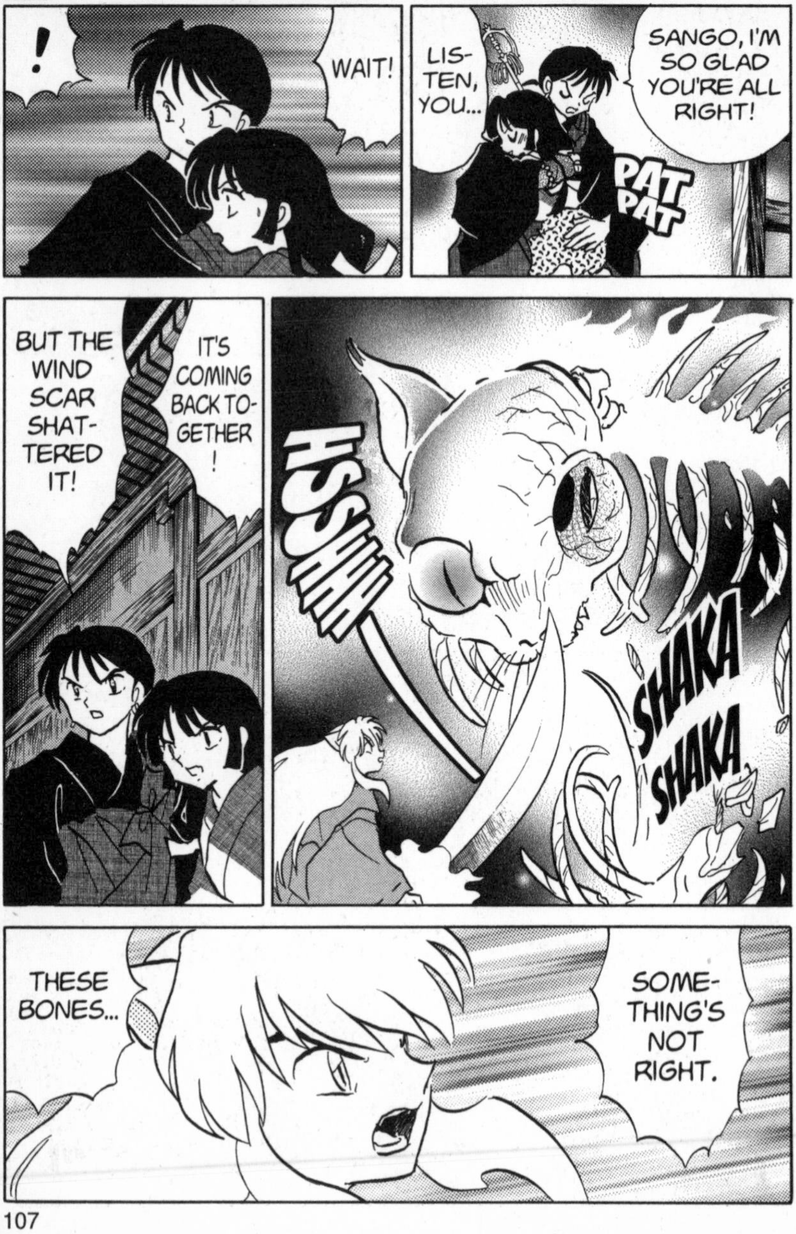
SANGO, I'M SO GLAD YOU'RE ALL RIGHT!
LIS-TEN, YOU...
PAT PAT
WAIT!
!
HSSH
SHAKA SHAKA
IT'S COMING BACK TO-GETHER!
BUT THE WIND SCAR SHAT-TERED IT!
SOME-THING'S NOT RIGHT.
THESE BONES...

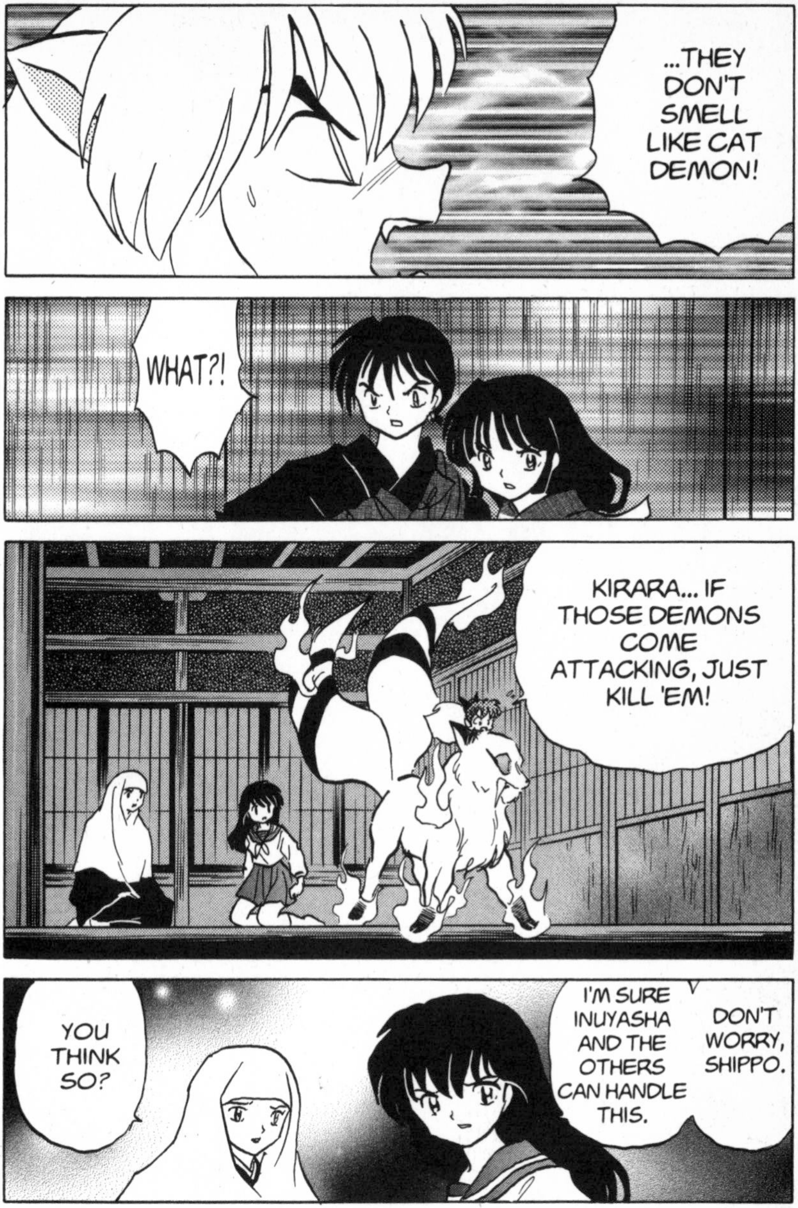
...THEY DON'T SMELL LIKE CAT DEMON!
WHAT?!
KIRARA... IF THOSE DEMONS COME ATTACKING, JUST KILL 'EM!
DON'T WORRY, SHIPPO.
I'M SURE INUYASHA AND THE OTHERS CAN HANDLE THIS.
YOU THINK SO?

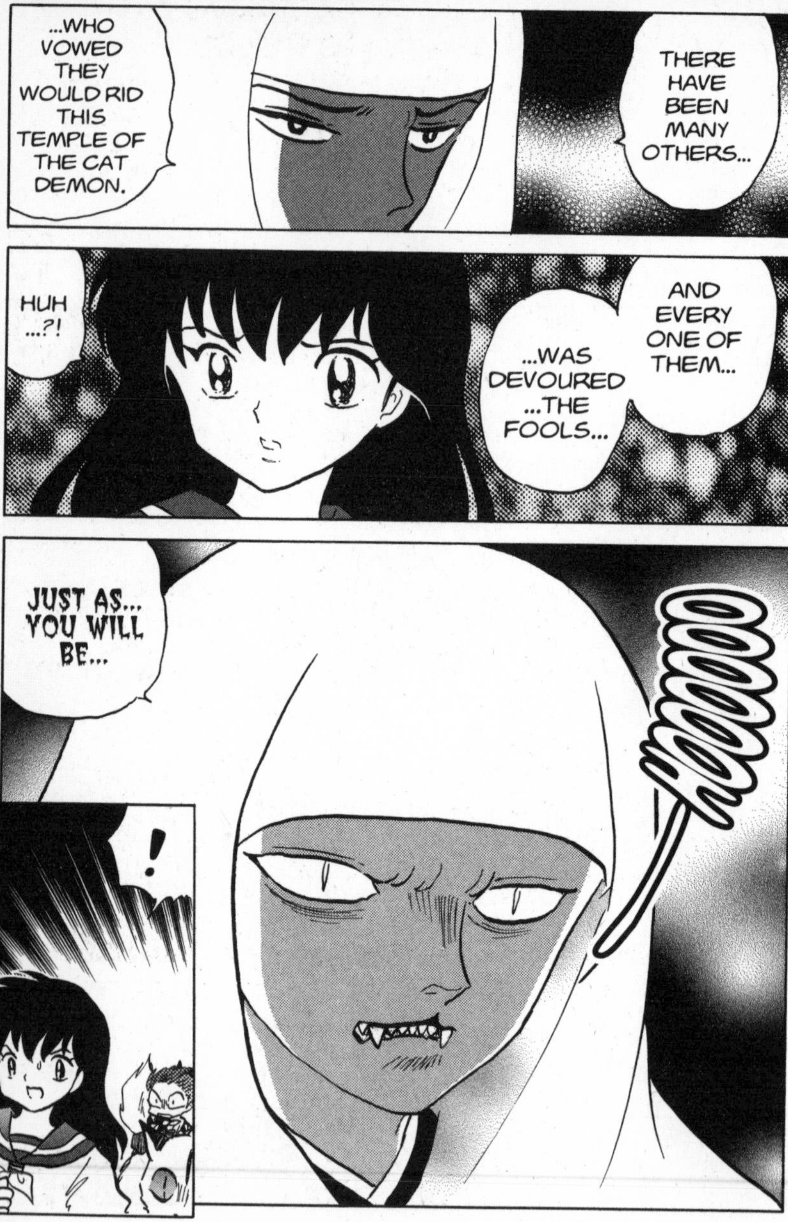
THERE HAVE BEEN MANY OTHERS...
...WHO VOWED THEY WOULD RID THIS TEMPLE OF THE CAT DEMON.
AND EVERY ONE OF THEM...
...WAS DEVOURED ...THE FOOLS...
HUH ...?!
JUST AS... YOU WILL BE...
!

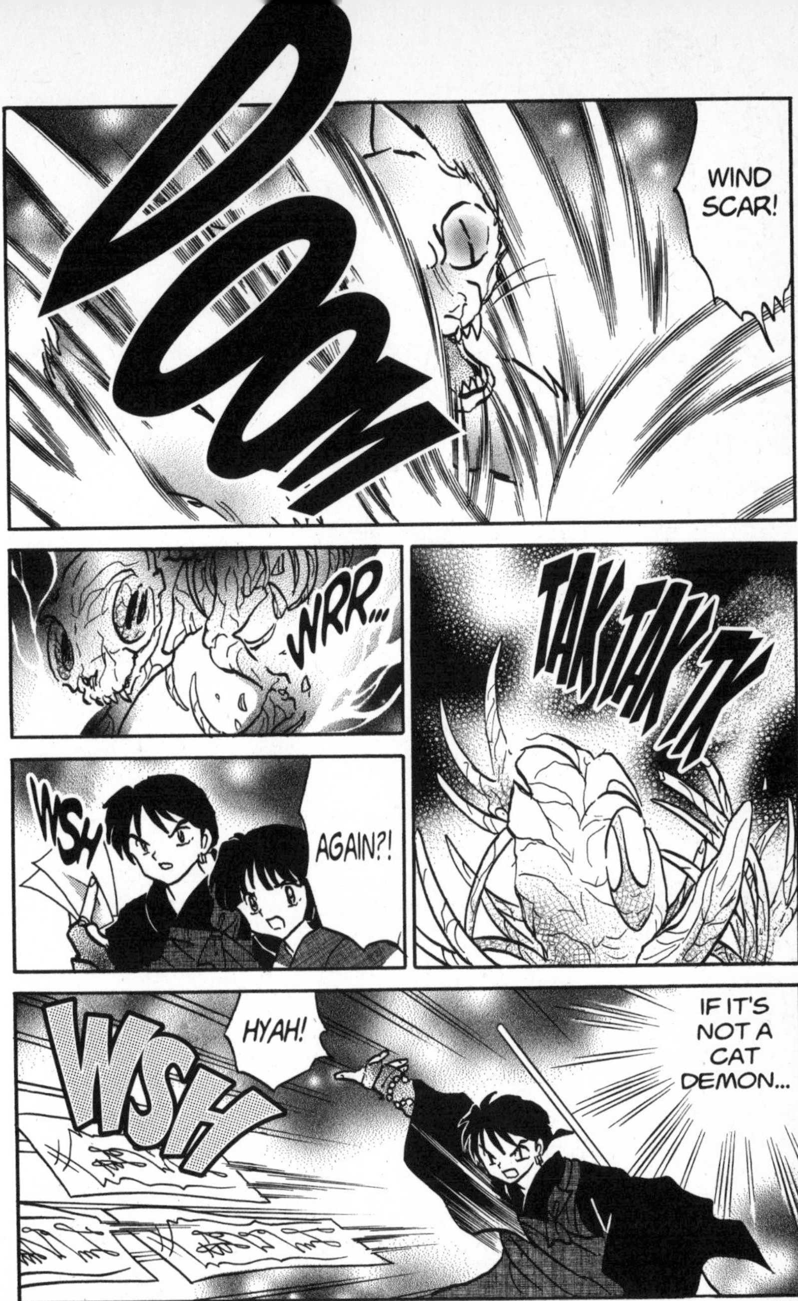
WIND SCAR!
DOOM!
TAK TAK TK
WRR...
AGAIN?!
WSH
IF IT'S NOT A CAT DEMON...
HYAH!
WSH

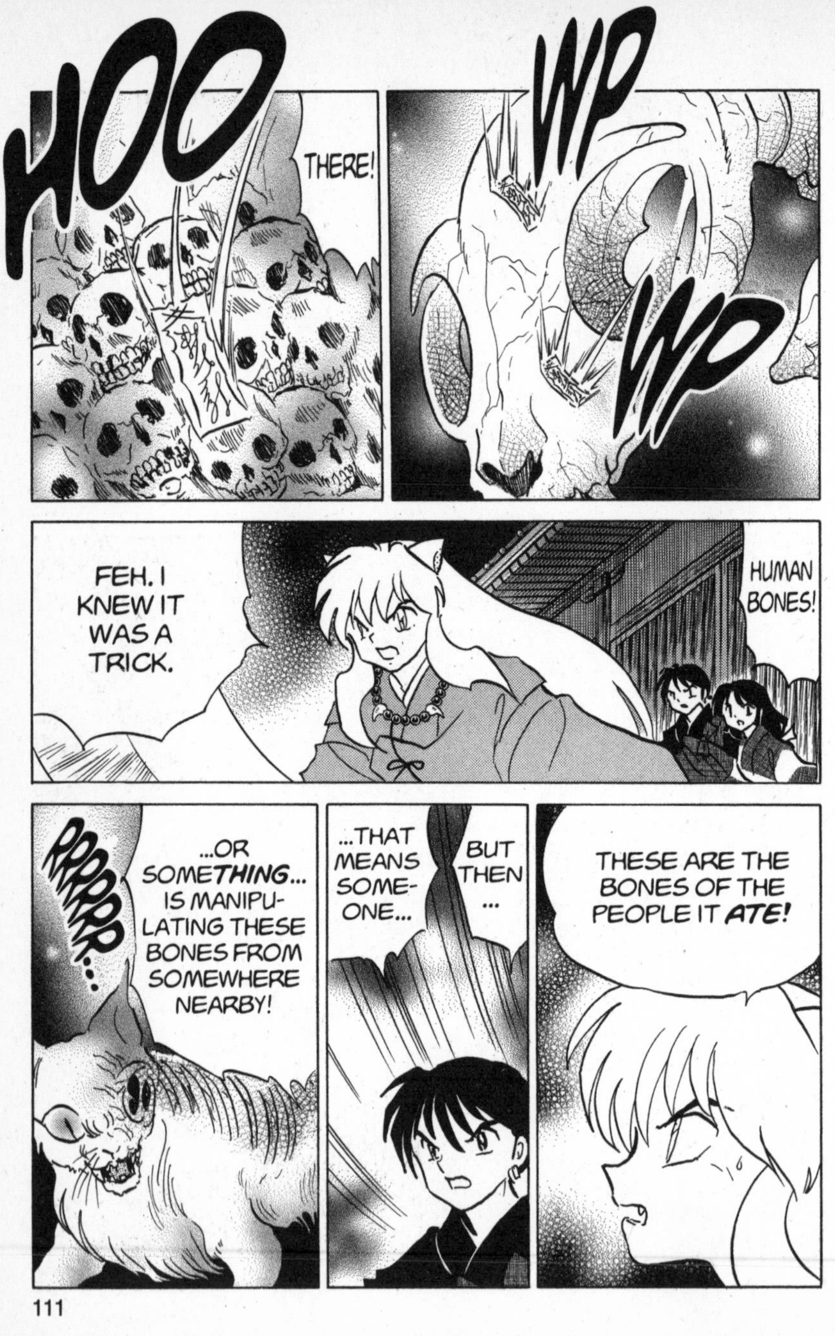
WP
WP
HOO
THERE!
HUMAN BONES!
FEH. I KNEW IT WAS A TRICK.
THESE ARE THE BONES OF THE PEOPLE IT ATE!
BUT THEN...
...THAT MEANS SOMEONE...
...OR SOMETHING... IS MANIPULATING THESE BONES FROM SOMEWHERE NEARBY!
RRRRRR...

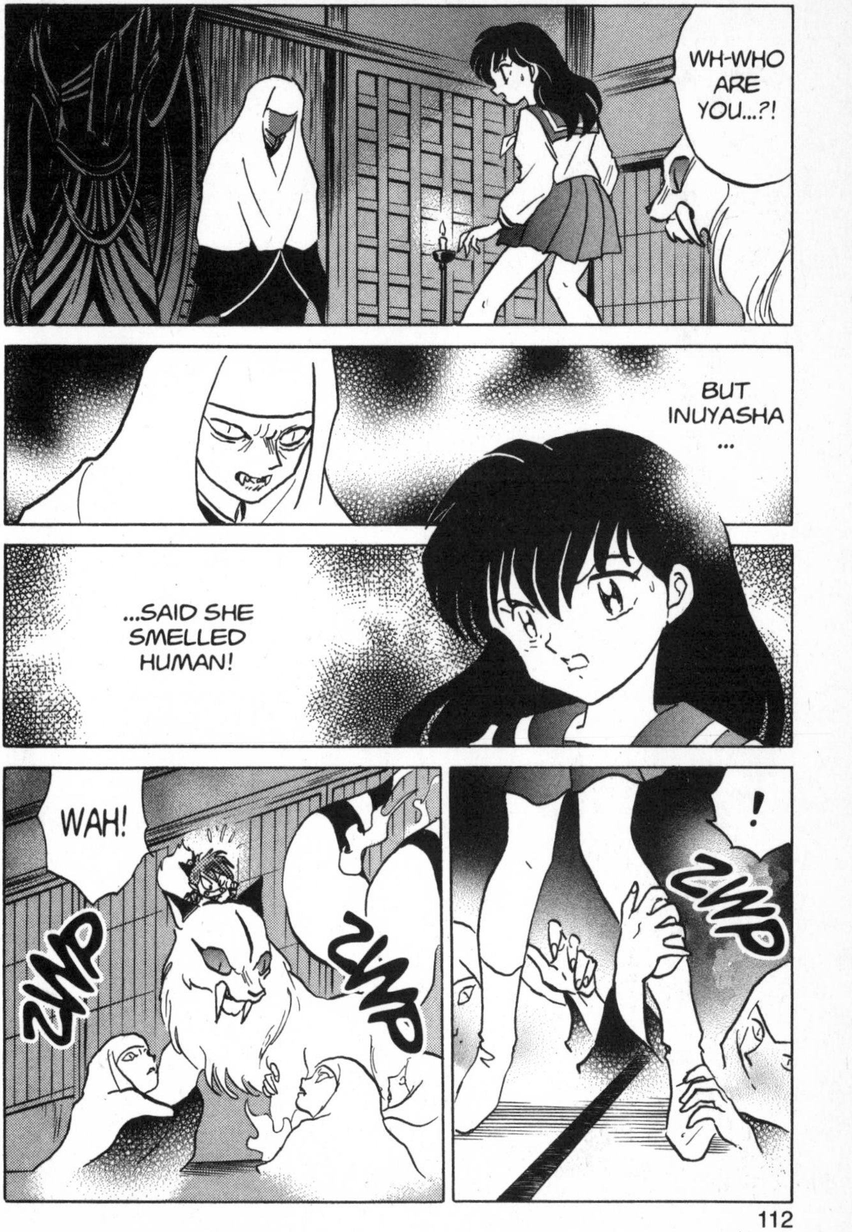

WH-WHO ARE YOU...?!
BUT INUYASHA ...
...SAID SHE SMELLED HUMAN!
!
ZWP
WAH!
ZWP
ZWP

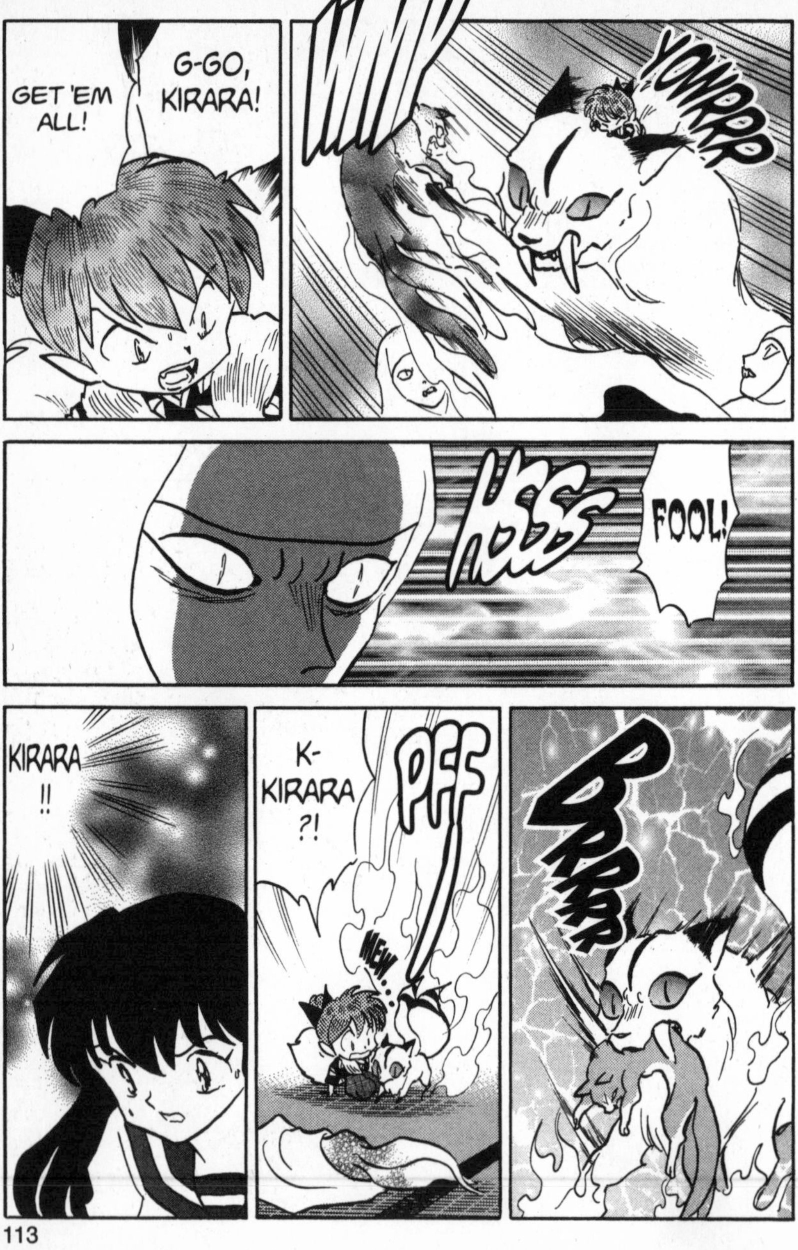
WHMP
YOWRRR
G-GO, KIRARA!
GET 'EM ALL!
FOOL!
HISSS
BRRRRR
PFF
K-KIRARA?!
MEW...
KIRARA!!

HEE HEE. HE'S JUST A KITTEN...
...COMPARED TO MY 300 YEARS!
HWOOO
I CAN'T...
...MOVE...
NOW.
TIME FOR DINNER.
BAM BAM BAM
KAGOME!
MY LADY NUN!
!
IT WON'T OPEN?!

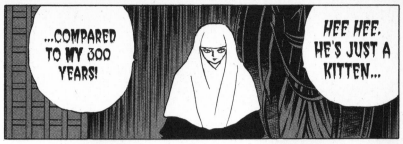

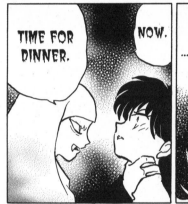

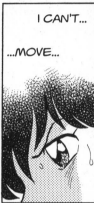

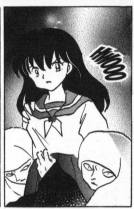

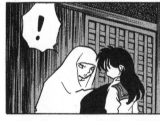

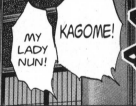

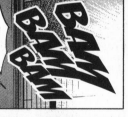

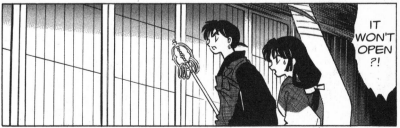

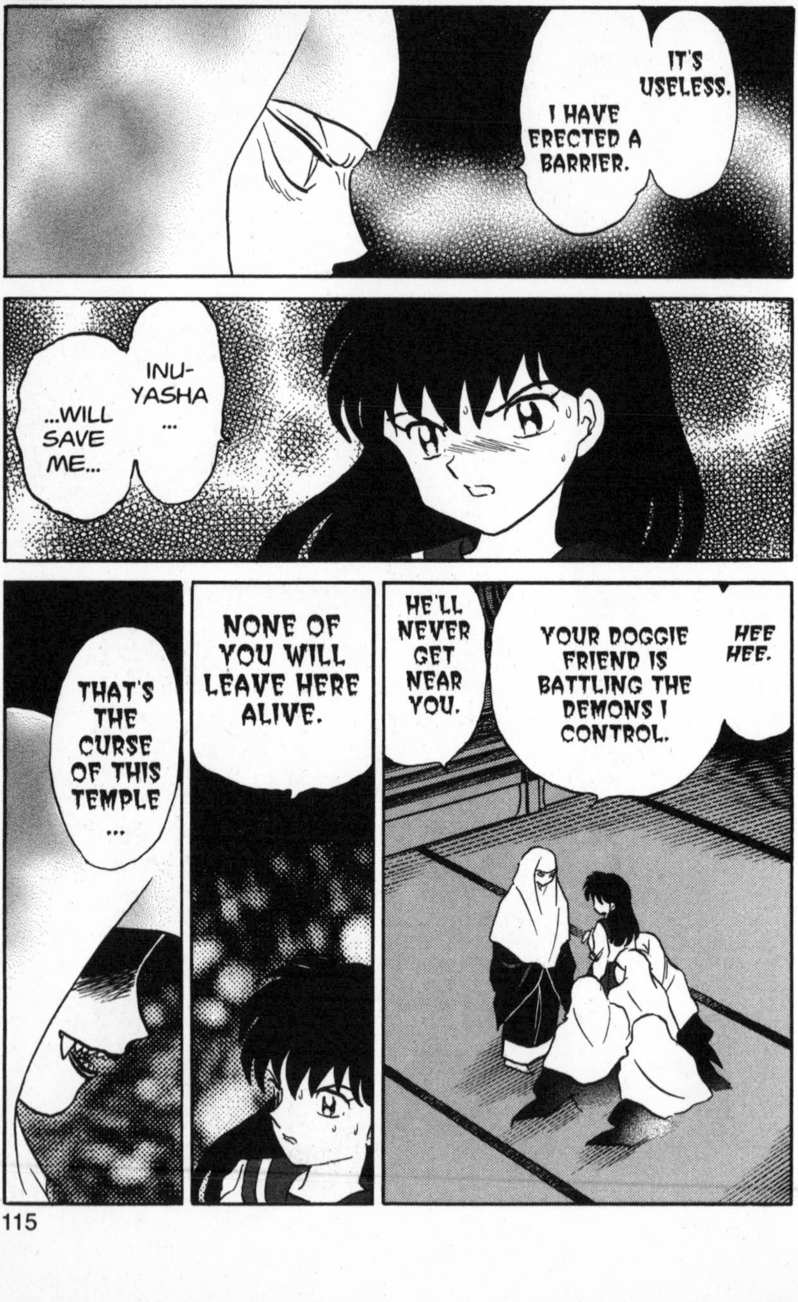
IT'S USELESS.
I HAVE ERECTED A BARRIER.
INU-YASHA ...
...WILL SAVE ME...
HEE HEE.
YOUR DOGGIE FRIEND IS BATTLING THE DEMONS I CONTROL.
HE'LL NEVER GET NEAR YOU.
NONE OF YOU WILL LEAVE HERE ALIVE.
THAT'S THE CURSE OF THIS TEMPLE ...

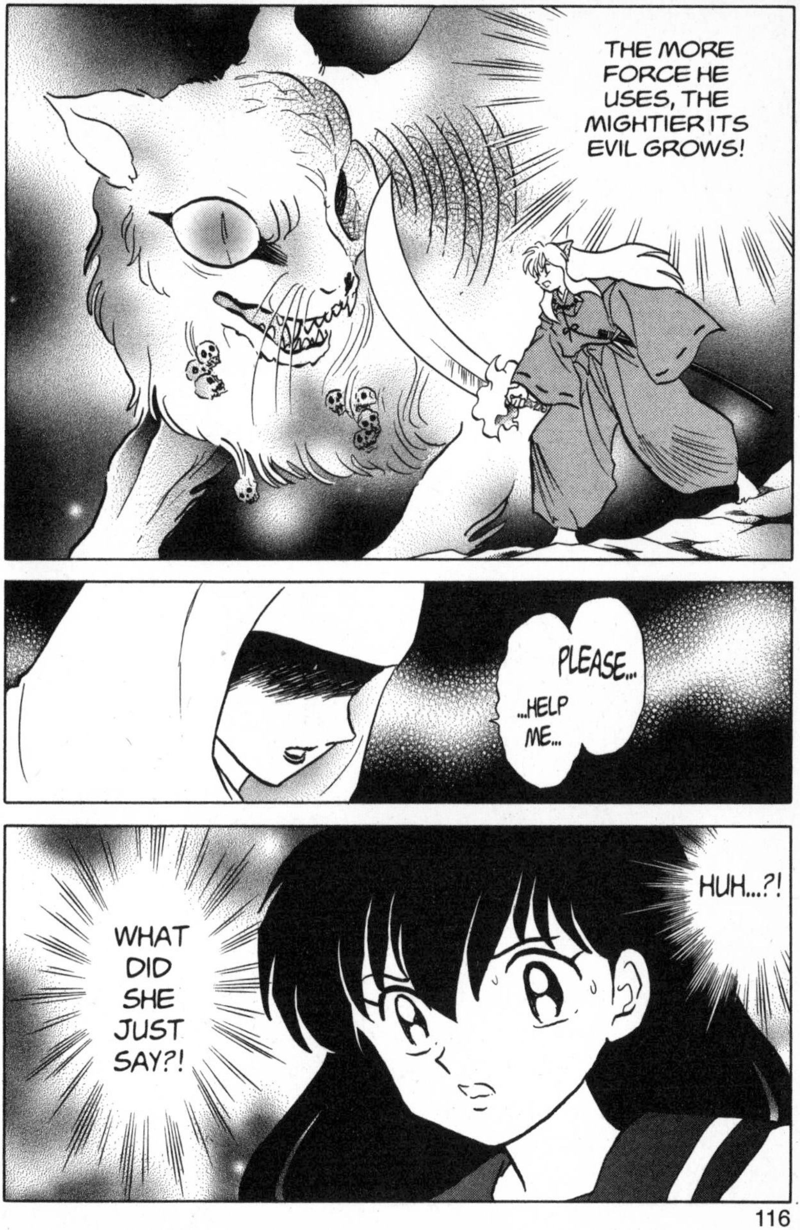
THE MORE FORCE HE USES, THE MIGHTIER ITS EVIL GROWS!
PLEASE...
...HELP ME...
HUH...?!
WHAT DID SHE JUST SAY?!

SCROLL 7

THE DRAGON-SCALED TETSUSAIGA

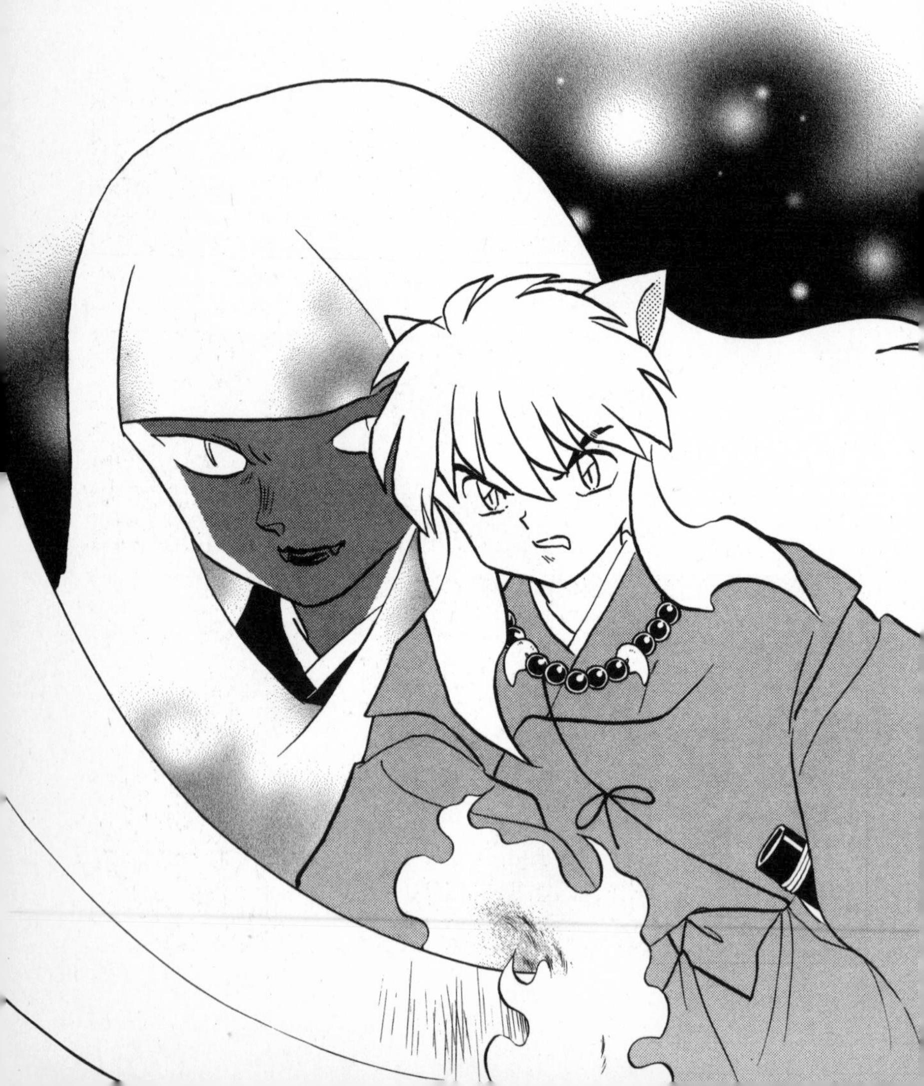

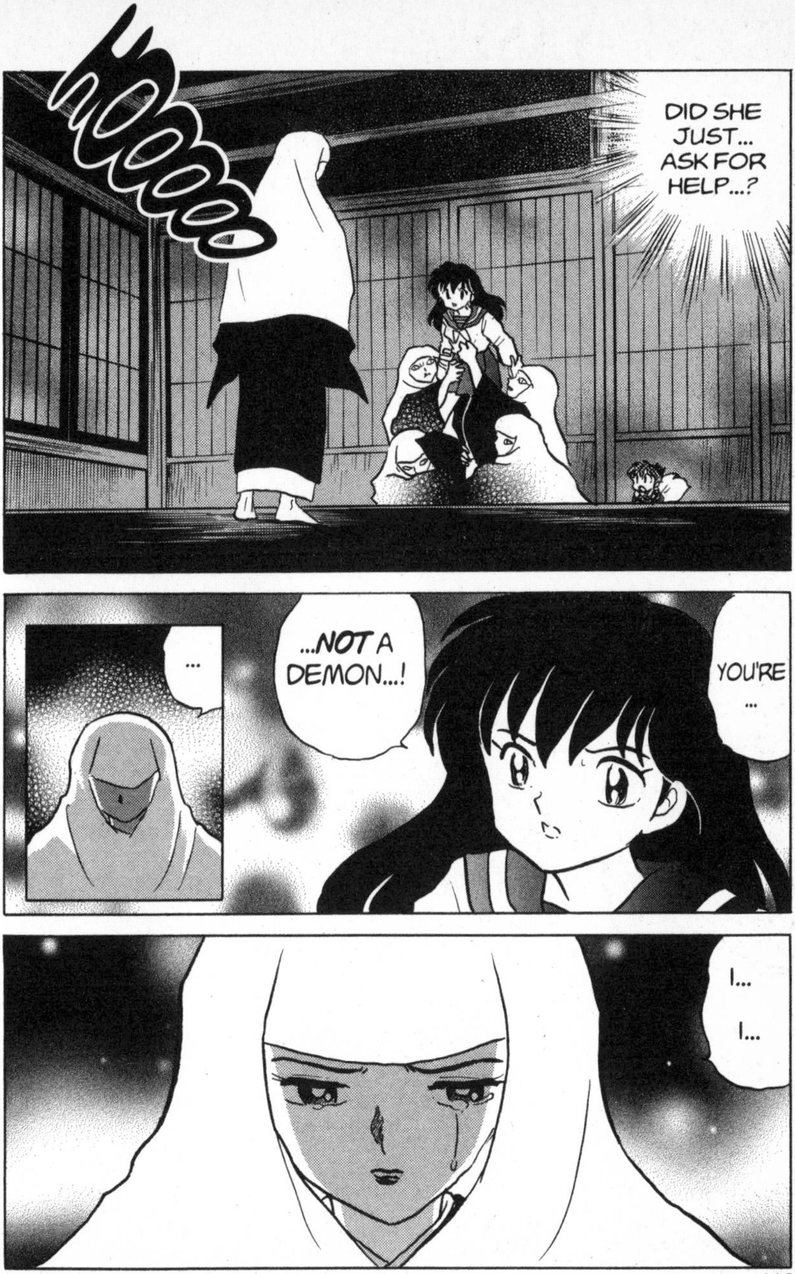
DID SHE JUST... ASK FOR HELP...?
HOOOOO
YOU'RE ...
...NOT A DEMON...!
...
I...
I...

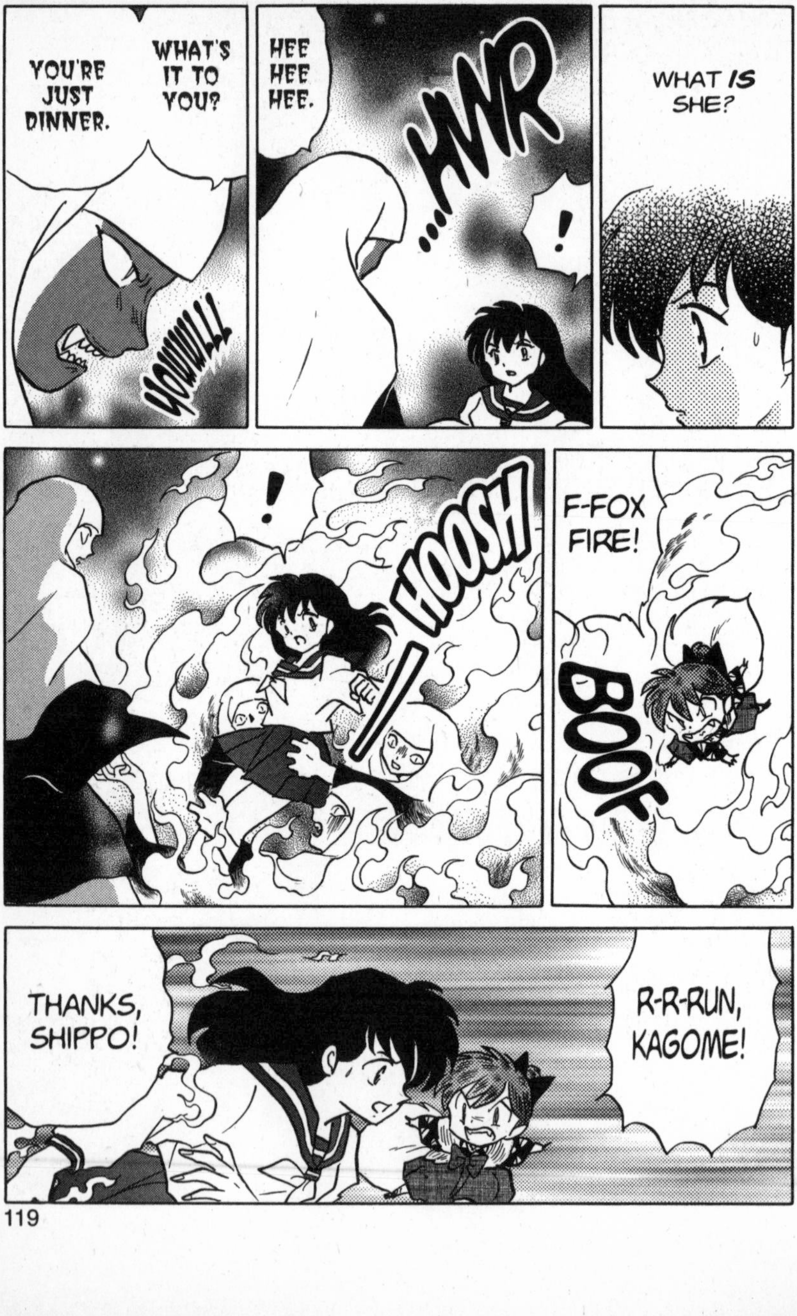
WHAT IS SHE?
HEE HEE HEE.
...HMR
!
WHAT'S IT TO YOU?
YOU'RE JUST DINNER.
HOWWWL!!
F-FOX FIRE!
BOOF
!
HOOSH
R-R-RUN, KAGOME!
THANKS, SHIPPO!

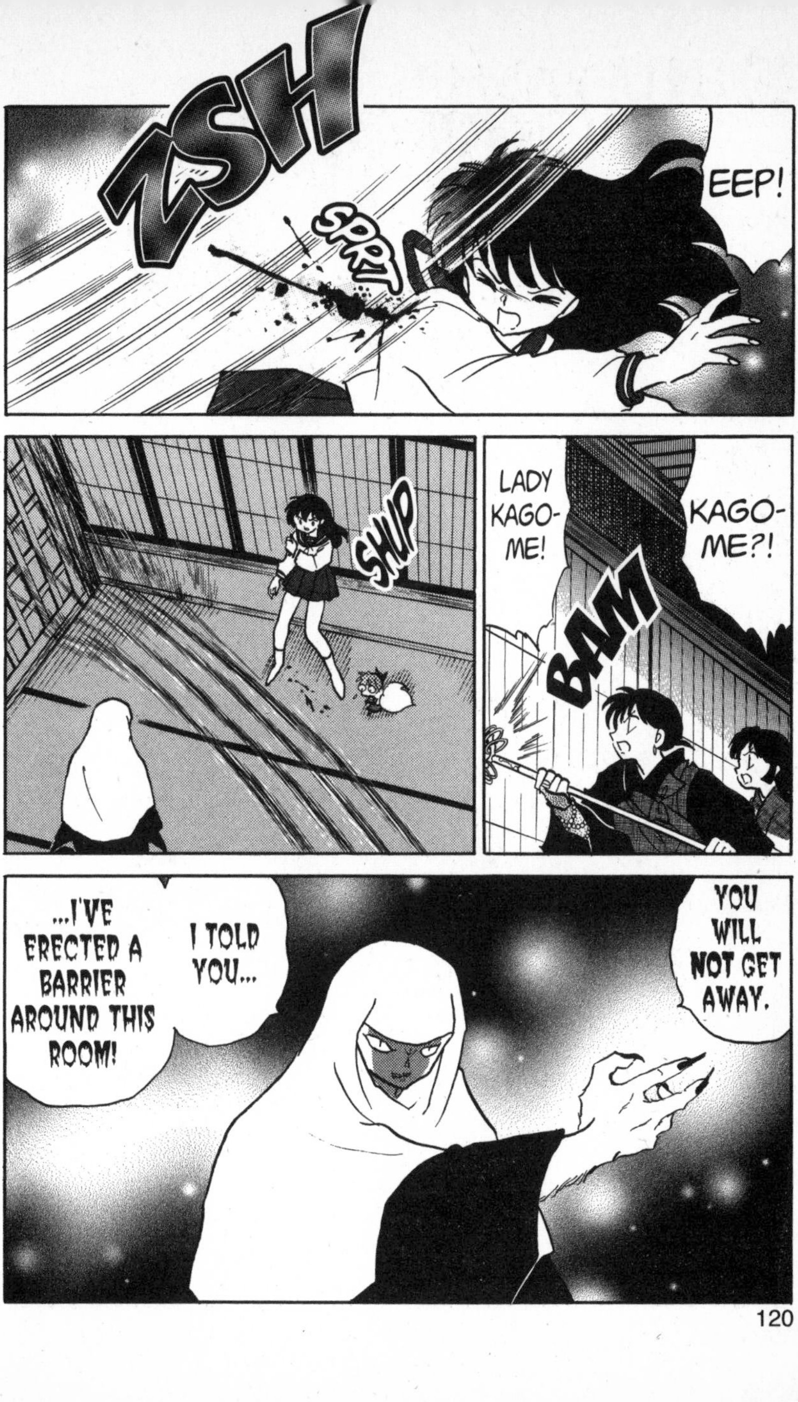
ZSH
EEP!
SPRT
KAGO-ME?!
LADY KAGO-ME!
BAM
SHUP
YOU WILL NOT GET AWAY.
I TOLD YOU...
...I'VE ERECTED A BARRIER AROUND THIS ROOM!

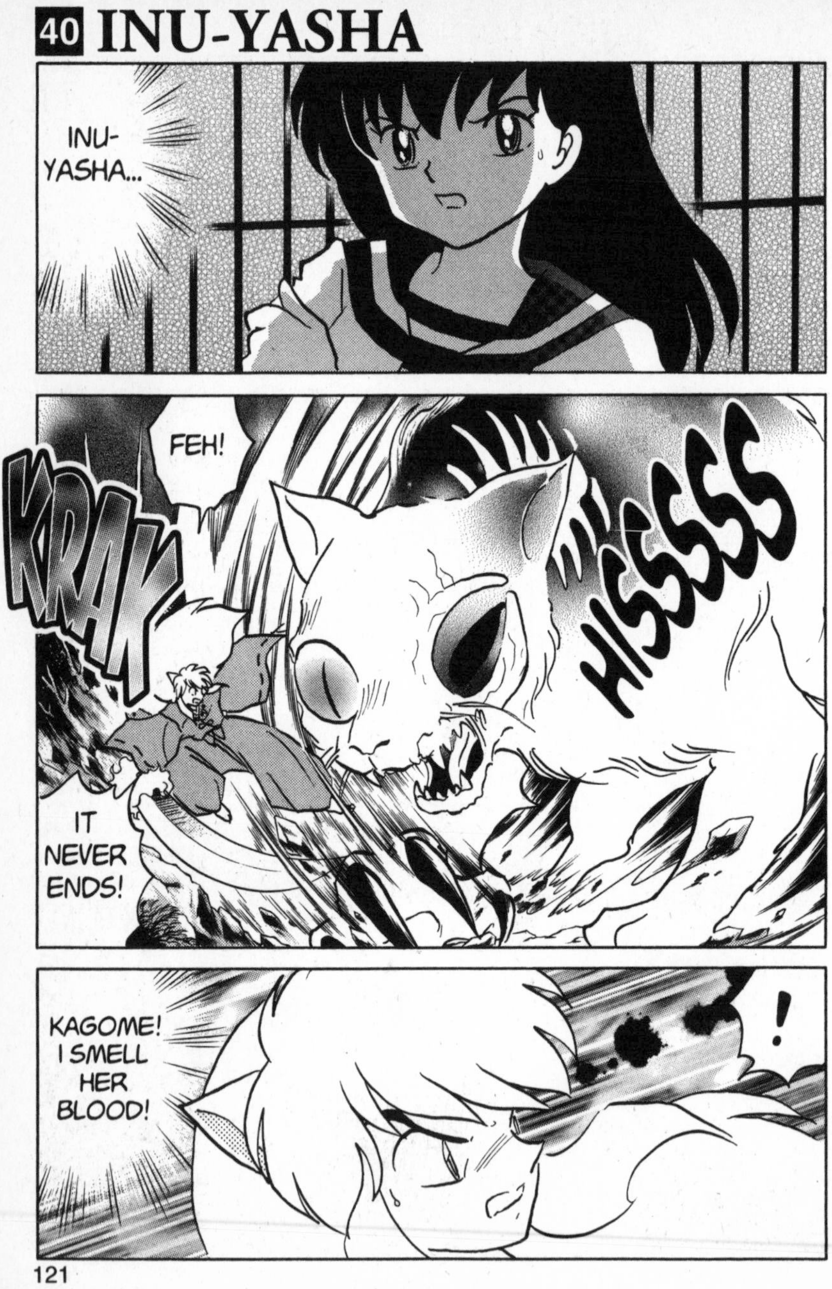
INU-YASHA...
HISSSSS
FEH!
KRAK
IT NEVER ENDS!
!
KAGOME! I SMELL HER BLOOD!

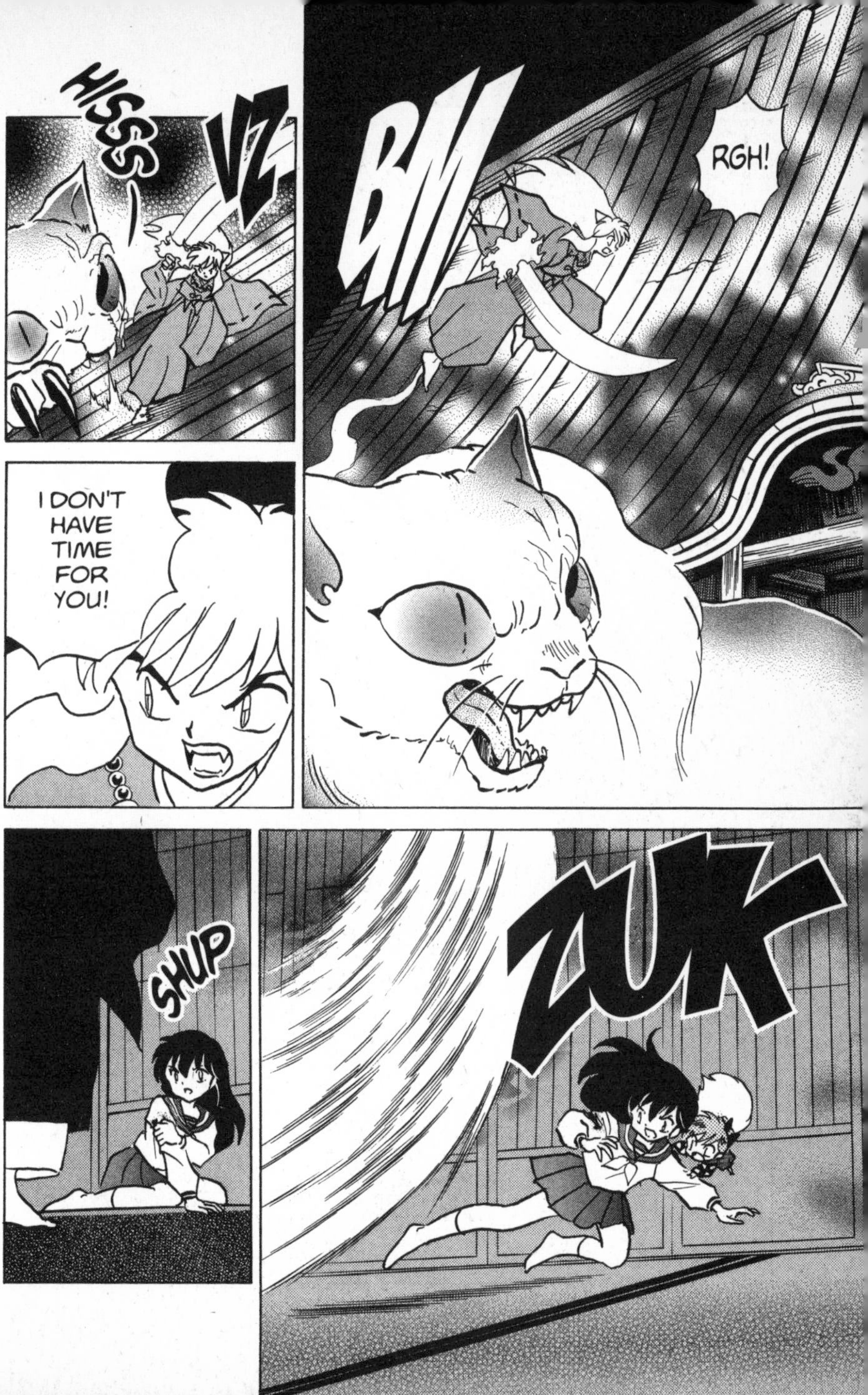
RGH!
BM
VZ
HISSS
I DON'T HAVE TIME FOR YOU!
ZUK
SHUP

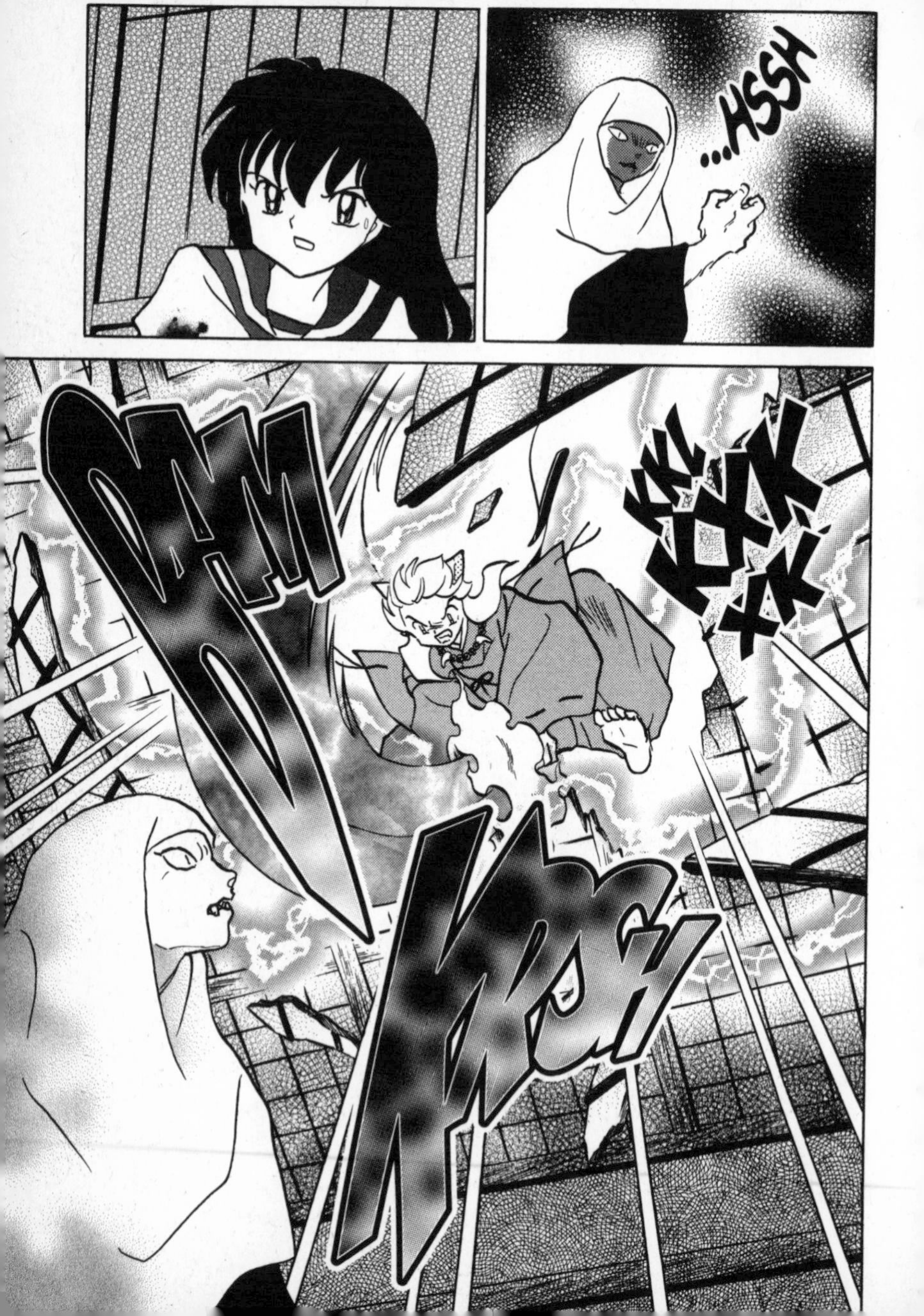
...HSSH
KRAK KRAK

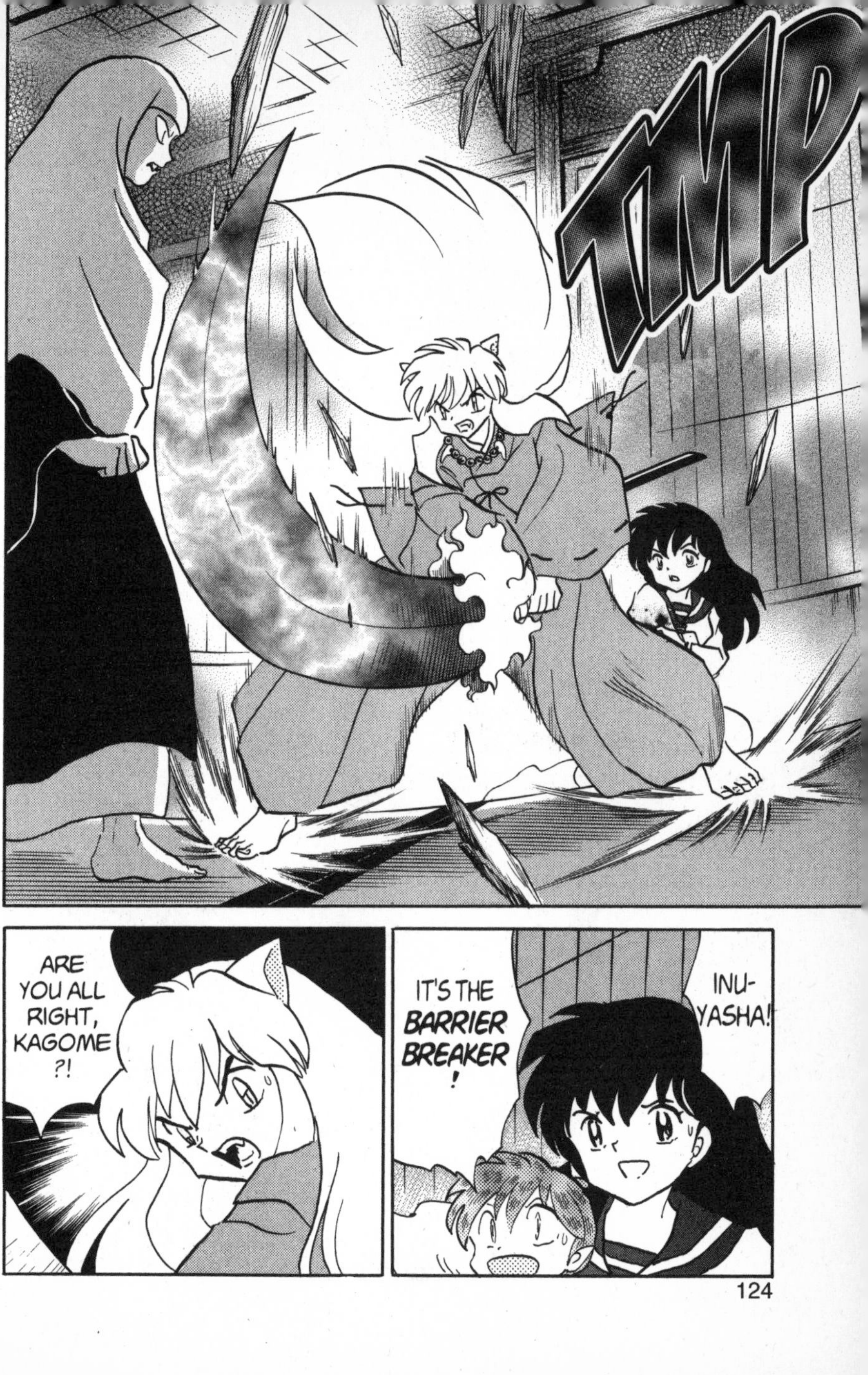
TMP
INU-YASHA!
IT'S THE BARRIER BREAKER!
ARE YOU ALL RIGHT, KAGOME?!

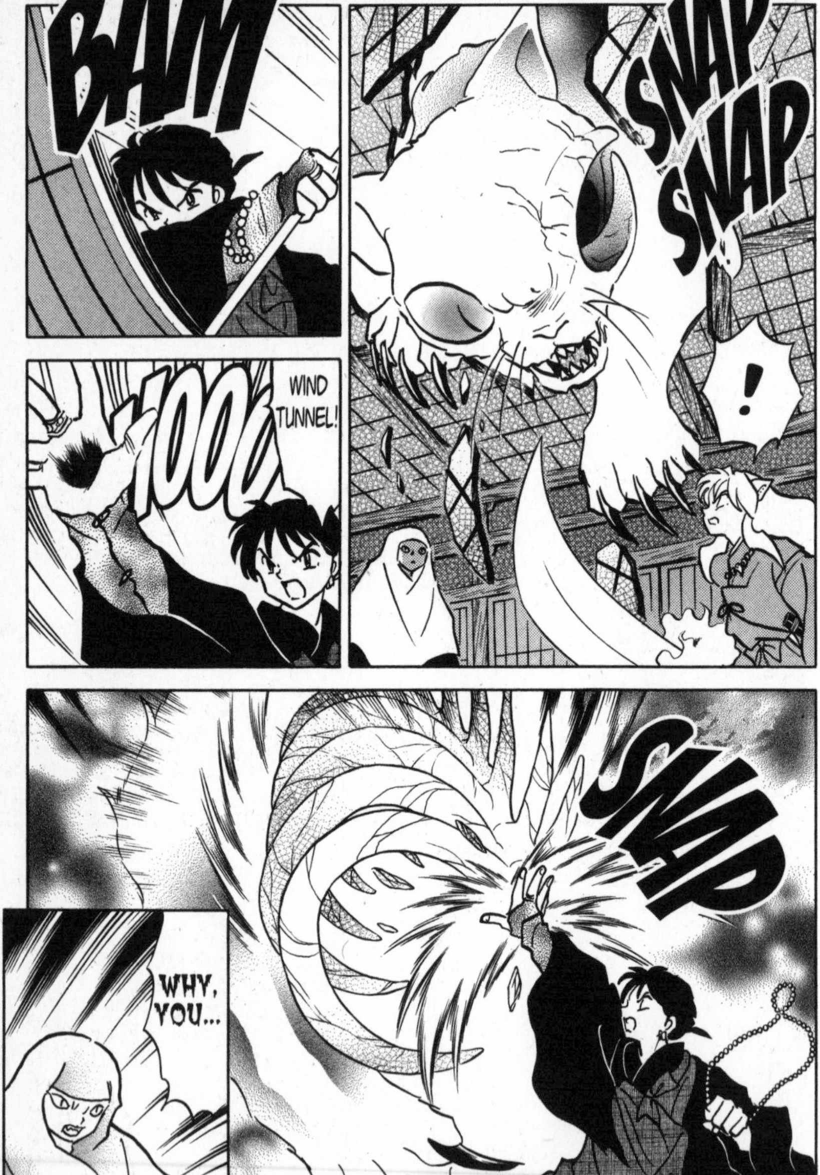
SNAP
SNAP
!
BAM
WIND TUNNEL!
SNAP
WHY, YOU...

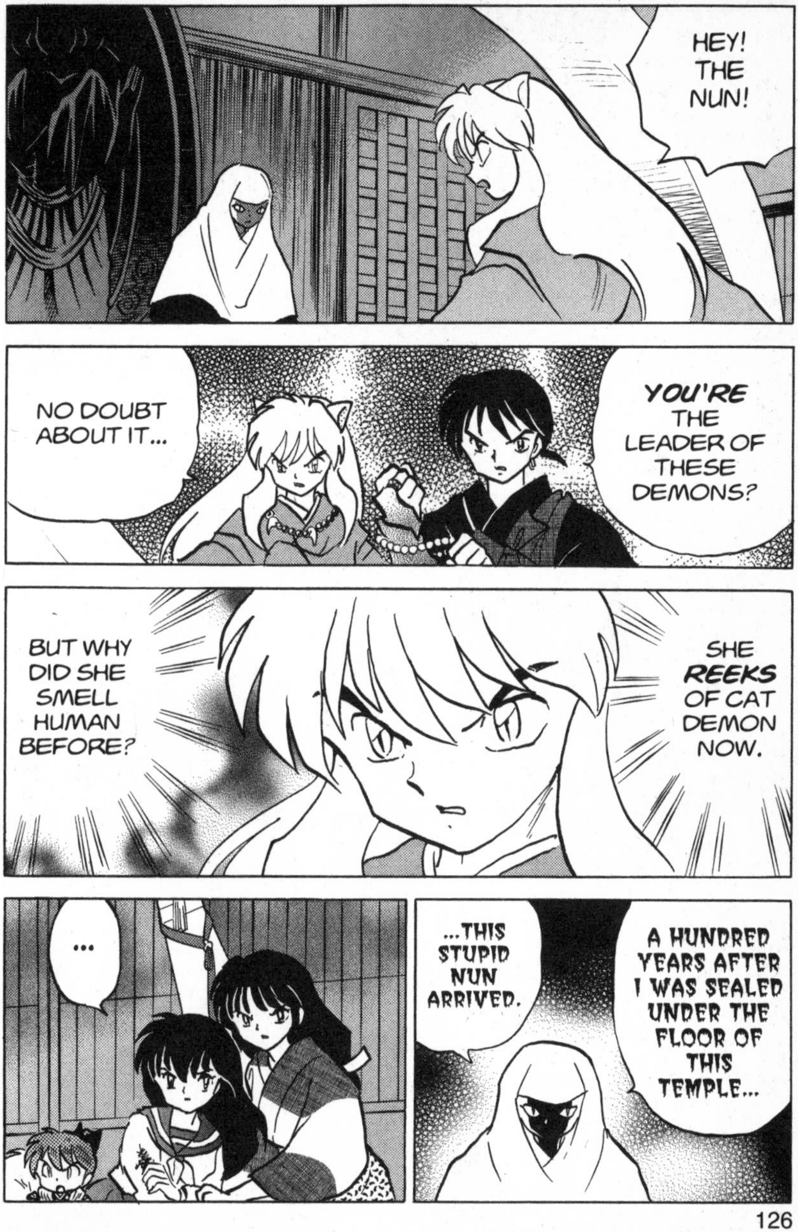
HEY! THE NUN!
YOU'RE THE LEADER OF THESE DEMONS?
NO DOUBT ABOUT IT...
SHE REEKS OF CAT DEMON NOW.
BUT WHY DID SHE SMELL HUMAN BEFORE?
A HUNDRED YEARS AFTER I WAS SEALED UNDER THE FLOOR OF THIS TEMPLE...
...THIS STUPID NUN ARRIVED.
...

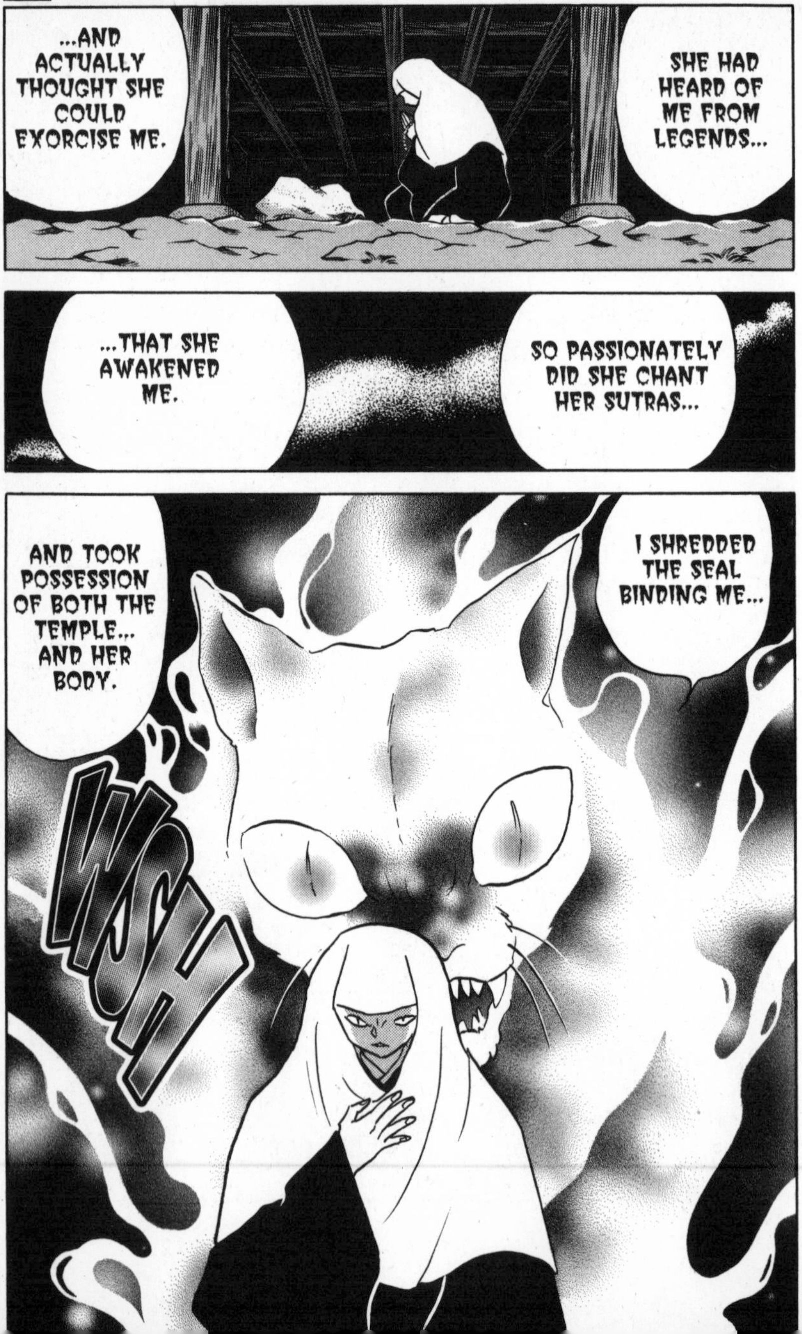
SHE HAD HEARD OF ME FROM LEGENDS...
...AND ACTUALLY THOUGHT SHE COULD EXORCISE ME.
SO PASSIONATELY DID SHE CHANT HER SUTRAS...
...THAT SHE AWAKENED ME.
I SHREDDED THE SEAL BINDING ME...
AND TOOK POSSESSION OF BOTH THE TEMPLE... AND HER BODY.
WSH

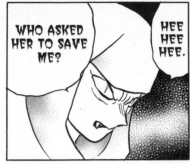

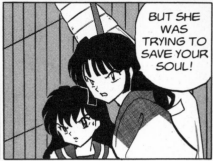

BUT SHE WAS TRYING TO SAVE YOUR SOUL!
HEE HEE HEE.
WHO ASKED HER TO SAVE ME?
I'VE HEARD ENOUGH!
PREPARE YOURSELF!
WAIT, INUYASHA!
THE NUN'S STILL ALIVE!
HEE HEE HEE. SHE'S MY CLOAK, THE DISGUISE I HIDE INSIDE...
...SO I LET HER LIVE.

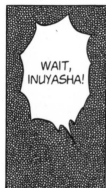

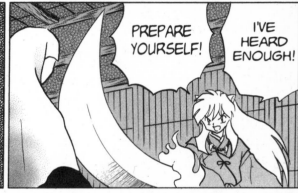

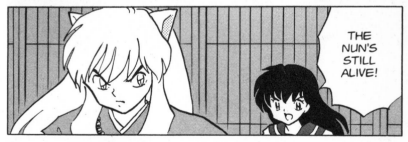

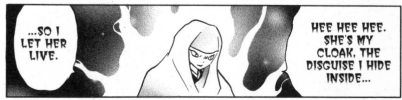

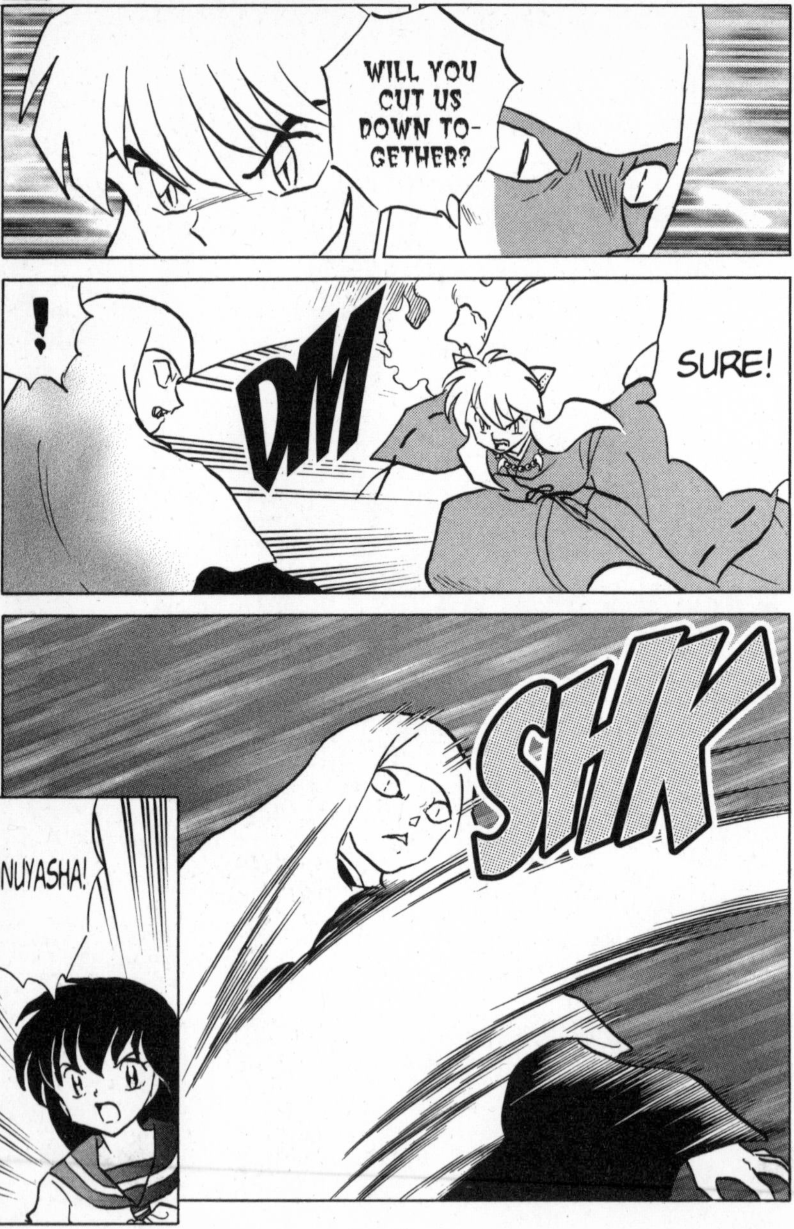
WILL YOU CUT US DOWN TO-GETHER?
SURE!
DM
!
SHK
I-INUYASHA!

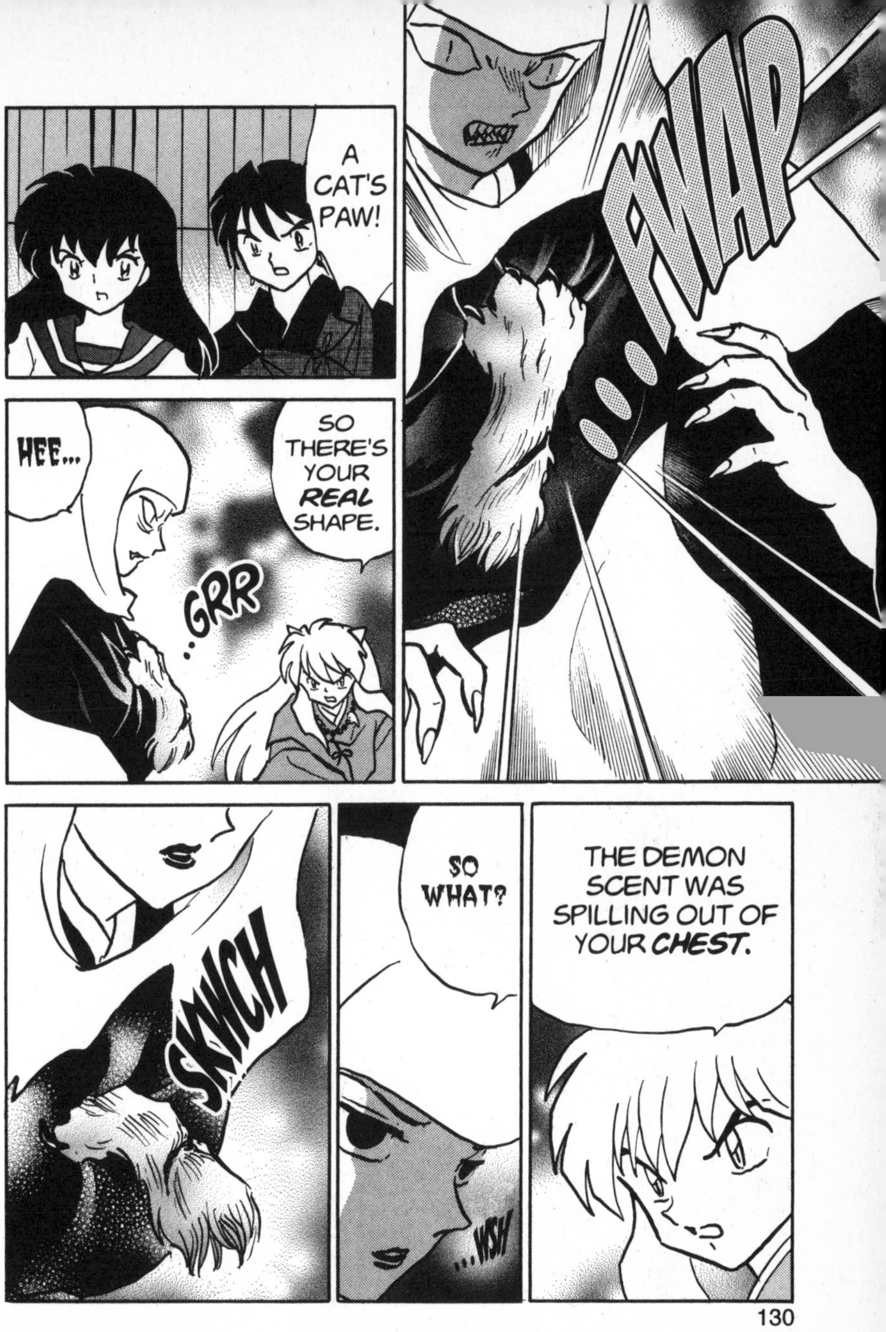
SNAP
...
A CAT'S PAW!
SO THERE'S YOUR REAL SHAPE.
HEE...
...GRR
THE DEMON SCENT WAS SPILLING OUT OF YOUR CHEST.
SO WHAT?
...WSH
SKWCH

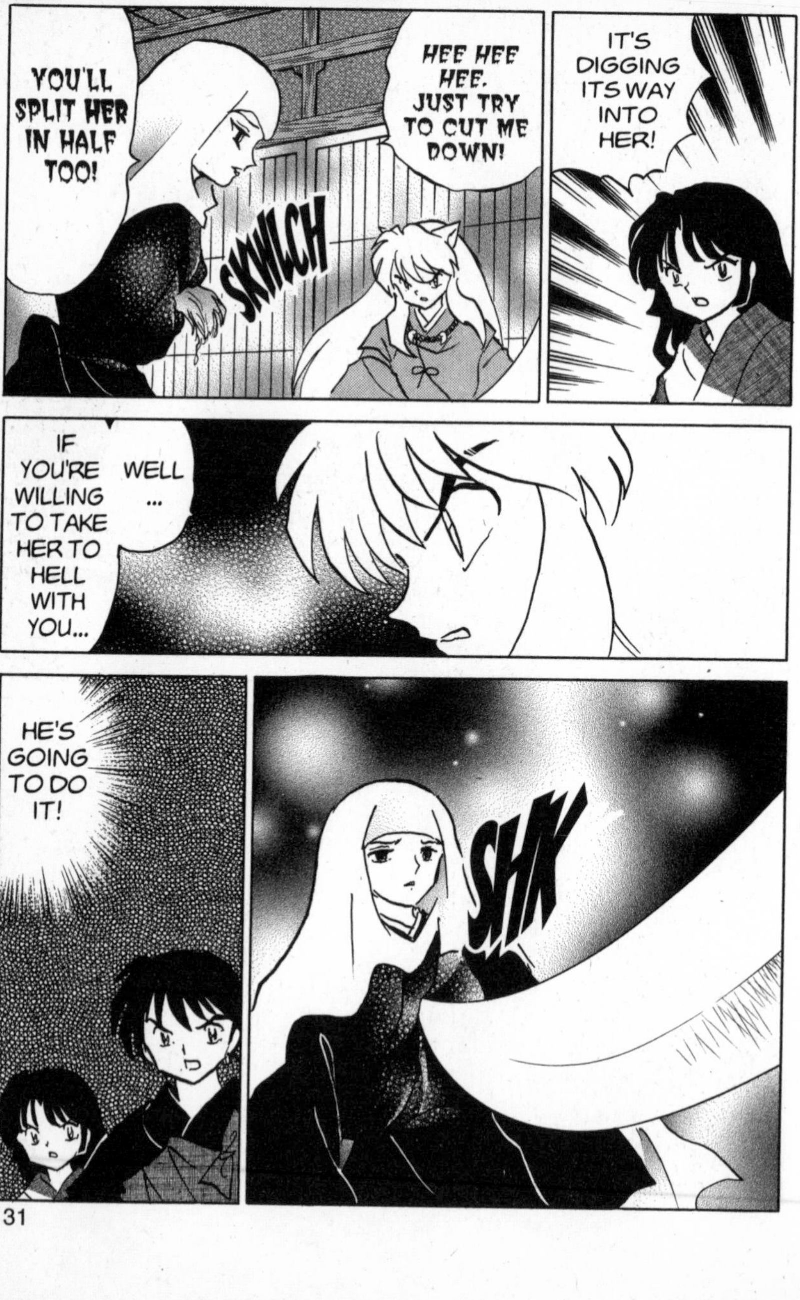
IT'S DIGGING ITS WAY INTO HER!
HEE HEE HEE. JUST TRY TO CUT ME DOWN!
YOU'LL SPLIT HER IN HALF TOO!
SKWLCH
WELL ...
IF YOU'RE WILLING TO TAKE HER TO HELL WITH YOU...
SHK
HE'S GOING TO DO IT!

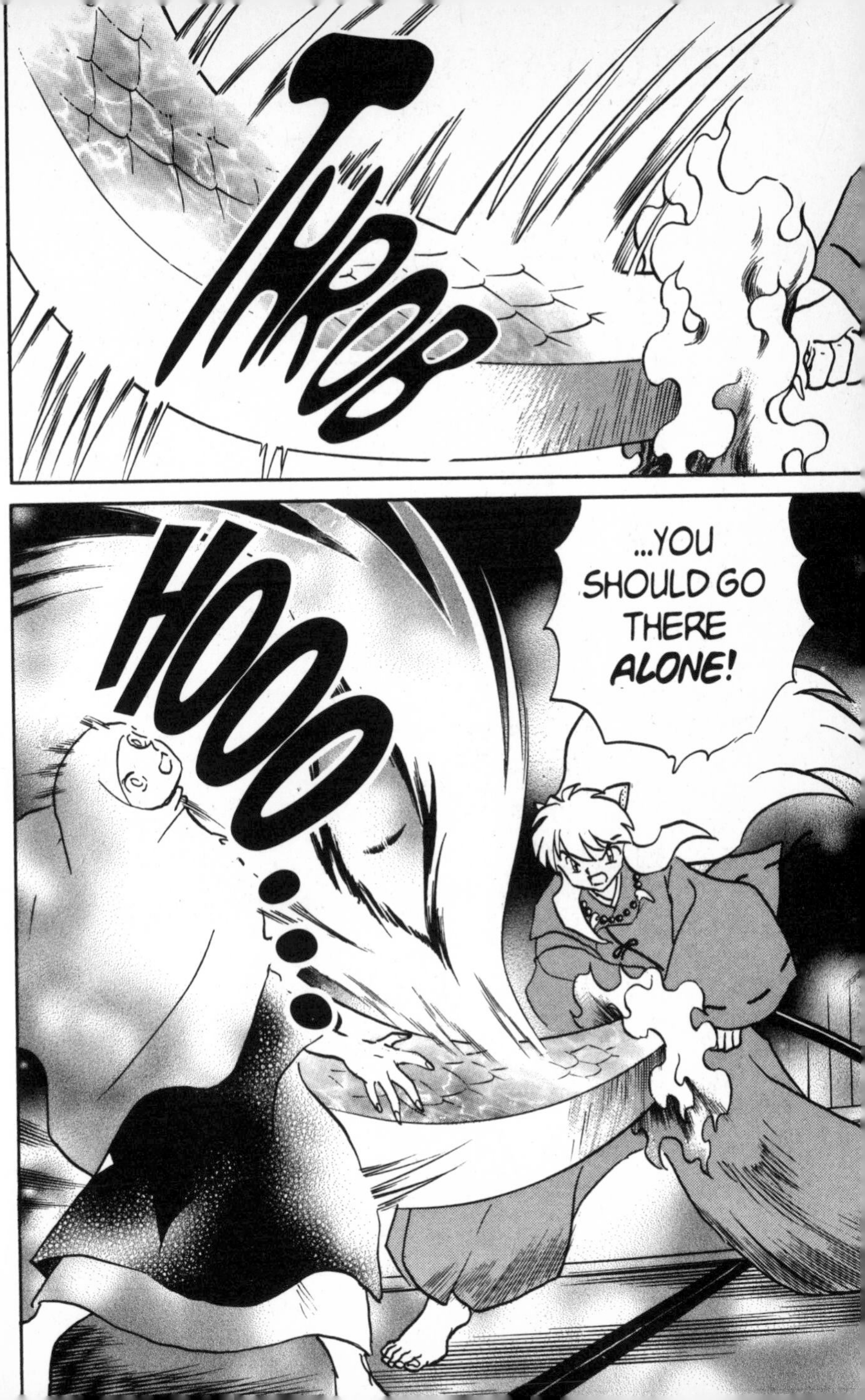
THROB
...YOU SHOULD GO THERE ALONE!
HOOO...

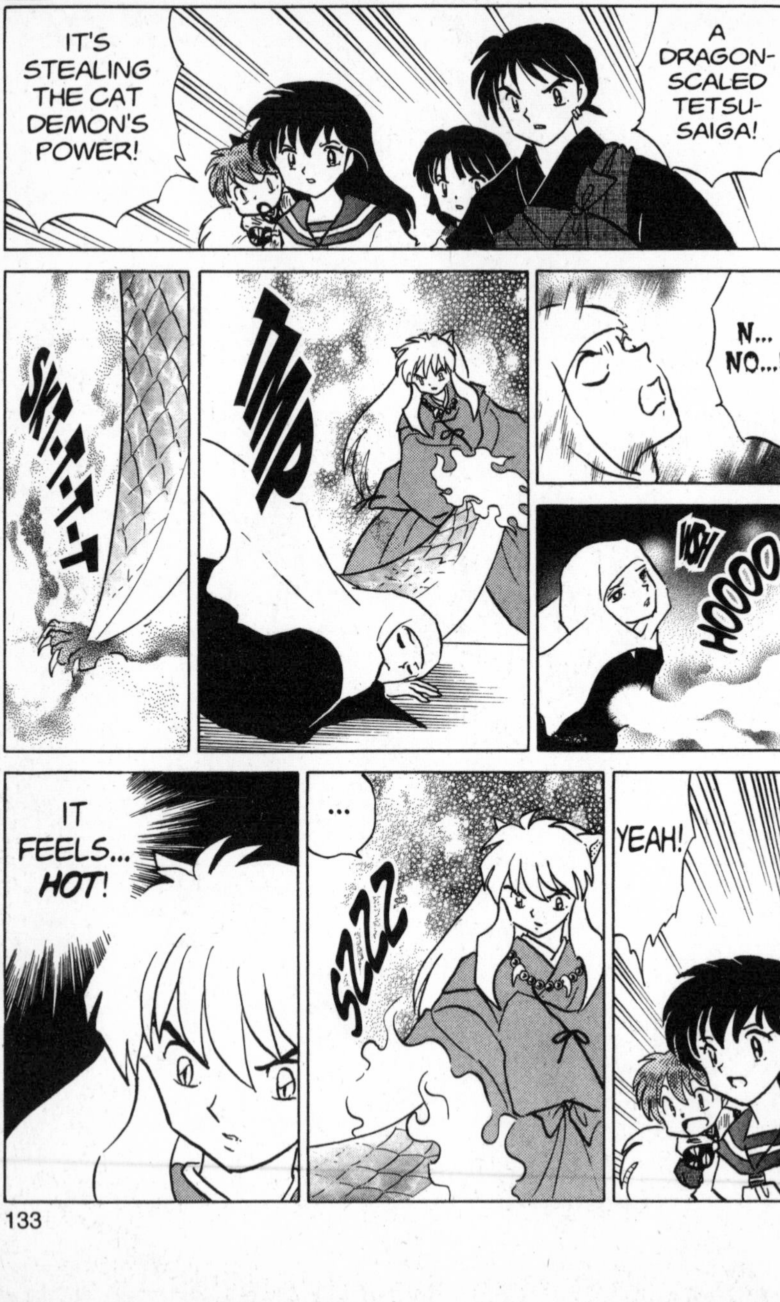
A DRAGON-SCALED TETSU-SAIGA!
IT'S STEALING THE CAT DEMON'S POWER!
N... NO...!
WSH
HOOOOO
TMP
SKT-T-T-T
YEAH!
...
SZZZ
IT FEELS... *HOT*!

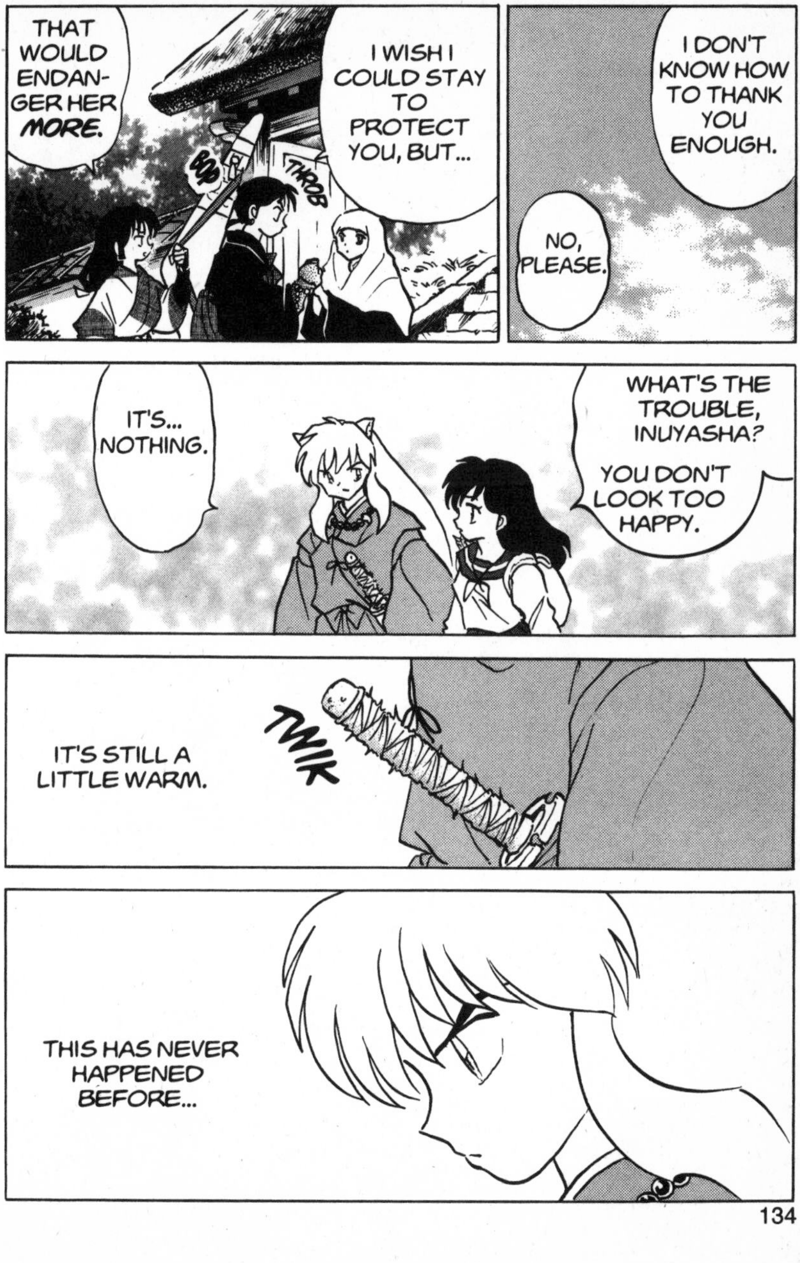
I DON'T KNOW HOW TO THANK YOU ENOUGH.
NO, PLEASE.
I WISH I COULD STAY TO PROTECT YOU, BUT...
THROB
THAT WOULD ENDANGER HER *MORE*.
WHAT'S THE TROUBLE, INUYASHA?
YOU DON'T LOOK TOO HAPPY.
IT'S... NOTHING.
TWIK
IT'S STILL A LITTLE WARM.
THIS HAS NEVER HAPPENED BEFORE...

SCROLL 8

VENOMOUS MIZUCHI

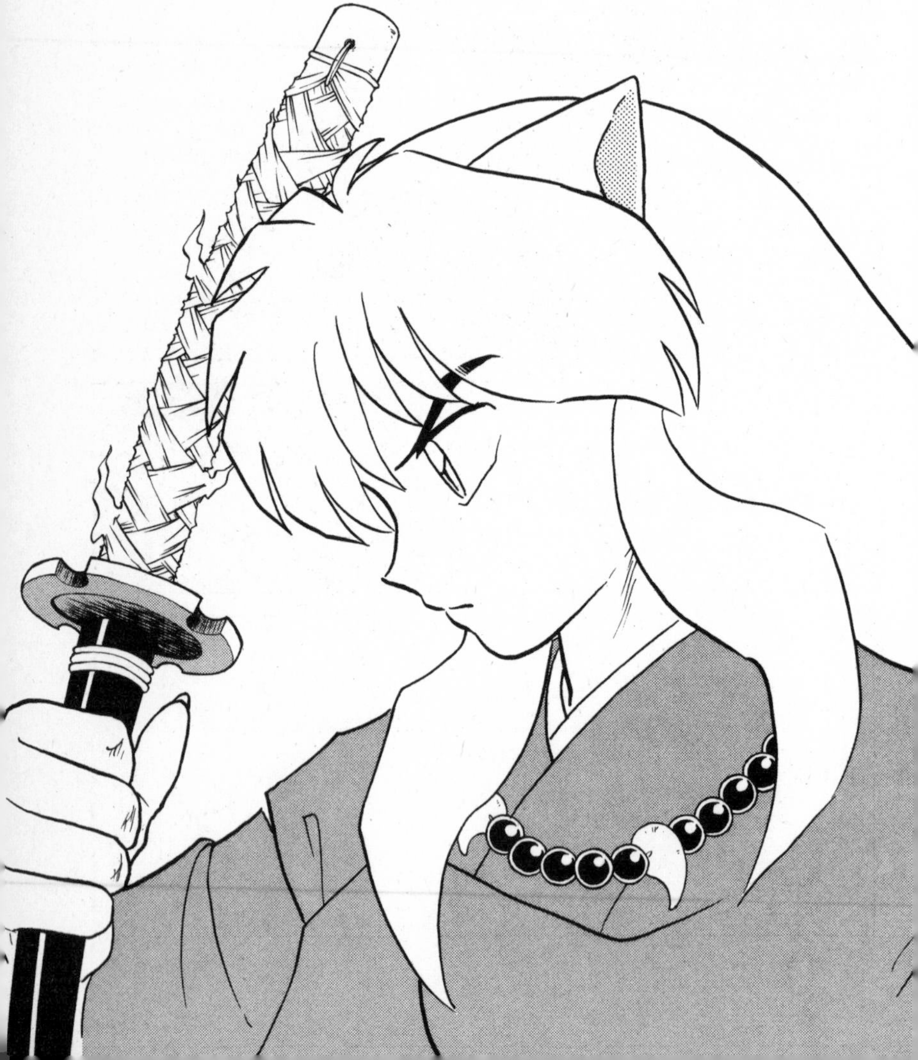

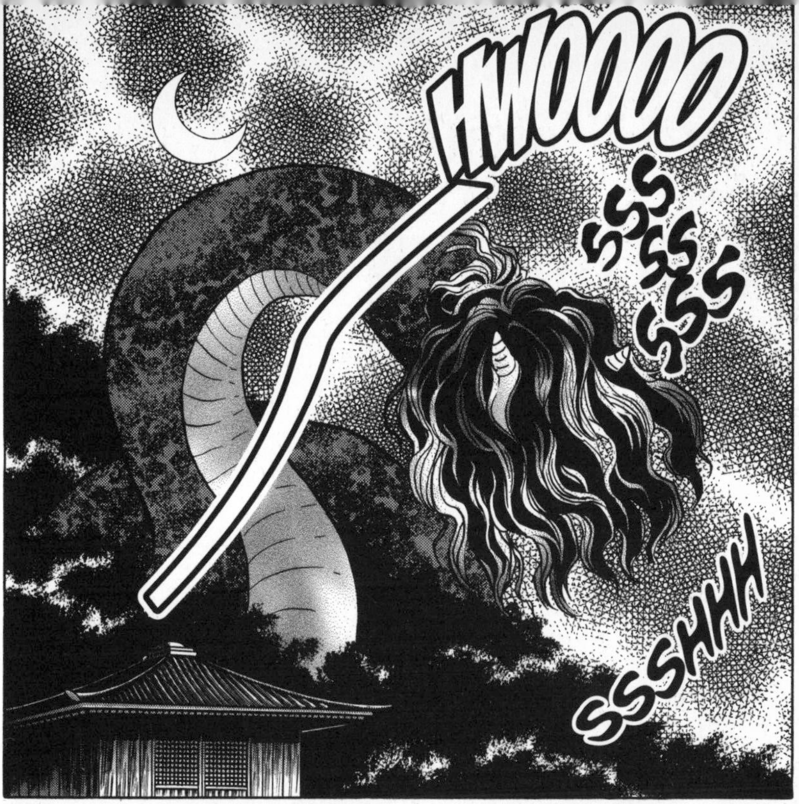
HWOOOO
SSS
SS
SSS
SSSHHH

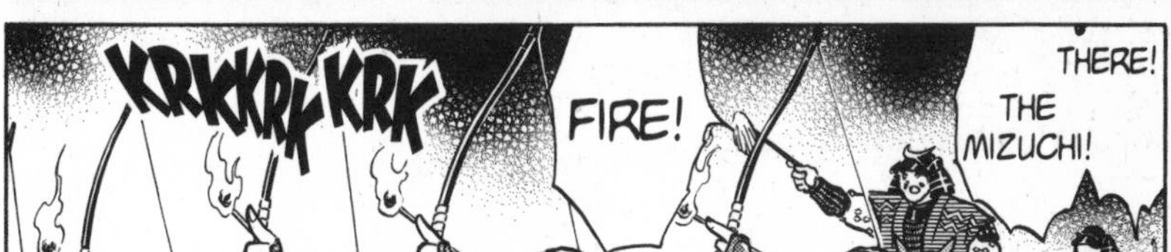
THERE!
THE MIZUCHI!
FIRE!
KRKKRK KRK

2

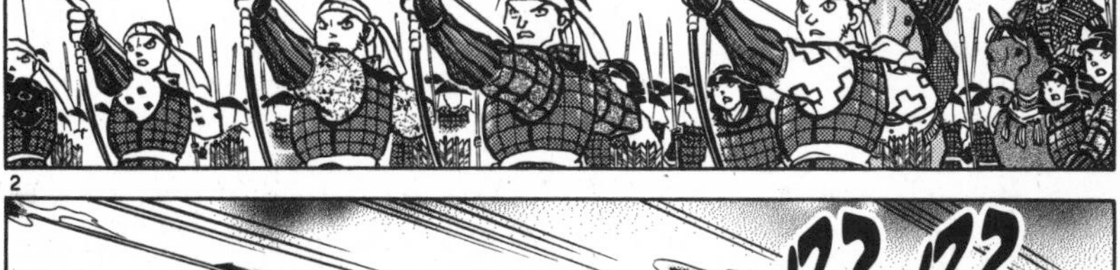
VZZ VZZ

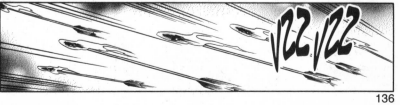

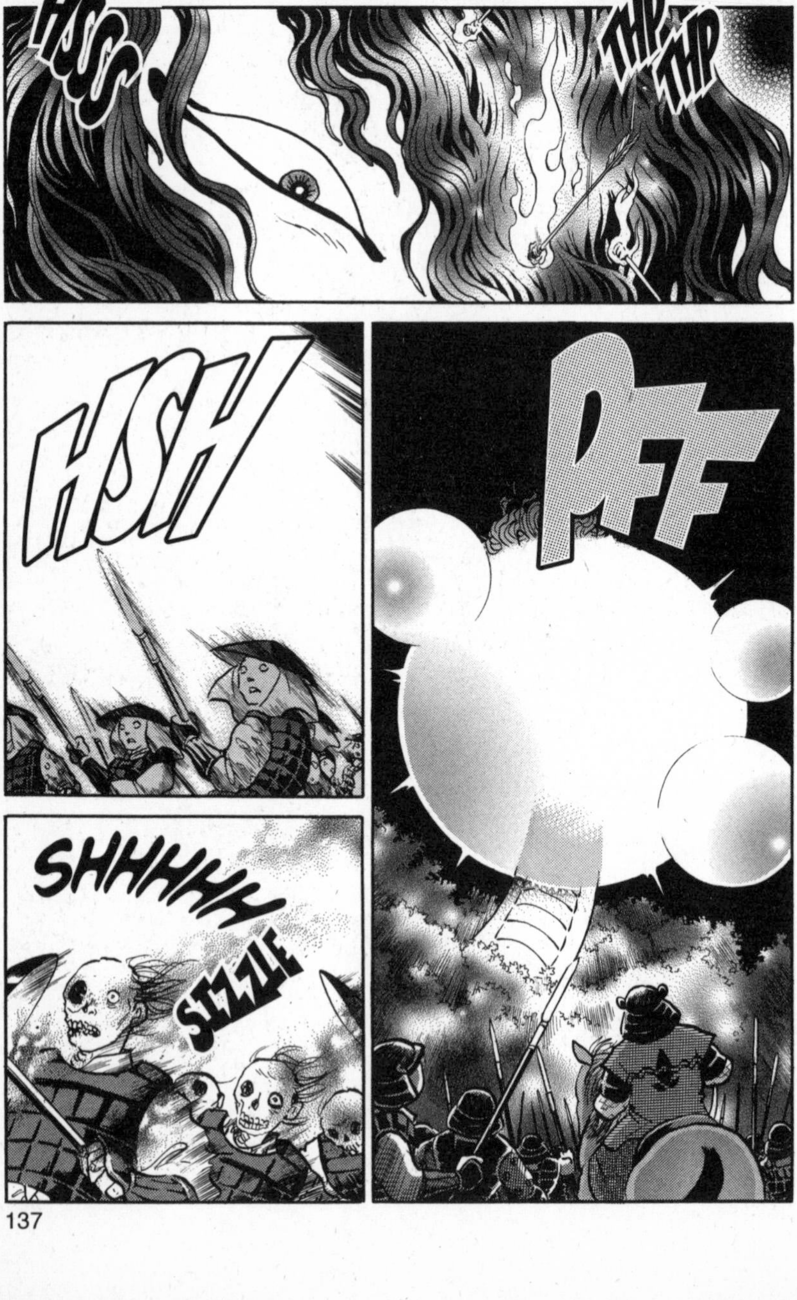
THP THP
HSSS
PFF
HSH
SHHHHH
SIZZLE

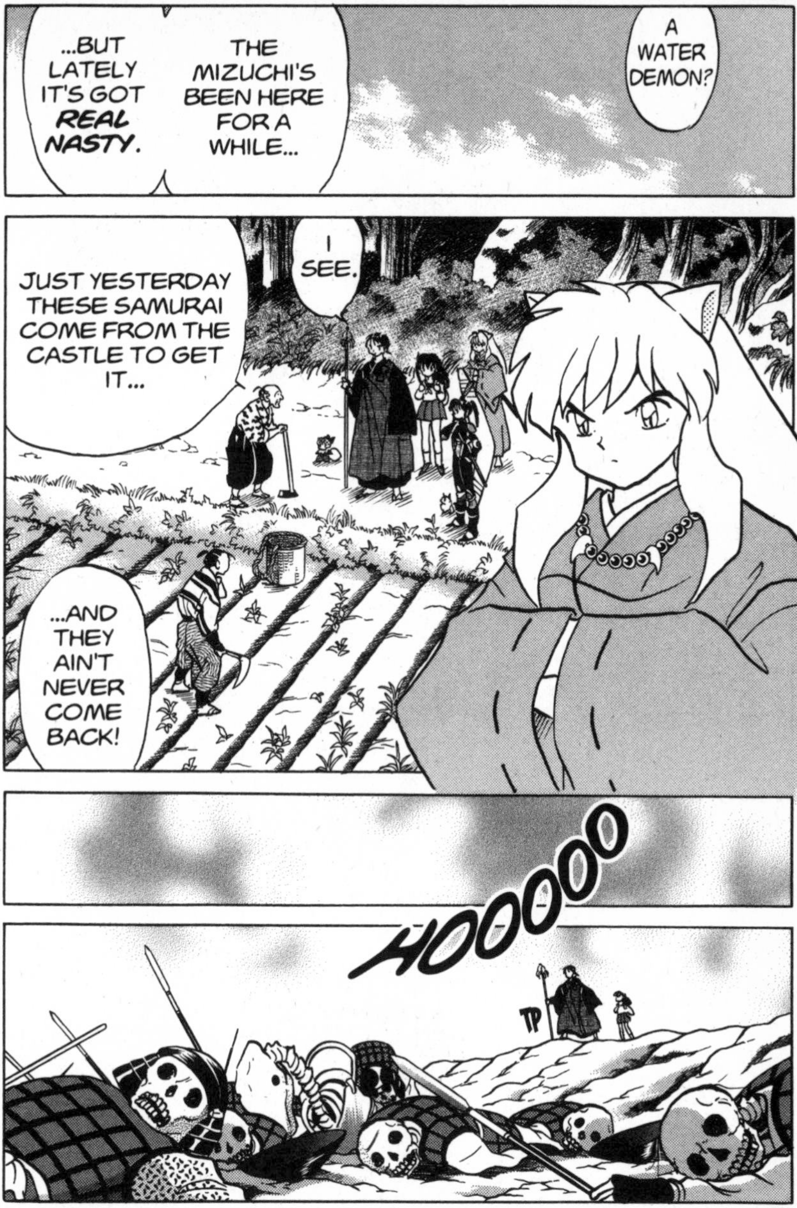
A WATER DEMON?
THE MIZUCHI'S BEEN HERE FOR A WHILE...
...BUT LATELY IT'S GOT REAL NASTY.
I SEE.
JUST YESTERDAY THESE SAMURAI COME FROM THE CASTLE TO GET IT...
...AND THEY AIN'T NEVER COME BACK!
HOOOOO
TP

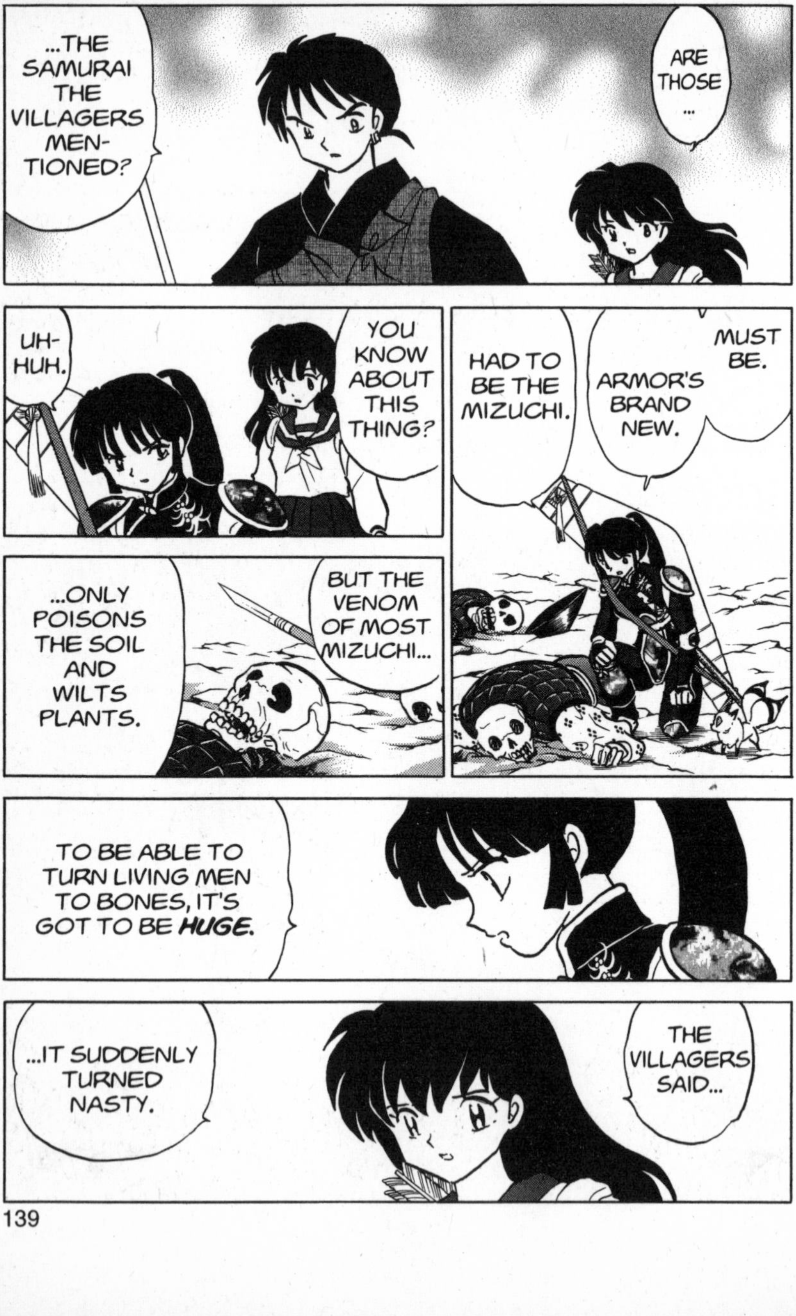
ARE THOSE ...
...THE SAMURAI THE VILLAGERS MEN-TIONED?
MUST BE.
ARMOR'S BRAND NEW.
HAD TO BE THE MIZUCHI.
YOU KNOW ABOUT THIS THING?
UH-HUH.
BUT THE VENOM OF MOST MIZUCHI...
...ONLY POISONS THE SOIL AND WILTS PLANTS.
TO BE ABLE TO TURN LIVING MEN TO BONES, IT'S GOT TO BE ***HUGE***.
THE VILLAGERS SAID...
...IT SUDDENLY TURNED NASTY.

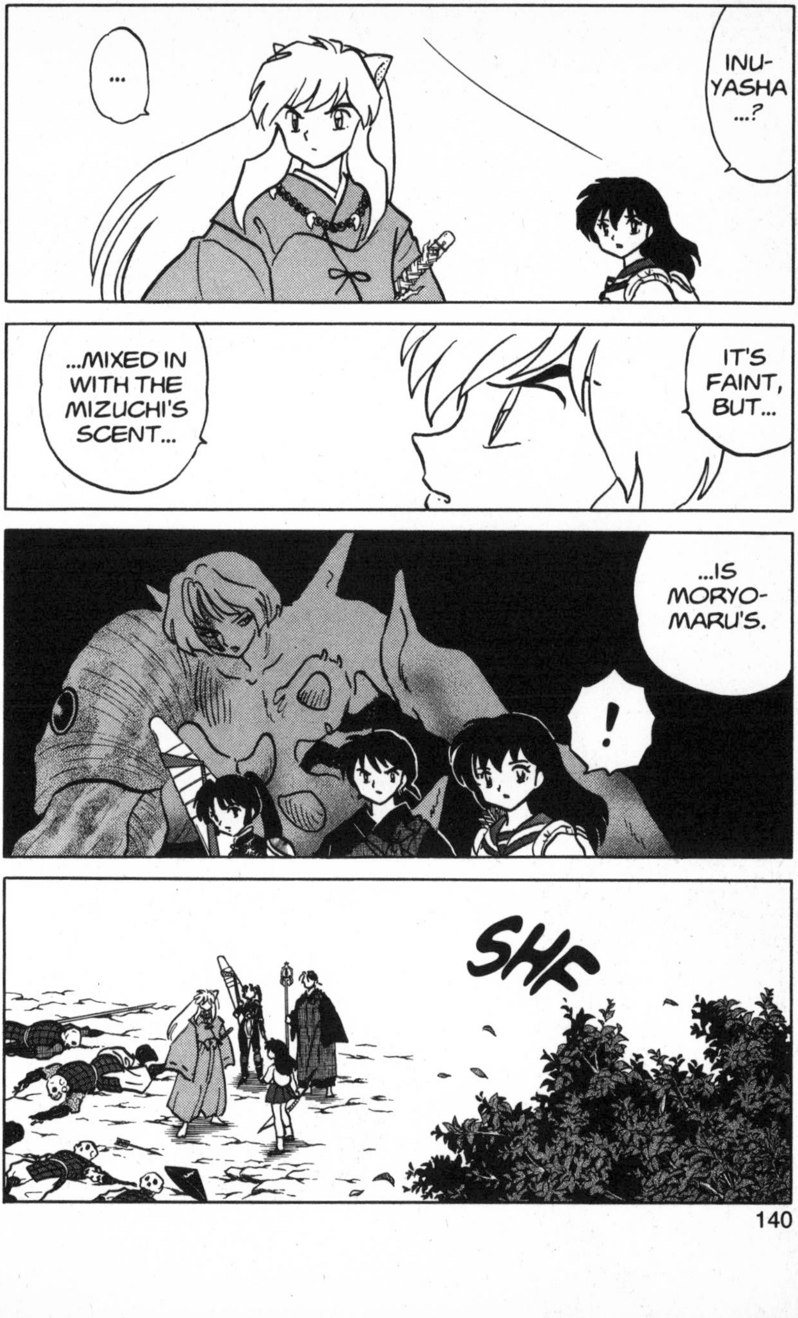
INU-YASHA ...?
...
IT'S FAINT, BUT...
...MIXED IN WITH THE MIZUCHI'S SCENT...
...IS MORYO-MARU'S.
!
SHF

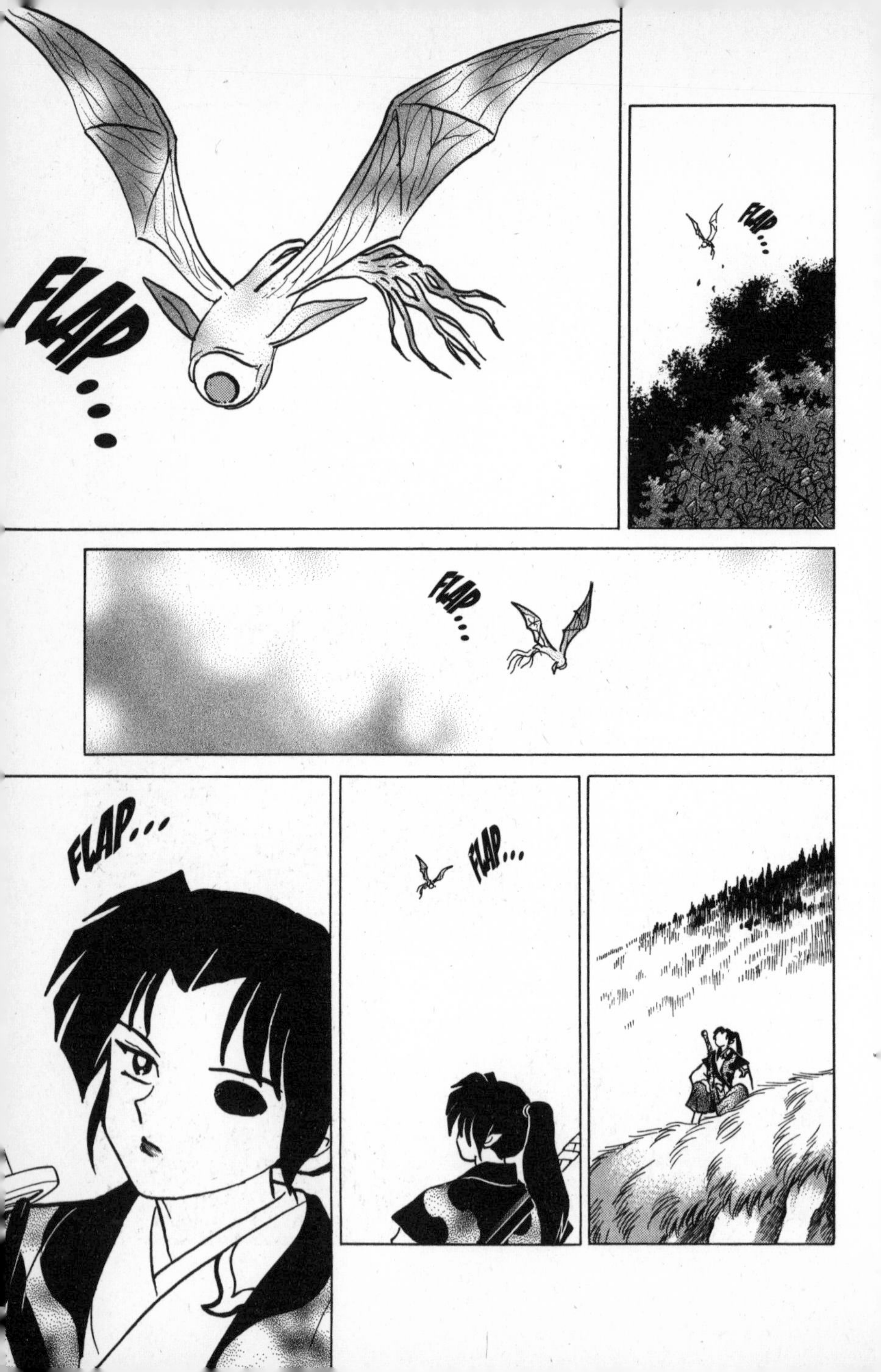
FLAP...
FLAP...
FLAP...
FLAP...
FLAP...

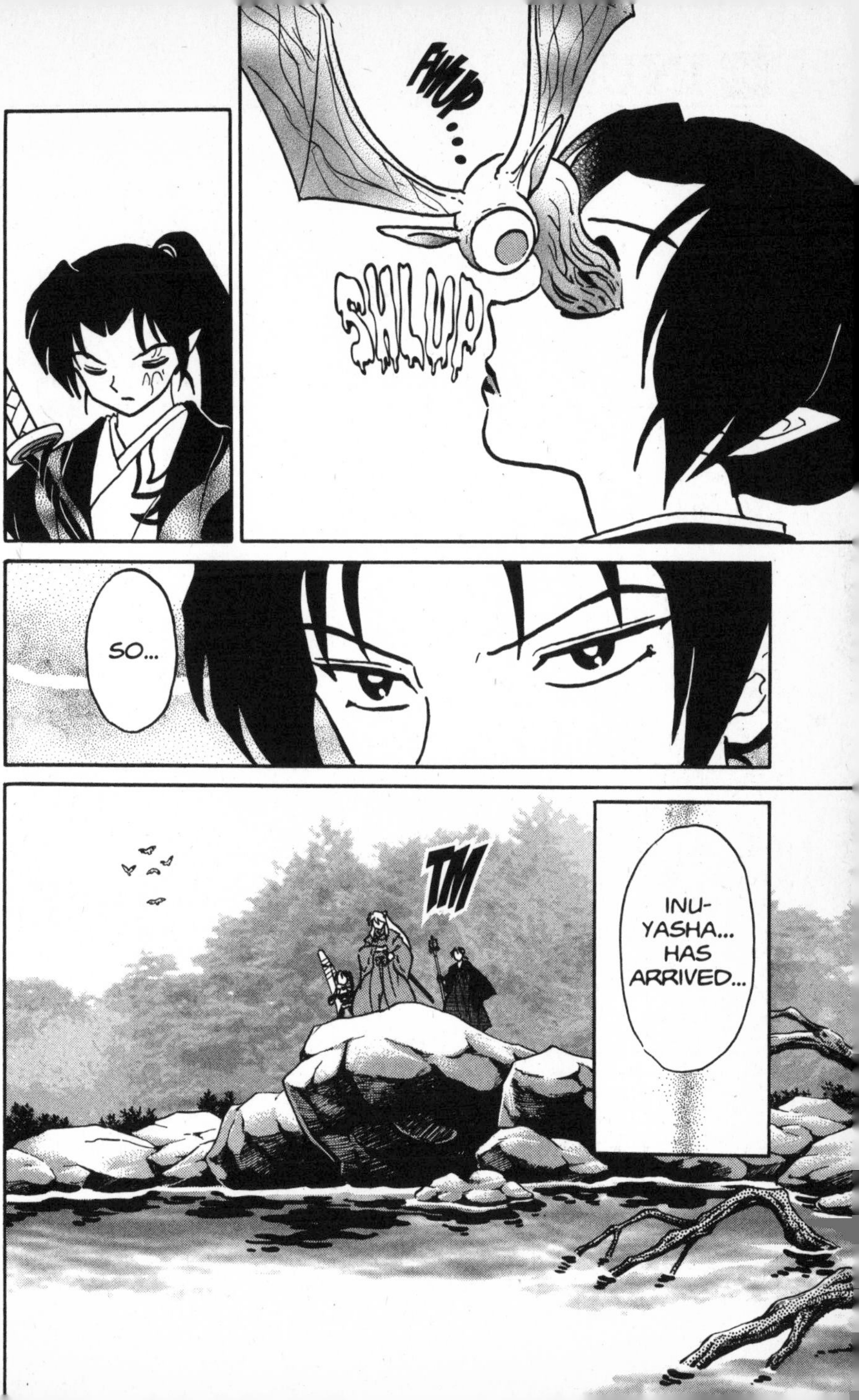
FWIP...
SHLUP
SO...
TM
INU-YASHA... HAS ARRIVED...

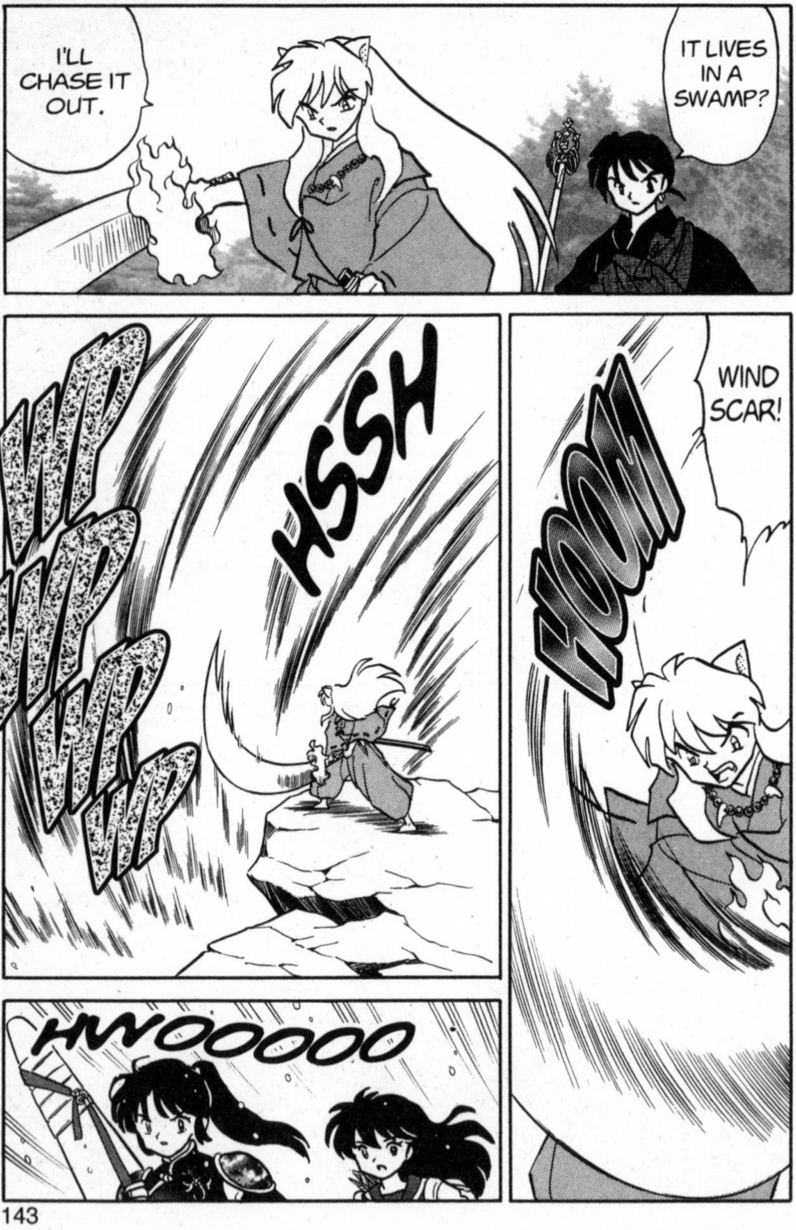
IT LIVES IN A SWAMP?
I'LL CHASE IT OUT.
WIND SCAR!
HOOM
HSSH
WIP WIP WIP WIP
HWOOOOO

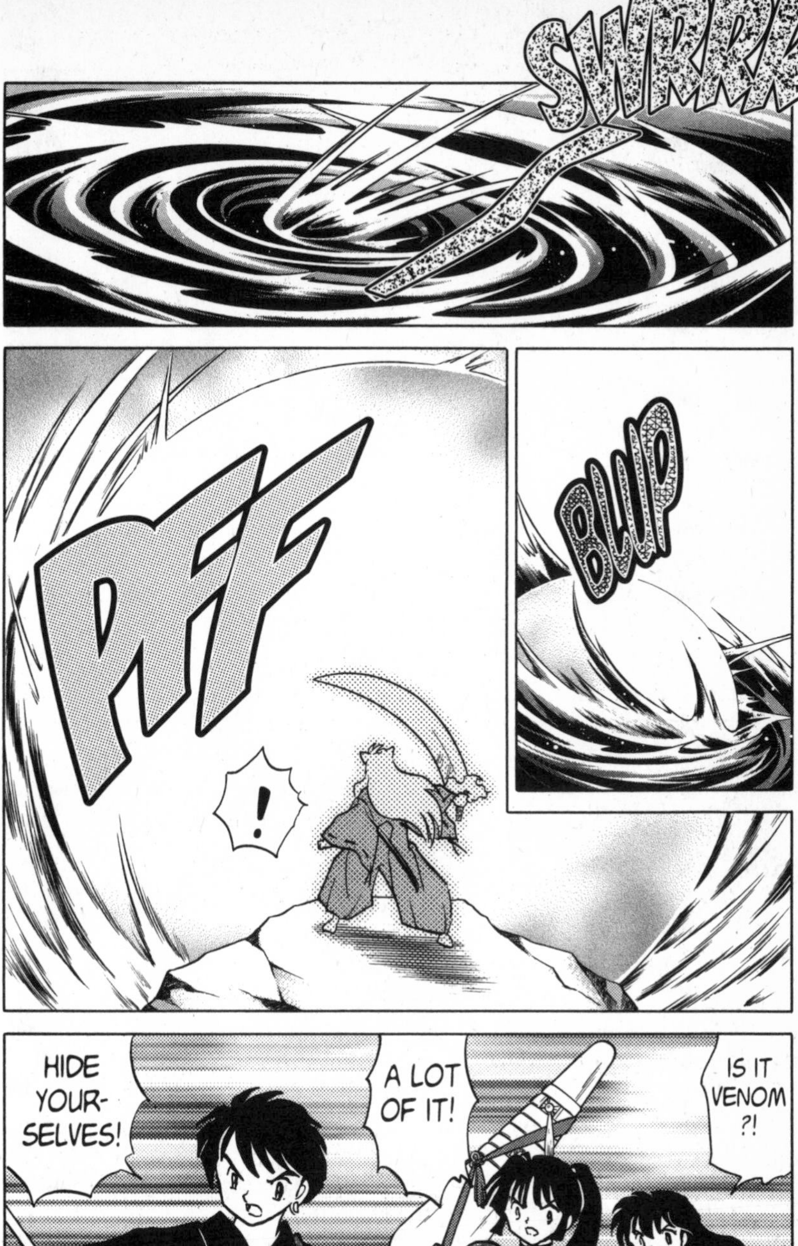
SWRRR
BLIP
PAF
!
IS IT VENOM ?!
A LOT OF IT!
HIDE YOUR-SELVES!

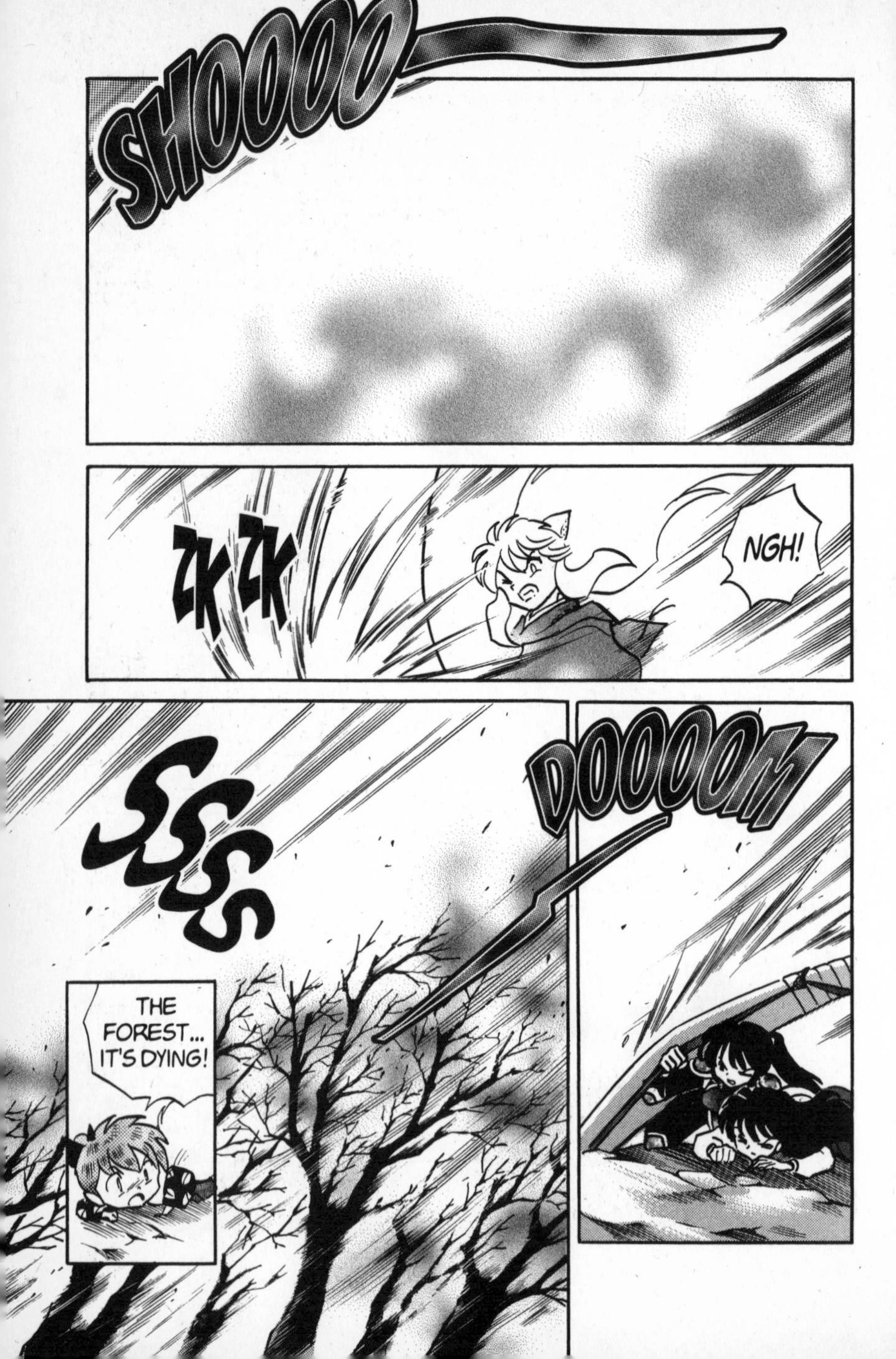
SHOOOO
NGH!
ZK ZK
DOOOOM
SSS
THE FOREST... IT'S DYING!

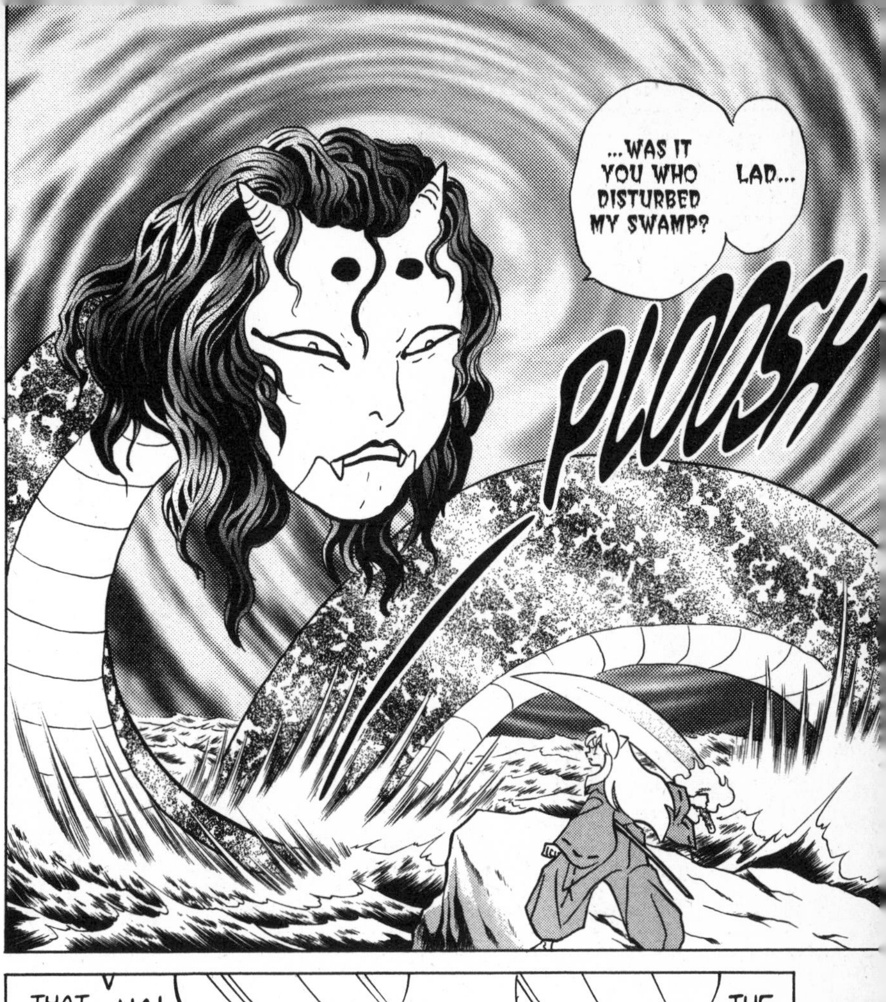
LAD...
...WAS IT YOU WHO DISTURBED MY SWAMP?
PLOOSH

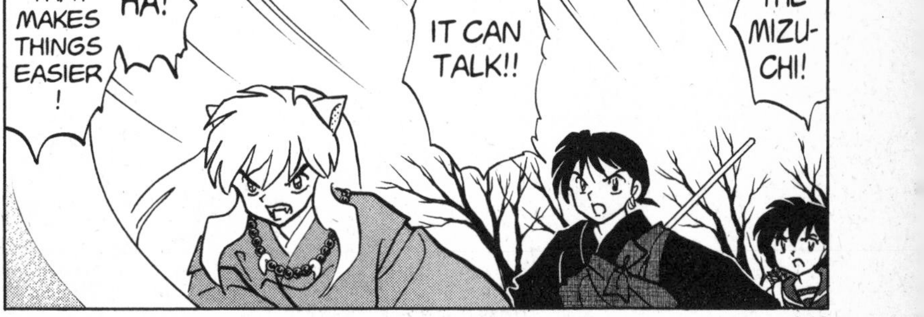
THE MIZU-CHI!
IT CAN TALK!!
HA!
THAT MAKES THINGS EASIER!

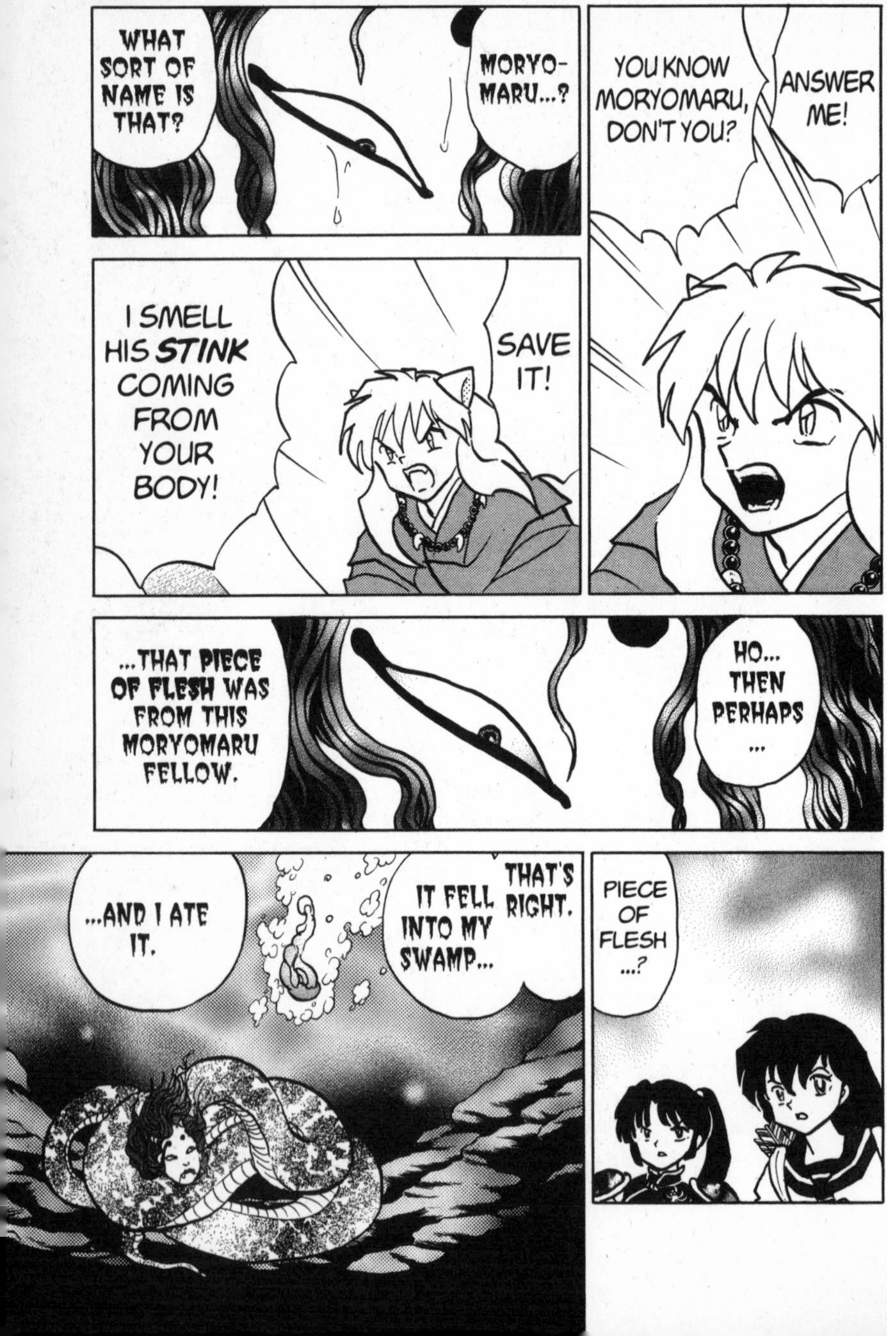
ANSWER ME!
YOU KNOW MORYOMARU, DON'T YOU?
MORYO-MARU...?
WHAT SORT OF NAME IS THAT?
SAVE IT!
I SMELL HIS STINK COMING FROM YOUR BODY!
HO... THEN PERHAPS ...
...THAT PIECE OF FLESH WAS FROM THIS MORYOMARU FELLOW.
PIECE OF FLESH ...?
THAT'S RIGHT.
IT FELL INTO MY SWAMP...
...AND I ATE IT.

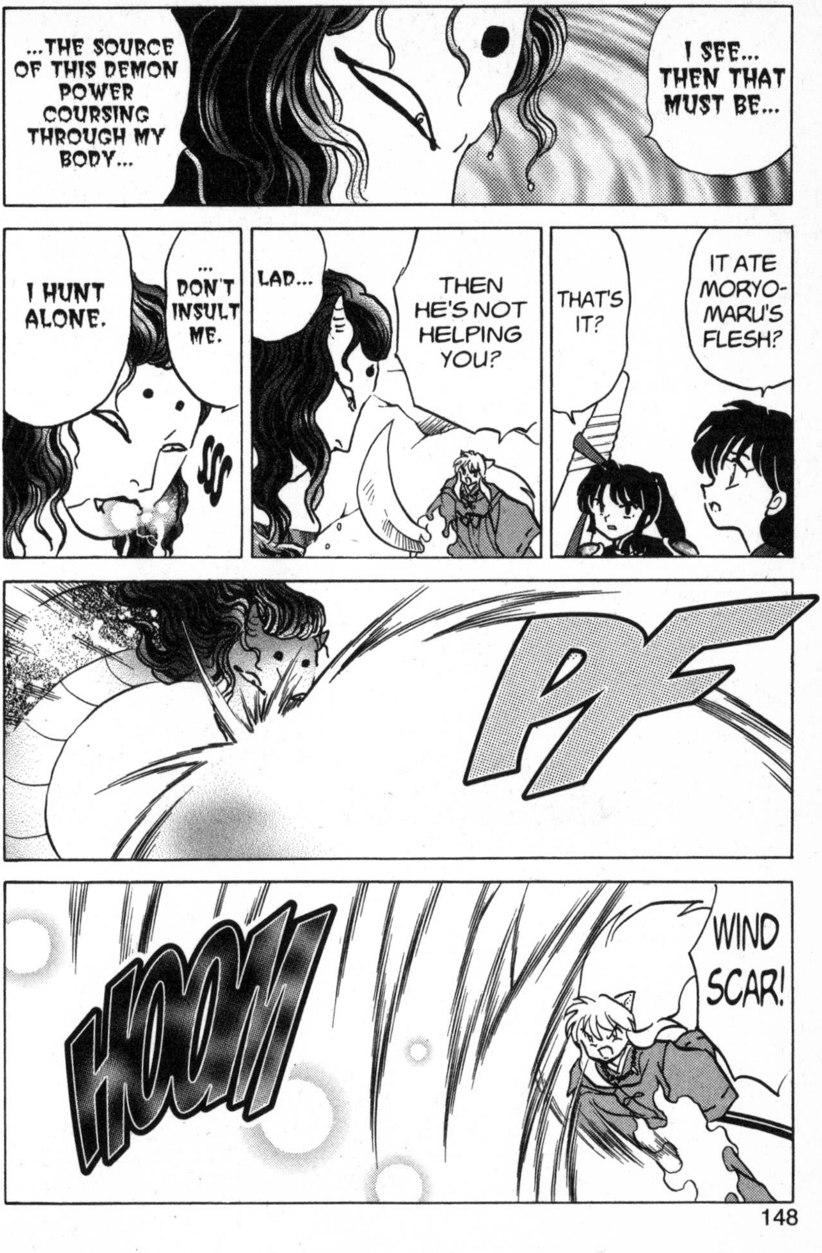
I SEE... THEN THAT MUST BE...
...THE SOURCE OF THIS DEMON POWER COURSING THROUGH MY BODY...
IT ATE MORYO-MARU'S FLESH?
THAT'S IT?
THEN HE'S NOT HELPING YOU?
LAD...
... DON'T INSULT ME.
I HUNT ALONE.
SSS
WIND SCAR!
HOOM

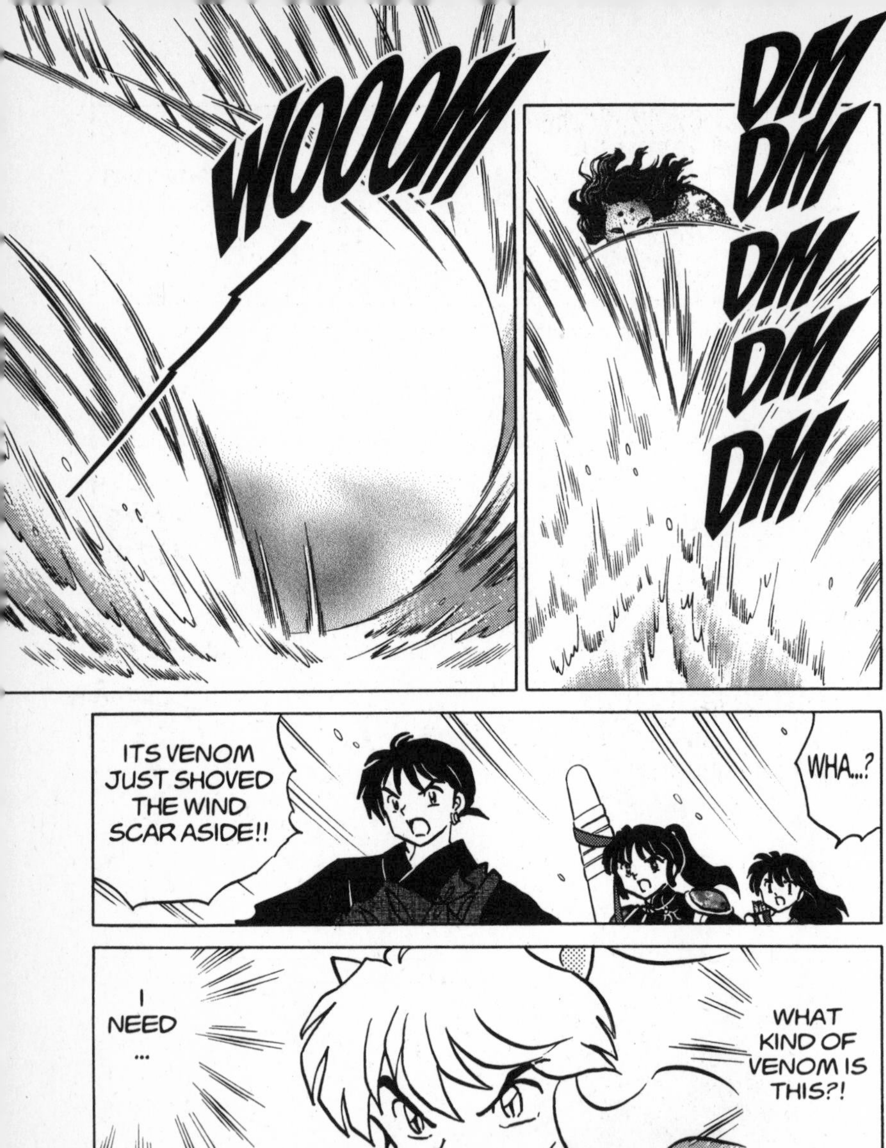
DM DM DM DM DM
WOOOM
WHA...?
ITS VENOM JUST SHOVED THE WIND SCAR ASIDE!!
WHAT KIND OF VENOM IS THIS?!
I NEED ...

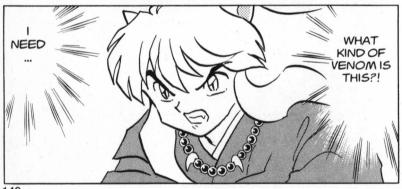

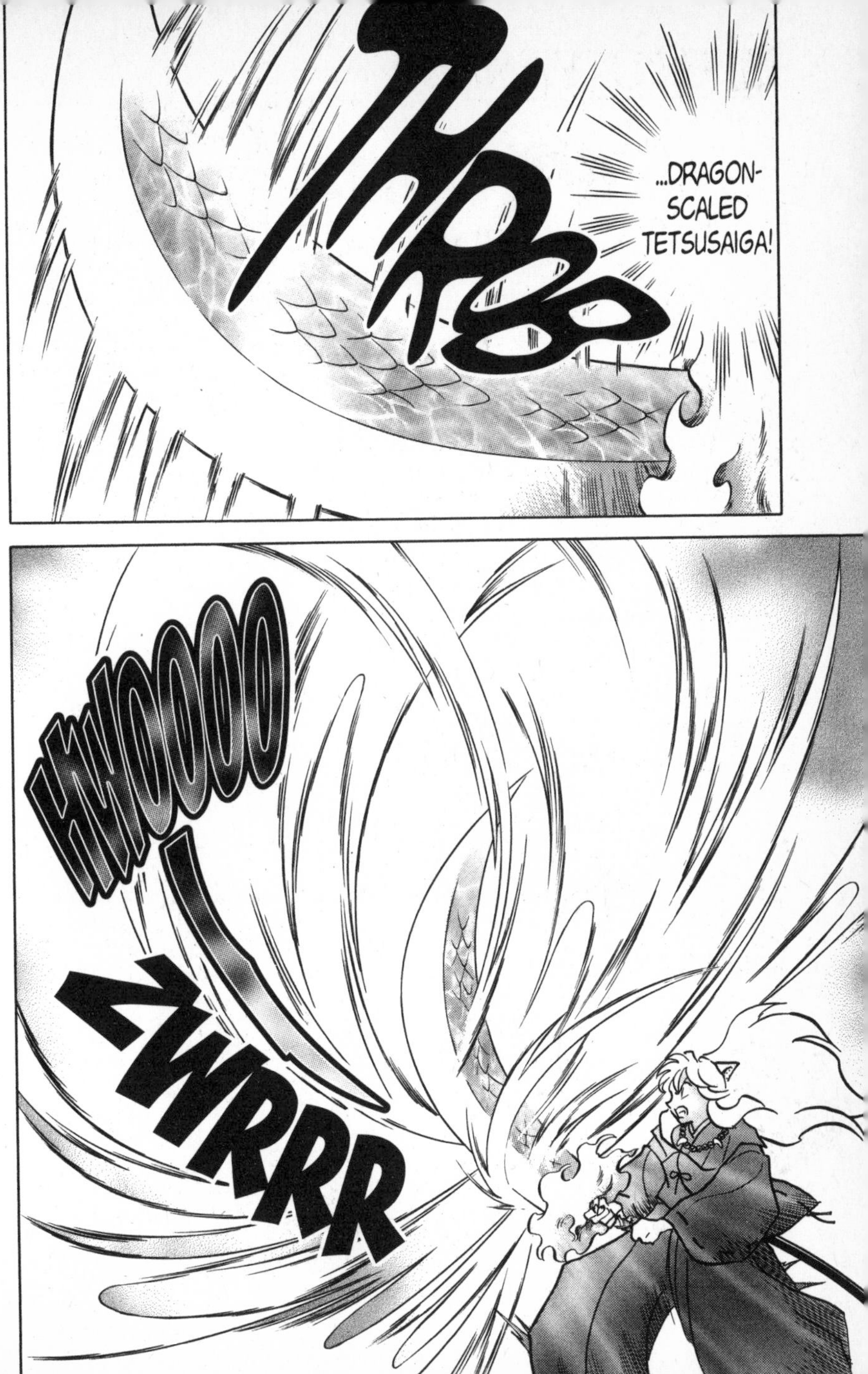
THROB
...DRAGON-SCALED TETSUSAIGA!
HWOOOO
ZWRRR

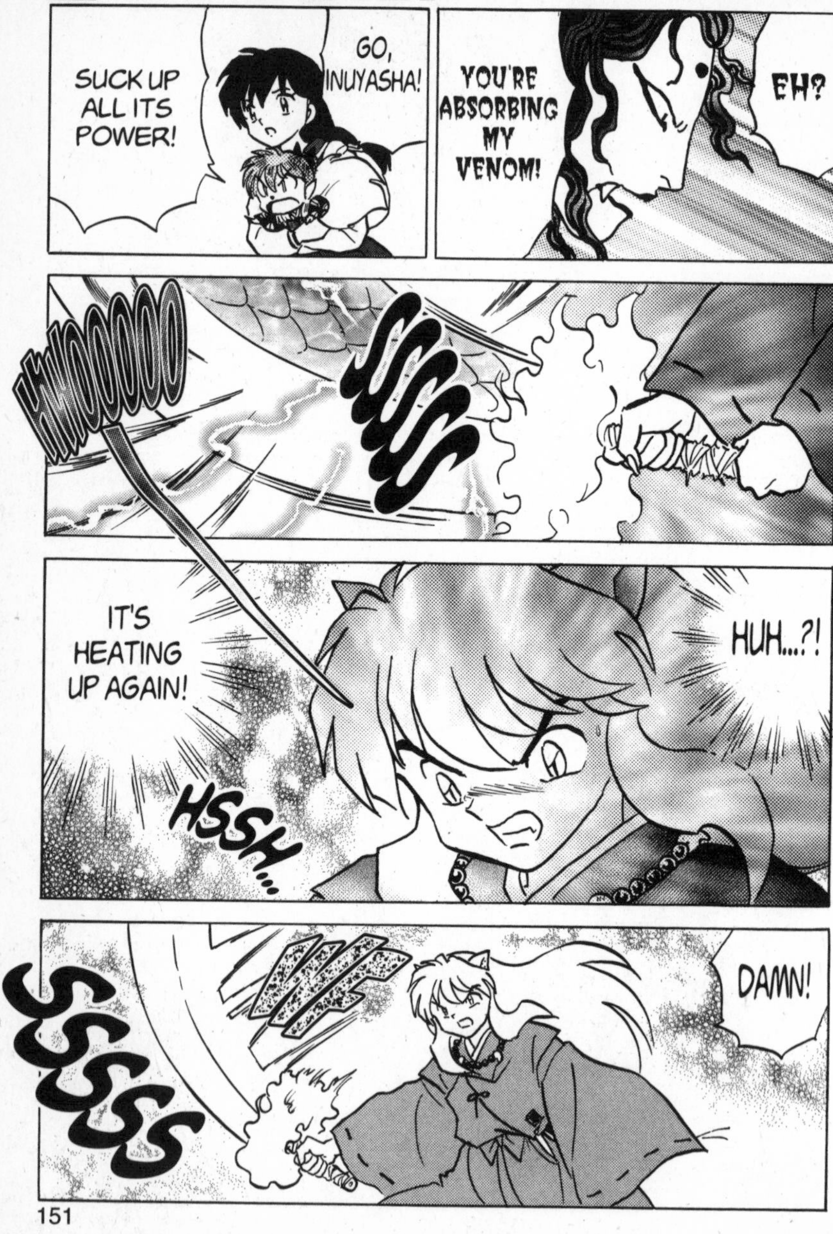
YOU'RE ABSORBING MY VENOM!
EH?
GO, INUYASHA!
SUCK UP ALL ITS POWER!
HWOOOOO
SSSSS
HUH...?!
IT'S HEATING UP AGAIN!
HSSH...
DAMN!
WF
SSSSS

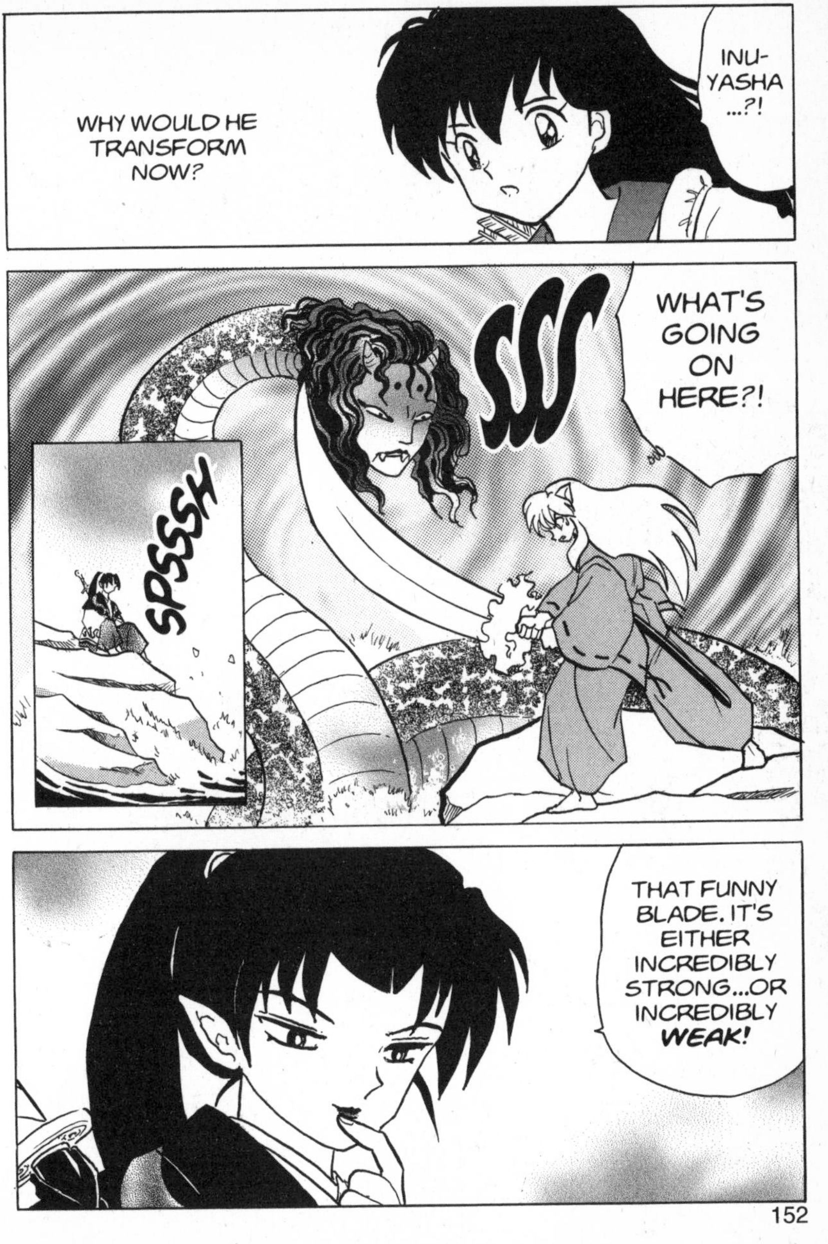
INU-YASHA ...?!
WHY WOULD HE TRANSFORM NOW?
WHAT'S GOING ON HERE?!
SSS
SPSSSH
THAT FUNNY BLADE. IT'S EITHER INCREDIBLY STRONG...OR INCREDIBLY WEAK!

SCROLL 9

BYAKUYA OF THE DREAMS

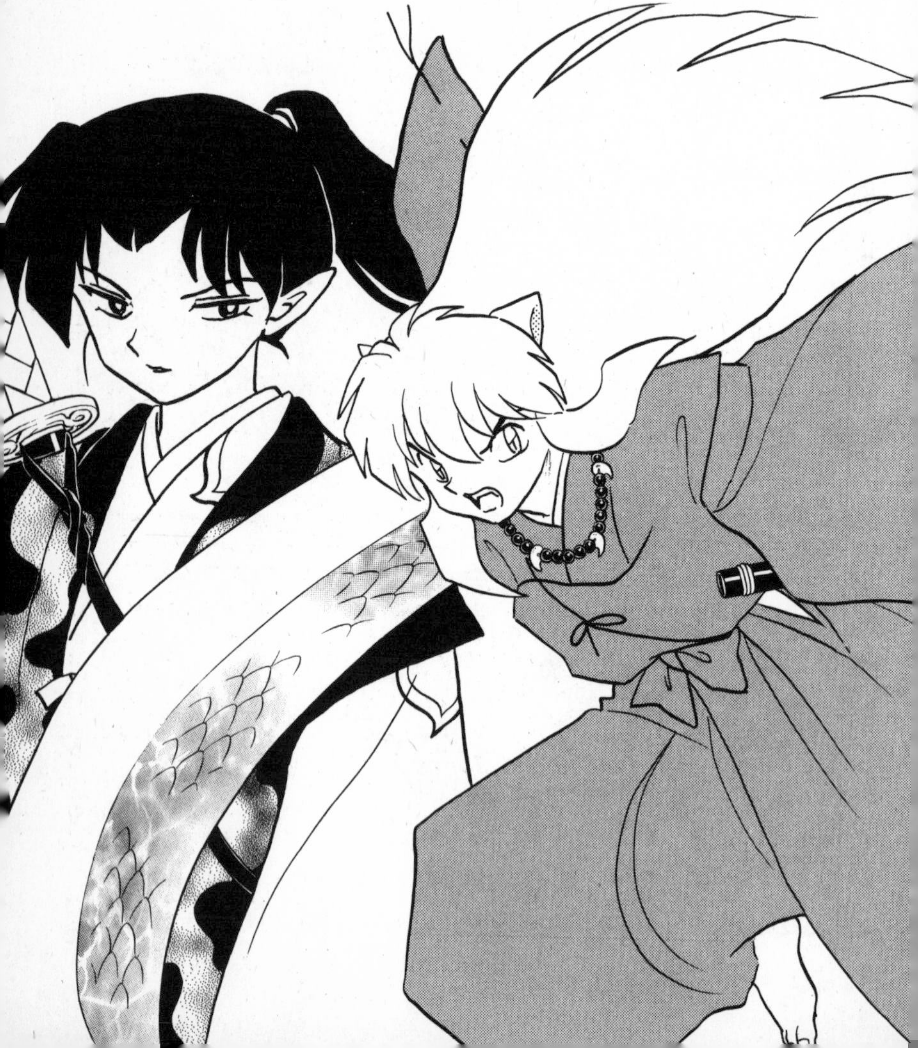

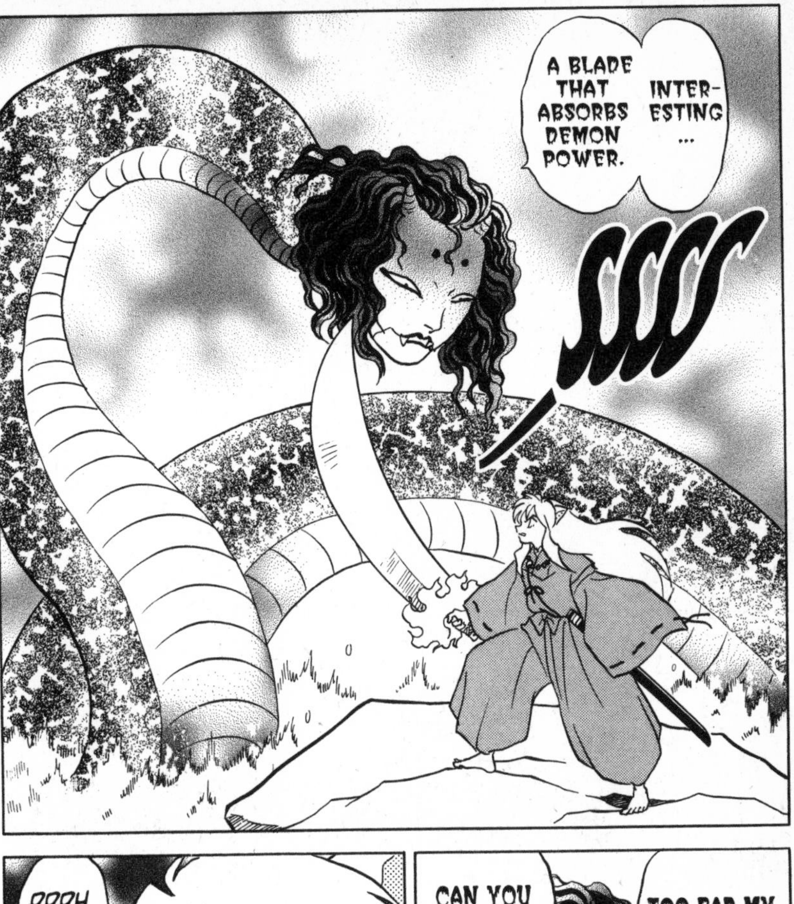
INTER-
ESTING
...
A BLADE
THAT
ABSORBS
DEMON
POWER.
SSSS
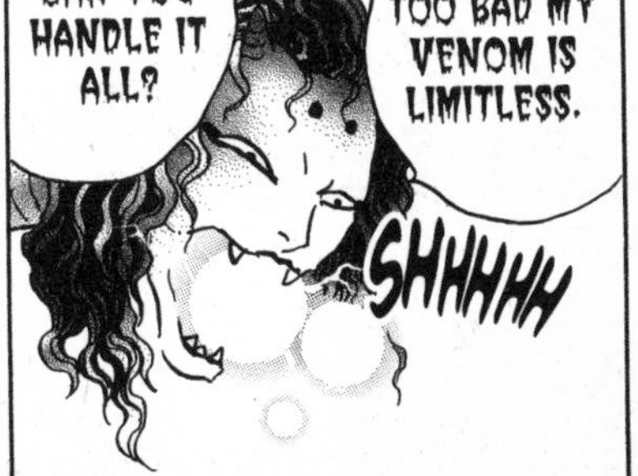
TOO BAD MY
VENOM IS
LIMITLESS.
CAN YOU
HANDLE IT
ALL?
SHHHHH
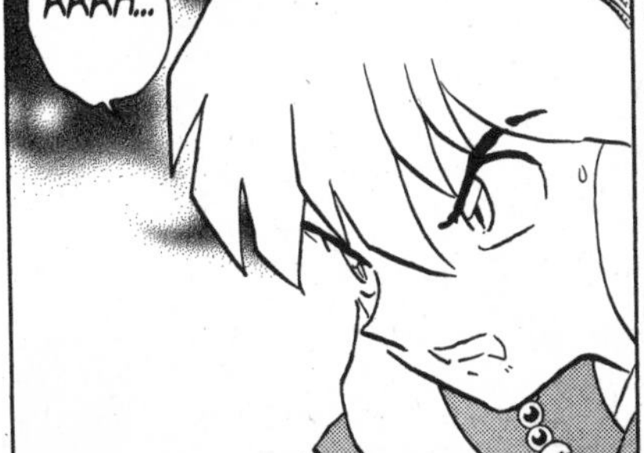
RRRH...

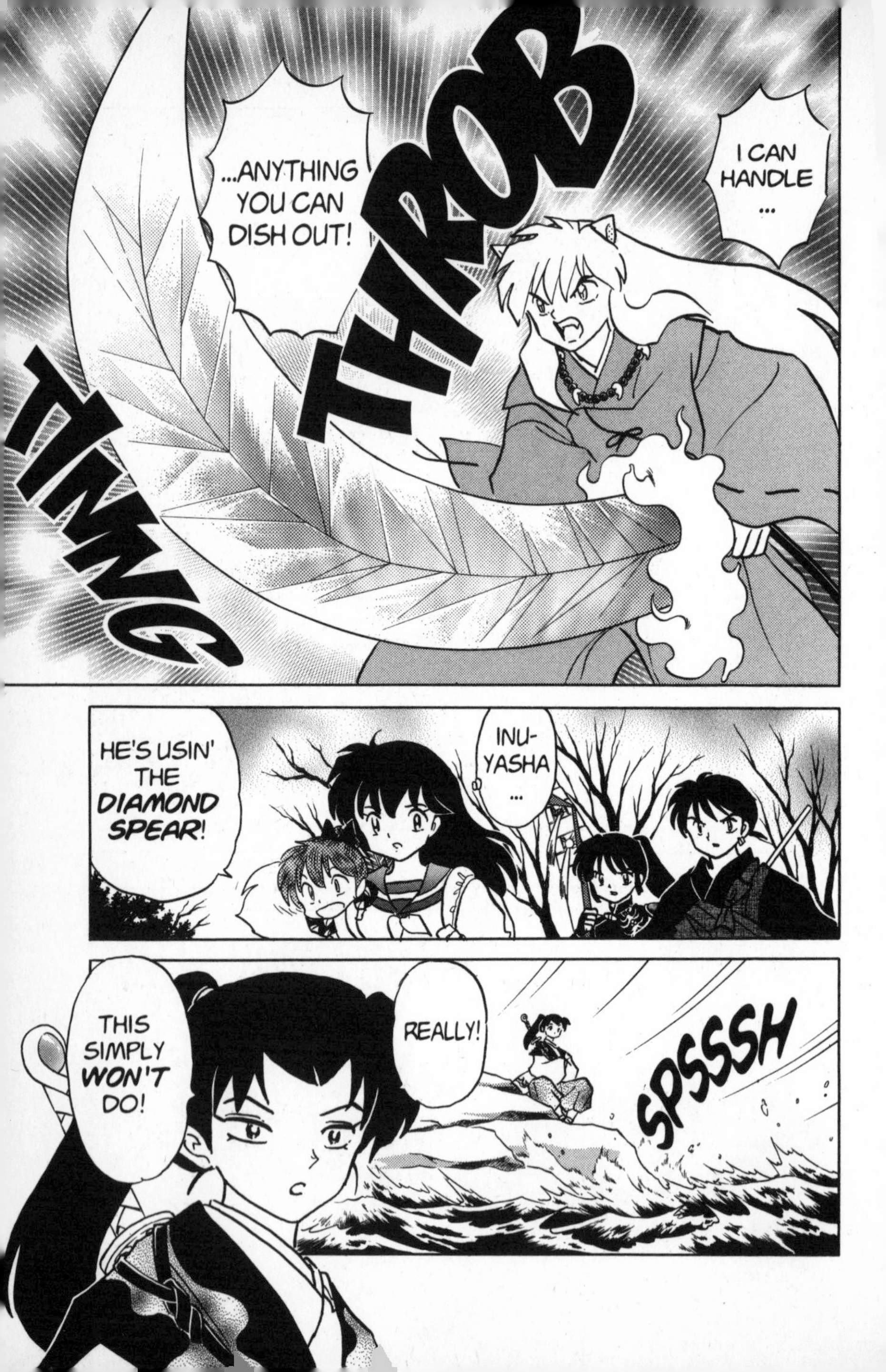
I CAN HANDLE ...
...ANYTHING YOU CAN DISH OUT!
THROB
TWNG
INU-YASHA ...
HE'S USIN' THE DIAMOND SPEAR!
SPSSSH
REALLY!
THIS SIMPLY WON'T DO!

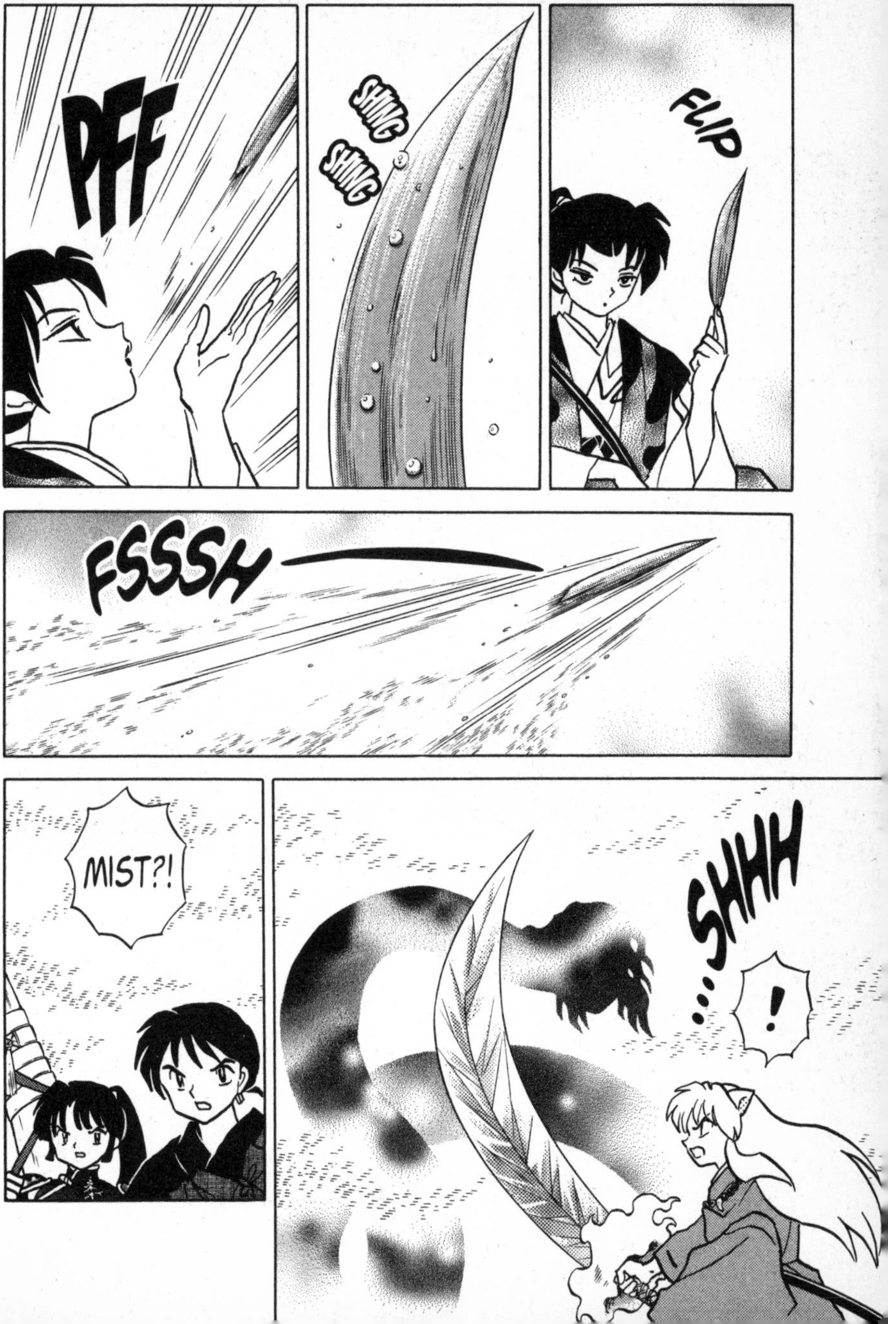
FLIP
SHING
SHING
PFF
FSSSH
SHHH
...
!
MIST?!

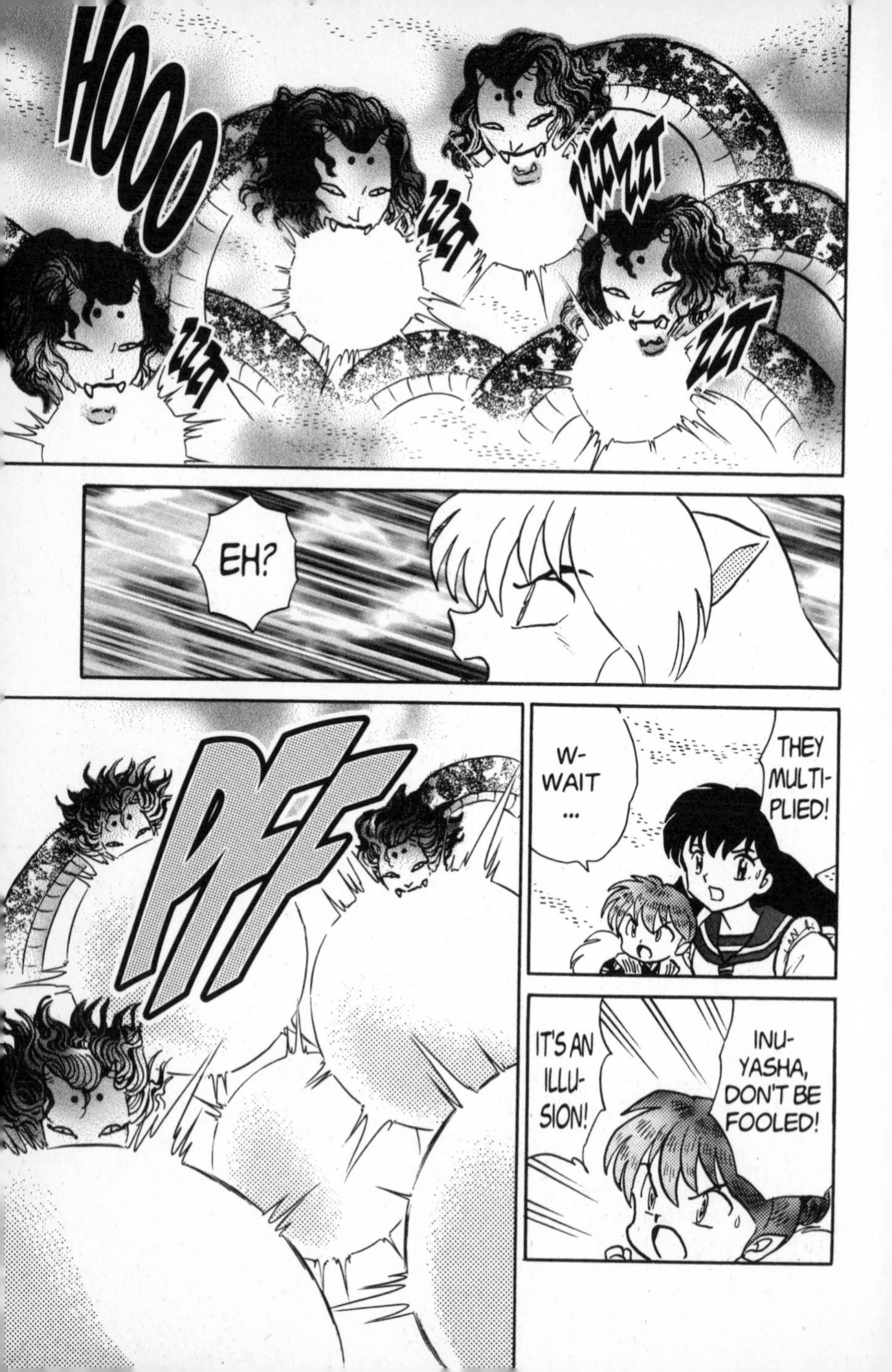
HOOO
ZZZT
ZZZT
ZZZT
EH?
THEY MULTI-PLIED!
W-WAIT ...
INU-YASHA, DON'T BE FOOLED!
IT'S AN ILLU-SION!

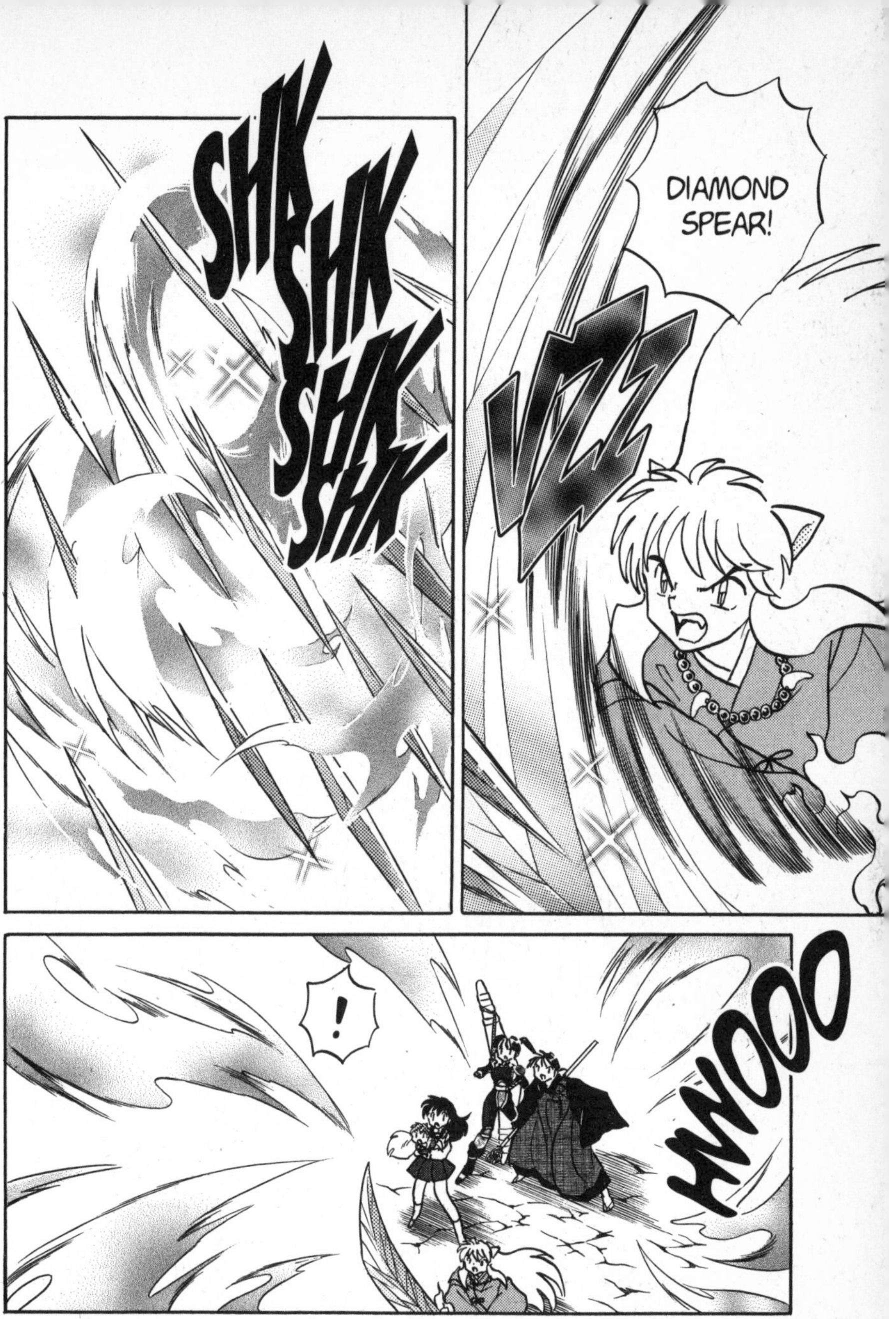
DIAMOND SPEAR!
VZZ
SHIK SHIK SHIK SHIK
!
HWOOO

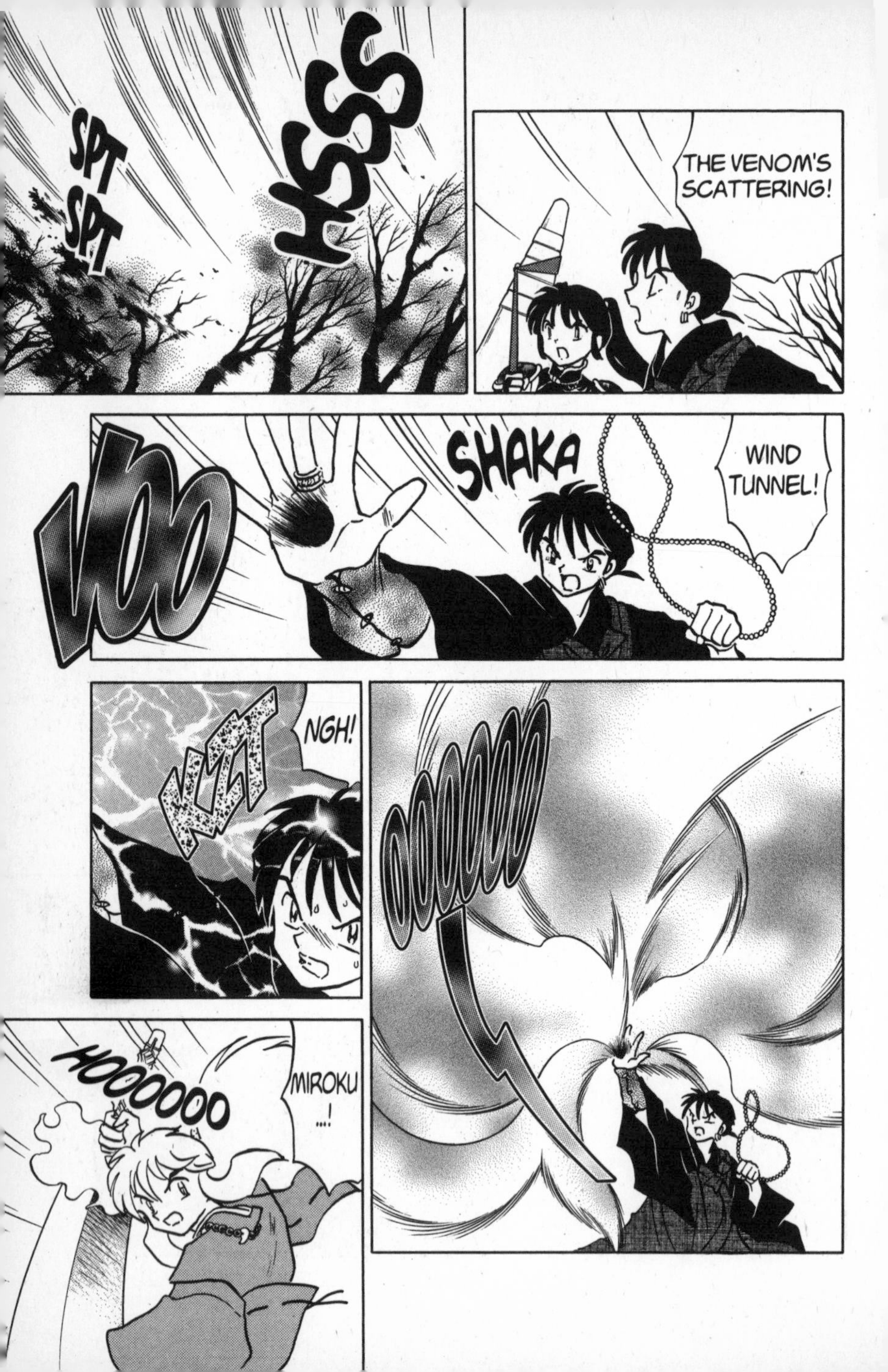
THE VENOM'S SCATTERING!
SPT SPT
HSSSS
WIND TUNNEL!
SHAKA
VOOO
NGH!
MIROKU ...!
HOOOOOO

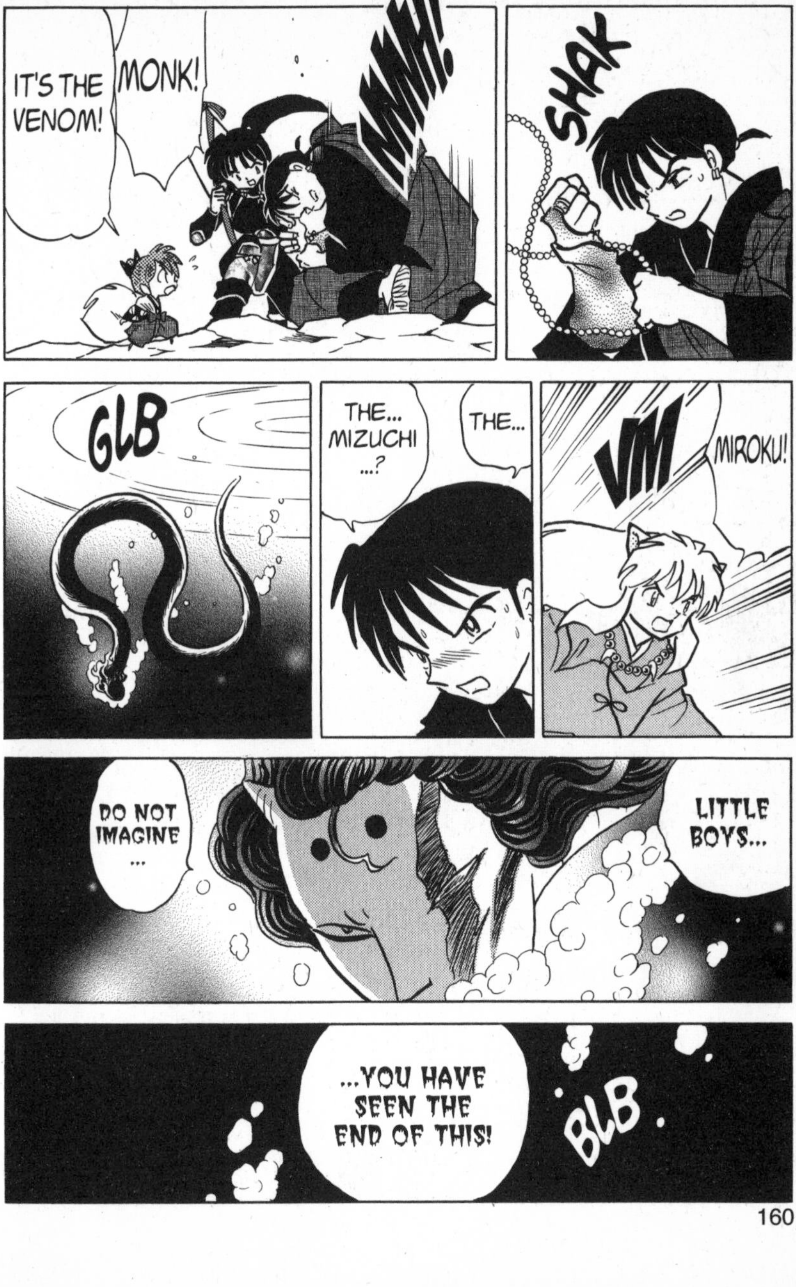
SHAK
MMMH!
MONK!
IT'S THE VENOM!
VM
MIROKU!
THE...
THE... MIZUCHI ...?
GLB
LITTLE BOYS...
DO NOT IMAGINE ...
BLB
...YOU HAVE SEEN THE END OF THIS!

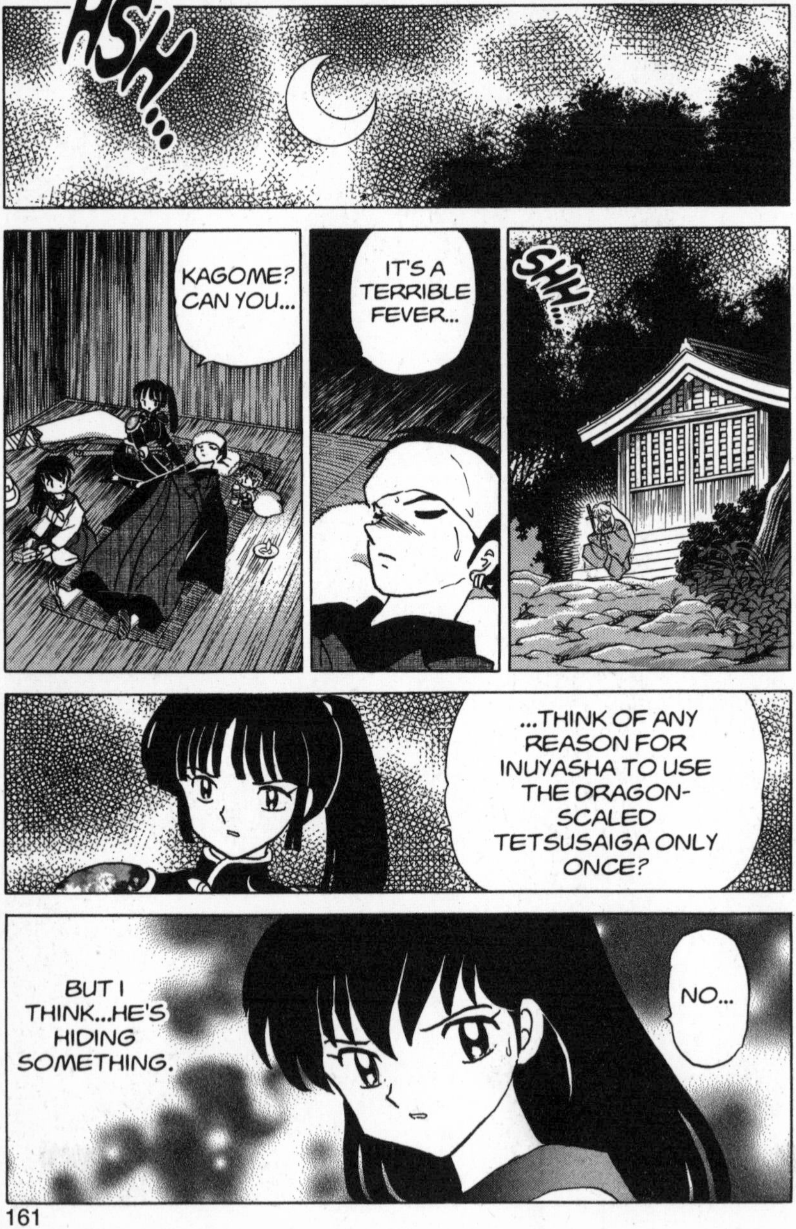
HSH...
SHH...
IT'S A TERRIBLE FEVER...
KAGOME? CAN YOU...
...THINK OF ANY REASON FOR INUYASHA TO USE THE DRAGON-SCALED TETSUSAIGA ONLY ONCE?
NO...
BUT I THINK...HE'S HIDING SOMETHING.

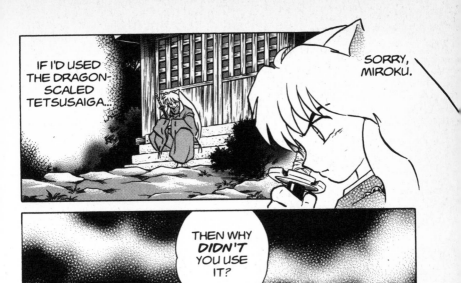

IF I'D USED THE DRAGON-SCALED TETSUSAIGA...

SORRY, MIROKU.

THEN WHY *DIDN'T* YOU USE IT?

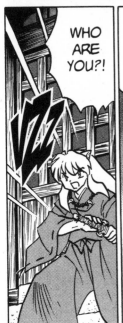

WHO ARE YOU?!

VZZ

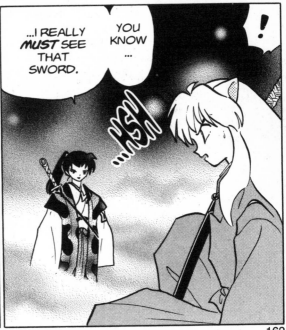

...I REALLY *MUST* SEE THAT SWORD.

YOU KNOW...

!

KSH KSH

162

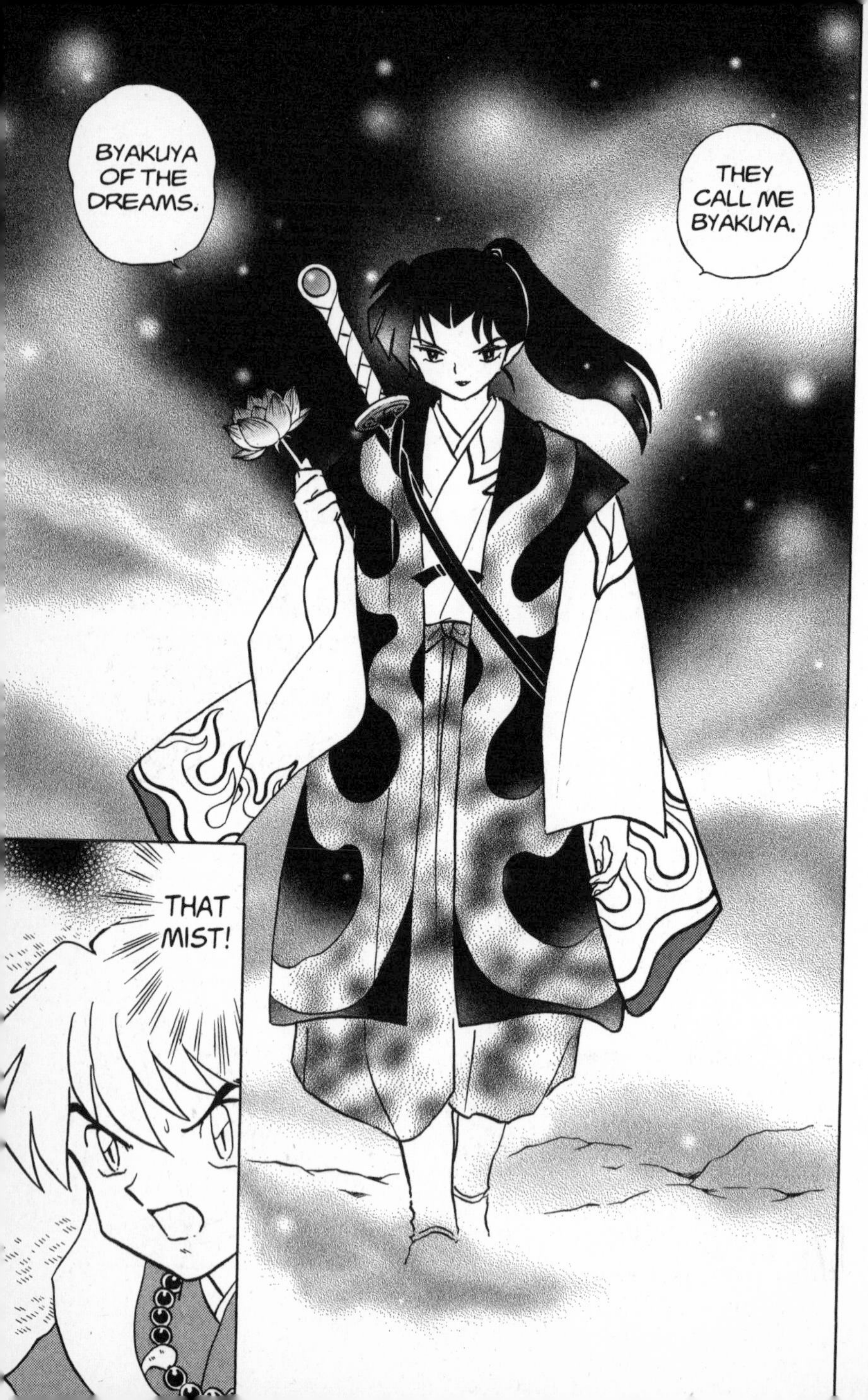
THEY CALL ME BYAKUYA.
BYAKUYA OF THE DREAMS.
THAT MIST!

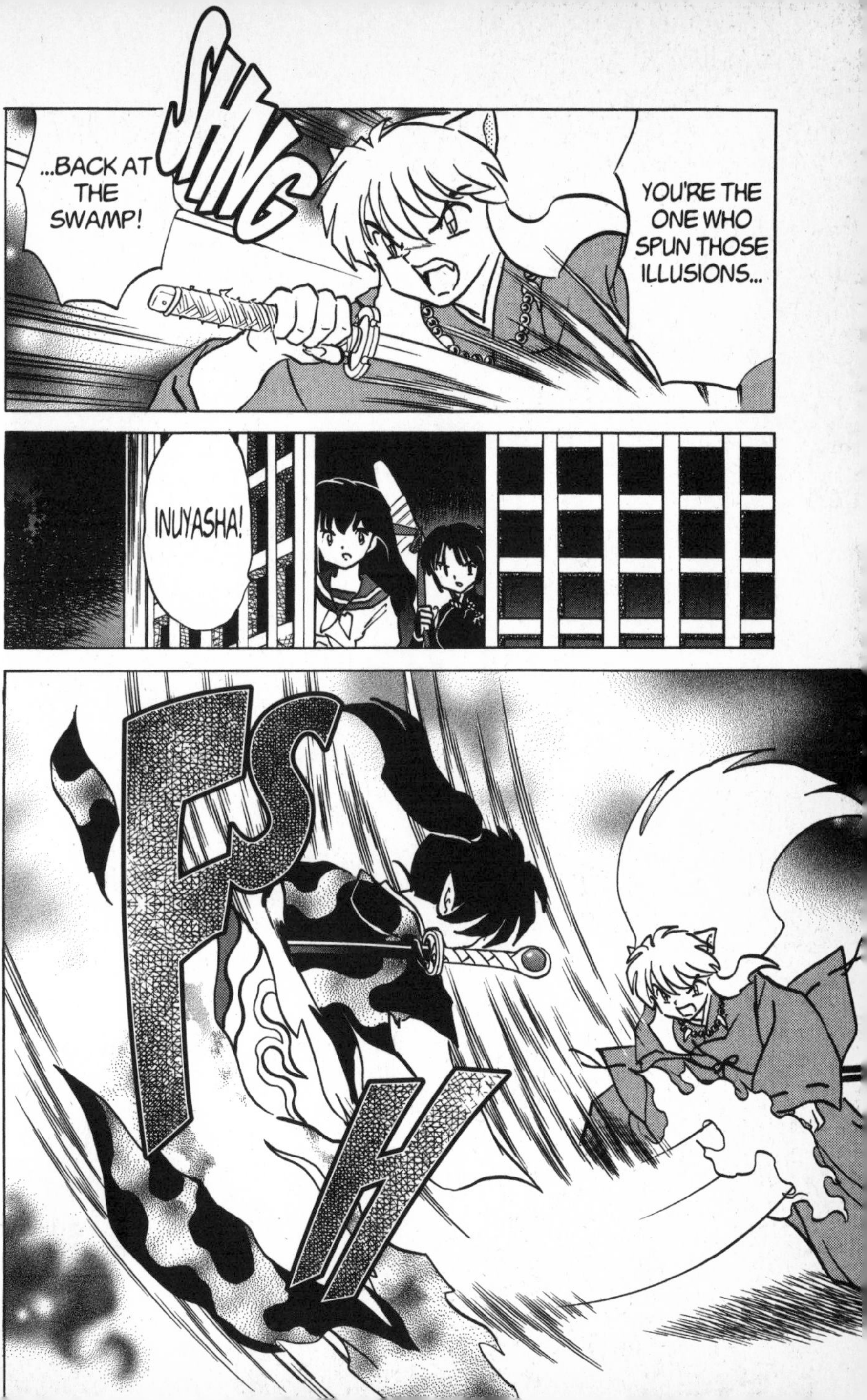
YOU'RE THE ONE WHO SPUN THOSE ILLUSIONS...
...BACK AT THE SWAMP!
SHING
INUYASHA!
FSH

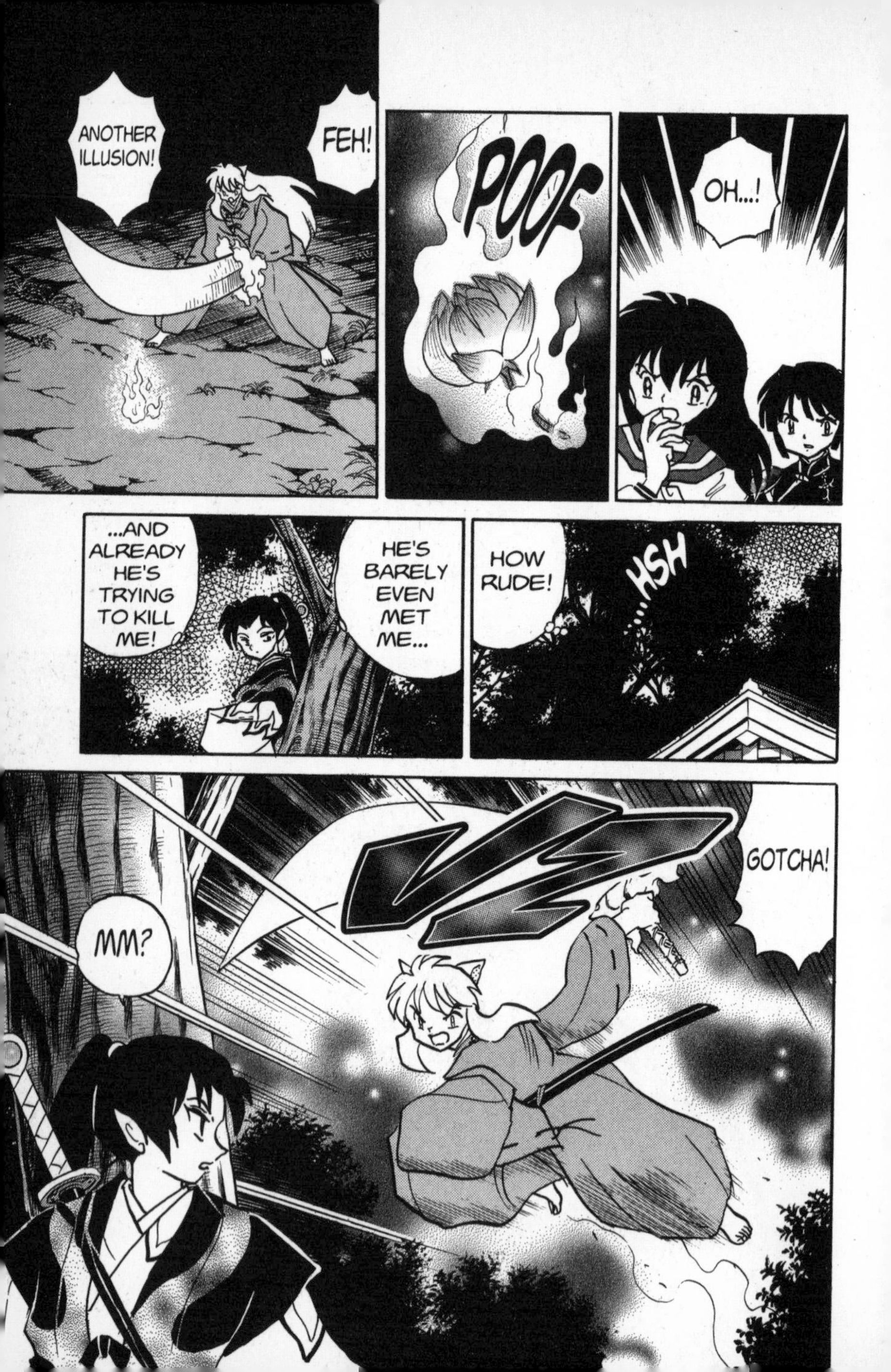
OH...!
POOF
FEH!
ANOTHER ILLUSION!
HOW RUDE!
HSH
HE'S BARELY EVEN MET ME...
...AND ALREADY HE'S TRYING TO KILL ME!
GOTCHA!
MM?

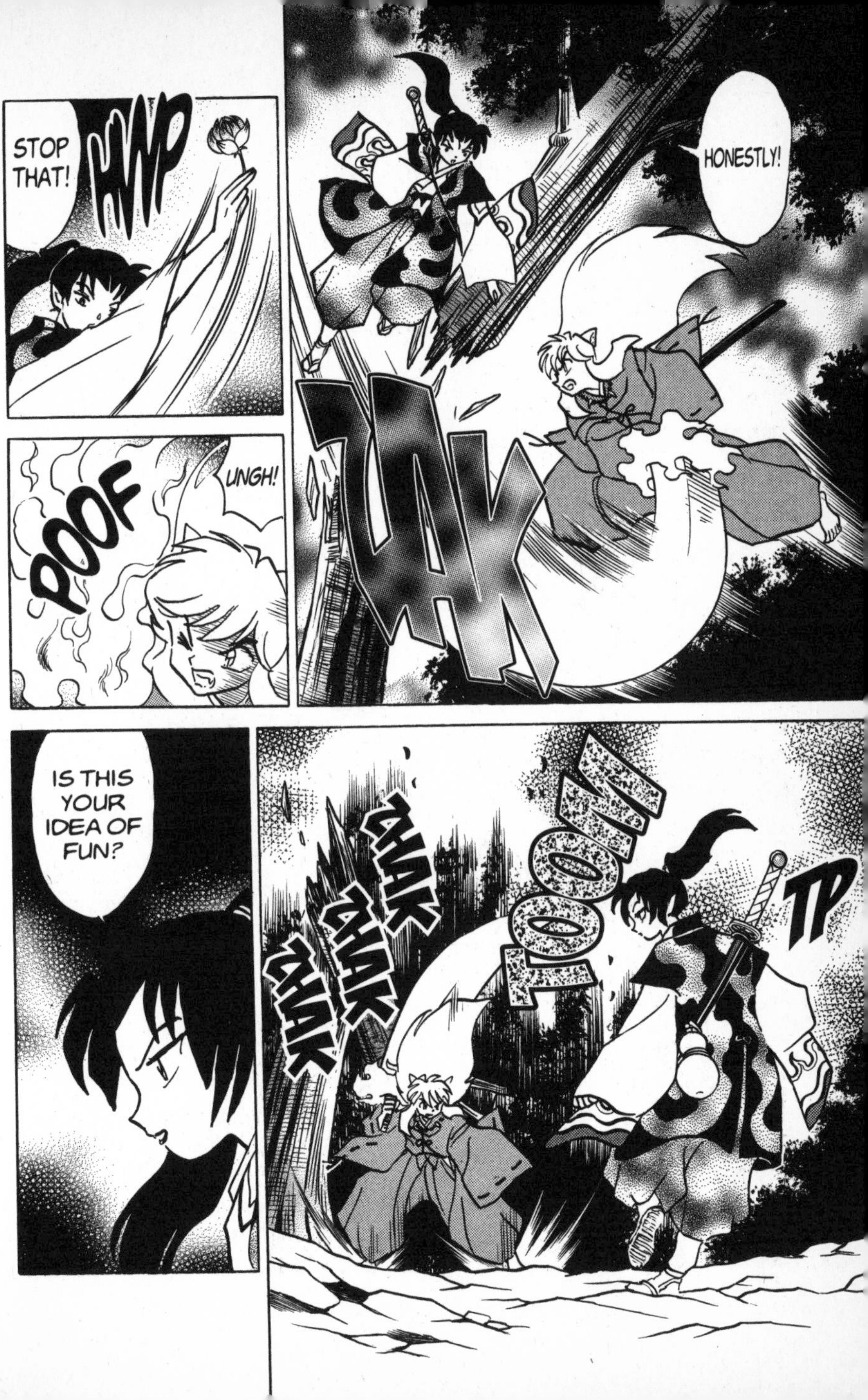
HONESTLY!
ZAK
HWIP
STOP THAT!
UNGH!
POOF
TP
TOOM
ZHAK ZHAK ZHAK
IS THIS YOUR IDEA OF FUN?

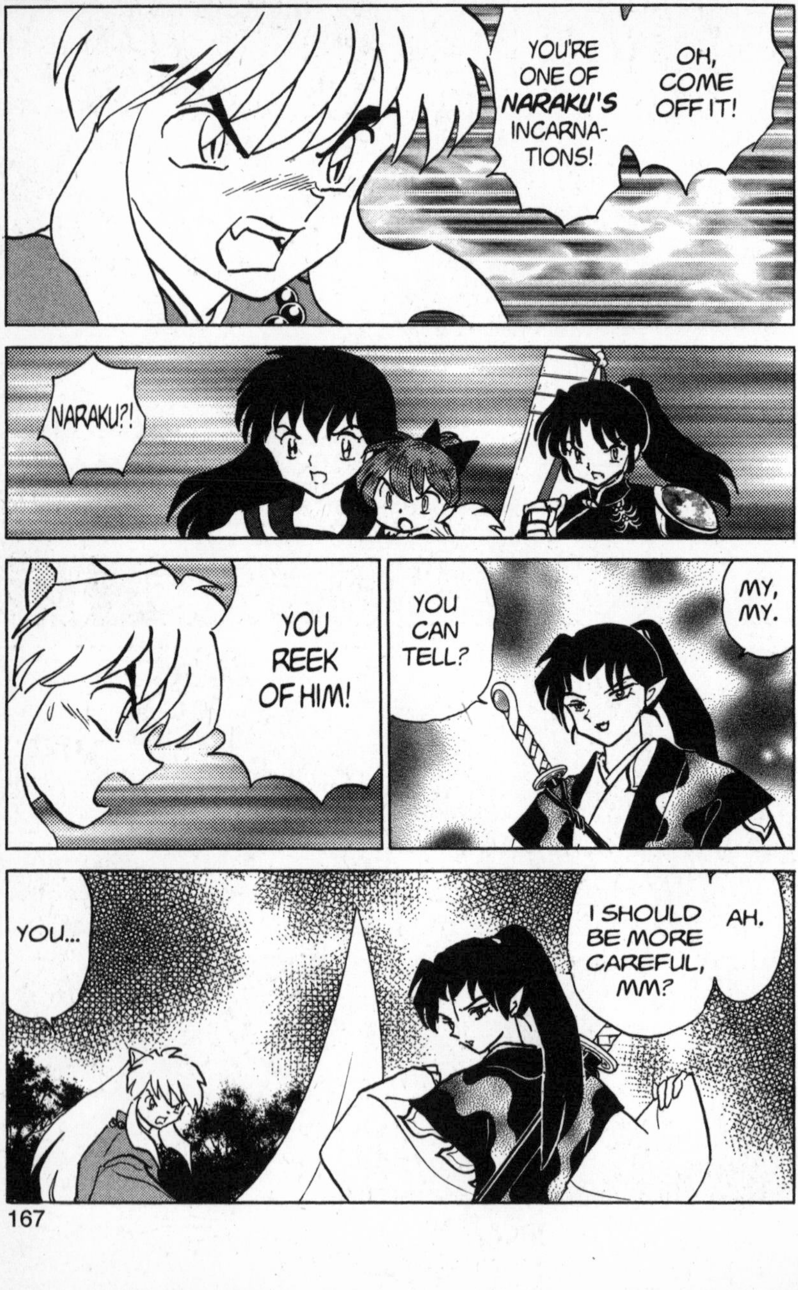
OH, COME OFF IT!
YOU'RE ONE OF NARAKU'S INCARNATIONS!
NARAKU?!
MY, MY.
YOU CAN TELL?
YOU REEK OF HIM!
AH.
I SHOULD BE MORE CAREFUL, MM?
YOU...

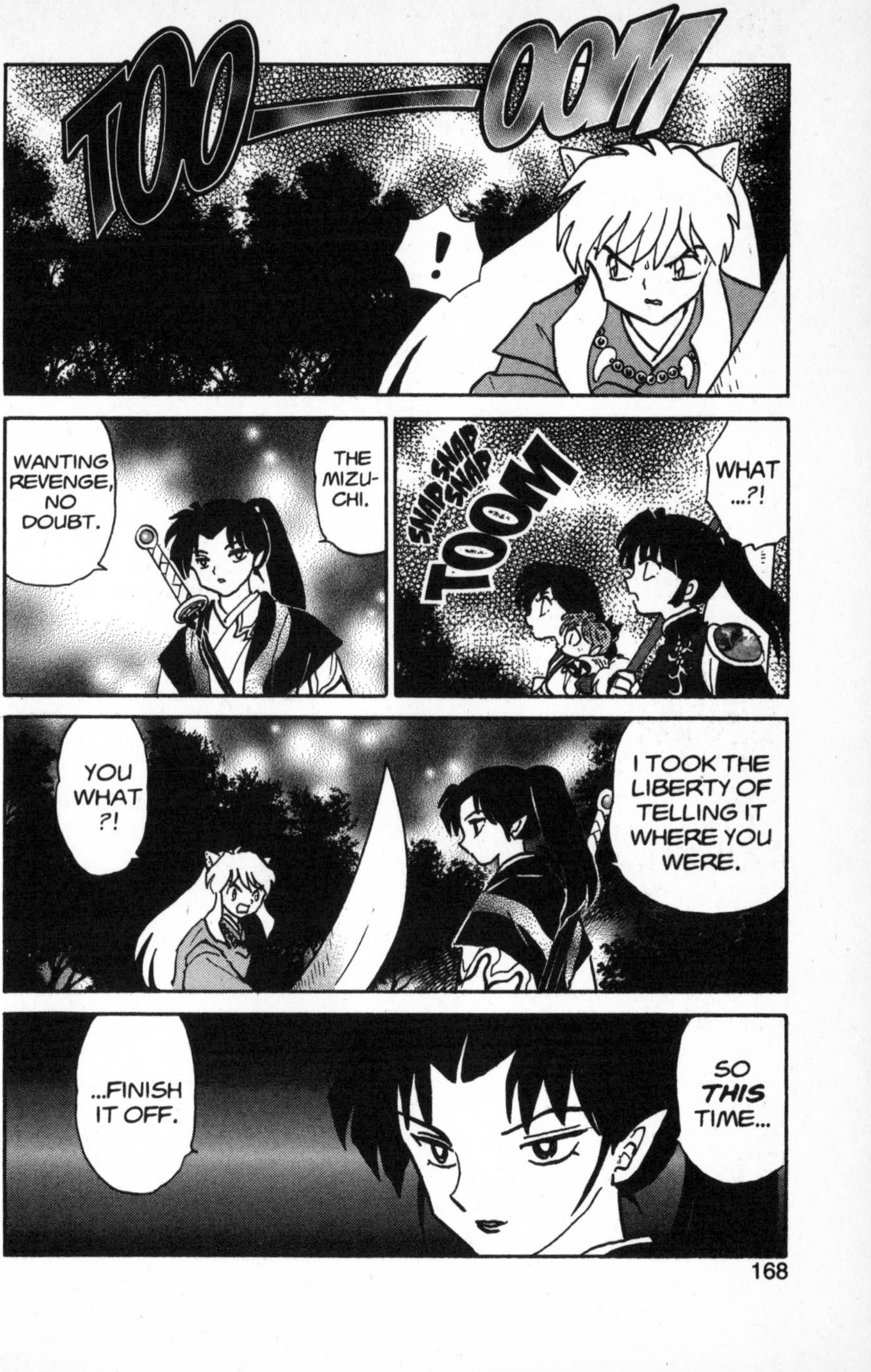
TOO——OOM
!
WHAT ...?!
SNAP SNAP SNAP
TOOM
THE MIZU-CHI.
WANTING REVENGE, NO DOUBT.
I TOOK THE LIBERTY OF TELLING IT WHERE YOU WERE.
YOU WHAT ?!
SO THIS TIME...
...FINISH IT OFF.

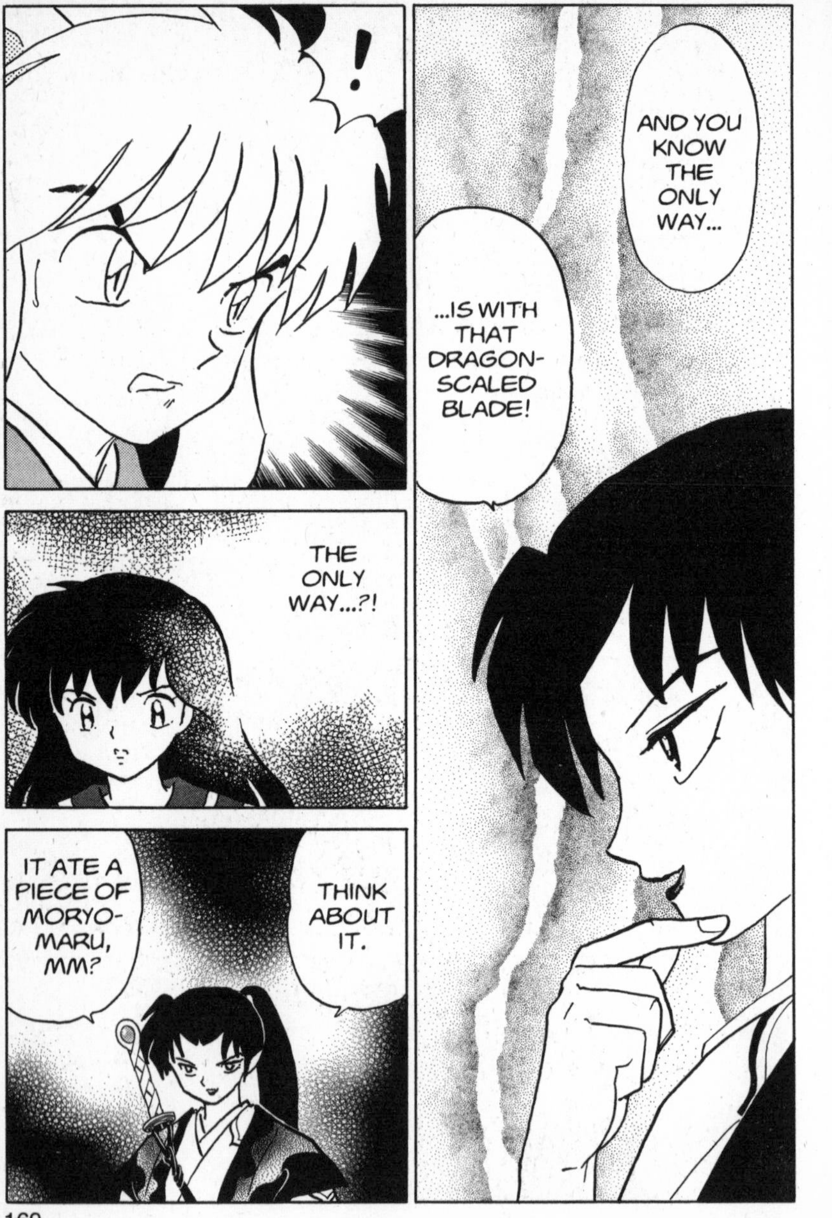
AND YOU KNOW THE ONLY WAY...
...IS WITH THAT DRAGON-SCALED BLADE!
!
THE ONLY WAY...?!
THINK ABOUT IT.
IT ATE A PIECE OF MORYO-MARU, MM?

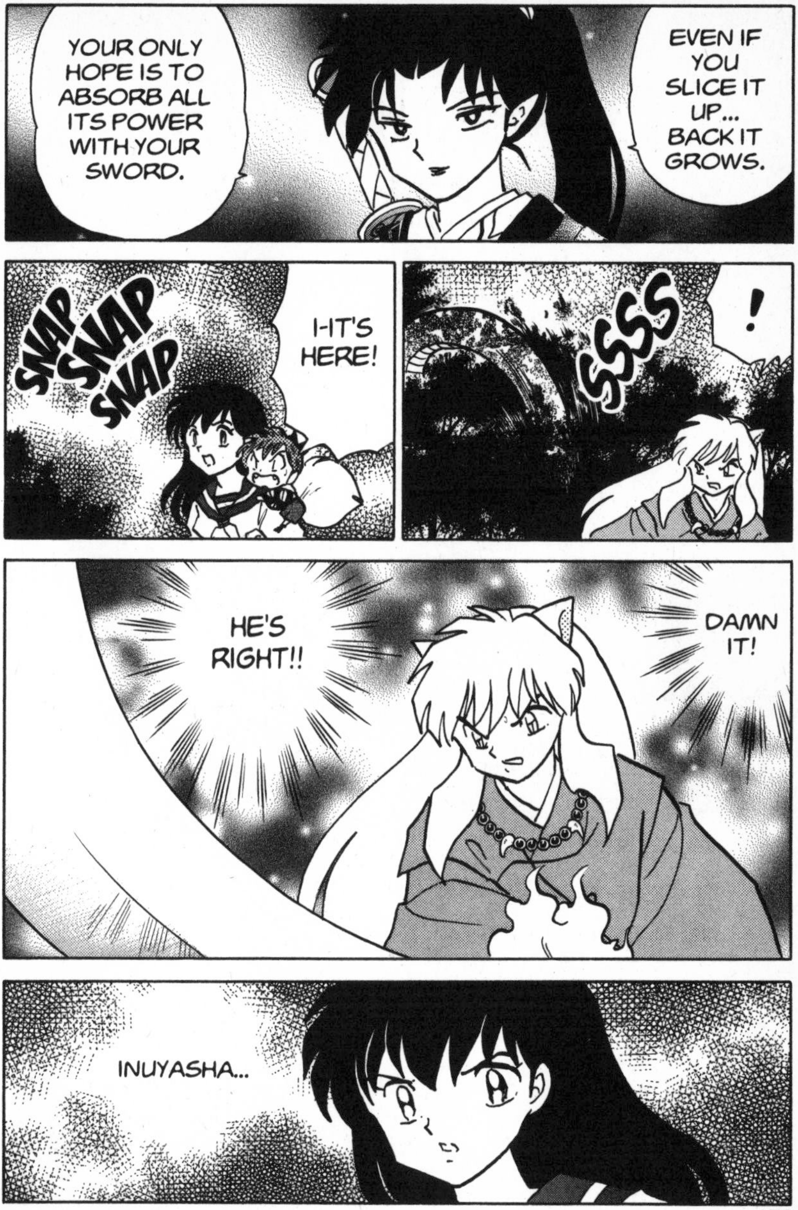
EVEN IF YOU SLICE IT UP... BACK IT GROWS.
YOUR ONLY HOPE IS TO ABSORB ALL ITS POWER WITH YOUR SWORD.
SSSS
!
I-IT'S HERE!
SNAP SNAP SNAP
DAMN IT!
HE'S RIGHT!!
INUYASHA...

SCROLL 10

TETSUSAIGA RELEASED

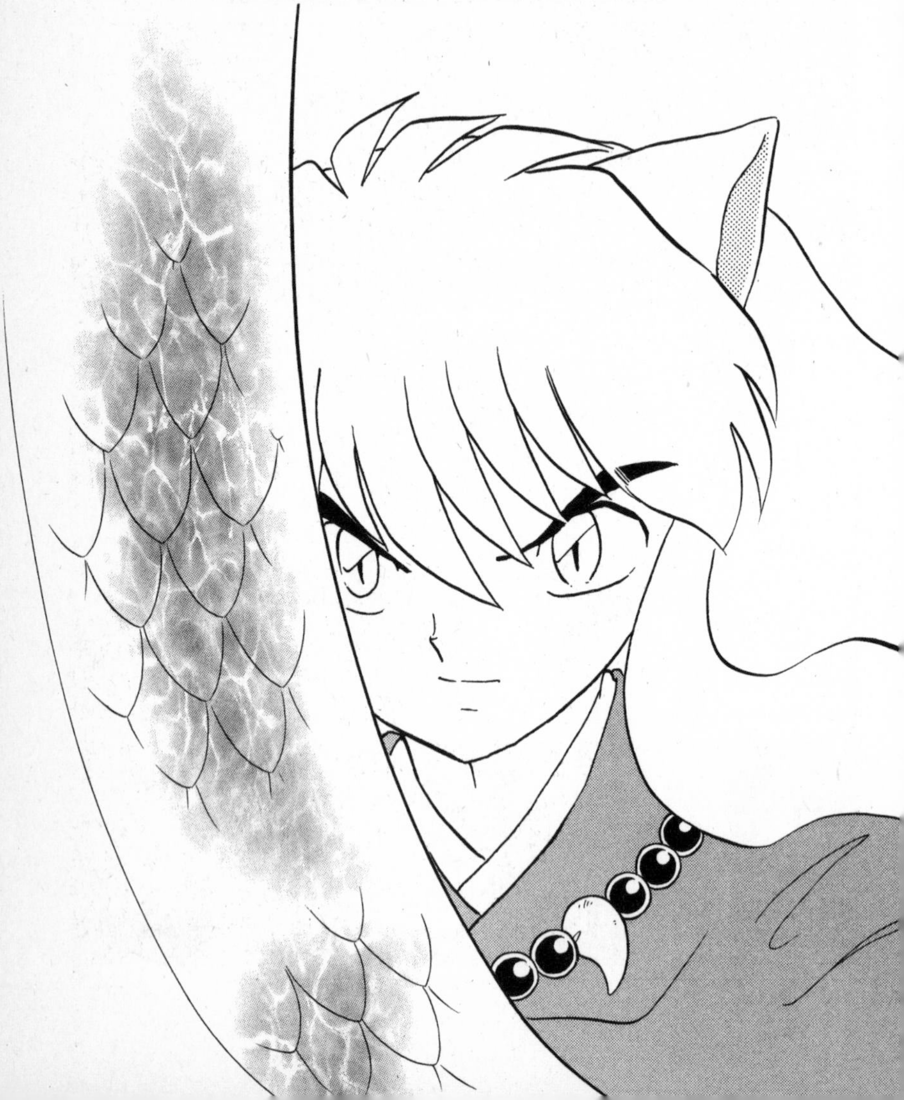

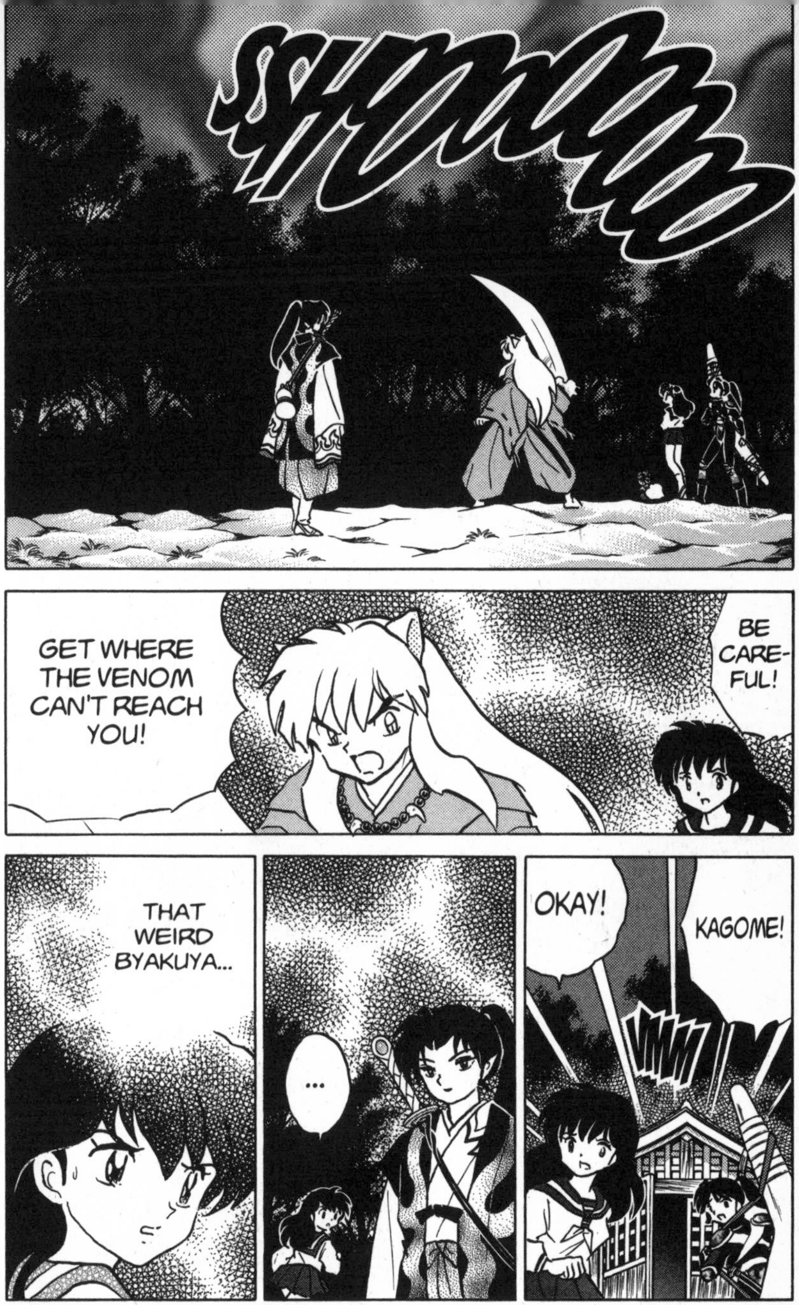
BE CARE-FUL!
GET WHERE THE VENOM CAN'T REACH YOU!
KAGOME!
OKAY!
VMMM
...
THAT WEIRD BYAKUYA...

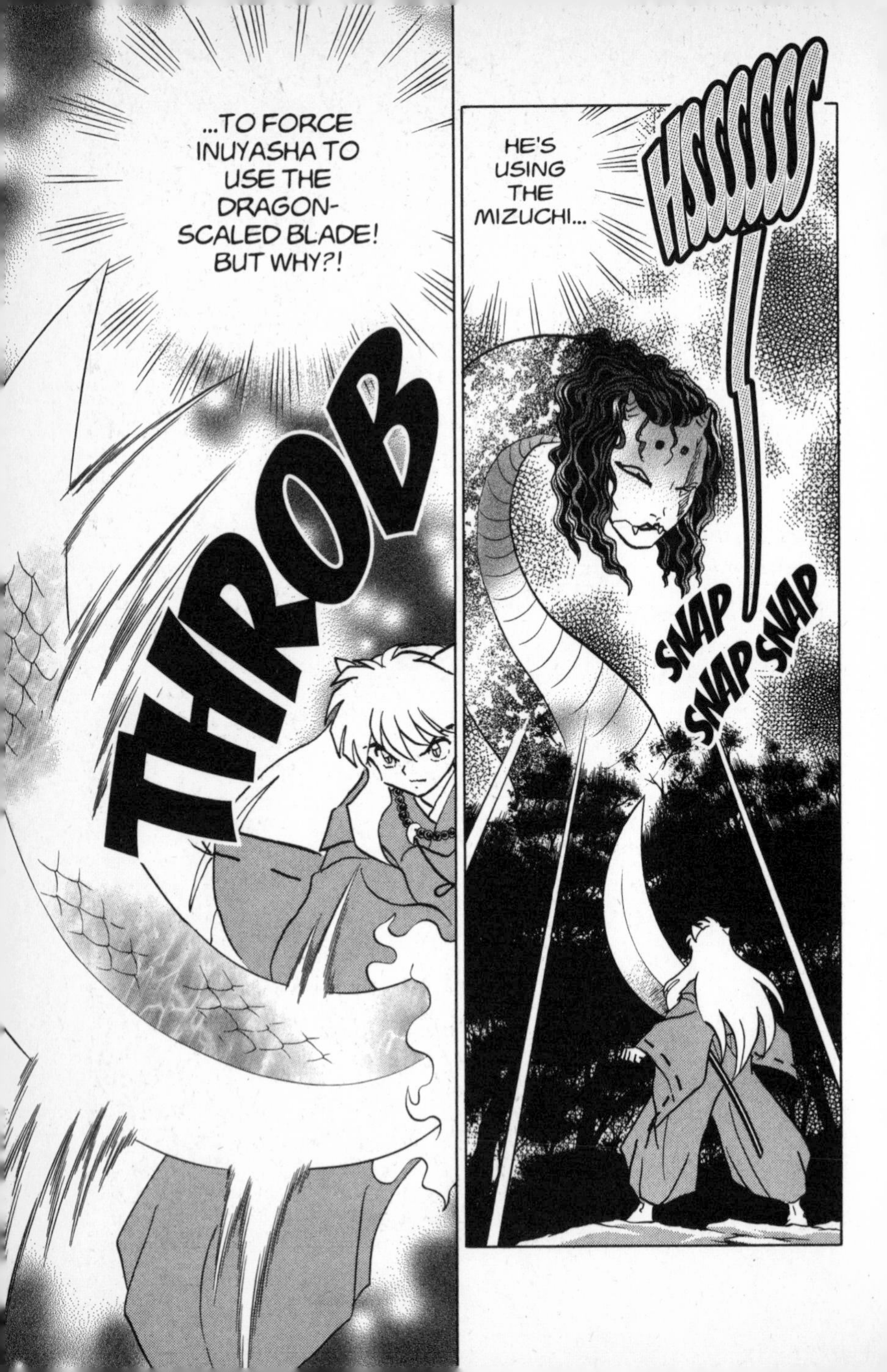
HE'S USING THE MIZUCHI...
HISSSSSS
SNAP SNAP SNAP
...TO FORCE INUYASHA TO USE THE DRAGON-SCALED BLADE! BUT WHY?!
THROB

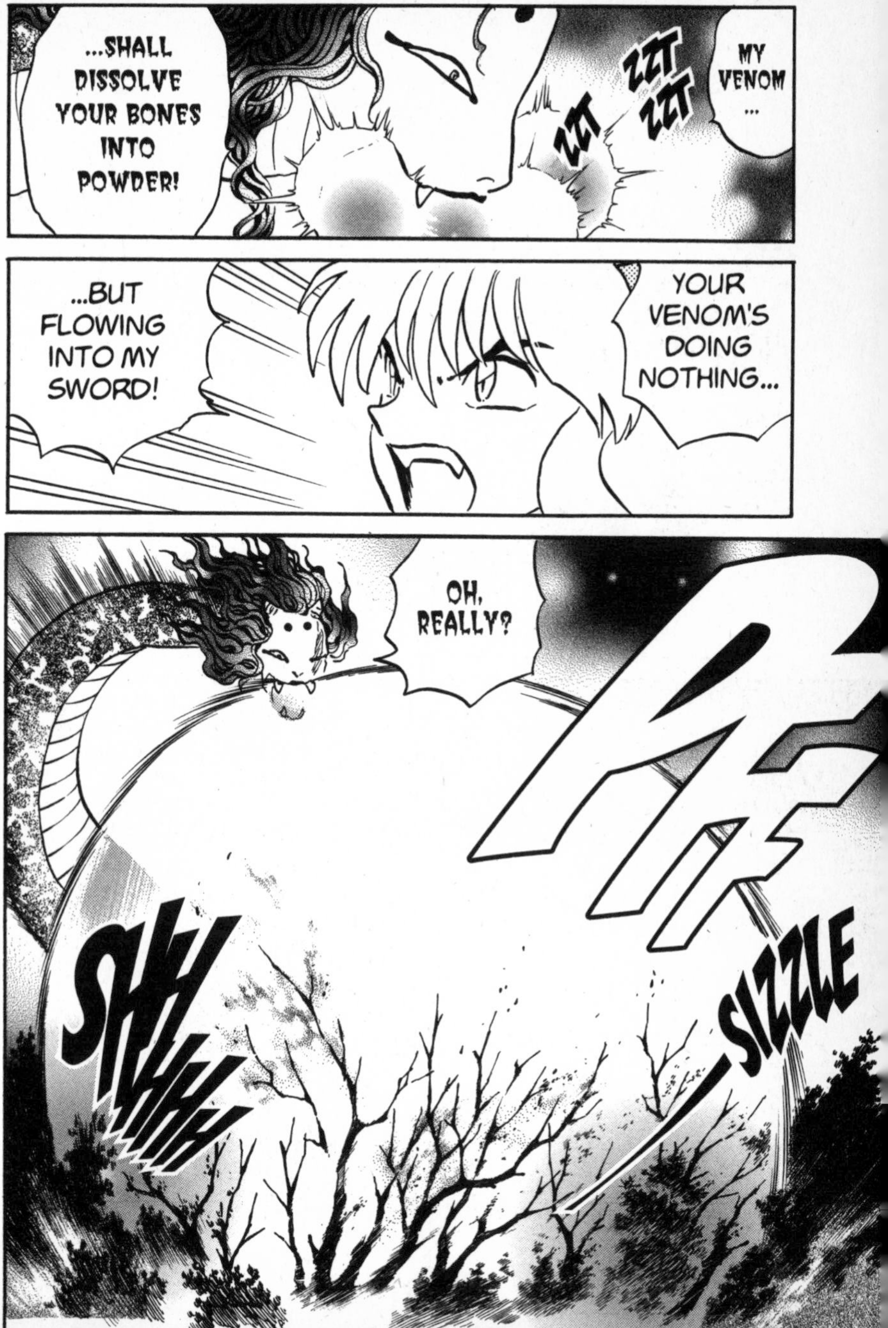
MY VENOM ...
ZZT ZZT ZZT
...SHALL DISSOLVE YOUR BONES INTO POWDER!
YOUR VENOM'S DOING NOTHING...
...BUT FLOWING INTO MY SWORD!
OH, REALLY?
SIZZLE

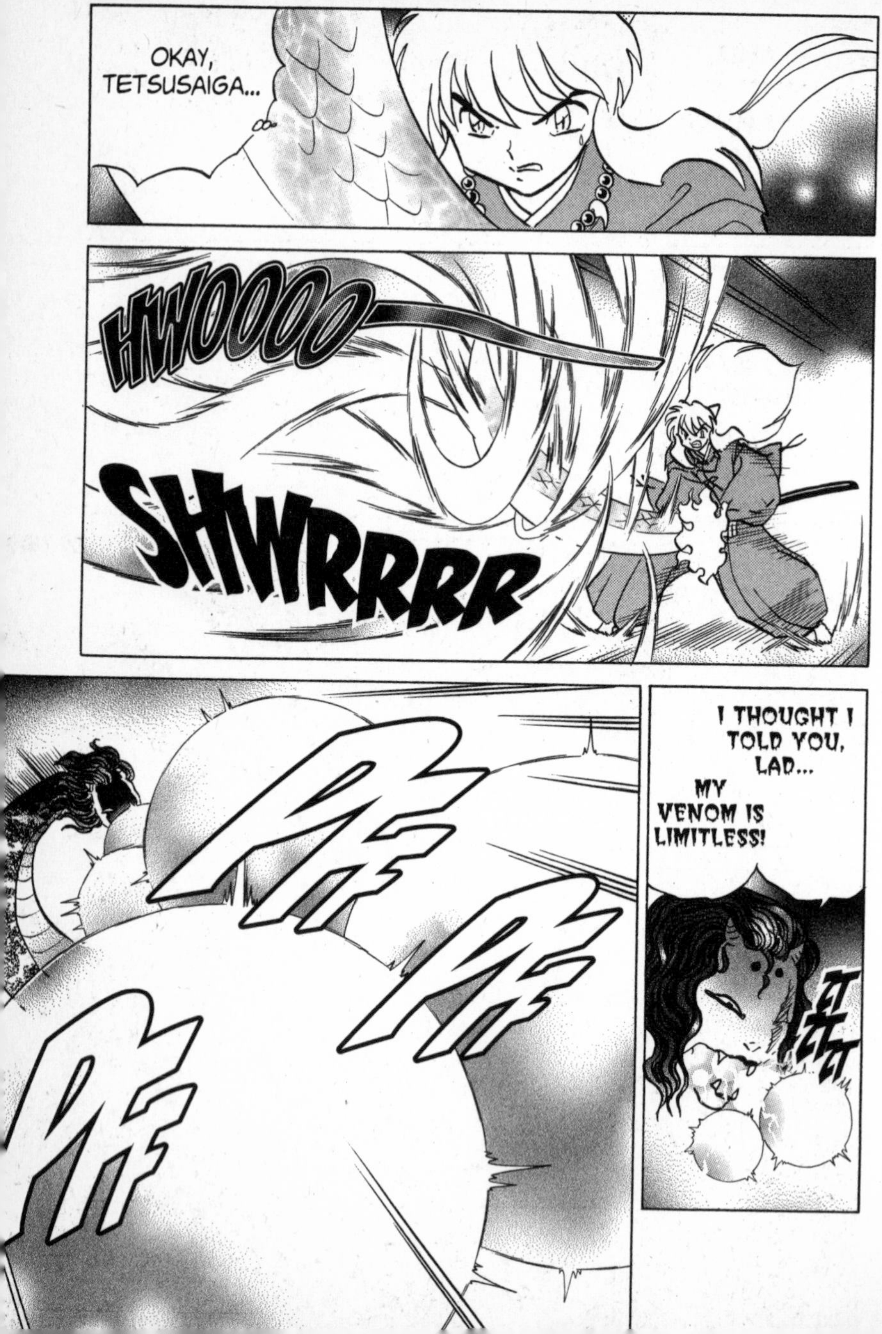
OKAY, TETSUSAIGA...
HWOOOO
SHWRRRR
I THOUGHT I TOLD YOU, LAD...
MY VENOM IS LIMITLESS!

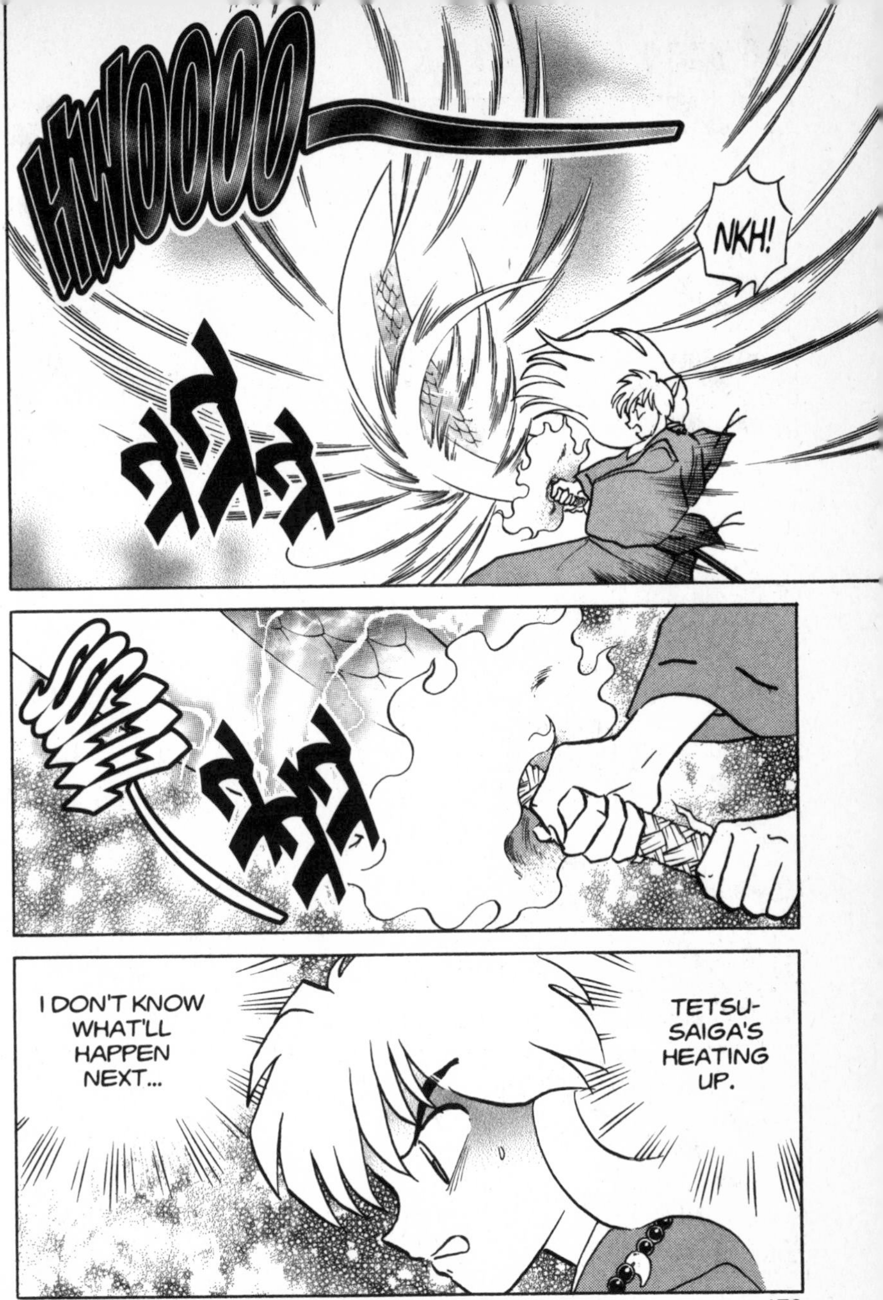
HWOOOO
NKH!
TETSUSAIGA'S HEATING UP.
I DON'T KNOW WHAT'LL HAPPEN NEXT...

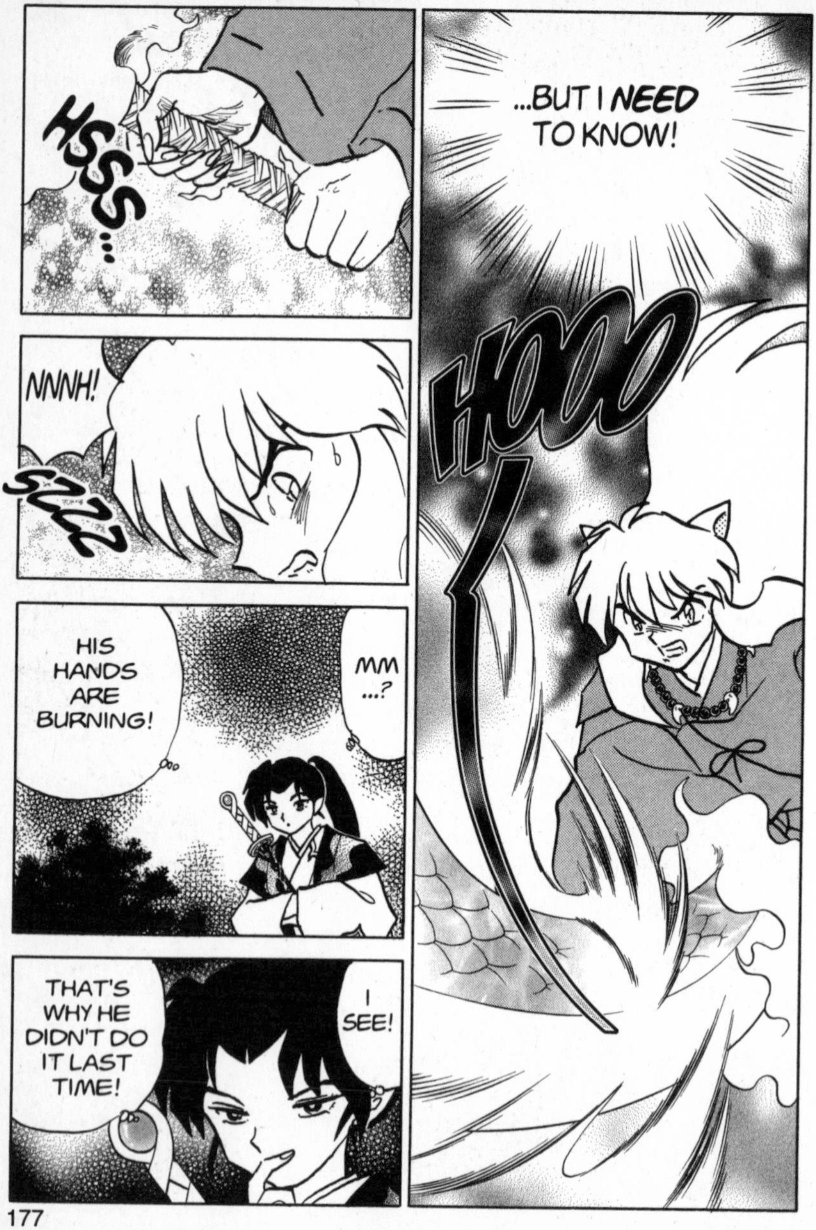
...BUT I NEED TO KNOW!
HOOO
HSSS...
NNNH!
SZZZ
MM ...?
HIS HANDS ARE BURNING!
I SEE!
THAT'S WHY HE DIDN'T DO IT LAST TIME!

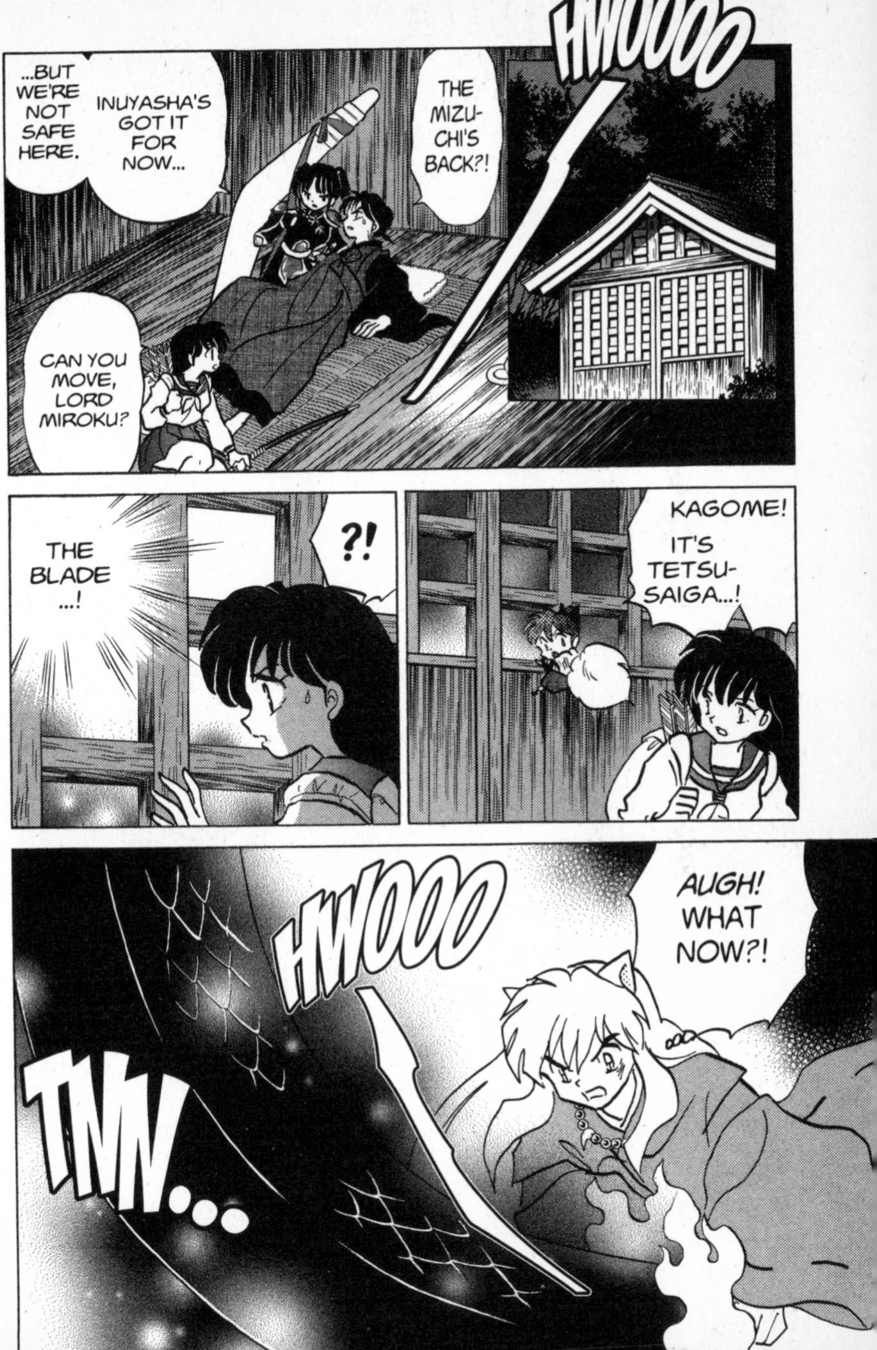
HWOOOO
THE MIZU-CHI'S BACK?!
INUYASHA'S GOT IT FOR NOW...
...BUT WE'RE NOT SAFE HERE.
CAN YOU MOVE, LORD MIROKU?
KAGOME!
IT'S TETSU-SAIGA...!
?!
THE BLADE ...!
AUGH! WHAT NOW?!
HWOOO
TMN...

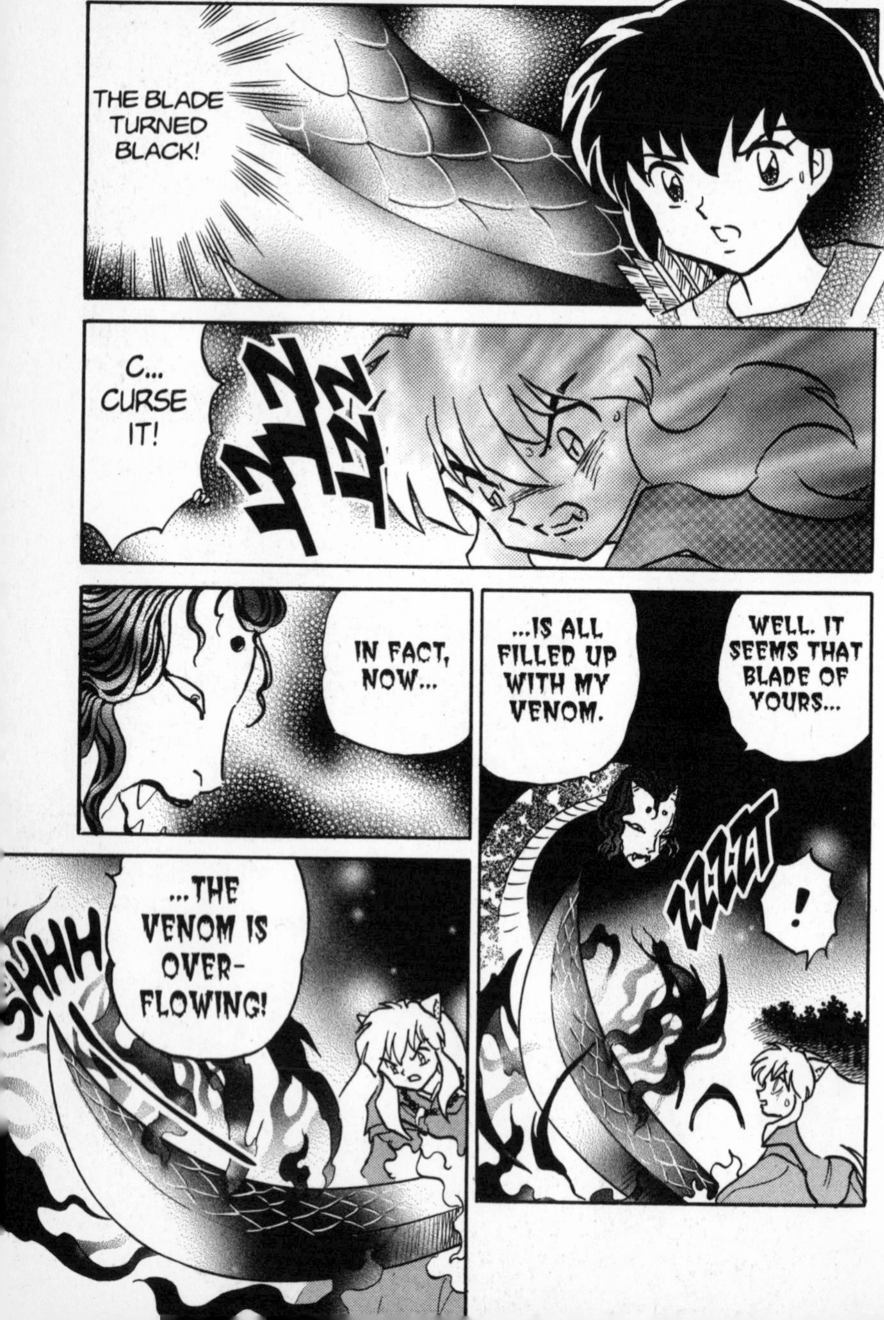
THE BLADE TURNED BLACK!
C... CURSE IT!
WELL. IT SEEMS THAT BLADE OF YOURS...
...IS ALL FILLED UP WITH MY VENOM.
!
IN FACT, NOW...
...THE VENOM IS OVER-FLOWING!
SHHH

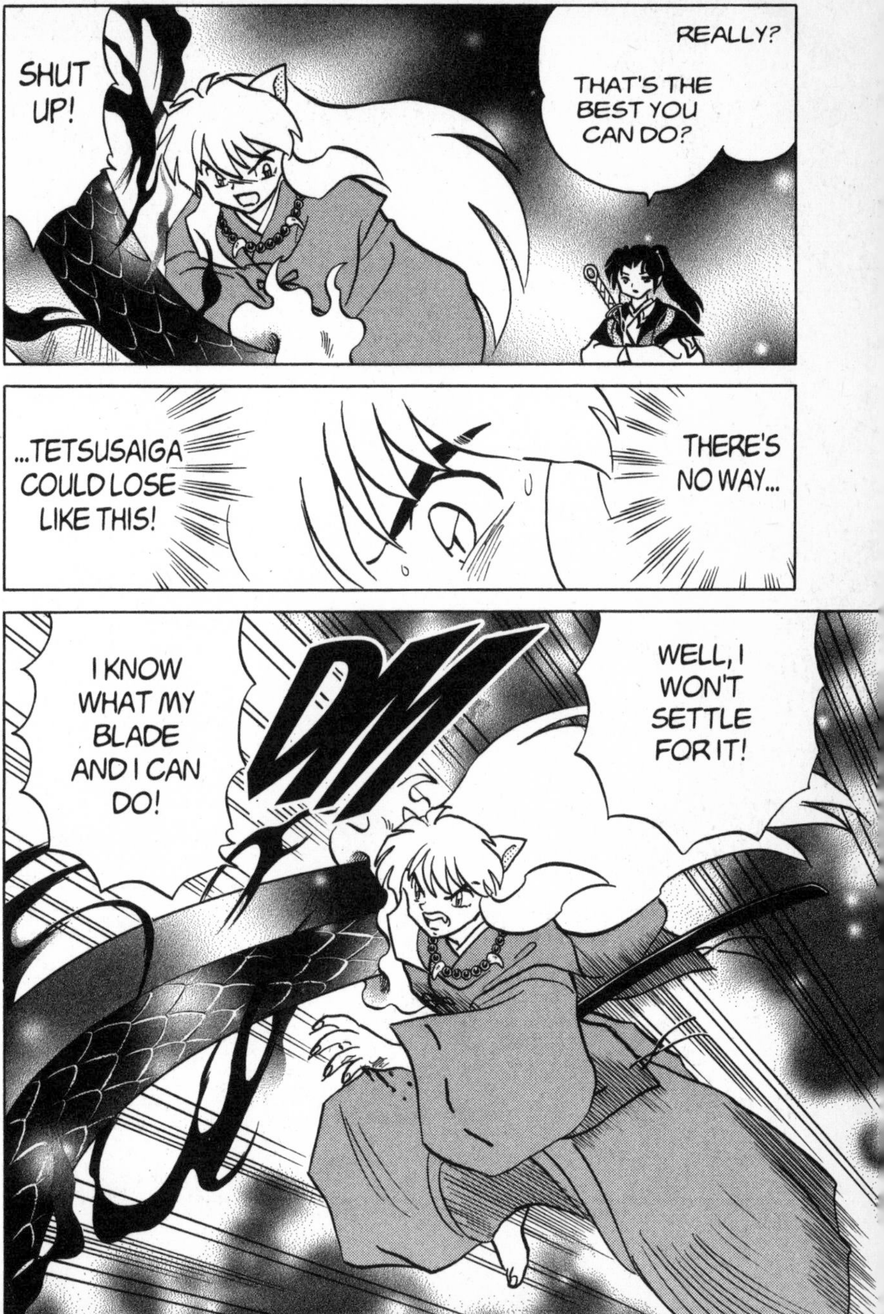
REALLY?
THAT'S THE BEST YOU CAN DO?
SHUT UP!
THERE'S NO WAY...
...TETSUSAIGA COULD LOSE LIKE THIS!
WELL, I WON'T SETTLE FOR IT!
I KNOW WHAT MY BLADE AND I CAN DO!

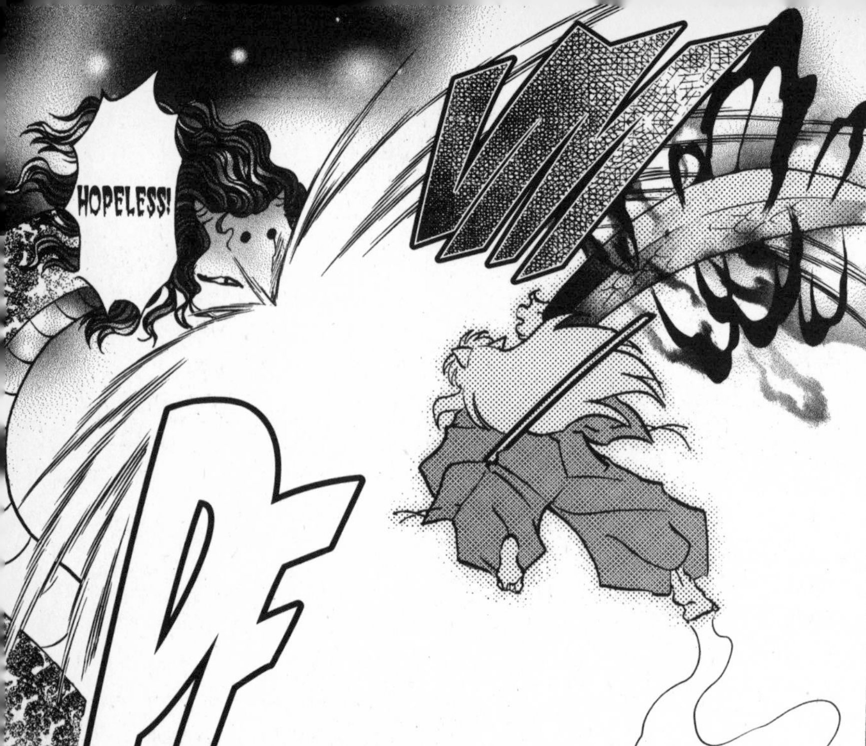
HOPELESS!

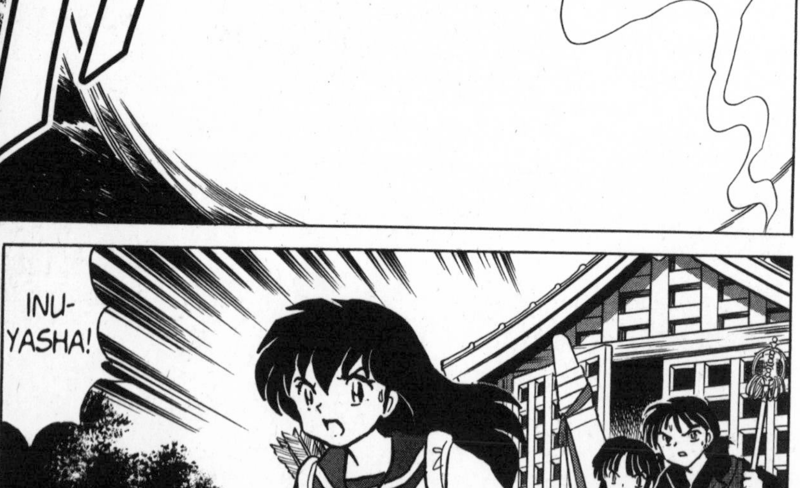
INU-
YASHA!

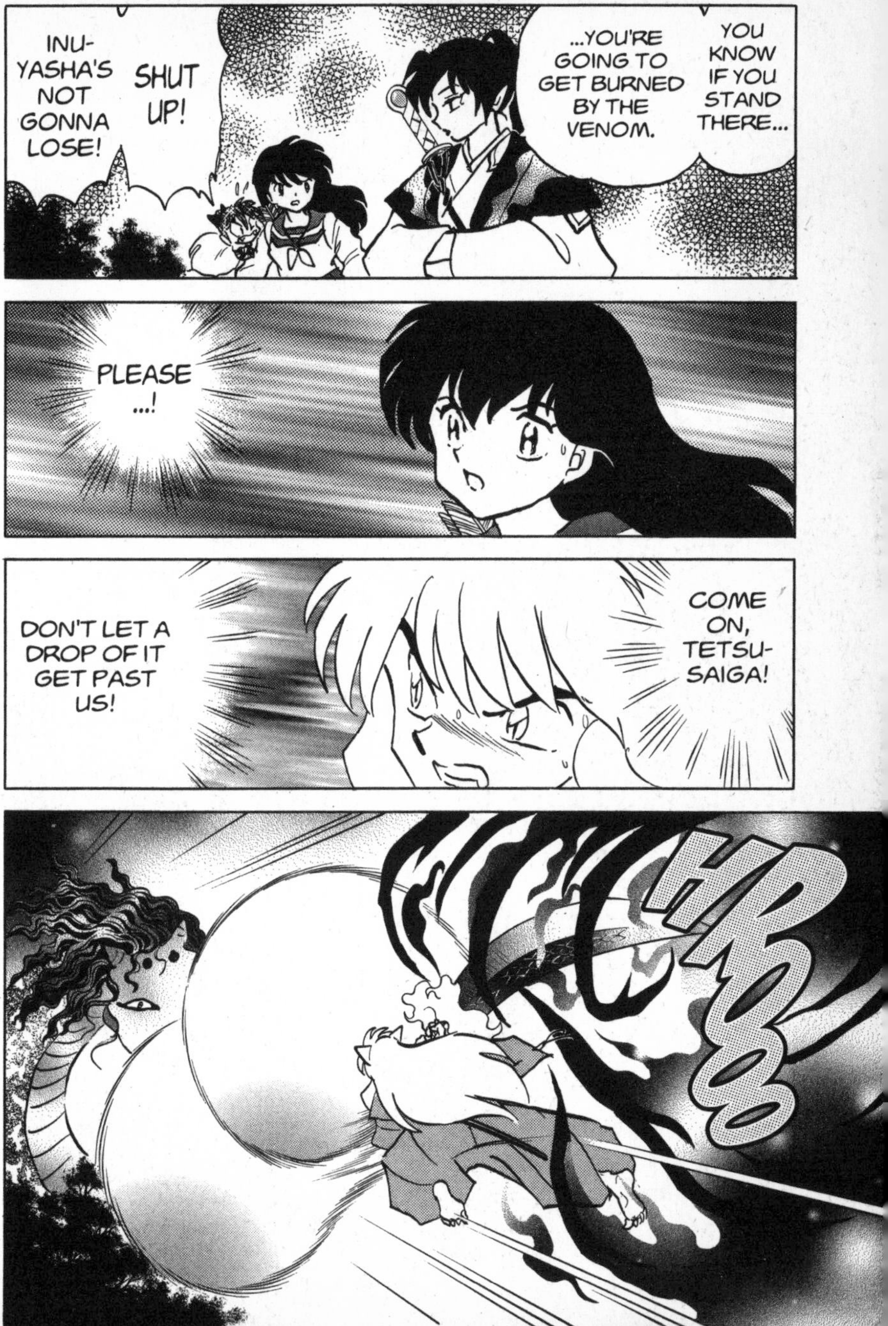
YOU KNOW IF YOU STAND THERE...
...YOU'RE GOING TO GET BURNED BY THE VENOM.
SHUT UP!
INU-YASHA'S NOT GONNA LOSE!
PLEASE ...!
COME ON, TETSU-SAIGA!
DON'T LET A DROP OF IT GET PAST US!
HROOO

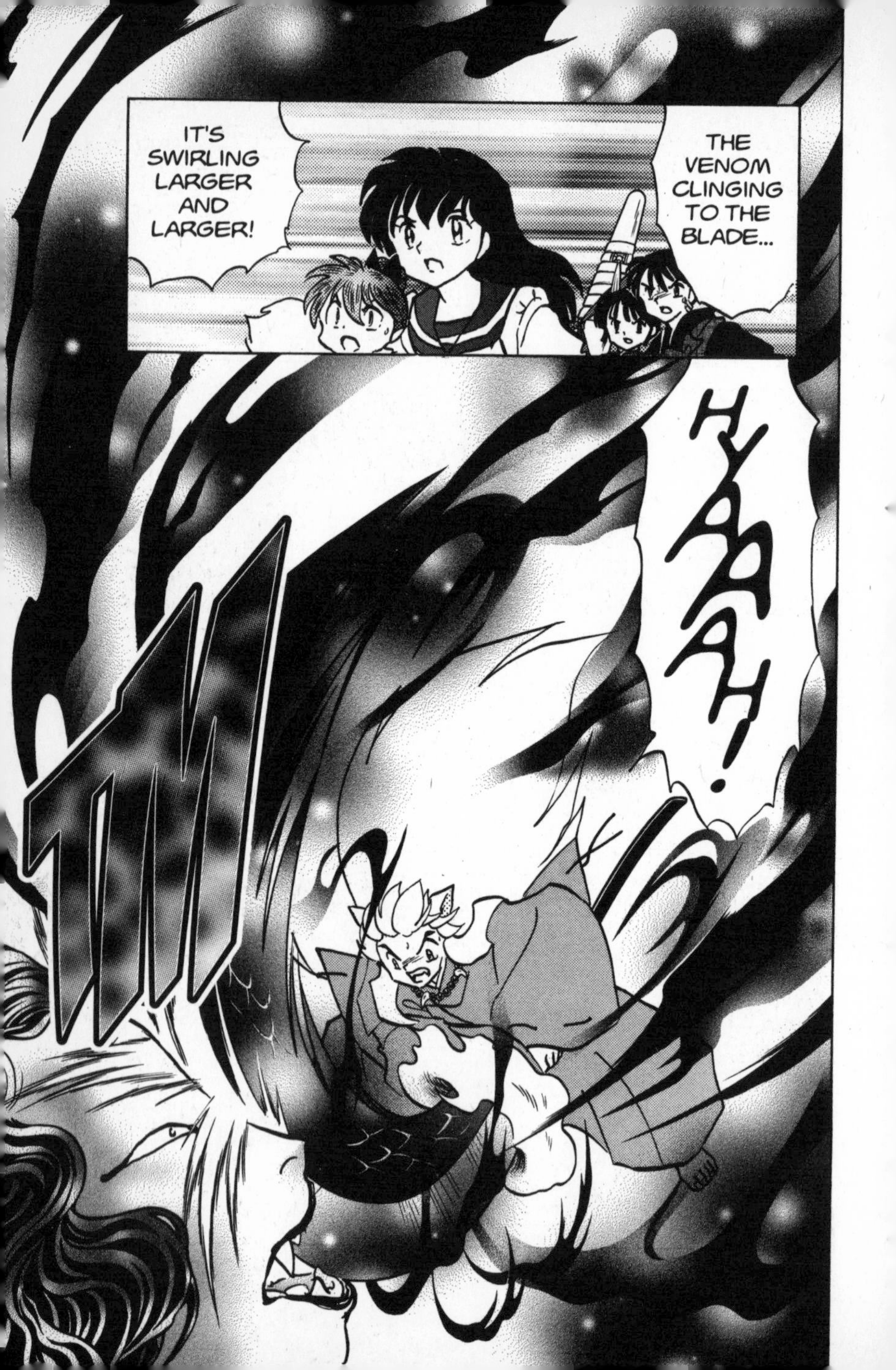
THE VENOM CLINGING TO THE BLADE...
IT'S SWIRLING LARGER AND LARGER!
HYAAAH!

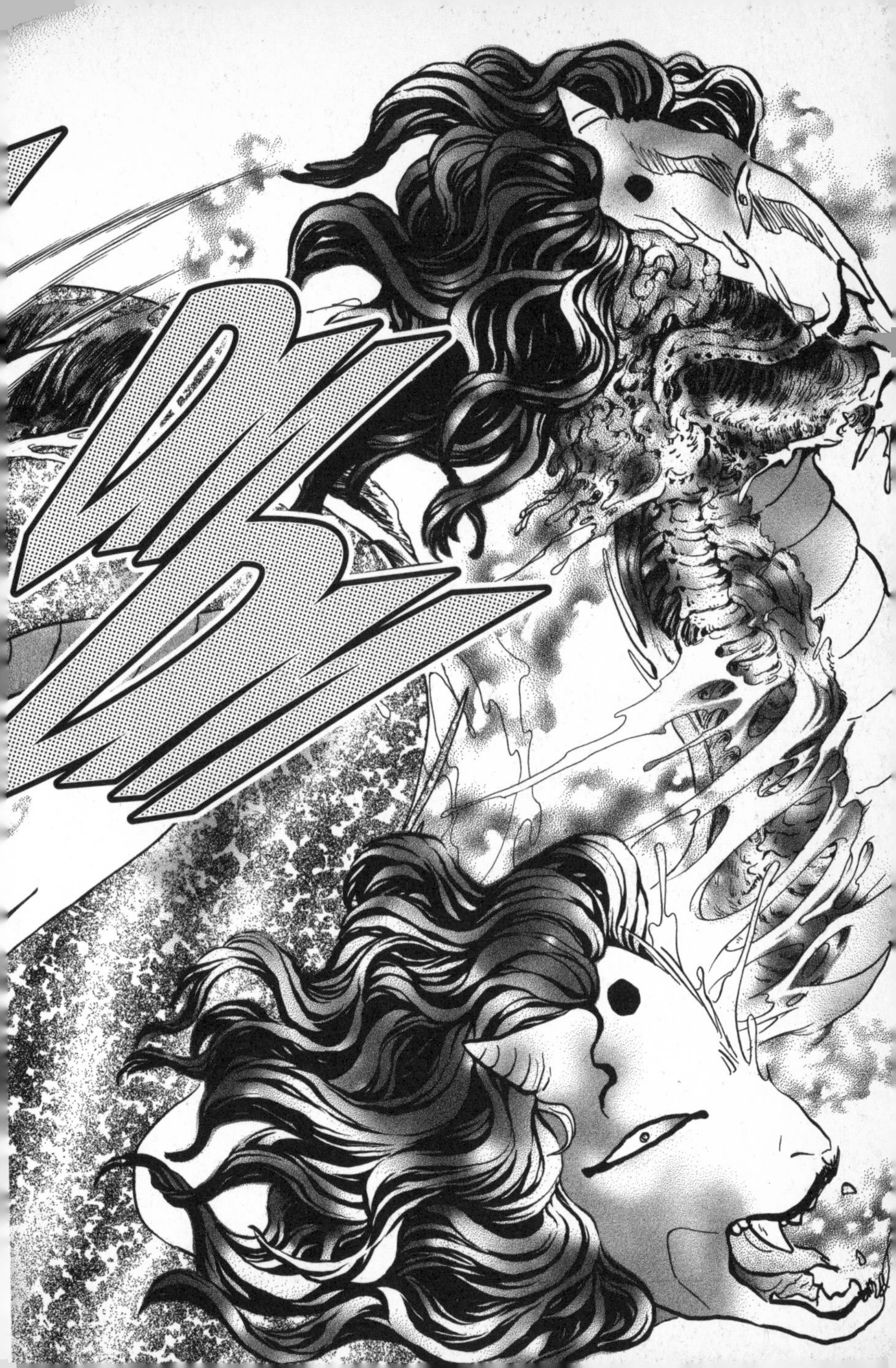

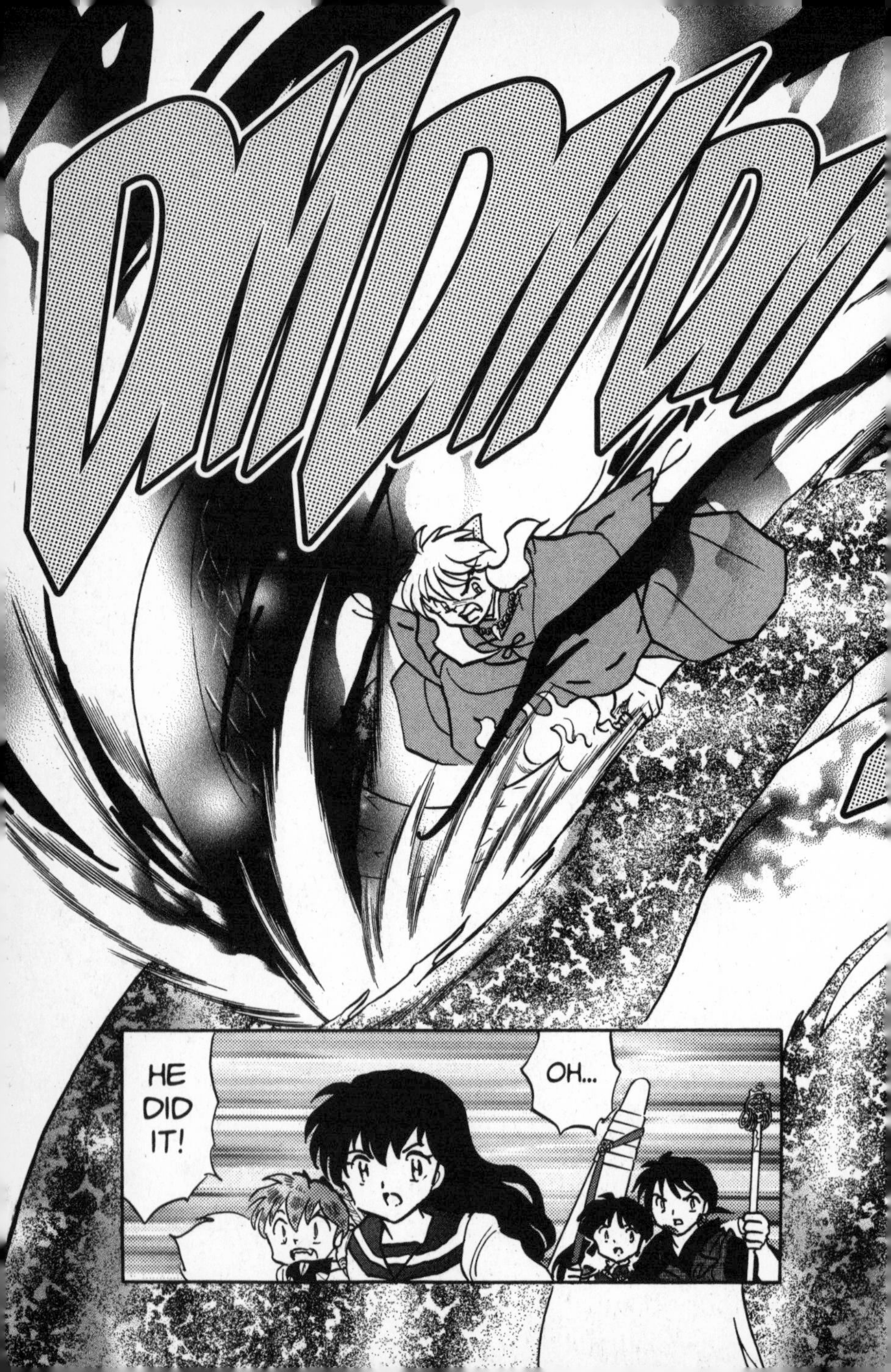
OH...
HE DID IT!

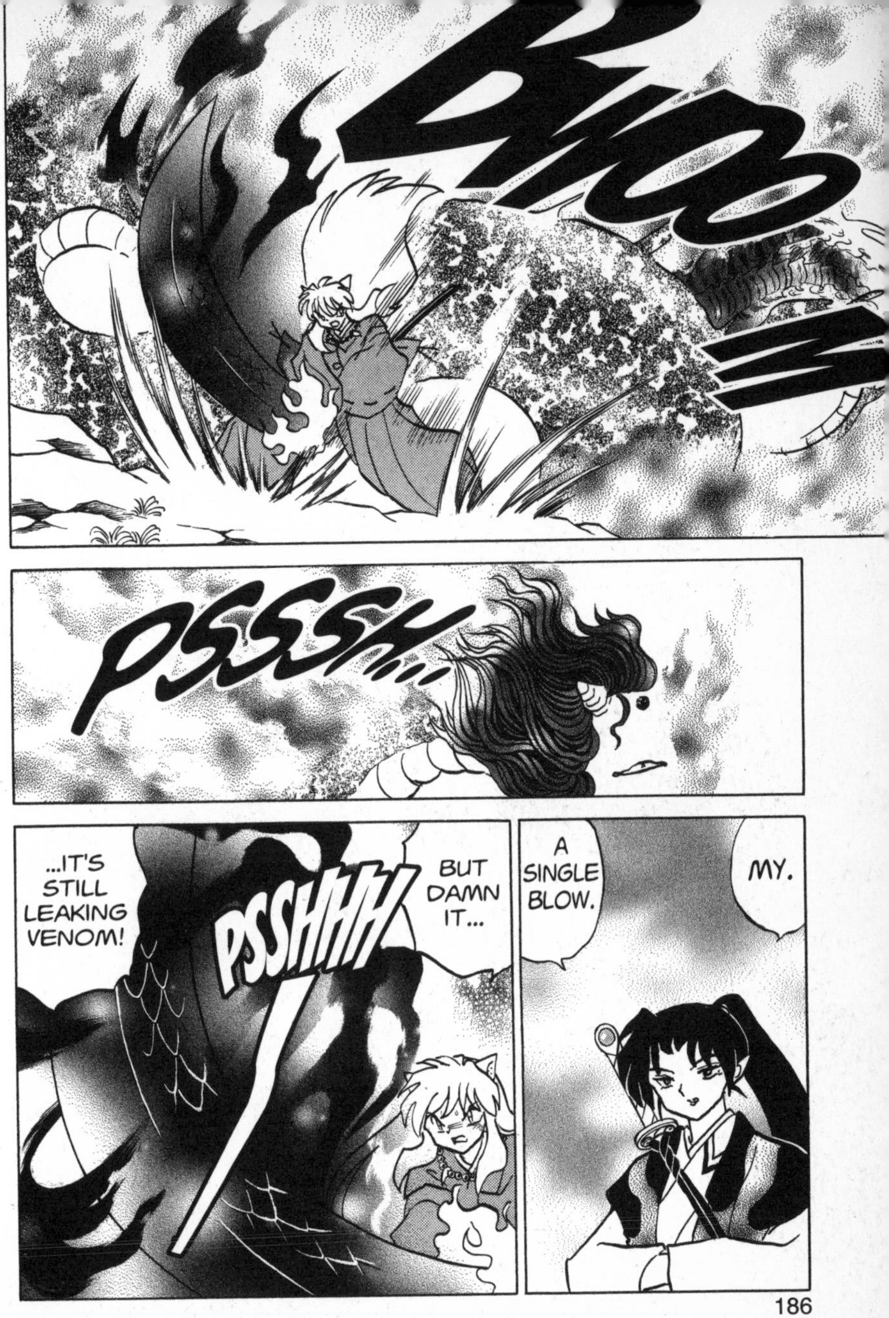
BHOOM!!
PSSSH...
MY.
A SINGLE BLOW.
BUT DAMN IT...
PSSHHH
...IT'S STILL LEAKING VENOM!

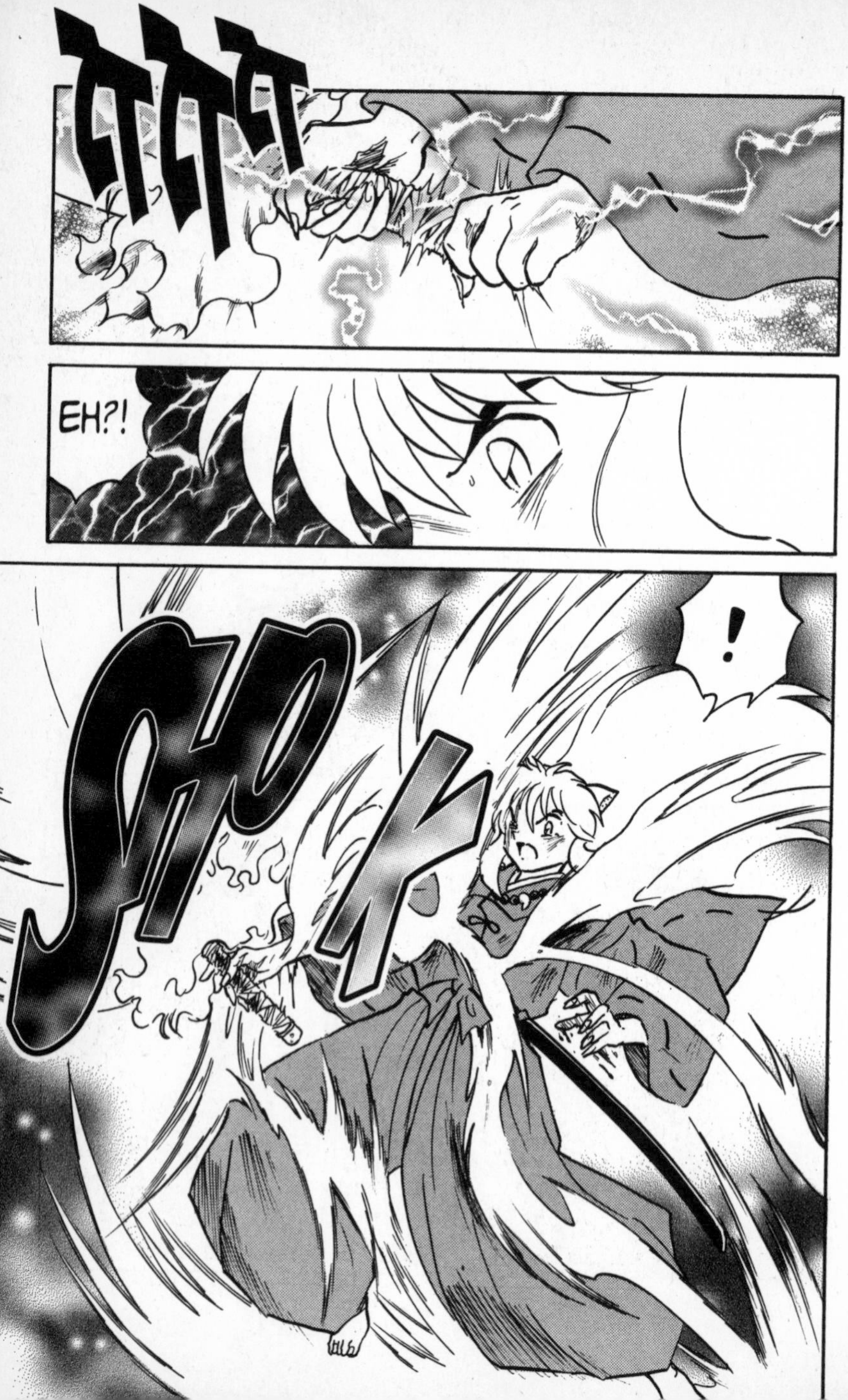
EH?!
!

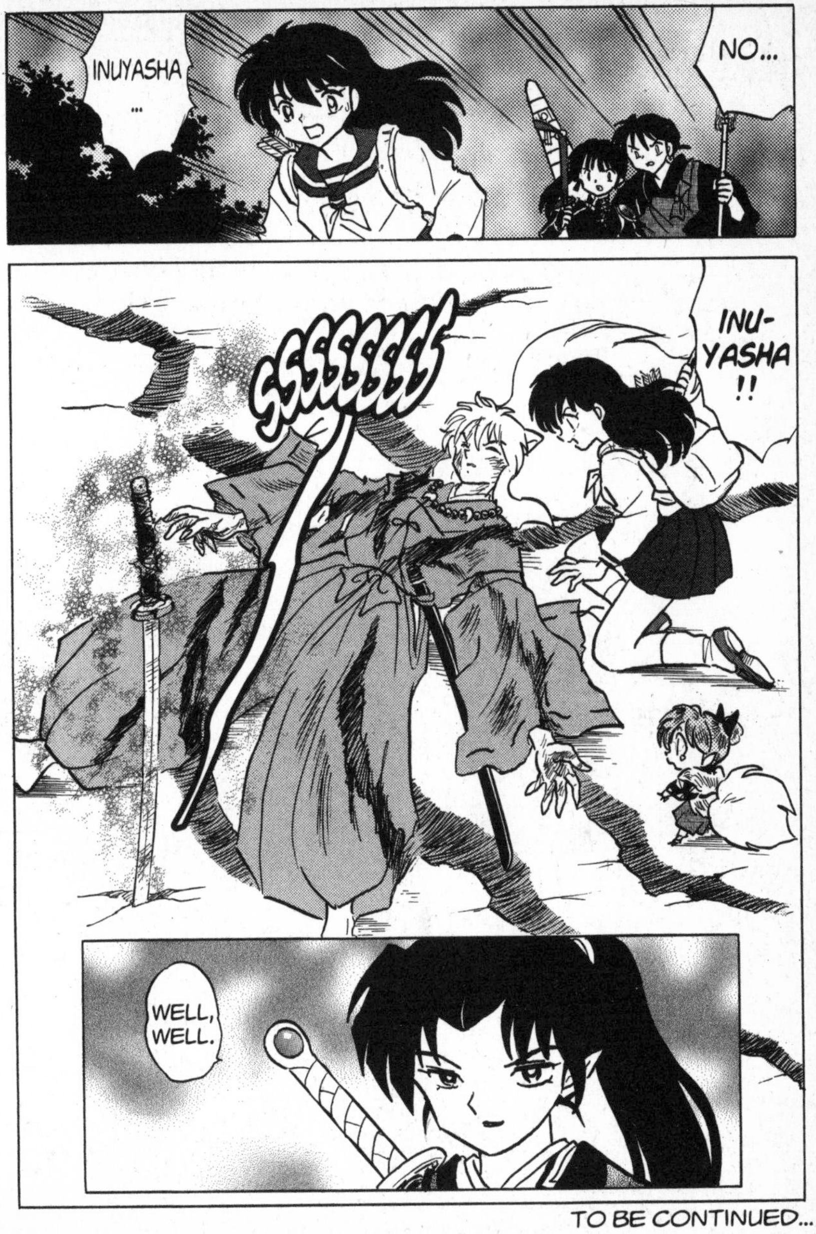
NO...
INUYASHA ...
INU-YASHA !!
SSSSSSSS
WELL, WELL.

TO BE CONTINUED...

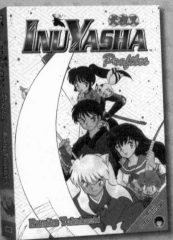
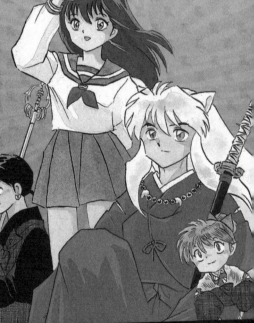

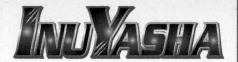

VOL. 40
Shonen Sunday Edition

Story and Art by
RUMIKO TAKAHASHI

English Adaptation by Gerard Jones

Translation/Mari Morimoto
Touch-up Art & Lettering/Bill Schuch
Cover and Interior Graphic Design/Yuki Ameda
Editor/Shaenon K. Garrity

VP, Production/Alvin Lu
VP, Publishing Licensing/Rika Inouye
VP, Sales & Product Marketing/Gonzalo Ferreyra
VP, Creative/Linda Espinosa
Publisher/Hyoe Narita

INUYASHA 40 by Rumiko TAKAHASHI
© 2005 Rumiko TAKAHASHI
All rights reserved. Original Japanese edition
published in 2005 by Shogakukan Inc., Tokyo.
The stories, characters and incidents mentioned in
this publication are entirely fictional.

Printed in the U.S.A.

Published by VIZ Media, LLC
P.O. Box 77010
San Francisco, CA 94107

10 9 8 7 6 5 4 3 2 1
First printing, September 2009

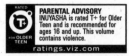

PARENTAL ADVISORY
INUYASHA is rated T+ for Older
Teen and is recommended for
ages 16 and up. This volume
contains violence.
ratings.viz.com

www.viz.com   WWW.SHONENSUNDAY.COM

D1529544